The Survival of American Democracy

The Survival of American Democracy

Presidential Abuse of Power and Reforms

David Contosta

BLOOMSBURY ACADEMIC
NEW YORK • LONDON • OXFORD • NEW DELHI • SYDNEY

BLOOMSBURY ACADEMIC
Bloomsbury Publishing Inc., 1359 Broadway, New York, NY 10018, USA.
Bloomsbury Publishing Plc., 50 Bedford Square, London, WC1B 3DP, UK.
Bloomsbury Publishing Ireland, 29 Earlsfort Terrace, Dublin 2, D02 AY28, Ireland.

First published in the United States of America 2026

A catalog record for this book is available from the Library of Congress.

ISBN: HB: 978-1-6669-4442-6
ePDF: 979-8-216-26904-5
eBook: 978-1-9787-5941-1

Typeset by Deanta Global Publishing Services, Chennai, India.

For product safety-related questions, contact productsafety@bloomsbury.com.

To find out more about our authors and books, visit www.bloomsbury.com and sign up for our newsletters.

To generations of students whom I have had the privilege of teaching about the American presidency, and who have taught me so much in return. And to dozens of colleagues and friends, along with daughters, sons, and cousins, who have put up with my questions and all too frequent utterances about the progress of this book.

Contents

Preface and Acknowledgments

For much of my life, I have been fascinated with the concept of an American experiment in government, an attitude put forward by the delegates themselves to the Constitutional Convention in Philadelphia during the very hot summer of 1787. They did not—and could not know—if their experiment with the presidency would be successful and only hoped that future generations could address abuses of presidential power.

I was fortunate to have an inspiring high school civics teacher in James "Jim" Love, at a time when civics education was virtually universal and taken very seriously throughout the United States. I was also fortunate as a college undergraduate to be taught by a group of dedicated and exhilarating professors of history and political science who encouraged my interests. Among them were Rio Christenson, Alan Engle, Richard Gustafson, David Fahey, and Harris Warren. It was Professor Warren who introduced me to Henry Adams and to Adams's often trenchant criticisms of the American experiment in government. These criticisms were inspired in no small measure by Adams's descent from two presidents of the United States, along with personal acquaintances—and even friendships—with several presidents during his own times, made convenient from a perch where he lived across Lafayette Square from the White House. Subsequently, under the direction of Professor Robert Reid, I wrote a master's thesis about Adams, and a decade later, my first published book became "Henry Adams and the American Experiment."

It was the brilliant and prolific writer-historian John Lukacs who hired me to teach history at Philadelphia's Chestnut Hill College, half a century ago now. He advised me, on the basis of his own experience, that it was more than possible—indeed advisable—to teach and write for publication at one and the same time. Teaching, he believed, gave rise to ideas about publishing, and publishing, in turn, enriched one's teaching. Through the years, many other colleagues at the college have been generous listeners and constructive critics about my various writing ventures. Most recently, these include Jeffrey Caroll, Lorraine Coons, Alexander Varias, and Barbara Lonnquist. I have also learned as much from generations of students as I think they have learned from me, especially in my classes about the American presidency. And I fear that I have all too often afflicted my family with too many tales of "Dad's latest writing projects."

I have often thought that my teaching and living in Philadelphia, with occasional treks down to Independence Hall, where the presidency was birthed, have played a subtle but important role in my continuing interest in the American presidential experiment. I also have cozy remembrances of those warm summer evenings when my father and I sat on our screened-in back porch taking in the drama of presidential party nominating conventions on a small, black-and-white portable TV, at a time when these conventions actually picked presidential candidates.

Finally, I wish to thank my superb editors for their many contributions to this book: Sidney Williams and Emilia Rivera.

Introduction

Promise and Perils

A Republic if You Can Keep it.

Benjamin Franklin, September 1787

The newly elected President of the United States has:

Boasted about being a very successful businessman, even though six of the businesses that he owned—or with which he was closely associated—went bankrupt.

He became famous by starring in a supposed "reality" television program called *The Celebrity Apprentice* that had nothing to do with reality. Yet millions of viewers became convinced that the star was a business genius.

He used false names to make phone calls to New York City media to advertise his latest exploits.

He created a fake university that had no accreditation, did not give grades, and did not award diplomas or certificates. When sued for fraud, he settled out of court for $25 million.

Just before the 2016 presidential election, he bragged on the *Access Hollywood* tape, "When you're a star, they let you do it. You can do anything. Grab them by their pussy. You can do anything."

The Washington Post newspaper counted over 30,000 false or misleading claims that he made during his first presidential term.

He used projection to defend himself against charges of lying: He was not lying. The "fake news," as he called the mainstream media, was lying.

Among his favorite phrases for denouncing the media was to call it "the enemy of the people," a term also used by Soviet dictator Joseph Stalin and Adolf Hitler's Propaganda Minister Joseph Goebbels.

He called his political opponents "vermin" and said immigrants were "poisoning the blood" of the United States, echoing language used by Hitler against those he considered undesirable and whom he would later try to exterminate completely.

He said that those who had served in the military were "losers" and "suckers."

As remedies for Covid, the most deadly global pandemic in a century, he recommended injecting powerful and dangerous cleaning agents into the body.

He wanted to use the Insurrection Act of 1807 to call out regular military troops against protesters but was talked out of it by his top military advisors.

He boasted, "I could stand in the middle of Fifth Avenue and shoot somebody, and wouldn't lose any voters."

He urged supporters at his rallies to "rough up" protesters and said he would pay their legal bills if they did so.

Although he clearly and definitively lost his bid for reelection in 2020, as measured in both the popular and electoral vote—a conclusion supported by some sixty federal judges (many of them members of his own political party)—he orchestrated an armed attack on the U.S. Capitol to reverse the results of the election and stay in power. The attack resulted in vicious assaults on Capitol police, four deaths, and life-threatening danger to Vice President Mike Pence.

He was impeached twice by the House but not convicted by the Senate, the first time for making $400 million in aid to Ukraine contingent on their investigating President Biden's son Hunter. The second time was for orchestrating that deadly assault on the Capital building in an effort to overturn a presidential election that he lost resoundingly.

He was indicted by two federal grand juries. One was for the January 6, 2021, attack on the capital, and the other was for illegally taking classified documents at the end of his presidency to his home at Mar-a-Lago in Florida and refusing to turn them over to the National Archives, in clear violation of the Presidential Records Acts of 1978 and 2018. He was not tried in either case because he was elected president a second time in 2024.

A criminal court in New York City found him guilty of thirty-four counts of falsifying business records to cover up a sexual relationship with a porn star. Yet he was not sentenced because of his election to a second term as president.

In a New York City civil trial, he was found guilty of sexually abusing and defaming E. Jean Carroll.

All these facts are just the "tip of the iceberg." And in any prior presidential election, any one of them would have been enough to disqualify him or derail his candidacy.

One would have every reason to conclude that the delegates to the Constitutional Convention, who created the US constitutional system of government in Philadelphia during the summer of 1787, would be shocked and appalled if they could have foreseen someone like Donald Trump as President of the United States.

But maybe not delegate Benjamin Franklin: On a mid-September day in 1787, a Mrs. Powell of Philadelphia recognized delegate Franklin at the end of the Constitutional Convention and asked, "Well, Doctor, what have we got, a republic or a monarchy?" To which Franklin quipped, "A republic if you can keep it."[1]

Franklin may have answered in this way because he knew that the main goal of the convention was to create a more powerful central government with a powerful chief executive at its helm. Franklin also must have realized that the delegates had just provided the president with essentially the same powers that then belonged to the crowned heads of Europe, once including the kings and queens of England, a fact that would probably surprise many if not most Americans today. However, the convention delegates believed they could restrain, or hopefully blunt altogether, abuses of these awesome presidential powers through a system of checks and balances. Unfortunately, many of these safeguards have proven ineffective over the years—and for various reasons addressed throughout this book.

Defiant Celebrity

Nevertheless, the question remains as to how so many voters could ignore the above evidence of Donald Trump's behavior in deciding the 2016 and 2024 elections. One preliminary answer comes from a recent book called *The Drama of Celebrity* by Sharon Marcus. In it, she discusses what she calls "Defiant Celebrities," who "appeal not only to the marginal and the outcast, but to anyone who has ever wanted to bypass conventions, gatekeepers, and experts."[2] There are many examples in history of such celebrities, including actress Sarah Bernhardt, author, playwright, and lecturer Oscar Wilde, bank robbers Bonnie and Clyde, actor James Dean (as in the movie *Rebel Without a Cause*), and Elvis "the Pelvis" Presley. In addition, there are the Beatles, with their *then* unconventional grooming and dress, and the lyrics of such songs as, "Do what you want to do. And go where you're going to go." And in 1966, John Lennon proclaimed that his Beatles were bigger than Jesus."[3] In 2015, the very popular singer Madonna announced, "I don't follow the rules. I never did, and I'm not going to start." She also used obscene language with abandon during public appearances.[4] Although the above represent some random examples, they all testify to the allure of defiant celebrity.

Americans voted for Trump for many reasons, but his "bad boy" behavior may very well have had great appeal to a significant number of them. Trump gave such voters permission to say whatever they wished, as well as to gleefully insist that no one was going to tell them what they could do or not do. This was especially true if such strictures came from well-educated elites on the two coasts whom they often thought were mocking them and whom they believed had too much power over American life and culture. Furthermore, it did not seem to matter to such voters that they had little in common with a billionaire from New York City, since he shared their contempt for proper speech and behavior, and they admired his disregard for social conventions. In addition, he disliked—or pretended to dislike—the same people, positions, and ideas that they did.

Then there is the possibility that even though Trump has said and done so many things that would have sunk any other candidate in the past, some voters may have simply said, "Oh, that's just Trump. He doesn't mean it." In addition, many Americans now receive their news through "silos" made up of their favorite cable news channels or their favorite social media sites. Reinforcing such habits is the factor of "cognitive dissonance," a universal human trait that explains why individuals as well as whole groups of people have strong tendencies to reject any facts that contradict their devotion to certain ideas or personalities. All these circumstances will be addressed later in the book.

Growth and Abuse of Power

The chapters that follow are about executive power, the growth of that power over the nearly two and a half centuries since the creation of the American presidency, the use and abuse of presidential power, the checks and balances that were created to check such abuses and explanations of their failure to do so in various cases. In this way, the author seeks to tell the story of the American presidential experience and in the process to address Benjamin Franklin's haunting comment at the end of the Constitutional Convention—"A Republic If You Can Keep It." (While the words republic and democracy are often conflated in the public mind, they represent two different aspects of the American political system, concepts to be explored more fully in the next chapter.)

The book pays special attention to the creation of the presidency at the Constitutional Convention, with a particular emphasis on the powers of the executive office, the expectations for presidential behavior, the checks and balances provided in the document, and an examination of their inadequacies. There is also a dissection of the motives for creating the Electoral College, along with the continuing dangers to the American political system presented by this method of electing presidents.

Alarming, too, is the early appearance of cults of personality surrounding certain presidents. Such cults can be associated in varying degrees with George Washington, Andrew Jackson, and Theodore Roosevelt, all of which point to the possibility of a far more dangerous cult surrounding Donald Trump. Significantly, other famous and widely admired presidents, such as Thomas Jefferson, Abraham Lincoln, and Franklin Roosevelt, did not cultivate or attract cults of personality, which only underlines the unique characteristics and dangers of the phenomenon.

Helping to fuel personality cults, as well as less harmful forms of popularity among both candidates and sitting presidents, have been various techniques for cultivating seductive images. The appearance of still photography, and later of movies and television, all became important tools for such images. Added to the list in later years are cable news and social media, referenced briefly above. Cable networks and social media sites, combined with the Supreme Court's decision in 2010 that allowed unlimited, anonymous campaign contributions, have also permitted prospective candidates to largely circumvent screening and approval by political party organizations.[5] It is highly unlikely, for example, that the Republican Party would have nominated a person like Donald Trump for president. Another factor in weakening the role of parties was the elevation of primary elections in the early 1970s as the main route to a presidential nomination.

It also appears that presidents who seriously abuse power and were impeached (but not convicted)—or who were threatened with impeachment—emerged from childhood and youth as angry and resentful individuals. Among them are Andrew Jackson, Andrew Johnson, Richard Nixon, and, unsurprisingly, Donald Trump. These factors should call on responsible media outlets as well as voters at large to pay closer attention to the deep backgrounds of candidates.

At the same time, the success of domestic reform movements as well as American foreign policy (especially in times of war) have depended on powerful presidents who knew how to build large majorities in Congress, persuade legislators to embrace their programs, and win over public opinion. In this way, Theodore and Franklin Roosevelt, Woodrow Wilson, and Lyndon Johnson achieved wide-ranging social and economic reforms. In addition, Wilson and the two Roosevelts were masters of foreign policy and military success in wartime, though Wilson failed to carry through in peacetime.

However, the war-making powers, which the delegates to the Constitutional Convention believed they had reserved exclusively for Congress, were very early invaded by presidents and abused to drag the country into unnecessary wars, often by deception and sometimes through outright lies. Such presidents include James K. Polk with the Mexican-American War; William McKinley with the Spanish-American War and the associated brutal conquest of the Philippines; Truman, Eisenhower, Kennedy, Johnson, and Nixon with the Vietnam War; and George W. Bush with the Iraq War. These conflicts, which depended mainly on presidential initiatives, will be explored in considerable detail.

The final chapters of the book analyze the three elections in which Donald Trump ran for president, especially the reasons why he won in both 2016 and 2024 and what his victories say about American politics, American life, and the possible future of American democracy. They also suggest some much-needed reforms in the country's political system, including the Constitution itself. The success or failure of such reforms will go far toward answering where the American Presidential Experiment might be headed, and with it American democracy.

Despite flaws in the experiment, the great majority of Americans have believed in the exceptionalism of their country's democratic systems—that while democracies might be seriously compromised or overthrown in other countries, such a fate could never befall the United States. Nearly a century ago, Sinclair Lewis, as explored in his novel, *It Can't Happen Here*, certainly knew better, as have several other writers whose insights will be presented later.

Fortunately, most of the individuals serving as President of the United States have largely observed the norms of behavior expected for someone in high public office. In addition, most presidents have generally respected the boundaries of executive power. Furthermore, many of them have used their influence and authority to bring about laudatory results. It was largely because of presidential initiative that 4 million enslaved Americans received their freedom, that Americans achieved civil rights in many areas of life, that the American people, in collaboration with their allies, liberated the world from fascist tyranny, and that the United States has achieved unparalleled prosperity. Through the leadership of some presidents, the nation came to promote conservation and preservation of the natural environment—along with much else. Other presidents, however, turned their backs on those recently freed from bondage, sent peaceful Native Americans to their deaths, promoted racist immigration policies, defied Supreme Court orders, started needless wars, and created dangerous cults of personality. Given these conflicting examples, one might compare presidential power to a double-edged sword with the capacity for both good and ill.

Not surprisingly, the chapters that follow do not offer an overall history of the American presidency. Rather, as proposed above, they attempt to give salient examples of the uses and abuses of presidential power. By highlighting such examples, the book necessarily fails to mention certain presidents, while it gives generous space to others. Some presidents also appear in more than one chapter. In addition, all the chapters do not follow each other in a strict chronological order, since some of them are largely topical in nature but, for the most part, honor a chronological sequence within topics.

As a final introductory note, the author briefly opens each chapter in the present tense to convey a sense of immediacy. In that way, it is hoped that the reader will relate more readily to the presidents being discussed, the times in which they lived and governed, and the important roles they played in the American presidential experiment.

Notes

1 This exchange was recorded in the diary of James McHenry, a fellow signer of the Constitution, https://www.thenewamerican.com/.../7631-a-republic-if-you-can-keep-it.
2 Sharon Marcus, *The Drama of Celebrity* (Princeton: Princeton University Press, 2019), 26. See also pages 21–44.
3 Quoted in ibid., 21.
4 Ibid.
5 *Citizens United v. FEC* (1910).

1

Republic or Monarchy

The Presidency and the Constitution

It was well known that there were individuals [at the convention] who betrayed a bias toward monarchy

James Madison, *Notes on the Debates about the Federal Constitution of 1787*

The Revolution has been won from Great Britain, but the feeble union created under the Articles of Confederation—the initial framework for a central government—has failed to address the many trials besetting the young nation. This first version of American government does not have the power to tax (only to beg the states for funds) or to regulate commerce among the several states. By the middle of the 1780s, the national government, such as it exists, is so short of funds that it faces bankruptcy and cannot even pay the interest on bonds sold to finance the War for Independence. Consequently, the country's credit rating is essentially zero. At the same time, the states are quarreling over control of adjoining waterways, and some are charging customs duties, that is, tariffs, on imports from neighboring states as if they were foreign countries. If this were not enough, an economic depression has settled over the land. In Massachusetts, Revolutionary War veteran Daniel Shays has led a rebellion of several thousand poor farmers, who have marched on the US armory at Springfield with the aim of seizing weapons and overthrowing the state government in Boston to protest seizures of their land for not being able to pay their property taxes.

Under the circumstances, it is not surprising that delegates to the Constitutional Convention aimed to create "a more perfect union" and establish "domestic tranquility," both phrases that would appear in the "Preamble" of their proposed framework of government.[1] In doing so, the delegates clearly violated the charge Congress had given to them the previous February, "for the sole and express purpose of revising the Articles of Confederation."[2] Instead, they scrapped the articles and produced a new framework of national government. In this sense, what became the Constitution of the United States of America would emerge from something of a bloodless coup.

The Convention

The delegates who assembled in Philadelphia in May 1787 found no modern examples of strong chief executives, other than in countries headed by monarchs, who could provide the energetic leadership to guide the country and its government out of its chaotic weakness. Thus, it is understandable that the president would be granted essentially the same sorts of executive powers that belonged to kings. As granted in Article II of the Constitution, which deals with the presidency, these include an absolute power of pardon and a veto over legislation, which could be countermanded only by a supermajority of the national legislature. Presidents would also have near-complete control over foreign affairs, which they would claim from their authority to send and receive ambassadors and to make treaties with the "advice and consent" of the Senate. In addition, the president would have the power to make a wide array of administrative appointments. The president, like any monarch, would also be commander-in-chief of the military. Indeed, the chief executive of any country, whatever the title, would need to exercise many if not most of these same powers.

Although the delegates attempted to work out ways to check such powers, future presidents would find ways to evade these so-called checks and balances. It is no wonder that James Madison, seen then and now as the main architect of the Constitution, wrote in *The Federalist Papers*, a series of newspaper articles explaining the proposed constitution and urging ratification, about an unnamed state office holder who complained that the Constitution was setting up "a direct and irresistible tendency to monarchy . . ."[3]

Given this fear of overweening or abusive presidential power, citizens of the early twenty-first century might understandably assume that more democracy in government would have been a primary way the delegates to the Constitutional Convention sought to curb executive overreach. Given that the word democracy does not appear anywhere in the Constitution, the closest the delegates came to referencing some sort of democratic sentiment comes in the "Preamble" to the document, which begins with the words, "*We the people* of the United States" and ends with the phrase ". . . do ordain and establish this constitution for the United States of America."

Nor does the word republic, to which Franklin had referred while conversing with that Philadelphia resident at the end of the convention, appear in the document. (The closest reference to a republic comes indirectly in Article IV, Section 4, which states that, "The United States shall guarantee to every state a Republican form of Government," but it does not go on to define what that might mean or entail, or how it might reflect the nature of the proposed new national government.)

Without wading too far into the etymological weeds, "republic" comes from a Latin word that roughly translates as "relating to public matters" and by extension, "relating to the public good," as opposed to favoring the interests of those in charge of government and their cronies. The term "democracy" comes from Greek and literally means "rule by the people." It is therefore understandable that the two words would become conflated through assertions that promoting the public good in a republic requires underlying democratic principles and institutions. In this respect, the two concepts might be said to echo the words of Abraham Lincoln's Gettysburg Address in which he proclaimed, "government of the people, by the people, and for the people"—that is a democratic government of and by the people that promotes the public good in a republic. Lincoln's famous words should demolish once and for all the long-held conservative argument that the United States is a republic and not a democracy. When operating properly, both aspects of government become closely intertwined.

Nevertheless, the central goal of the delegates to the Constitutional Convention was not, as referenced above, to create a democracy, as democratic governments are generally understood more than two centuries later, but to create a powerful central government with a powerful chief executive at its head. The result has been much confusion about American democracy as it has emerged over the years, along with how it ought to operate within the context of growing presidential power. Commensurate with that theme is the reality that the Constitution, as originally formulated, was a pre-democratic document. This situation is not surprising since no other democracies then existed in the world as models and since, as will be discussed, the authors of the Constitution had doubts about the ability of the common people to rule—or even to select those who would rule.

It should be kept in mind that even delegates to the convention were not elected by the people of the various states but by the individual state legislatures at a time when the right to vote for these legislatures was severely limited with respect to race, gender, and property qualifications. In addition, the Constitution, as initially written, permitted only those who had the right to vote for their state legislatures to vote for the national House of Representatives. At the time, all the states reserved the elective franchise to white adult males who owned property, the required amount and value of which varied from state to state. Consequently, it has been estimated that only about 6 percent of adults had the right to vote at the time of the Constitutional Convention. Regarding the Senate, the upper house of the national legislature, members were to be chosen by the state legislatures. There would be no direct input from voters in selecting the Senate until 1913, when the Seventeenth Amendment to the Constitution provided for the direct election of senators by the voters in each state.

When it came to selecting a president, the choice was in the hands of an Electoral College with no connection to a popular vote until the states gradually decided to allow voters—initially only white, property-owning males—to select their states' presidential electors. For Alexander Hamilton, writing in *Federalist* No. 68, the Electoral College would be a way of preventing a man with "low talents for intrigue, and the little arts of popularity" from ever becoming president of the United States. (How wrong he was.) Commenting on Hamilton's fears more than two and a quarter centuries later, historian Anne Applebaum would write in her book, *The Twilight of Democracy*, "The electoral college was originally . . . designed as a kind of review board, a group of elite lawmakers and men of property who would select the president." They "would select the president, rejecting the people's choice if necessary, in order to avoid the 'excesses of democracy.'"[4]

The judicial system created at the Constitutional Convention was even less democratic since federal judges, along with justices of the Supreme Court, were to be selected by presidents and confirmed by members of the Senate (who themselves were not popularly elected until 1913). The justices were to serve "during good behavior," which could mean for life if a justice so wished and were not impeached and removed from the court (which has never occurred). What is more, presidents who nominated judges and justices were themselves put in power by an Electoral College with only an indirect link to the popular vote.

Since the Constitution went into effect in 1789, substantial changes have in fact led to a far more democratic system: First came the abolition by states of property qualifications for voting, largely completed by the 1830s. After the Civil War, the Fifteenth Amendment of 1870 enfranchised black men (but not women of any race). However, the federal government soon gave up on enforcing this amendment. Congress would not again mandate the rights of African Americans to vote until the Voting Rights Act of 1965. However, by the early twenty-first century, various state legislatures would undermine this law by imposing voting restrictions, and Congress would fail to renew various provisions of the Voting Rights Act after the Supreme Court declared them unconstitutional in 2013.[5] In 1920, the Nineteenth Amendment assured women of the right to vote after a long and arduous campaign to obtain it, but, of course, largely white women benefited from the amendment for many decades thereafter. Thus, if democratic governments are defined in large measure by a universal right to vote by citizens, the United States has had to struggle mightily to reach that goal.

Thickets of the Unknowable

In addition to not envisioning what most present citizens would consider a genuine, modern democracy, the authors of the Constitution refrained from setting down a detailed framework for the new government, in part realizing correctly that they could not anticipate every future contingency. Especially when it came to the presidency, they were feeling their way as if in partial darkness. It should be no surprise, then, that the American presidency would take on a life of its own in the years ahead. It would evolve in ways that the delegates could not have imagined, leading to much confusion and debate over what should be expected of presidents or what they should be permitted to do—or not do—which could be exploited by some presidents over the years to abuse their power.

Attempting to grope their way through thickets of the unknowable in creating the presidency, the convention delegates looked for guidance in two main directions: to their own experiences with government and to the lessons of history. Of the fifty-five delegates, twenty-eight of them had served in the old Congresses during the American Revolution or later under the Articles of Confederation—and many had held some position in state government. The lessons of history reminded them that demagogues had subverted the ancient Athenian democracy and that Julius Caesar and rampant corruption had undermined the Roman Republic and paved the way for unchecked imperial rule.[6] For a chilling account of Rome's fortunes, the delegates only needed to read British historian Edward Gibbon's *Decline and Fall of the Roman Empire*, the first volume of which had been published in 1776, the same year the Americans declared their independence. The final volumes of this massive work appeared in 1788 and 1789, as the new American government under the Constitution was being debated and taking shape. According to Gibbon, unbridled corruption was one of the primary reasons for the demise of Rome, and by comparison in the minds of many delegates, a principal complaint against British rule over the colonies.[7] Added to this swirl of conversation were what the delegates remembered about—or had heard tell of—corrupt and authoritarian royal governors in America before the Revolution.

Despite such fears, the delegates rejected a proposal to create an executive council (which existed under many state governments at the time) whose approval the president would need before making major decisions.[8] Instead, Article II of the Constitution, which deals with the presidency, simply declared, "The executive Power shall be vested in a President of the United States of America."[9] This provision was later interpreted to mean that there would be a "unitary executive," with the president in charge of and responsible for all the departments and individuals under the executive branch. However, the Constitution did not clarify or define just what this authority might entail.

Thus, the unitary executive power could be interpreted as saying, as it would be in the future, that presidents have the right to issue executive orders to and through the various departments and agencies under the executive branch, so long as they do not specifically violate any act of Congress or provision of the Constitution. Even here, as it turned out, it would be very difficult for either Congress or the federal courts to countermand such orders. In effect, presidents would come to exercise an "executive prerogative" that was not unlike the traditional "royal prerogative" of the British monarch, even though the delegates had, during their debates, specifically rejected the concept of a presidential prerogative.[10] Furthermore, presidents, in taking an oath of office, swear to "preserve, protect and defend the Constitution of the United States," which future presidents would argue gives them the right to decide which executive actions are, in their opinion alone, constitutional in pursuance of that oath.[11] Perhaps surprising to many if not most citizens over the years, the Constitution does not anywhere specifically authorize presidents to issue executive orders.

Another power not mentioned in the Constitution but that would loom large is the president as "head of state," a position that George Washington assumed by default in the absence of a monarch, who had filled that position in Great Britain. Closely aligned to this function, presidents became the chief ceremonial officers of the nation, which might involve varying degrees of pomp and circumstance associated with monarchies. Many citizens also came to view the president as the symbolic father of the American family, as well as its chief comforter and chief mourner in times of trial. Some future presidents would assume the mantle of religious authority as they offered prayers for the nation on various occasions.

All these extraconstitutional roles could add an elevated aura surrounding the office that only strengthened emotional attachments to presidents and that enhanced their power and reach. If this were not enough, Article II of the Constitution, which deals with the presidency, was largely and hastily assembled at the end of the convention in September by the Committee on Detail, which worked under the pressure of fellow delegates wanting their work to be over so they could go home. In addition, the uncomfortable conditions under which they had labored all summer made them all the more anxious to leave Philadelphia. To debate freely without public criticism, they had agreed to close all the windows in the hall. Even if the windows had been left open, it would have done little good, since many residents of the city remarked that it had been the hottest and most humid summer they could remember—not to mention the armies of flies that would have invaded the hall from streets filled with horse manure.

In the words of historian Forrest McDonald, "Article II was hastily put together in slipshod fashion. . . . The article proceeds to enumerate certain powers, but not others, and it fails to mention . . . some traditional executive powers . . ."[12] Such a "slipshod" approach to the powers of the presidency would become a major source of ballooning executive authority, and with this authority, expanding opportunities for the abuse of power. Jack N. Rakove, in his *Original Meanings*, a detailed and highly regarded study of the making of the Constitution, concurs. He writes, "The first sentence of Article II of the Constitution . . . badly stated that, 'The executive power shall be vested in a president of the United States of America' without explaining what executive power is."[13]

Alexander Hamilton had expressed a far simpler solution to executive authority that had no chance of adoption at the Constitutional Convention, given his advocacy of a powerful American monarchy. Speaking to the delegates on June 18, he gave a six-hour speech in which he said the British governmental system was the best in the world and proposed a hereditary monarchy for the United States. Such a king, insisted Hamilton, would have "so much power that it will not be in his interest to risk much to acquire more. . . . He is above corruptions." Hamilton also condemned a democratically elected legislature: "The voice of the people has been said to be the voice of God. . . . It is not true in fact. Can a democratic assembly . . . be supposed to steadily pursue the public good?"[14] Hamilton later abandoned his advocacy of hereditary monarchy, but Madison had recorded the remark in his convention notes and others present that day heard and remembered it. It is possible that Hamilton was not entirely serious in his advocacy of hereditary monarchy and simply put the notion out there for others to reject. Perhaps Hamilton's motives or sincerity can never be known. Still, in the future, political opponents would cite this speech many times to accuse Hamilton of being both a monarchist and a fawning Anglophile.

According to biographer Ron Chernow, no one at the convention criticized Hamilton's speech the following day, possibly finding it too extreme to merit serious rebuttal.[15] Another reason may be that, despite the war for independence, many Americans, including virtually all the delegates, continued to admire certain ideals of British government. Americans had concluded, however, that Great Britain had betrayed its own principles and left them with no choice but to rebel. Madison would later write, "It was well known that there were individuals [at the convention] who betrayed a bias toward monarchy."[16] And no one was more impressed with the ideals of the British system of government and law than Alexander Hamilton.[17] Yet despite his controversial speech, Hamilton would go on to support the completed constitution enthusiastically and strongly advocate for its ratification as one of the authors of *The Federalist Papers*, perhaps as a pragmatic decision to embrace the possible.

And in what also appears to be a radical about-face, Hamilton went on to praise Madison's framework of checks and balances in an effort to minimize abuses of power by presidents as well as other governmental authorities. Hamilton himself wrote in *Federalist* No. 51 (one of the eighty-five newspaper articles about the Constitution which he, James Madison, and John Jay wrote in support of ratifying the Constitution) that they must "oblige [the government] to control itself." There had also been many references during the convention about how virtue among officeholders might help to control their behavior. This quality would be especially important for filling the presidency, in Hamilton's words, with men "preeminent for ability and virtue."[18] George Washington, who presided over the Constitutional Convention, had also concluded that the country needed virtuous men at the helm, whom he described as "the wise and the good."[19] At the time, virtue was understood to mean putting the public welfare above one's own selfish interests.[20]

However, as Tom Ricks points out in his *First Principles*, a book about the intellectual underpinnings of the Constitution, some delegates already harbored doubts about the efficacy of virtue in controlling presidents and others in government. John Adams, well known for his pessimistic tendency, was one of them (although he was in Paris during the Constitutional Convention representing the United States, along with Thomas Jefferson, as joint American ministers to France). Adams had written to his wife Abigail a decade earlier at the time of the Declaration of Independence, "The new Government . . . will require a Purification from our Vices and an augmentation of our Virtues . . ." However, he believed that all men were "extremely addicted to Corruption and Venality [and so] I am not without apprehension from this Quarter."[21] Adams was saying that certain commonly understood standards of proper behavior and restraint would be essential among office holders if they were to resist abusing power, however much he doubted that the public could depend on them in actuality.

Indeed, Madison himself, even though possessed of a sunnier temperament than Adams, likewise came to doubt during the Constitutional Convention that the country could count on leaders always forswearing self-interest and abuse of power. Thus, he went on at great length to explain how his proposed system of checks and balances might serve as a barrier to presidential overreach.[22] These ideas were not completely original to him and the other delegates, since they drew strong inspiration from such political theorists as Englishman John Locke and the French Baron Montesquieu. However, and perhaps again surprising to Americans nearly two and a half centuries later, the phrase "checks and balances" appears nowhere in the Constitution—nor does the associated term, "separation of powers." One would have to plow through the *Federalist Papers* and through Madison's extensive *Notes of Debates* at the convention, as well as how the understanding and application of these concepts evolved over time. (And to be fair, one could not expect the document of the Constitution to spell out in great detail how "checks and balances" and a "separation of powers" could or should operate.) Still, the delegates hoped that the president could be given enough power to lead the country and enforce the laws, but that this executive power could be sufficiently blunted or curbed when necessary to prevent abuse.

Checks and Balances

As spelled out in Article I of the Constitution, which dealt with the legislative branch, Congress could override (or check) presidential vetoes by a two-thirds vote of both the Senate and House of Representatives. However, because of the emergence of political parties extremely loyal to presidents—neither envisioned nor welcomed by the convention delegates—such overrides would turn out to be both difficult and infrequent.

Also mandated in Article I, the Senate had to confirm treaties made by the president, again by a two-thirds vote. Unimagined at the time was the possibility that future presidents could circumvent this treaty confirmation process by making executive agreements with foreign heads of state in place of formal treaties. Then there were issues of foreign policy, which the Constitution left relatively unresolved—a glaring example of the hurried "slipshod" construction of Article II—including who was supposed to recognize foreign governments, who had the authority to proclaim American neutrality, and who should control information essential to making decisions about foreign policy.

The Senate would confirm high-level presidential appointments, including cabinet secretaries, justices of the Supreme Court, and judges of the lower federal courts. Even here, presidents in the future might circumvent Senate confirmation in some instances by making "interim" appointments when Congress was not in session. In addition, because of political loyalty, members of a president's party in the Senate would prove unlikely to refuse confirmation to such appointees.

The Constitution stated that only Congress could declare war, and that Congress alone possessed the "power of the purse"—that is, the sole authority to tax and authorize spending, which supposedly could be used to prevent or curb various presidential initiatives, including a march toward war. Alexander Hamilton insisted that the legislature "[has] the sole power of declaring war," with the president having "the direction of war when authorized or begun."[23]

Writing nearly a decade after the convention, Madison reflected on how presidents could be tempted to use war to abuse their powers, despite checks and balances: "Of all the enemies of true liberty," he declared, "war is, perhaps, the most to be dreaded, because it comprises and develops the germ of every other." Specifically, he warned that during times of war "the discretionary power of the Executive is extended; its influence in dealing out offices, honors and emoluments is multiplied; and all the means of seducing the minds, are added to those of subduing the force, of the people."[24] Madison would have been especially alarmed to know that future presidents would take the country to war without a congressional declaration of hostilities, or that presidents would use the prestige of their office to demand war, knowing that the public would not question their judgment and give full, patriotic support—at least, initially. This problem is explored in some detail during subsequent chapters.

However, at the time ratification of the Constitution was under debate, Madison was convinced that the national legislature would be supreme among the three branches of government and therefore an extremely reliable check on presidents. After all, Article I of the Constitution, which defined and listed the powers of the legislative branch, is by far the longest article in the document and is more than twice as long as Article II, which concerns the presidency. As such, Hamilton believed that the legislative branch would be superior. He wrote in *Federalist* No. 48, "The legislative department derives a superiority in our government. . . . Its constitutional powers being at once more extensive, [it is] less susceptible to precise limits . . ." In addition, with the executive power "being restrained within a narrower compass, and being more simple in its nature . . . [any] projects of usurpation . . . would immediately betray and defame [it]." Furthermore, he argued that the "legislative department alone has access to the pockets of the people, and has . . . full discretion over the pecuniary awards of those who fill the other departments [of government]."[25] That is, what would come to be called "the power of the purse."

In addition, Madison believed that the legislative branch, and especially the more numerous members of the House of Representatives, could use their direct connections to constituents to "plead their cause most successfully with the people." Consequently, they were "more immediately the confidential guardians of the rights and liberties of the people."[26] As he put it, "the legislative authority necessarily predominates."[27] Earlier, during the debates at the Constitutional Convention, he had confidently asserted, "It would rarely if ever happen that the Executive constituted as ours is proposed to be would, have firmness eno[ugh] to resist the legislature . . ."[28] Hamilton agreed and wrote, "The most POPULAR branch of every government, partaking of the republican genius, by being generally the favorite of the people, will be as generally a full match, if not an overmatch, for every other member of the Government."[29] Yet, the great popularity of certain presidents could make it extremely difficult for Congress to check executive abuses of power. In that sense, public opinion could—and would—cut both ways. Furthermore, the legislative branch had to depend on presidents to "take care that Laws be faithfully executed," as stated in Article II, Section 3 of the Constitution. Nevertheless, presidents could and would decide what needed to be done to execute the laws, and Congress had little power to force presidents to carry out the laws that it passed if a president simply refused to do so.

Another supposed check against presidential overreach was a provision for removing presidents from office through impeachment by a majority vote of the House of Representatives, and through conviction by a two-thirds vote in the Senate for "Treason, Bribery, or other High Crimes and Misdemeanors." The inclusion of "misdemeanors," which refers to undefined forms of bad behavior, meant that a president could be impeached and removed for actions that did not violate some criminal statute. Tellingly, one of Madison's main arguments for including impeachment in the Constitution was to prevent any president from "betray[ing] his trust to foreign powers."

Writing in *Federalist* No. 39, Madison somewhat breezily assured readers that "The President of the United States is impeachable at any time during his continuance in office."[30] And if impeached and convicted by the Senate, Hamilton likewise added in *Federalist* No. 69 that the president "would afterwards be liable to prosecution and punishment in the ordinary course of law."[31] Like any other citizen, the president would not be "above the law." What Hamilton and the other delegates did not want to take into consideration, given their dislike of political parties at the time, was that supposed legislative checks on presidents, including impeachment, were not likely to be effective if the president's party enjoyed substantial majorities in either the House or Senate. Furthermore, if the president were extremely popular with the public, legislators were likely to fear losing votes when standing for reelection if they went against a popular president. Hamilton specifically admitted in *Federalist* No. 65 that partisans of the president in the Senate were highly unlikely to vote for impeachment, regardless of the charges.

Disagreeing, future President James Monroe wrote years later that impeachment was the most critical piece among the checks and balances of the Constitution. It was "the main spring of the great machine of government. In this way, the machine will be kept in motion by its own powers and on a proper balance."[32] He could not have been more wrong, given the history of impeachment over the years.

Monroe's words about the Constitution creating a machine that would be kept in motion and on a proper balance stand as a perfect expression of the eighteenth-century Enlightenment's fondness for mechanistic analogies. A century later, poet James Russell Lowell would rephrase Madison's words to say that the Constitution is a "machine that would go of itself."[33] It is uncertain if Lowell meant this comment seriously or if it was intended as a tongue-in-cheek criticism, but experience should have already demonstrated that the Constitution was not a machine that would automatically "be kept in motion by its own powers and on a proper balance." In any case, Monroe's belief would certainly not ring true in the early twenty-first century as President Donald Trump escaped convictions in the Senate following two impeachments, the second of which was for attempting the violent overthrow of the results of a presidential election.

Then there would be the many instances in which the legislative branch ceded authority to the executive in a faraway age when various domestic regulatory programs, along with the country's emergence as an economic colossus and a great world power, would seem to dictate such arrangements. Besides, any president automatically became the most well-known figure in the national government, if not in the entire country (and later in the entire world). Indeed, while most citizens could name the president, many did not know—or could not remember—the name of their own member of Congress. If these situations were not enough, Congress would be at a great disadvantage in vying with presidents for publicity, especially in a future age of visual media that could and often did surround the nation's chief executives with an aura of celebrity that could contribute to dangerous cults of personality.

Perhaps surprising to later generations, the Constitution did not spell out how the federal judiciary could check the executive branch. Rather, Article III merely stated that the judicial power was to "extend to all Cases, in Law and Equity" arising under the Constitution, laws of the United States, or "Treaties made." Citing such jurisdiction, the Supreme Court would later assert in the case of *Marbury v. Madison* (1803) its power of "judicial review" over presidential authority, as well as over other governmental actions, on a case-by-case basis.[34] Even so, the Supreme Court, as well as the lower federal courts, would often prove reluctant to come down against presidential overreach, ironically citing the separation of powers doctrine regarding the executive, legislative, and judicial branches of government and their somewhat ill-defined roles in hopefully checking and balancing one another. Furthermore, the federal courts, including the Supreme Court, could not enforce their decisions, since such enforcement was the responsibility of the executive branch, as headed by the president. Then, in 2024, in the case of *Trump v. United States*, the high court would rule that the president was immune from judicial prosecution or restraint when engaged in official executive actions. (And there could be no doubt that Trump would assert that anything he did as president would qualify as an official executive action.)

Besides claiming powers that were not clearly authorized by the Constitution, the Supreme Court would become increasingly the most undemocratic institution of US government. Its members were to serve for "good behavior," as noted above, which has been interpreted to mean for life or until they decided on their own to retire from the court (except in cases of very unlikely impeachment) to supposedly insulate them from momentary whims of popular opinion. However, given the average life expectancy in the 1800s of just thirty-five years, the first justices would serve only an average of 8.3 years.[35] In comparison, justices appointed after 1970 have averaged 25.3 years on the high court, more than a generation after presidents appointed them, and in many cases long after greatly shifting attitudes and needs in American society.[36]

Another important check against the president, as well as against the federal government generally, came via the First Amendment to the Constitution, added in 1791. This amendment forbade Congress from "abridging the freedom of speech, or of the press; or the right of the people peaceably to assemble, and to petition the government for a redress of grievances." (The amendment did not forbid the president from making such abridgments, since it was doubtless assumed that presidents had no such authority.) Freedom of the press, which later extended to all forms of media, would form the basis for what came to be called the "Fourth Branch of Government." A free press could criticize presidents openly and hold them accountable for their actions in the arena of public opinion. However, in a later age, presidents could and would circumvent a degree of media scrutiny by finding ways to "speak" directly to the American people without the filters of journalists. Such would become especially true by virtue of various forms of electronic and social media that would not be created for many decades after the Constitutional Convention and that none of the delegates could have fathomed.

Yet another check against any sort of governmental tyranny, according to Madison, was factionalism, to be accepted as natural human behavior and harnessed for the good. In this way, he insisted, competing interests would keep any one faction from taking over government and abusing its power. Thus, the more conflicting interests throughout the country, the better. As he wrote in *Federalist* No. 10, "Extend the sphere, and you take in a greater variety of parties and interests; you make it less probable that a majority of the whole will have a common motive to invade the rights of other citizens." Even if such common motives for invading rights existed, he believed that in a country so large, "It will be more difficult for all who feel it to discover their own strength and to act in unison with each other." In this way, competing interests would supposedly serve as a check against the abuse of power. Again, one should keep in mind that such predictions came in an age before mass-circulated periodicals, television, and especially social media would allow factions and interests to more easily discover their own strength and act in unison with each other.

Struggling to Shape the Presidency

The question of term limits for the presidency came up during convention debates as another mechanism for thwarting presidential overreach. One obvious argument for such limits stemmed from a fear that presidents might use the advantages of incumbency to occupy the office virtually for life. In the end, the delegates decided to give presidents a four-year term, but with no limit on the number of terms they could serve. There were two basic reasons for this decision: The more familiar reason stemmed from the desire to maintain a president in office in case of an ongoing emergency that the incumbent would, in theory, be best able to manage. A less well-known reason for allowing unlimited terms was that the potential for reelection would cause presidents to "behave themselves" and to observe certain norms of proper disposition as a way of securing the public's favor in the next election. As it turned out, Washington, the country's first chief executive, established a two-term precedent that was not superseded until Franklin Roosevelt won a third and then a fourth term (in 1940 and 1944 respectively), which triggered the Twenty-Second Amendment, ratified in 1951, that essentially limits presidents to two full terms.[37]

Thomas Jefferson received two copies of the proposed Constitution while in Paris and was alarmed at the lack of term limits for the president. Expressing his concerns to John Adams, he wrote, "Reason and experience prove to us that a chief magistrate, so continuable [sic], is an officer for life. When one or two generations shall have proved that this is an office for life, it becomes on every succession worthy of intrigue, of bribery, of force, and even of foreign interference."[38] Another of his objections was the lack of a bill of rights, though he believed the problem could be rectified through the amendment process, which did indeed take place under Madison's leadership, and ten amendments forming the Bill of Rights were ratified as part of the Constitution in 1791. Yet as Jefferson reflected further on the Constitution, he grew enthusiastic about it, and upon returning to the United States, he would become the nation's first Secretary of State. Nevertheless, his fears about the power of incumbency were not misplaced, as time would tell.

Since the possibility of foreign influence on the presidency had been a serious worry for the delegates throughout the convention debates, they required as a further check that the president must be a "natural born citizen of the United States" who would not be tempted to favor the land of his birth against American interests. The president also had to be "Fourteen Years a Resident within the United States."[39] This residency requirement was in response to worries that even a natural born citizen might have lived many years abroad before returning to the United States and becoming president, and thereby have come under the influence of foreign interests.

A further protection against foreign influence was the foreign Emoluments Clause, which applies to any federal officeholder, including the president. It reads, "No Person holding any Office of Profit or Trust under [the United States], shall, without the Consent of the Congress, accept of any present, Emolument, Office, or Title, of any kind whatever, from any King, Prince, or foreign State."[40] The giving of expensive gifts was then a mainstay of European diplomacy that personified to Americans the corruption of monarchical countries, which the delegates wanted to banish from their new government, lest it fall into corruption and decline or become in thrall to foreign interests, intrigues, and entanglements.[41]

The question of how to select a president, eventually concluding with the creation of the Electoral College, turned out to be especially vexing. The topic came up at the convention on twenty-one separate days and led to thirty different votes on the matter.[42] During the convention debates, a proposal that kept coming up was to have Congress choose the president, but the delegates rejected the idea because it would deprive presidents of independence and render them less likely to check legislative overreach. In other words, it would undermine a system of checks and balances. Some of the delegates also rejected a nationwide popular vote because they believed, for one thing, that voters spread over such a large territory, at a time of limited transportation and thus dissemination of news, would have no way of ascertaining the qualities of the various candidates. In the words of delegate George Mason, "It would be as unnatural to refer the choice of a proper character for Chief Magistrate to the people, as it would, to refer a trial of colours [sic] to a blind man."[43] And even if the delegates had opted for the election of presidents by popular vote, they assumed that the states would continue to limit the franchise to a small percentage of inhabitants.

Despite the importance of the issue, coming up with a mechanism for choosing presidents became the task of "The Committee on Unfinished Parts" in the waning days of the convention. Six of the eleven members of the committee, made up from one from each of the states then represented at the convention, voted in favor of electing the president by popular vote, perhaps with the comfort of knowing that the popular vote would be very limited by state qualifications for the franchise. However, the other five, who hailed from southern states and who were already very protective of states' rights, objected to election by popular ballot. The South was already fearful that the northern states might grow more populous than the southern states and at some future date use their strength in any popular election of presidents to threaten the institution of slavery. In addition, the three-fifths compromise, which allowed the slaveholding states to count those who were enslaved as three fifths of a person for the purposes of representation in the House of Representatives, would not help them when it came to the popular vote, since people in bondage were obviously not eligible to vote.

Some scholars have seen the creation of the Electoral College as something of a default position after the convention had rejected every other proposal, with a final decision made when the delegates were desperate to wind up business and go home.[44] Others, such as Shlomo Slonim, in a scholarly article about the creation of the college, have argued that this solution was in fact brilliant in its acceptability for the times as well as for the delegates, since it paralleled the compromises already made over representation in the two houses of the national legislature. To quote Slonim, "The Electoral College was an exact replica of Congress, since each state was entitled to as many votes in the Electoral College as it had in the House of Representatives and the Senate, with even the smallest state entitled to at least three votes."[45] This latter privilege stemmed from the fact that each state, regardless of size, was entitled to two senators even if it merited just one representative in the House. The southern states would benefit from the "three-fifths rule," which reflected their representation in the House of Representatives.

Another supposed virtue of the Electoral College, Hamilton argued in *Federalist* No. 68, was the prevention of corruption in selecting a person to lead the country, since each state would choose its own electors, equivalent to the number of its senators and members of the House of Representatives in Congress. Given that the electors were dispersed over several states, he believed it would be difficult to arrange any corrupt conspiracies to elect a certain individual as president. Another reason for approving the Electoral College, Hamilton asserted, was its function as an additional check against foreign intrigue, since the president would be selected by the Electoral College, rather than "any preexisting bodies of men [such as legislators] who might be tampered with beforehand [for example, by foreign agents] to prostitute their votes."[46] Hamilton elaborated on this point, saying, "The most deadly adversaries of republican government might naturally have been expected to make their approaches . . . chiefly from the desire in foreign powers to gain an improper ascendant in our councils."[47]

In addition, the Electoral College was an answer to fears that state sovereignty would suffer under a new and more powerful central government, as indicated by the southern states' refusal to go along with the popular election of the president at the convention. With an Electoral College, the states would be choosing the president, since each state would receive a body of electors equal to the number of its senators and members of the House of Representatives.

Furthermore, each state could decide how to appoint its electors, and initially the states used a variety of methods: In some cases, the state legislatures themselves designated electors; in other states, the voters selected them in statewide elections; and in still others, voters chose their presidential electors in specially designated districts within the state.[48] By 1836, all the states would allow the popular vote to determine the electoral vote, except for South Carolina, where the legislature continued to select electors until after the Civil War.[49] And since the states had different numbers of people in them, a variation that would widen over time, those living in small states would have an increasingly disproportionate voice in selecting presidents, given that their two senators would give them an additional two electoral votes no matter how small their populations.

Most Americans would be shocked to know that it remains constitutional more than two centuries after the Constitution went into effect for states to reverse course and have their legislators appoint the electors, so long as they passed a law or made a state constitutional change to that effect before an election.[50] In the aftermath of the 2020 presidential election, there were attempts by Donald Trump and the Republican Party to make such changes "after the fact," regardless of state electoral laws.

Because the states jealously maintained their "rights," the delegates to the Constitutional Convention had little choice but to allow them to determine who was qualified to vote, as well as to control the whole apparatus of casting and counting ballots. This decentralized system meant there would be few nationwide standards or rules for elections, with the exception of several amendments added later to the Constitution backed up by Congressional legislation, which required states to allow various classes of citizens to cast ballots, such as non-whites, women, and citizens eighteen years of age and over.[51] Even so, voting rules and methods could vary widely from state to state and result in considerable confusion and contention when it came to determining presidential winners, which would happen more than once and, in the process, undermine confidence in the electoral process, as would state laws and regulations for the purpose of voter suppression. Furthermore, as mentioned above, it was theoretically within their constitutional rights for states to reverse course and have their legislature select presidential electors with no regard to any popular vote. (On the other hand, state control over elections might serve as a protection against a power-hungry president who attempted to take over management of elections from the states.)

The delegates also could not know that, within two generations, nearly all the states would allow voters to choose the presidential electors, with most states adopting "winner-take-all" provisions that awarded all their electoral votes to whomever received the most popular ballots, no matter how small the margin of popular victory. In other words, a presidential candidate could win a critical handful of states by a relatively small number of popular votes, while the presidential opponent won other states by large majorities of popular ballots with no effect on the number of electoral votes won in those states. Once these shifts occurred, the candidate who won the "popular vote" nationwide could lose the electoral vote and be cheated, in the minds of many voters, out of the presidency, with the stigma of illegitimacy hanging over the person who was instead installed as chief executive. This disparity between the popular and electoral vote would occur five times over the years, most recently in 2000 and 2016. Such discrepancies put into question whether the United States was a full-fledged, modern democracy, not only in the opinion of many Americans but also among the citizens of various democracies around the world, who find the Electoral College to be absurd as well as unjust. This was a situation that the delegates to the Constitutional Convention did not and could not foresee.

The Constitution set down only three basic qualifications for would-be presidents: They had to be at least thirty-five years old, and, as referenced earlier, must be a "natural born Citizen" and have been "Fourteen Years a Resident within the United States."[52] The document made no requirement for prior experience in government. However, it is very likely that the delegates assumed that any president would have at least some personal and practical familiarity with the workings of government, given that the great majority of the delegates had served in governmental capacities of one sort or another before becoming delegates to the convention.

Surprisingly to later generations, familiar with primary elections and party nominating conventions, the Constitution did not specify any method for identifying presidential candidates—and still does not more than two centuries later. In this regard, all nominating procedures exist outside the Constitution. (i.e., they are extra-constitutional though not unconstitutional.) Initially, the electors in each state would cast votes for two individuals, one of whom had to be from another state. In effect, they would be nominating candidates at the same time they were casting their electoral votes. The person receiving a majority of electoral votes would become president, and the person with the next highest number of electoral votes would become vice president, the argument being that the vice president would then be as qualified for office as the president in case the runner-up had to succeed to that office. If no person received a majority of electoral votes, the House of Representatives would select the president (with each state delegation having one vote regardless of its population, yet another anti-majoritarian provision), and the Senate would select the vice president (in which the smaller states in population with two senators each would have a "louder" voice). Later, the Twelfth Amendment to the Constitution, ratified in 1804, required the electors to vote separately for president and vice president as a response to the 1800 election, which had resulted in an electoral vote tie between the presidential and vice-presidential candidate.[53]

Because of continuing frustration with the Electoral College, despite what had seemed to be a good solution for selecting a president in the waning days of the Constitutional Convention, there have been hundreds of attempts to reform or eliminate the scheme since the Constitution went into effect in 1789.[54] However, if any section of the country or any political party has deemed such actions to be contrary to their interests, there is no chance of change, and the United States appears stuck with an undemocratic and increasingly corruptible system for choosing its presidents.

However, to return to the early 1800s, the two political parties, which were largely organizations of legislators and other officeholders, began holding caucuses in Congress to nominate their party's candidate for president. They then instructed their party organizations in each state to choose electors who would vote for those nominated by their respective parties in Congress (dependent, of course, on each state's method for deciding how electoral votes would be allocated and apportioned). Indeed, the desire to influence presidential nominations and to choose members of the Electoral College in each state was an important reason why political parties emerged very early in the presidential election process.[55] This outcome was also unexpected at the Constitutional Convention, where, in the words of constitutional scholar Jack Rakove, "few [of the delegates] thought the electors would do anything more than nominate candidates."[56]

They also believed that in many cases, none of the candidates would win a majority of the Electoral College, resulting in the choice being made by Congress, in many if not most cases.

Nevertheless, under such a party caucus system for making presidential nominations, the personal qualifications and fitness for office of presidential aspirants would, at least, be fairly well-known by members of the House of Representatives and the Senate.[57] The Constitution did not provide for this strategy, but it at least solved the question of how to select presidential candidates—to repeat, an issue that the delegates had not adequately addressed—or really addressed at all. Later, national party conventions would nominate presidential candidates and still later primary elections conducted in the various states would largely take over the nominating function, methods that were also extra-constitutional. By not prescribing a method for nominating presidents, the Constitution would leave open possibilities for all manner of manipulation, second-guessing, and even corruption.

If the Constitutional Convention had chosen to create a parliamentary system of government, instead of what has come to be called a "presidential system," the method of selecting someone to head the government could have been much simpler. In that case, the leader of the majority party in the legislature, or a person designated by a coalition of parties, would become prime minister. It could also be argued that the person selected in a parliamentary system would always have some necessary experience, since that individual would likely have served as a member of the legislative body for many years, as well as very likely being a government minister already, and would be widely regarded by fellow party members as both competent and hopefully upstanding. A parliamentary government would also have resulted in most cases in a smoother and easier method for removing an ineffective or otherwise objectionable head of government, either through calling new elections or by a party removing the prime minister and selecting another from within their ranks. However, the British parliamentary system was not fully evolved at the time of the Constitutional Convention, and the delegates associated it with favoritism and corruption. Then, too, the delegates disparaged political parties, which are standard in evolved parliamentary systems.[58]

In not opting for a parliamentary type of government and in not anticipating the growth of a popular vote for president in all the states within several decades after ratification of the Constitution, the delegates to the Constitutional Convention unknowingly set the stage for what would later be called a "plebiscitary presidency." That is, they did not foresee that presidents claiming popular mandates could come to claim a separate democratic legitimacy and at times would be encouraged to circumvent or even defy Congressional checks on their authority.[59] Although such claimed mandates might weaken or even lapse because of changing opinions and changing national needs during an administration—or because of unacceptable behavior by presidents—there were no satisfactory solutions. Of course, one way of removing such "wounded" presidents was through the very unlikely remedy of impeachment—or, failing that, by waiting until the next election.

The Presidential Dilemma

The delegates of the Constitution had clearly struggled with the presidency. They knew the document they had forged was imperfect regarding the executive branch and much else, but they took comfort in believing that future generations could use the amendment process to correct their mistakes or to meet the needs of changing times. In a 1787 speech, convention delegate James Wilson told his audience, "If there are errors, it should be remembered that the seeds of reform [meaning the amendment process] are sewn in the work itself."[60] Reflecting on the making of the Constitution many years later, delegate Gouverneur Morris wrote to a friend, "Surrounded by difficulties, we did the best we could; leaving it with those who should come after us to take counsel from experience, and exercise prudently the power of amendment, which we had provided."[61]

Morris and the other delegates understandably did not want the document amended too easily, which is why they required a two-thirds vote of both the House and Senate to propose an amendment and ratification by three-fourths of the state legislatures. (Less known is an alternative constitutional provision that allows two-thirds of the state legislatures to call for a national convention to propose amendments, after which three-fourths of the state legislatures or three-fourths of specially called state conventions must ratify it.)[62] However, Morris and other delegates did not appreciate that political partisanship would make it extremely difficult to amend the document since political parties would tend to support or oppose amendments depending largely on whether they believed such amendments would advance their prospects at election time. Thus, the nation would struggle to come up with alternative approaches to tame abuses of the presidency.

While creating the office of president, the delegates to the Constitutional Convention faced a dilemma. They wanted to create a chief executive with enough power to preside over the government and give overall direction to the nation. At the same time, they feared that future presidents might so abuse their power as to become like kings. Whether fully recognized then, as well as now, a powerful presidency indeed represents the monarchical aspect of the American government.

Convention delegate Alexander Hamilton, who himself had called for a strong executive at the helm of a new government, was well aware of criticism that presidents might end up acting like kings. He reported in *Federalist* No. 67, that there had been tremendous controversy over defining the nation's highest office. "There is hardly any part of the system," he wrote, "which could have been attended with greater difficulty than the arrangement of [the presidency] . . ." He went on to report that critics of creating the office (with whom he did not agree) had conjured the image of a "diadem sparkling on [the president's] brow and the imperial purple flowing in his train"—"seated on a throne surrounded by minions and mistresses, giving audience to foreign potentates, in all the supercilious pomp of majesty."[63]

Even delegate James Madison, who is credited with conceiving and fighting for a system of checks and balances to block abuses of power, had written before the convention assembled that the new government needed to assume sweeping powers over the American continent much like those formerly wielded by the British monarch. "Let the national government be armed," he urged, "with a positive and complete authority in all cases where uniform measures are necessary, . . . as the King of Great Britain heretofore had."[64]

A century later, future President Woodrow Wilson (who almost seemed to be anticipating his own very powerful tenure in the White House) wrote while a graduate student in the 1880s that, "[the] president's functions were made of the highest dignity. . . . The president's "privileges [are] many and substantial—so great, indeed, that it has pleased the fancy of some writers to parade them as exceeding those of the British crown . . ."[65]

These references about the essentially monarchial powers of the presidency are very telling. So, too, are the many ways that presidents, as referenced above, could circumvent the Constitution because of certain silences and deficiencies in the document, which would contribute in the future to expansions in as well as to abuses of presidential power. Most worrisome, these silences and deficiencies could be manipulated to undermine both American democracy and a republican form of government as they emerged over the years, thus allowing presidents to enhance the inherently monarchial aspect of their office.

Certainly, respect for the Constitution as a foundation for the rule of law remains extremely important and is the key to basic rights and individual liberties, as well as defining and regulating basic institutions of national government. Yet in many respects, the Constitution has come to resemble a rambling old house greatly in need of repair if it is to safeguard American democracy more effectively and to check both actual and potential abuses of presidential authority. Because of this "deferred maintenance," those who have wanted to compromise or dismantle democracy have sometimes sought to use democratic ideas and processes as a means of undermining democracy itself.

Suggestions for repair of the Constitutional edifice will be offered in the final chapter of this book. But on the way to getting there, the author will tell the story of how various presidents over time have augmented the power of the office, for good or ill, and have tested and even defied the checks and balances that were supposed to keep the presidency within bounds.

Notes

1 These phrases would appear in the Preamble of the Constitution.
2 Quoted in Catherine Drinker Bowen, *Miracle at Philadelphia: The Story of the Constitutional Convention* (Boston: Little, Brown and Company, 1966), 5.
3 James Madison, *Federalist James,* No. 38.
4 Anne Applebaum, *Twilight of Democracy: The Seductive Lure of Authoritarianism* (New York: Doubleday, 2020), 14–15.
5 The case was *Shelby County v. Holder* (2013).
6 On what the delegates learned—or thought they learned—from classical antiquity, see Thomas E. Ricks' thorough and thoughtful account in *First Principles: What*

America's Founders Learned from the Greeks and Romans and How that Shaped Our Country (New York: HarperCollins, 2020).

7 For an excellent discussion of the ways in which Gibbon's Decline and Fall resonated with the delegates, see Zephyr Teachout, *Corruption in America: From Benjamin Franklin's Snuff Box to Citizens United* (Cambridge, MA: Harvard University Press, 2104), 32–4.

8 See Jack N. Rakove, *Original Meanings: Politics and Ideas in the Making of the Constitution* (New York: Vintage Books, 1996), 84, 269.

9 Article II, Section 1, Clause 1.

10 See Phillip J. Cooper, *By Order of the President: The Use and Abuse of Executive Direct Action* (Lawrence: University Press of Kansas, 2004), 6–7.

11 Article II, Section 1, Clause 8.

12 Forrest McDonald, in "Forword to the Liberty Fund Edition" of Charles C. Thach, *The Creation of the Presidency: A Study in Constitutional History* (Indianapolis: Liberty Fund, 2007), xiv.

13 Rakove, *Original Meanings*, 244.

14 *Papers of Alexander Hamilton*, ed. Harold C. Syrett et al., 27 vols. (New York: Columbia University Press, 1961–1987), 4:165, 186, 192. See also Ron Chernow, *Alexander Hamilton* (New York: Penguin Books, 2005), 232–5.

15 Chernow, *Alexander Hamilton*, 234. See also Bowen, *Miracle*, 114.

16 *The Writings of James Madison*, ed. Gaillard Hunt, 9 vols. (New York: G.P. Putnam's Sons, 1909–1910), 1:406.

17 Bowen, *Miracle*, 57.

18 Alexander Hamilton, quoted in Bowen, *Miracle*, 208.

19 Washington to Henry Lee, October 31, 1786, in W. W. Abbot et al., eds., *The Papers of George Washington: Confederation Series*, 6 vols. (Charlottesville: University Press of Virginia, 1992–1997), 4:318, and Washington to James Madison, November 5, 1786, in ibid., 4:331.

20 Ricks, *First Principles*, 5–6, 10.

21 Ibid., 130.

22 Ibid., 206–7.

23 Hamilton, Constitutional Convention, Plan of Government, *Hamilton Papers*, June 18, 1787, https://founders.archives.gov/documents/Hamilton/01-04-02-0099.

24 Madison, "Political Observations," April 20, 1795, in *Letters and Other Writings of James Madison* (New York: E. Worthington, 1884), 4:491.

25 Madison, *Federalist* No. 48.

26 Madison, *Federalist* No. 49.

27 Madison, *Federalist* No. 51.

28 Madison, *Notes of Debates in the Federal Convention of 1787* (Athens: Ohio University Press, 1985), 63.

29 Hamilton, *Federalist* No. 66.

30 Madison, *Federalist* No. 39.

31 Hamilton, *Federalist* No. 69.

32 Quoted in Arthur M. Schlesinger, Jr., *The Imperial Presidency* (Boston: Houghton Mifflin Company, 1973), 12.

33 James Russell Lowell, "A Machine That Would Go of Itself: The Constitution in . . ." www.jstor.org/stable/365428.

34 See Article III, Section 2. The Supreme Court asserted this right of judicial review over the presidency in the famous case of *Marbury v. Madison* (1803).
35 A life expectancy of thirty-five in 1800, of course, did not mean that no one lived well beyond that age, since greater childhood mortality and death in childbirth at that time substantially pulled down the average. Nevertheless, the state of medical science and general ignorance about public health meant that far fewer people lived well into old age during the early nineteenth century.
36 Steven Levitsky and Daniel Ziblatt, *Tyranny of the Minority* (New York: Crown Publishing Company, 2023), 159.
37 Under certain circumstances, a president could serve nearly ten years if individuals were to be vice president and then become president because of the death, resignation, or incapacity of the president, which propelled them into the presidency at a time when the former president had fewer than two years left in office. In this case, the former vice president could serve out these nearly two years and then run for two whole four-year terms.
38 Thomas Jefferson to John Adams, November 13, 1787, https://founders.archives.gov .doccuments.adams.
39 Article II, Section 1
40 Article I, Section 9, Clause 8.
41 See Teachout, *Corruption in America*, 17–31.
42 Shlomo Slonim, "The Electoral College at Philadelphia: The Evolution of an Ad Hoc Congress for the Selection of a President," *Journal of American History* (June 1986): 35.
43 George Mason, quoted in Lucius Wilmerding, Jr., *The Electoral College* (New Brunswick: Rutgers University Press, 1958), 5.
44 Levitsky and Ziblatt, *Tyranny of the Minority*, 157.
45 Slonim, "The Electoral College," 51.
46 Hamilton, *Federalist* No. 68.
47 Ibid.
48 On the matter of how the states selected electors in the early years, see Wilmerding, *The Electoral College*, 42–67. Despite being published six decades ago, the Wilmerding volume on the Electoral College remains the most thorough and incisive account on the subject.
49 Ibid., 64–5.
50 Ibid., 55.
51 These were the Fifteenth Amendment (1870), which forbade the states from denying the right to vote on the basis of "race, color, or previous condition of servitude"; the Nineteenth Amendment (1920), which gave women the right to vote; and the Twenty-Sixth Amendment (1971), which lowered the voting age to 18.
52 Article II Section 1.
53 The House of Representatives broke the tie after thirty-six ballots, awarding the presidency to Jefferson, who was widely understood to be the preferred candidate.
54 Thomas H. Neale and Andrew Nolan, *The National Popular Vote (NPV) Initiative: Direct Election of the President by Interstate Compact (PDF)* (Report) (Washington, DC: Congressional Research Service, 2019).
55 Rakove, *Original Meanings*, 268.
56 Ibid., 265.

57 On the caucus system, see Eugene H. Roseboom, *A History of Presidential Elections* (New York: The Macmillan Company, 1970), 33, 38, 42–3, 51, 55–6, 59, 68, 74–5, 83.

58 For a good comparison between parliamentary and presidential systems, see Arend Lijphart, ed., *Parliamentary Versus Presidential Government* (Oxford: Oxford University Press, 1992).

59 On the concept of "plebiscitary presidentialism," see Juan Jose Linz, "The Perils of Presidentialism," *Journal of Democracy* 1 (Winter 1990): 60–2; Juan Jose Linz and Arturo Valenzuela, *The Failure of Presidential Democracy* (Baltimore: Johns Hopkins University Press, 1994).

60 Speech of James Wilson, October 6, 1787, www.let.rug.nl/usa/documents/1786-1800/the-anti. See also Jesse Wegman, "Will We Ever Amend the Constitution Again?" *New York Times*, August 8, 2021.

61 Gouverneur Morris to W. H. Wells, February 24, 1815, https://www.consource.org/document/gouverneur-morris-to-w-h-wells-1815-2-24.

62 See Article V of the Constitution for the amending process. The only time state conventions were used to ratify an amendment was for the Twenty-First Amendment in 1933, which repealed the Eighteenth Amendment that provided for the prohibition of alcohol.

63 Hamilton, *Federalist* No. 67.

64 Bowen, *Miracle*, 14.

65 Woodrow Wilson, *Congressional Government: A Study in American Politics* (Mineola: Dover Publications, 2006 [1885]), 47.

2

Demi-God and Dissenter

Formative Presidential Styles

[President Washington] has exactly copied the style of monarchs . . . [and] has in short only differed in kings in wanting a kingdom, which his friends were seeking to provide for him.

National Gazette, February 2, 1793

George Washington sets out from his home at Mount Vernon, Virginia, on April 14, 1789, making his way to New York City, then the temporary capital of the United States, where he will take the oath of office as the nation's first president. The Constitution has designated March Fourth as Inauguration Day, but only during the first week of April have enough senators arrived to form a quorum necessary to count the electoral votes sent in by the states. As everyone expects, the electors have selected Washington unanimously.

One biographer observed that the president-elect's journey to New York was much like a "royal progress by which ancient kings took symbolic possession of their realm."[1] Allowing for some exaggeration, Washington's "progress" to the capital was awe-inspiring to those who witnessed it. Escorts on horseback went forth from each town and village to meet him, at which point Washington stepped down from his coach and mounted "Prescott," his great white parade horse. Lining the streets were flags, emblems, and congratulatory slogans. There were invariably speeches, toasts, and fetes for the honored guest. An estimated twenty thousand people watched him pass through Philadelphia.[2]

The inauguration finally took place in New York on April 30. As Washington's coach made its way from the "President's House" to Federal Hall, five military units and a band made up of drummers and bagpipers accompanied him. Decorating his coat were metal buttons stamped with images of eagles, and at his side, a ceremonial sword. Appearing on a balcony, where he would take the oath of office, crowds cheered and artillery boomed from the Battery at the tip of Manhattan as well as from ships in the harbor below.[3] That day and in the years to follow, not a few men and women believed that God had sent Washington to save the nation, and at his death, many attributed characteristics of divinity to him.

Twelve years later, fellow Virginian Thomas Jefferson took the oath of office as the country's third president in Washington, DC, having become the nation's seat of government only a year before. There was nothing resembling a "royal progress" for Jefferson from his Virginia home at Monticello, partly because he was already in the new capital, where he had been serving as John Adams's vice president. However, it is unlikely that he would have savored or encouraged such veneration. An artillery unit and a contingent of riflemen did parade in front of his lodging in Washington, but eschewing a fine coach, Jefferson simply walked to the unfinished Capitol with a group of friends. He wore a plain suit of clothes and did not carry a sword at his side.[4] According to the *Alexandria Times* newspaper, "his dress was, as usual, that of a plain citizen without any distinctive badge of office."[5] Jefferson's unremarkable style at the inauguration was a harbinger of how he would conduct himself in office, and in striking contrast to the pomp that would surround the Washington presidency. Although Jefferson greatly admired Washington, he would dissent from a growing public belief that his predecessor had been Heaven-sent to deliver America from its enemies and to form a new nation, as if he were president by divine right.

Although Jefferson cut a very different figure than Washington as president, the awe with which many Americans regarded the nation's first chief executive suggested that many citizens craved a degree of pomp and circumstance surrounding the nation's highest office. It was almost as if they missed the regal trappings associated with kingship. This craving would later be satisfied in part with celebrity and cults of personality surrounding some future presidents.

Two Virginians

Although both Jefferson and Washington belonged to the Virginia aristocracy, Washington had come into the world with far fewer prospects than Jefferson enjoyed. Despite and perhaps because of limited horizons, Washington desired from an early age both great wealth and the fame that would accompany it.[6] In the words of biographer John Ferling, "He was madly ambitious and obsessed with recognition and renown."[7] His father, Augustine Washington, had been a man of substance in colonial Virginia, but at his death when George was eleven years old, the bulk of his property and wealth went to the two sons from his first marriage. George, who was born of his father's second marriage, received only a small, worn-out farm and some ten enslaved people. There was also no money for continuing his formal education, let alone sending him to school in England, where his two older brothers had gone.

George chose his older brother Lawrence as a model of ascent, as well as a touchstone for good manners and habits of speech appropriate for addressing wealthy and powerful men in Virginia. He also read books about ancient and modern ethics and the men who personified them. When he was just fourteen, George determined to follow Lawrence's example by joining the British Navy, but his mother refused her consent. Then, when Lawrence died in 1752, the twenty-year-old George inherited his brother's large plantation at Mount Vernon, ever after associated with the future president. Seven years later, he married Martha Custis, a wealthy widow who brought even more land as well as many enslaved men, women, and children into the marriage.

In addition, Washington bought large swaths of land in Virginia's western frontier. By his late twenties, he was one of the wealthiest men in Virginia. In 1758, a year after his marriage, he won election to the House of Burgesses, the colony's colonial legislature, giving him considerable prestige as well as a voice in politics.

Adding to Washington's allure was an impressive physique. At a time when the average height for adult men in colonial America was about 5 feet 7 inches, Washington stood 6 feet 3 inches. He weighed approximately 175 pounds, with broad shoulders and well-proportioned, muscular arms and legs that made him look especially imposing in the saddle. Although charming when the occasion called for it, no one would have called Washington handsome; rather he exuded a sense of rugged strength and an aura of leadership. In the opinion of Jefferson, Washington was no intellectual and would later write of him, "His mind was great and powerful without being of the very first rate. . . . It was slow in operation, being little aided by invention or imagination, but sure in conclusion."[8]

In 1774, Washington became one of seven Virginia delegates to the First Continental Congress in Philadelphia. There the assembly protested what they considered depredations by the Mother Country, including the Quebec Act of 1774, which placed the Ohio Country and all the rest of the land north of the Ohio River under the control of the Province of Quebec, which Britain had annexed after its victory in the French and Indian War. The Congress also condemned the various taxes levied by Parliament on the colonies, in addition to the so-called Coercive Acts that sought to punish Boston for the Tea Party and other acts of defiance.

When the Continental Congress reassembled in May of 1775, Washington packed a handsome buff and blue officer's uniform that he himself had designed, guessing correctly that the Congress would soon call on him to become the commander of an American army, and wore it each day to sessions in what would later be known as Philadelphia's Independence Hall. In addition to his prior military experience, Congress felt reassured by Washington's modesty when he proclaimed himself unequal to the task in accepting his commission from the legislators. This was not, in fact, a calculated or false modesty, since Washington well appreciated the challenge ahead of him. Nor were his pronouncements disingenuous throughout the war about longing for the comforts of Mount Vernon. Even so, his professed fears of inadequacy, along with his stated desire to return to civilian life, went very far in allaying worries that he might seek to make himself a king. His refusal to accept a salary, being content with reimbursement for personal expenses, only reinforced the belief that Washington had no interest in using his command for personal aggrandizement.

Several recent military historians have found fault with Washington's abilities as a military strategist during the Revolution that resulted in various defeats. These included reversals on Long Island, New York; at Fort Lee, New Jersey; at Brandywine west of Philadelphia (which led to British occupation of the then American capital); and at his failed counterattack at Germantown northwest of Philadelphia. Yet Congress was careful not to fault Washington in public for these disasters, believing the people needed to see him as a heroic figure who would protect the country and lead it to victory.

Although French assistance was the critical factor in the surrender of British General Cornwallis at Yorktown in October 1781, most Americans believed the credit should go to Washington, with only a little assistance from France. Two years later, after Britain had recognized American independence and the war had come to an official end, Washington submitted his resignation to Congress, now meeting in Annapolis, Maryland, and immediately returned to Mount Vernon and civilian life. He had already come to symbolize the American union and had become the personal glue that held the nation together in dangerous and uncertain times. His task accomplished, he willingly gave up power, unlike so many other military leaders in the past, such as Julius Caesar and Napoleon Bonaparte.

In contrast to Washington, Thomas Jefferson began life in far more promising circumstances. As the eldest son, he inherited some 5,000 acres of land. His father's family, as well as his mother's kin, the Randolphs, had long been leaders in the colony, giving Jefferson a strong sense that he had both the duty and the example to be a leader himself. He had a thirst for learning everything he could, and in the fall of 1760, he entered the College of William and Mary in Virginia's capital at Williamsburg. There, Professor William Small introduced him to the tenets of the eighteenth-century Enlightenment, which would become a life-long inspiration. Another of his teachers who attended those evenings at the palace was George Wythe, a celebrated lawyer under whom Jefferson "read" law in preparation for his acceptance to the Virginia bar.

All these advantages contributed to Jefferson's rapid rise in politics, becoming a member of the House of Burgesses at age twenty-six and one of Virginia's delegates, at age thirty-three, to the Second Continental Congress in Philadelphia, where he subsequently became the principal author of the Declaration of Independence.[9] He agreed with many colonial leaders up and down the coast that the imperial government in London was denying them the rights and privileges of Englishmen and had already shown himself to be an adept writer who could eloquently proclaim them. He was also a brilliant conversationalist, which attracted other men to admire and promote him. In the decade that followed, Jefferson served as governor of Virginia and the American Minister to France.

Although later generations would see Jefferson as the intellectual hero of the American Revolution, he would never come close to rivaling Washington's reputation in the pantheon of Founding Fathers, a position that the first president reinforced through an aura of dignity and formality from his initial days in office. This demeanor came naturally to him. At the same time, Washington believed that such an approach to the presidency was necessary, being very aware that he would be setting precedents for those who came after him.

A "Republican Court"

Because the country was young, and its new government was even younger, Washington thought it was important to establish an atmosphere of protocol and respect—even of mystique—surrounding the presidency, although much of it was adapted from the royal courts of Europe. For instance, every Tuesday afternoon between three and four o'clock he held formal levees, a term that described functions at royal courts at the time. On these occasions, he wore a black velvet suit, a white vest, and yellow gloves, with knee breeches and silver buckles on his shoes. At his side hung a ceremonial sword, and on his head rested a stylish cocked hat. Footmen in livery wearing white wigs attended dinner guests, both features of royal courts in Europe at the time. The president did not shake hands but bowed stiffly to guests. He did not accept invitations to private homes for fear of mixing informally with other guests or that he might be seen as playing favorites by accepting some invitations and not others, and he invariably referred to his wife Martha as "Lady Washington." When he traveled through the streets of Philadelphia, which was the nation's capital from 1790 to 1800, he rode in a carriage drawn by six matching horses, with his family's coat of arms emblazoned on the side.[10]

Vice President John Adams, as the presiding officer of the Senate, had thought there should be an elevated title for the president and proposed several possibilities. Among these were "His Elective Majesty," "His Mightiness," and "His Highness the President of the United States and Protector of the Rights of the Same." Congressman Peter Muhlenberg, who had served as one of Washington's generals, reported that Washington himself favored "His High Mightiness," which was the title used by the then Stadtholder of the Netherlands.[11] However, the House of Representatives rejected all of them, settling simply on "the President of the United States," which was just as well since it reinforced Washington's reputation for modesty.[12] Even so, no one who called on the president could feel he was meeting an equal, given that Washington avoided anything resembling familiar or friendly conversation as part of his belief that a dose of mystique was essential to projecting power.

Not everyone in political circles approved of the ceremonial trappings adopted by the chief executive, finding them both elitist and wasteful. Edmond Randolph of Virginia, a former delegate to the Constitutional Convention and later one of Washington's secretaries of state, complained with some exaggeration that "there was more pomp and ceremony" at the presidential residence than in the court of Britain's George III.[13] US Senator William Maclay of Pennsylvania criticized Washington's levees as "a feature of royalty . . . [and] certainly anti-republican."[14] A letter writer to the *Boston Independent Chronicle* insisted that such "ideas of pomp, parade and luxury," as were on display at the presidential residence, "are rather to be spurned, than courted and fostered by a young republic."[15] Also very critical of the pomp surrounding the Washington presidency was the *National Gazette*, an opposition newspaper sponsored by the newly formed Republican Party (not to be confused with the later party of the same name) whose leading member was Thomas Jefferson. The newspaper insisted Washington "has exactly copied the style of monarchs . . . [and] has in short only differed in kings in wanting a kingdom, which his friends were seeking to provide for him."[16]

Presidential Precedents

Despite these allegations of regal behavior, Washington did not want to make himself a king and was happy to return to his Mount Vernon plantation at the end of his second term. This voluntary surrender of power at a time when there were no term limits for presidents, even though Washington sincerely wanted to retire to his home, only cemented his public reputation for disinterest in personal glory. His refusal to seek a third term established a precedent that would not be broken for another 144 years until Franklin Roosevelt won a third term, followed by a fourth.

Another precedent established by Washington was the issuance of executive orders, which had the force of law, even though they lacked Congressional approval, and in the process greatly elevated the power of the presidency. These were, in effect, exercises of the presidential prerogative, not unlike the royal prerogative, which the delegates to the Constitutional Convention had expressly opposed during their debates. Nor had the finished Constitution specifically authorized the issuance of such orders. Rather, it was an implied power that Washington and his successors derived from the concept of a unitary executive, by virtue of which the president controls the entire executive branch and, as such, can give orders to all executive departments and agencies (so long, hypothetically, that they do not violate the Constitution or acts of Congress).

It has also been claimed that the authority to issue executive orders stems from the presidential oath of office wherein the president swears to "take care that the Laws be faithfully executed," consequently giving presidents permission to instruct subordinates about the resources and means of carrying out laws passed by Congress. In addition, the president's powers as commander-in-chief of the armed forces, as well as his role as chief architect of the country's foreign policy, would give presidents increasing latitude for issuing executive orders in these two very broad areas.

Washington issued eight executive orders in all, more than all five presidents who succeeded him. This record reflected his view of the presidency as a source of substance and form for the new national government, along with his need to establish the executive branch in working order. His earliest directive was a message to cabinet heads to send him annual written reports of their activities. Another early order took the form of a proclamation for the date of Thanksgiving in 1790. The same year he declared that American citizens must abide by treaties made by the federal government. Two others, in 1792 and 1794, referred to the so-called Whiskey Rebels in Western Pennsylvania who were refusing to pay the congressionally mandated excise tax on "distilled spirits." The most controversial of Washington's orders was his Proclamation of Neutrality in April 1793 that declared the country's neutrality in the wars between Britain and France, and threatened legal action against American citizens who assisted any country at war. Washington made this proclamation while Congress was not in session and in the face of considerable opposition by some Americans who favored France.

Jefferson, then Washington's secretary of state, opposed the president's neutrality proclamation based on his "strict construction" views of the Constitution, which held that only specifically delegated authority set forth in the document could be legitimately exercised by anyone in government, thereby accusing Washington of exceeding his powers as president. Jefferson's objections to the Declaration of Neutrality were twofold: First, the declaration meant that the United States would not go to war, a decision which violated the specific constitutional provision that Congress, and Congress alone, had the authority to declare whether (or not, Jefferson would add) the country went to war. Second, a neutral stance by the United States failed to honor the mutual assistance treaty that the country had made in 1778 with France during the American Revolution. This treaty, which had resulted in vital support from the French during the War for Independence, could not be overturned, Jefferson argued, without the advice and consent of the Senate and thus was unconstitutional.

Alexander Hamilton, who believed in a strong central government as well as in substantial power for the president, defended the constitutionality of the neutrality declaration. He did so by cleverly differentiating the "vesting clauses" in the Constitution for the legislative branch as compared to the executive branch. Article I, as he pointed out, declares that, "All legislative powers herein granted shall be vested in a Congress of the United States." However, Article II, he observed, leaves out the words *herein granted*, and more generally states, "The executive Power shall be vested in a President of the United States." This difference, turning on the phrase *herein granted*, Hamilton argued, means that the executive power is extraordinarily broad and vested wholly in the president, "subject only to the exceptions and qualifications which are expressed in the Constitution," which he deemed to be very few.[17] For Hamilton, there were few legitimate checks on presidential power.

Jefferson enlisted James Madison, then a member of the House of Representatives as well as a fellow member of their nascent Republican Party, to respond to Hamilton's arguments. He wrote to Madison, "For God's sake my dear sir, take up your pen and cut the worst of these heresies to pieces."[18] Madison followed up these urgings by publishing a series of five pamphlets under the pseudonym of Helvidius, accusing Hamilton and his supporters of being secret monarchists because of their inflated views of executive authority. Having a supporter criticize his political opponents through pamphlets or newspaper articles under anonymous authorships was typical of Jefferson, who greatly disliked and always sought to avoid direct confrontations. Thus, from the beginning, executive orders proved controversial and could draw strong opposition.

However, none of this criticism could dent the increasing public reverence for Washington. Whenever he traveled, as during his trip through New England in the autumn of 1789, units of local militia escorted him into every town, with Washington riding in on horseback with cannons booming. He then spoke to adoring crowds on village greens, with leading citizens hosting a tea or dinner in the president's honor, receptions much like those the previous spring when he traveled to his inauguration in New York.

Divine Right and Cults of Personality

Even in retirement, Washington continued to symbolize the American union, when people and communities all over the land celebrated his birthday on February 22 each year, replacing the earlier celebration of the king's birthday. In the words of Washington scholar Barry Schwartz, Washington's Birthday "was a national event, equaled only by July Fourth in enthusiasm and resplendence. The birth of the nation and the birth of Washington had become commemorative touchstones for the American people."[19] The solemn commemoration of Washington's birth also suggested that some citizens, perhaps unconsciously, continued to long for a king-like figure.

Washington's death at home on December 14, 1799, touched off days of deep mourning throughout the country, with tributes that described a man who by then had taken on the attributes of a demi-God.[20] Although Washington's very modest funeral took place at Mount Vernon, mock funeral processions and memorial services, climaxed with eulogies, took place in communities all over the country. Many speakers compared Washington to Jesus. Like Christ, he had been destined by God to become a savior—in this case, of his country—and by honoring Washington, one also honored his Creator in Heaven. Lithographs depicted Washington being carried into the "Other World" dressed in biblical or classical garb. These images invariably carried the title "Apotheosis of Washington," a term meaning "elevation to divine status." Most impressive of all is the Apotheosis inside the US Capitol Building, a large fresco in the interior eye of the dome, painted in 1865 and showing an ascendant Washington in glory.

Not everyone agreed with the glorifications of Washington at the time of his death, including David Tappan of the Harvard Divinity School, who warned that the country might be cursed for "deifying the creature at the expense of the Creator."[21] Congregationalist minister David McClure went so far as to say that the worship of Washington had become so extreme that God had caused his death. John Adams, who had genuinely admired Washington, also disapproved of what he thought was excessive adulation of the man. Years later, in 1812, Adams wrote, "Among the national sins of our country . . . is the idolatrous worship paid to the name of George Washington by all classes and *nearly* all parties of our citizens, manifested in the impious applications of names and epithets to him which are ascribed in scripture only to God and to Jesus Christ."[22]

Very few in the public at large shared these qualms, and virtually all the biographies written over the next six decades were replete with praise and awe for Washington. The most popular of these was Mason Weems' *Life of Washington*, first published in 1800 and expanded in subsequent editions. Weems was an Episcopal clergyman who intended his book as a series of morality tales for American youth. Best known of these was the mythical cherry tree story in which young George used his little hatchet to cut down his father's prized fruit tree, and when confronted about it, told the truth. More significant, though less famous, was Weems's description of Washington as "the hero, and the Demigod," much like the Roman god, "Jupiter Conservator," the "Savior of the world."[23] Weems was hinting very strongly that Washington had become president by divine right, a status long claimed by the crowned heads of Europe.

In many respects, Weems's praise for Washington, along with all the other adulation of the country's first president, fulfills certain characteristics of a cult of personality, which results from campaigns to create an idealized or heroic image of a leader who is never wrong and who deserves unquestioning support and constant adulation. Such a cult is typically created through unyielding flattery and praise and can result in extreme abuses of power and claims of absolute authority. In Washington's case, he had both encouraged and passively accepted such adulation, while others had criticized the pomp and circumstance with which he surrounded himself. Then there were those who strongly criticized the belief that he had been some sort of God-like savior. Still, Washington voluntarily relinquished the presidency after two terms. Thus, a very real cult of personality that grew up around Washington did not pose a genuine danger to the country. At the same time, the Washington cult demonstrated very early on that Americans were not immune to personality cults surrounding a president.

Jeffersonian Democracy

When Washington died, Jefferson was home at Monticello, thereby avoiding the various public ceremonies celebrating the first president's life. As a religious skeptic, he could hardly embrace what had become a religious cult of Washington. He had also rejected claims that the framers of the Constitution were divinely inspired. In addition, he would later create his own version of the New Testament Gospels by going through them with a razor and cutting out all the miracles or anything else that struck him as supernatural, including the Resurrection. This left only the narration of Jesus's life and teachings, which Jefferson clipped out and pasted in his alternative text. The result was what came to be known popularly as "The Jefferson Bible," although it was unpublished until the early twentieth century.[24]

When becoming president himself, Jefferson rejected the trappings of European court life, which had surrounded the Washington presidency. Both he and his supporters, along with their political foes, referred to his election as "the Revolution of 1800," since he and his Republican Party had defeated the Federalist John Adams in his bid for reelection. According to Jefferson, his election to the presidency and the majorities that his Republican Party swept into both the House and Senate had saved the principles of the American Revolution, which he charged were being undermined by the Hamiltonian Federalists' use of overweening executive power, and in the process exposing the country to the dangers of monarchy. Indeed, Jefferson must have remembered Hamilton's comment during an after-dinner conversation in 1792 that he thought the greatest man who had ever lived was Julius Caesar.[25] Jefferson already feared the possibility of a monarchy or dictatorship in the United States, and Hamilton's comment did nothing to reassure him, which was an important motive for his decision to run for president in 1800. He won the still limited popular vote by 61.1 percent to incumbent Adams's 38.6 percent, but the electoral vote was much closer at seventy-three to sixty-five.

In his 1801 inaugural address, Jefferson sought to calm political passions by saying, "We are all Republicans; we are all Federalists." Nevertheless, he was clear about the sweeping program of his party. Indeed, he had sought the presidency in the belief that it was necessary to achieve power to make his political philosophy a reality. He and his party would limit the authority of the national government while supporting states' rights and pursuing a "frugal" administration. Yet Jefferson the dissenter often ended up governing much like a Federalist and in the process greatly enhanced the power of the presidency. The principal difference was that he used his party leadership to obtain what he wanted through the vehicle of "popular" support in Congress.

In the end, the defeated Federalist Party did not contest the turnover of power. Unfortunately, outgoing President John Adams, very hurt at being spurned by the voters, left Washington early in the morning of Jefferson's inauguration and did not attend the ceremony. Despite the slight, other leading Federalists had known Jefferson personally, and many of them knew that he could be a pragmatist who was very likely to operate within the established constitutional system. After all, Jefferson and the Federalist Hamilton had served together in President Washington's cabinet—Jefferson as Secretary of State and Hamilton as Secretary of the Treasury. Thus, the new system passed an essential first test of any democracy (in this case a proto-democracy)—the peaceful transfer of power.[26] However, the possibilities of manipulating the electoral vote would remain for the future.

As was his habit, Jefferson did not make public pronouncements about what he thought Congress should do, which in any case would have been thought unseemly at the time. Instead, he worked quietly with his party's leadership on Capitol Hill. Initially, he hoped to surmount heated partisanship but could not allay the Federalist opposition. Still, he never quite gave up, believing that Federalists would respond positively to the gracious hospitality of dinners at the President's House (not yet known as the White House), but to little effect. Such party obstruction would become a permanent fixture in American politics, at times more intense than at others, despite the framers' hopes that it would not.

Jefferson's presidency also serves as a reminder that the office itself, in addition to unforeseen events confronting the nation, has often made demands that thwart the best-laid plans. In practice, and as leading Federalists who knew him realized, Jefferson was indeed a practical individual rather than a stickler for political ideology or party doctrine. He believed in the art of compromise and always tried to restrain himself from the personal dislike of political opponents. As he wrote to his daughter Patsy, "Every human being, my dear, must be viewed according to what it is good for, for none of us, no one of us, is perfect; and were we to love none who had imperfections this would be a desert for our love."[27]

Such a view also accorded with his dislike for personal confrontation, though he did not always follow his own advice, however hard he tried. Nevertheless, throughout his public career, Jefferson used others as much as possible to promote his views, either through their own personal contacts or by writing letters, pamphlets, and newspaper articles expressing his views. He sometimes wrote anonymously for or against a given piece of legislation, as when he secretly composed resolutions for the Kentucky legislature that protested the Alien and Sedition Acts of 1798 and proposed state nullification of these hated laws.

During his presidency, Jefferson was determined to reverse the damage he believed had been done under his two predecessors, including the pomp and ceremony that had marked the presidency under Washington and his successor John Adams, whose protocol had been little different from Washington's. Gone were the formal levees and liveried servants, and when Jefferson received visitors in the morning, they might find him comfortably and even shabbily dressed. One senator who called on the president was shocked to discover him "dressed, or rather undressed, with an old brown coat, red waistcoat, old corduroy small clothes [that is, knee breeches], much soiled, woolen hose and slippers without heels."[28] Jefferson also dispensed with powdering his hair or wearing a ceremonial sword. At dinners, he followed the practice of "pell-mell," expecting his guests to find their own places at a large oval table so there was no possibility of anyone sitting at its head. He even stated this policy in writing to members of his administration: "When brought together in society, all are perfectly equal, whether foreign or domestic, titled or untitled, in or out of office."[29] Guests who preferred a bit more formality discovered to their relief that the president did dress elegantly for dinner.

Jefferson also discontinued the practice of personally delivering an Annual Message before Congress (later known as the State of the Union Address), as Washington and Adams both had done. He saw this change as a way of demonstrating the separation of powers and his respect for the legislative branch. In addition, he was not a good public speaker but an excellent and persuasive writer, another reason he preferred to submit his message in writing. No subsequent president would address Congress in person for more than a century, until Woodrow Wilson brought back the practice in 1913.[30]

During the first years of his administration, Jefferson stood by what he understood to be a strict adherence to the Constitution, in contrast to Hamilton's loose (or broad) interpretation of the document. This stance required a reduction in taxes, since in Jefferson's mind high taxes represented excessive power in the national government, given that the taxes and the funding that depended on them were reflections of governmental activity. Accordingly, he worked with the Republican Congress to abolish internal excise taxes as well as certain direct property taxes, at the same time his administration reduced the national debt year by year. To do so, Jefferson greatly reduced the size of the army and navy, which had grown under the Adams administration because of French attacks on American shipping. Even so, foreign trade flourished during the early years of Jefferson's presidency, causing tariff revenues to more than make up for the tax cuts elsewhere, with surpluses applied to lowering the debt.

However, like Adams and Washington before him, Jefferson had to wrestle with the consequences of ongoing wars between Britain and France, while fearing that being dragged into this conflict would wreck his plans for lower taxes and debt reduction as part of his goal of reducing the strong arm of the central government. In addition, he believed in peace as a guiding principle. Biographer Fawn Brodie has written of him, "Jefferson's passion for peace affected every aspect of his presidency."[31] He sincerely believed that an enlightened republic need not resort to war or to regard war as a natural human pursuit—the mark, he believed, of a primitive society.

Yet foreign matters kept intruding on Jefferson's plans in ways that made him forsake personal and political principles, act in certain ways like the despised Federalists, and, in the process, use all the potential powers of the presidency. The first of these foreign crises involved New Orleans. Through a treaty with France in 1800, the Spanish had given back (or retroceded) to France the vast Louisiana Territory, which the French had been forced to turn over to Spain in 1763 when they lost the Seven Years War (a.k.a., the French and Indian War in America). In 1802, authorities in New Orleans revoked the right of Americans to deposit goods in the city that had come down the Mississippi River, with disastrous consequences for farmers in what was then called "the West." Following Napoleon's failure to put down a slave rebellion in Santo Domingo (now Haiti), with tremendous French losses, the French Emperor decided to rid himself of any obligation to defend France's New World colonies and agreed to sell the entire Louisiana Territory to the United States for $15 million. The territory extended from the Mississippi-Missouri River Valley to the Rocky Mountains, nearly doubling the size of the United States.

Since the Constitution was silent on the question of buying land from a foreign power, a strict-constructionist Jefferson had serious qualms about the deal and for a time urged a constitutional amendment to legitimize the purchase. However, members of his own Republican Party in Congress refused to consider such an amendment and justified the transaction by employing familiar Federalist arguments. They proposed that buying Louisiana was in the general welfare; it was necessary and proper to the common defense; it was essential to continued national prosperity; and it fell within the treaty-making power of the president followed by ratification in the Senate. Swallowing his hesitations, Jefferson accepted these arguments and acquired the vast, new domain. He had used Hamiltonian arguments to achieve his own ends. As Jefferson explained this expansion of executive powers, "On great occasions every good officer must be ready to risk himself in going beyond the strict line of the law, when the public preservation requires it . . ." Shockingly from the author of the Declaration of Independence, who had denounced tyranny, he added that there were "extreme cases where the laws become inadequate to their own preservation and where the universal recourse is a dictator, or martial law."[32]Jefferson also acquired Louisiana without the permission of those living there and then appointed a military governor who ruled Louisiana territory for several years without any representative institutions. Apparently, his own words in the Declaration of Independence about needing the "consent of the governed" did not apply there, at least for the time being.

Another issue stemming from the Louisiana Purchase led Jefferson to assert executive privilege in 1807 when he refused to testify personally in court against Aaron Burr, his former vice president. Burr was charged with treason (subsequently acquitted) for allegedly trying to carve out an independent country from the middle of the Louisiana Purchase and parts of the Southwest, which still belonged to Spain. Explaining his refusal to testify, Jefferson wrote to US Attorney George Hay, "As I do not believe that the district courts have the power of *commanding* the Executive government to abandon superior duties and attend to them, at whatever distance, I am unwilling by any notice of the subpoena to set a precedent which might sanction a proceeding so preposterous."[33] This statement of executive privilege would lay down a precedent that presidents would assert many times in the future, to the consternation of the judicial branch of government.

Jefferson was less successful in dealing with other serious complications from the continuing war between Britain and France. The British forcibly stopped American ships and took off (or "impressed") any sailors they suspected of being deserters. Life in the British Navy was extremely harsh and even brutal; consequently, many sailors deserted and found work on American merchant ships. Some estimates hold that as many as one-fourth of the 50,000 to 100,000 seamen on American ships were, in fact British deserters. However, those boarding ships too often removed genuine American citizens who betrayed even a hint of an English, Scottish, or Irish accent but who were not, in fact deserters.

Jefferson also had to deal with France's Berlin Decree of 1806, which forbade all trade with Great Britain, including by neutrals. Britain responded the following year with its Orders in Council, which blocked all trade, also including neutrals, with France or any of its allies. Jefferson believed that the United States was in no condition to fight a war and knew that war would wreck his program of lowering both taxes and the national debt. Instead, he turned to economic pressure against both Britain and France by obtaining from Congress the Embargo Act of 1807, which forbade American shippers from trading anywhere in the British Isles or on the European Continent as a way of keeping his country out of what he denounced as "the present paroxysm of the insanity in Europe."[34]

However, the Embargo proved nearly impossible to enforce and was extremely unpopular in New England, which relied heavily on maritime trade for its livelihood, as well as in the South, which depended on exporting its crops to Europe. Jefferson used the navy to enforce the law and disregarded the Constitution's Fourth Amendment protections that required search warrants to thwart "unreasonable searches and seizures"—behavior by British authorities against which American colonists had protested leading up to the American Revolution and which Jefferson himself had condemned in the Declaration of Independence. By any definition, enforcement of the embargo, carried out by executive order, was an extraordinary use of the presidential prerogative, which one could argue was clearly unconstitutional. Partly as a result, Congress repealed the Embargo in early 1809, just three days before Jefferson left office. Even so, Jefferson had extended the powers of the presidency with acquiescence from a pliant Congress controlled by members of his own Republican Party (again, not to be confused with the later party of the same name).

Presidential Preeminence

Unlike Washington, Jefferson did not inspire a cult-like status, which he would have disdained. Following his death on July 4, 1826, the fiftieth anniversary of the Declaration of Independence, his interment took place in the small burial ground at Monticello, similar to Washington's simple burial at Mount Vernon. However, unlike the aftermath of Washington's death, there were no massive memorial services around the country in Jefferson's honor.

The precedents and behaviors in office of both Washington and Jefferson, although they differed in certain respects, greatly expanded presidential authority and established precedents for future holders of their high office. The issuance of executive orders established what amounted to a presidential prerogative that delegates to the Constitutional Convention had rejected during debates. There was also an assertion of executive privilege against being required to testify in court. Jefferson especially used his party's domination of Congress to obtain legislation, a method that many future presidents would use. In addition, Jefferson justified going beyond provisions in the Constitution in cases of national need, as with the Louisiana Purchase and the search and seizure of maritime cargo without warrants. There was also his assertion that a national emergency one day might require a recourse to dictatorship. The appearance of strong political parties among members of Congress, which would fail to check a president of their own party or which would almost automatically approve the actions and requests of a fellow party member in the presidency, also blunted checks on executive authority.

In addition, the Washington presidency showed that not all Americans were immune to cults of personality or the desire to see presidents surrounded by certain trappings of royalty. And in a distant future, new systems for image making would all but guarantee that presidents would be celebrities to some degree as candidates (or even before), as well as during their terms in office.

Were Benjamin Franklin still alive to comment on the Washington and Jefferson presidencies, he might have recalled saying during the Constitutional Convention, "The executive will always be increasing here, as elsewhere till it ends in a monarchy."[35] This is not to say that either Washington or Jefferson wished to be kings. Fortunately, Washington stepped down peacefully from power after two terms in office, and Jefferson's inauguration in 1801 began the precedent of a peaceful transfer of power from one party to the other.

Nevertheless, it seems clear that presidents were well on their way to being something of a preeminent source of authority in the United States government. This situation should not be surprising, since one of the main goals of the Constitution makers had been to create a chief executive with sufficient power to unify and direct the nation, supposedly with checks and balances to rein in abuses of presidential power. Time would tell if future presidents would continue to skirt supposed checks on executive authority and if there would be effective pushbacks against them.

Notes

1 Barry Schwartz, *George Washington: The Making of an American Symbol* (New York: The Free Press, 1987), 49.
2 Ibid.
3 John Ferling, *The Ascent of George Washington: The Hidden Political Genius of an American Icon* (New York: Bloomsbury Press, 2009), 275. See also Griswold Rufus

Wilmot, *The Republican Court Or, America Society in the Days of Washington* (New York: D. Appleton and Company, 1856), 138–42.

4 See Fawn M. Brodie, *Thomas Jefferson: An Intimate History* (New York: W. W. Norton and Company, 1974), 335.

5 Quoted in Willard Sterne Randall, *Thomas Jefferson: A Life* (New York: Henry Holt and Company, 1993), 547.

6 For this account of Washington's early ambitions, I am very indebted to Ferling's *The Ascent of George Washington*.

7 Ibid., 368.

8 Jefferson to Walter Jones, January 2, 1814, https://founders.archives.gov/documents/Jefferson/03-07-02-0052.

9 I am indebted to several biographies of Jefferson in the writing of this chapter: In addition to works by Brodie and Randall, cited above, these are John B. Bowles, *Jefferson: Architect of American Liberty* (New York: Basic Books, 2017); Brodie, *Jefferson*; Joseph E. Ellis, *American Sphinx: The Character of Thomas Jefferson* (New York: Basic Books, 1998): Jon Meacham, *Thomas Jefferson: The Art of Power* (New York: Random House, 2012).

10 Wilmot, *Republican Court*, 149–50. Written a little more than half a century after the institution of the presidency under Washington, this book is a goldmine of detail about the comings and goings of the president, as well as about upper-class society in both Philadelphia and New York in the late eighteenth century. See also the more recent Ferling, *The Ascent of George Washington*, 278–81.

11 Wilmot, *Republican Court*, 153–4.

12 Also on Washington's attention to formality and decorum while president, see Ferling, *The Ascent of George Washington*, 279–81.

13 Edmund Randolph to James Madison, July 23, 1789. *The Papers of James Madison* (Charlottesville: University of Virginia Press, 1979), 12:2.

14 Edgar S. Maclay, ed., *Journal of William Maclay, United States Senator from Pennsylvania, 1789–1991* (New York: D. Appleton and Company, 1890), 69, 351.

15 *Boston Independent Chronicle*, July 15, 1790.

16 Benjamin Franklin Bache, "Remarks Occasioned by the Late Conduct of Mr. Washington, as President of the United States," *National Gazette*, February 2, 1793.

17 It has been argued that Robert Morris, who was the chief drafter of the Committee of Style, which rendered the Constitution into its finished and more polished style, purposely omitted the phrase "herein granted" in the vesting clause for the presidency. It is well known that Morris was a strong believer in executive authority and that the omission was intentional in the hope that it would "give the president a field of activity wider than that outlined by his enumerated powers." Charles C. Thatch, *Creation of the Presidency*(Indianapolis: Liberty Fund, 2007), 138–9. Hamilton is quoted in Frederick A. O. Schwarz, Jr. and Aziz Z. Huq, *Unbalanced: Presidential Power in Time of Terror* (New York: The New Press, 2008), 179.

18 Thomas Jefferson to James Madison, July 7, 1793, https://founders.archives.gov/documents/Madison/01-15-02-0037.

19 Schwartz, *George Washington*, 78.

20 For a discussion of these memorials, see Ibid., 91–103.

21 Ibid., 100.

22 Quoted in ibid., 194.

23 Mason L. Weems, *Life of Washington* (Philadelphia: Joseph Allen, 1800), 212.
24 Jefferson's handwritten title, completed in 1820, was "The Life and Morals of Jesus of Nazareth."
25 See Meacham, *Jefferson*, 260.
26 Levitsky and Ziblatt, *Tyranny of the Minority*, 22.
27 Jefferson to Martha Jefferson Randolph, https://founders.archives.gov/documents/Jefferson/01-17-02-2003.
28 Senator William Plumer to Jeremiah Smith, December 9, 1802, quoted in Randall, *Thomas Jefferson*, 553–4.
29 Thomas Jefferson, Rules of Etiquette, 1803, quoted in ibid., 554.
30 Randall, *Thomas Jefferson*, 548.
31 Brodie, *Jefferson*, 412.
32 Jefferson to W. C. Claiborne, February 3, 1807; to James Brown, October 27, 1808; to J. B. Colvin, September 20, 1810, in Jefferson, *Writings*, Memorial Edition (Jefferson Memorial Association, 1903), 11:151, 12:183, 418.
33 Quoted in Meacham, *Jefferson*, 422.
34 Brodie, *Jefferson*, 418.
35 Benjamin Franklin, quoted in James Madison, *Debates*, June 4, 1787.

3

Old Hickory and the Great Emancipator

Power for Evil and Good

The authority of the Supreme Court must not, therefore, be permitted to control the Congress or the Executive . . ., but to have only such influence as the force of their reasoning may deserve.

Andrew Jackson, Veto Message Regarding the Bank of the United States, July 10, 1832

Whether the President in fulfilling his duties as Commander-in-Chief, in suppressing an insurrection . . . is a question to be decided by him. . . . *He must determine what degree of force the crisis demands.*

US Supreme Court, *The Prize Cases*, March 10, 1863

The Supreme Court has spoken: The Cherokee Nation has a valid treaty with the United States guaranteeing their right to live on tribal lands in Georgia. The president refuses to carry out the decision, and the Cherokee are forced under military guard to trek west in the middle of winter. Approximately 4,000 of them die along the way. A quarter of a century later, another president defies an order from the Chief Justice to grant *habeas corpus* rights to a man arrested for organizing men to fight against the Union.[1]

Andrew Jackson uses his authority to strip both the legal and human rights of vulnerable men, women, and children and send them to their deaths. Abraham Lincoln wields his power to save the Union and to free millions from bondage, even if it means defying the highest judicial authority in the land and violating the Constitution itself. Jackson is often filled with rage and vindictiveness, while Lincoln has tried to avoid war and pleads for healing a broken nation. They are the most powerful presidents in the nineteenth century and among the most powerful chief executives in all American history, and they create precedents that future presidents can use for good or ill.

Andrew Jackson and Abraham Lincoln both rose from humble backgrounds on what was then the American frontier and faced numerous challenges while growing up. Both men lost their mothers at a young age, while Jackson's father died before he was born. Both were familiar with the Bible and the main tenets of Christianity. But while Jackson remained a somewhat conventional believer, Lincoln became a lifelong skeptic. Both won praise for their leadership in war, Jackson as a general during the War of 1812 and Lincoln as commander-in-chief during the Civil War.

Beyond such similarities and differences, however, the two men used their power very differently, partly because of the events and trends of their times. Equally important—if not more important—was how their character formations shaped their overall approaches to life. In his widely respected book, *The Presidential Character*, political scientist James David Barber writes, "*Character is the way the President orients himself toward life*—not at the moment, but enduringly." Barber continues, "Character is the person's stance as he confronts experience. . . . The man develops a combination which makes psychological sense for him, a dynamic arrangement of motives, beliefs, and habits in the services of his need for self-esteem."[2] For Barber, the character of a president is the most important predictor of how an occupant of the White House will behave. Therefore, the best way to predict a president's character, Barber asserts, is to explore how it emerged during the person's childhood, adolescence, and early adulthood.[3]

The Making of Andrew Jackson

Popular comparisons have often been made between Abraham Lincoln and Andrew Jackson, if only because both were born on what was then the frontier and because both came to represent the idea that any boy, no matter how humble his origins, could grow up someday to become president of the United States. Yet Jackson's early frustrations were far more daunting than Lincoln's, and they gave birth to numerous, life-long resentments.[4] Because Jackson's father died before he was born, he, along with his brother Robert and their mother Elizabeth, had to depend on the charity of one of Elizabeth's sisters who had married into the more prosperous Crawford family. The Crawford sister had become an invalid, and the two families struck an agreement whereby Mrs. Jackson would become the "housekeeper and poor relations."[5]

Then, as Andrew entered his early teens, the Waxhaws, an area straddling the border between North and South Carolina where the Jacksons and Crawfords lived, was pitched into the bloody maelstrom of the American Revolution. Some members of the community fought alongside the invading British armies and others, such as the Jacksons and Crawfords, hitched their fortunes to the revolutionary cause. In late May of 1780, some three hundred British troops under Lieutenant Colonel Banastre Tarleton invaded the Waxhaws area and killed 113 men, including the wounded who begged for mercy but were bayoneted to death as they cried out. Andrew's sixteen-year-old brother Hugh also died in the fighting.

Nearly a year later, while serving as a young messenger boy for American forces during the Revolution, Jackson, along with his brother Robert, fell into the hands of British troops. When an officer ordered Andrew to polish his boots, the fourteen-year-old Andrew refused because he was a prisoner of war and was not required to obey such a command. The angry officer swung his sword at him, and he intercepted the blow with his left hand. However, the blade grazed Jackson's skull and left a mark that he would carry for the rest of his life. Robert, now ordered to polish the boots, likewise refused the order and received a sword blow to the head, which knocked him to the floor. Both Jacksons were force-marched some forty miles to a prison camp. Their mother managed to secure the boys' release, but Robert died two days after they returned home. After managing to nurse Andrew back from the edge of death, their mother left for Charleston to take care of two Crawford nephews who had fallen ill. She herself died in Charleston in the fall of 1781.

By then, Andrew had obtained about six years of elementary education. Yet he would struggle throughout life with spelling, along with the finer points of grammar, and would become the least well-educated person up to that time to attain the presidency. However, he read widely as an adult and was not as book-deprived as critics often contended. He was familiar with many biblical passages and picked up an assortment of religious beliefs from the long Presbyterian Church services to which his mother and her family took him every Sabbath day.

Now an orphan and deprived of his mother's love, Andrew was shunted among various Crawford relatives, none of whom treated him as a son or offered him loving encouragement. In reaction, he often seethed with anger and flew into fits of rage so intense that he would be reduced to slobbering. He also fought frequent brawls with other boys and liked to brag that no one could whip him. It is no wonder that he never returned to the Waxall after leaving for good—or that he seldom mentioned the location in later years. It was a place where he had not felt valued or wanted, and where he lost—or learned about the loss—of his entire immediate family.

Jackson's anger, resentment, and violent behavior spilled over into early adulthood. In Salisbury, North Carolina, where he "read law" with an established attorney at a time when there were no law schools in his part of the world—and few anywhere in the United States—he gained admission to the bar in 1787 and soon gained a reputation as a wild young man. He reacted to losing his first court case by challenging the opposing attorney to a duel, which they managed to avoid in the end. For a bit of fun, he once invited the town's prostitutes to a Christmas ball sponsored by socially prominent families, who were not amused when these ladies of the night showed up. An old resident of the town remembered that Jackson was "the most roaring, rollicking, game-cocking, card-playing, mischievous fellow that ever lived in Salisbury."[6]

Jackson fought duels resulting in injury and death, many of them triggered by remarks over the circumstances of his marriage. He met his future wife Rachel in Nashville, Tennessee, where he had moved in 1788 to practice law. There he boarded with the widow Donelson, whose husband John was a member of one of the most prominent families in the area, and whose beautiful daughter Rachel caught Jackson's eye and won his heart. Two years after their marriage, the couple discovered she had not been divorced from her first husband, Lewis Robards, having mistaken Robards' petition for divorce as an actual divorce decree. When the divorce finally did go through, the couple arranged a second—and this time legal—marriage ceremony.

Political enemies used the fact that the couple had initially been "living in sin" to attack their morality. One of those who alluded to Jackson's matrimonial record was Charles Dickinson, who bled to death in May 1806 after Jackson shot him in a duel. Jackson might have ignored the slurs, but there was no way he would refrain from avenging this slander against his wife, at a time and place where "real men" on the frontier were expected to demand satisfaction for such verbal assaults. There was also his brawl with the two brothers, Thomas Hart and Jesse Benton, one morning in Nashville, stemming from a quarrel Jesse had had with one of Jackson's friends. Jackson went after Jesse with a whip and then pulled a gun on him. Benton shot Jackson in the upper left arm, and he nearly bled to death.

Despite the controversial circumstances of his marriage, Jackson's now intimate connection with the Donelson family did much to advance him both socially and politically. When Tennessee achieved statehood in 1796, Jackson won election to its one seat in the House of Representatives in Washington. Soon thereafter, one of Tennessee's US senators was expelled from the body, and Jackson was selected to replace him. However, Jackson thoroughly disliked what he saw as disingenuous politicking in both the House and Senate, and when he did rise to speak, his style was one of anger. His disgust with the Senate, worry about debts back home, and a per diem compensation of $6.00 as a senator at a time when Congress met for just sixty to ninety days a year led Jackson to resign his seat and accept a judicial appointment to Tennessee's Superior Court. The court position not only assured a steady income, but riding the judicial circuit allowed him to make valuable political connections.

After six years on the court, the ever-restless Jackson resigned and unsuccessfully sought appointment by the Jefferson administration to become governor of "Orleans," consisting of the lower part of the Louisiana Territory. He also became the part owner of a general store (which ultimately failed), bred horses, and from time to time made money from the slave trade. Eventually, his plantation, "The Hermitage" outside Nashville, became the mainstay of his finances. At the estate, which came to total some 1,000 acres, he grew cotton, corn, and wheat with a workforce of some 150 enslaved persons.

In 1802, using his accumulated political skills, Jackson persuaded field officers to elect him a major general of the Tennessee militia despite having no military training or experience. The position led to Jackson's extremely controversial behavior as an officer, along with Jackson's greatest triumph. During the War of 1812 against Great Britain, controversy arose from his decisions to defy the orders of higher authorities to dole out summary executions and to take bold initiatives without permission. For instance, when the Secretary of War ordered him in March 1813 to halt his march at Natchez, Mississippi, and to dismiss his men, Jackson ignored the Secretary and escorted them back home as an army still under his command. In September of the following year, Jackson had several men shot who believed their enlistment had expired by lodging a questionable charge of desertion.

Two months later, Jackson attacked Pensacola, Florida, still under Spanish control, without asking permission from the government in Washington. In 1817, he took his men into Florida again, this time in pursuit of members of the Seminole tribe. While there, he also fought Spanish troops and executed two British nationals who, he charged, had supported the Seminoles. Jackson went on to take Florida for the United States without official permission, though he believed that vague messaging from Washington had authorized the seizure. President Monroe and most of the cabinet concluded that Jackson had indeed made war on Spain without permission, with Secretary of War John C. Calhoun wanting to have Jackson court-martialed.

Secretary of State John Quincy Adams, who had long believed the war power should belong to the president and not to Congress, disagreed and supported Jackson. In the end, Monroe concluded that Jackson's wide public support would make chastising him politically risky and accepted the fait accompli, which led to an official annexation of Florida with the Adams-Onis Treaty of 1819. This would not be the last time that great popularity would stand in the way of holding a public person to account. Nevertheless, in the House of Representatives, Monroe's opponent Henry Clay denounced Jackson's seizure of Florida as "a triumph of the principle of insubordination—a triumph of the military over the civil authority—a triumph over the powers of this house—a triumph over the constitution of the land."[7] Predictably, Jackson erupted in fury over Clay's speech and wrote to friends, "I hope . . . you will see him skinned here, & hope you will roast him in the West."[8] Jackson would despise Clay for the rest of his life. Clay's criticisms largely fell on deaf ears, while Jackson went on to become a great war hero because of his sweeping victory over a large British force at New Orleans in January 1815.

Over the years, Jackson had hoped for war against Great Britain, his sworn enemy ever since being captured as a youth during the Revolution; and more than a year before Congress finally declared war against Britain in 1812, he began readying his troops for combat. To Jackson, the war was all about vindicating American honor. In a summons to the militia, he wrote, "The advocates of kingly power shall not enjoy the triumph of seeing a free people desert themselves and crouch before the slaves of a foreign tyrant."[9] His victory over that great tyrant at New Orleans in early January 1815 was sweet indeed.

In fact, Jackson's triumph at New Orleans had no effect on the outcome of the war, since unknown to him and the country at large, the Treaty of Ghent making peace between Britain and the United States had already been signed on December 24, 1814, but the news had not yet arrived in this era of sailing ships. This fact was lost on nearly all Americans, as Jackson's feat of arms at New Orleans became a matter of tremendous pride for a nation that had suffered one reversal after another during the war. Jackson gloried in the plaudits that rained down on him as the Hero of New Orleans—the parades, the receptions, the toasts, the tributes, and the speeches overflowing with praise. Supporters immediately began to urge Jackson to run for president. Yet such applause could never fully satisfy Jackson's need for attention and validation. The origins of this need may well have come from a desire to blot out the humiliations he had suffered as a child and youth, along with the scorn heaped upon him and Rachel for the irregularities of their marriage.

Jackson's earlier reputation for personal violence did nothing to blunt his political prospects: On the contrary, he was widely admired for never backing down or apologizing for his behavior. These characteristics, along with fierceness in battle, personal stamina, and fatherly loyalty to his troops, earned him the nickname "Old Hickory"—after the tall tree with its notoriously hard wood and rough bark. This image was central to Jackson's growing cult of personality, whereby his followers displayed a strong emotional bond to him, would fall prey to cognitive dissonance to reject any criticism of him, and would support any of his actions, no matter how questionable. Jackson was also part of a growing westward movement, and many people in the West at that time admired him for his pugilistic exploits. In this sense, he was the personification of what would later be called a "defiant celebrity."

Pro-Jackson newspapers understandably portrayed him as a great military hero without equal for honesty and courage and who, as a supposed political outsider, would topple professional politicians and champion the needs of the common people. Cutting such a figure made sense at a time when most of the states had dropped earlier property qualifications for access to the ballot (at least for white men) and had assigned voters the role of choosing their presidential electors for each state.[10]Although the term "populist" would not become current until the late nineteenth century, Jackson's appeal was that of a populist figure reaching out to people who thought their interests and concerns had been disregarded or thwarted by an established elite (a charge that would be made by Donald Trump two centuries later). By 1824, Jackson seemed the perfect candidate for president.

Since the disappearance of the Federalist Party in the aftermath of the War of 1812, the remaining Jeffersonian Republicans had split into two major factions. These were the Democratic-Republicans (who later would call themselves Democrats) and the National Republicans, in addition to some smaller factions, which explains the four candidates vying for the presidency in 1824. Jackson, the Democratic-Republican, was clearly the most popular of the four candidates, but none of them won a majority of the Electoral College. Jackson scored ninety-nine electoral votes. John Quincy Adams came in at eighty-four, William Crawford at forty-one, and Henry Clay at thirty-seven. Jackson could boast of more popular votes than any of his challengers, but he lacked a majority of electoral votes. With no one winning the Electoral College, the decision went to the House of Representatives, as directed by the Constitution. Henry Clay, who was fourth in the running, threw his support to Adams, resulting in Adams's election by the House. Jackson and his supporters were furious, claiming that Adams had made a "corrupt bargain" with Clay, Jackson's old nemesis, by promising to appoint him Secretary of State in return for his assistance. Adams afterwards did appoint Clay to that position, but he and Adams were already very close in political philosophy and governing policy and had long been political allies. Clay also genuinely feared a Jackson presidency. He believed that Jackson would make himself into a dictator and destroy the young American republic. (Similar warnings would be made generations later about a prospective Trump presidency.) There has never been any evidence of an explicit deal between Clay and Adams, but there may well have been an unspoken understanding between them.[11]

However, Jackson remained convinced that a diabolical bargain had deprived him of his rightful victory, since he had won more popular votes as well as more electoral votes than any of the other candidates and was, in his mind, the clear choice of the people and that the presidency had been stolen from him. He denounced Clay as "the Judas of the West," adding, ["He] has closed the contract and will receive the thirty pieces of silver—his end will be the same"—that is by committing suicide, at least politically.[12] Following Adams's election by the House of Representatives, Jackson and his supporters in Congress vowed to sabotage every piece of legislation put forward by Adams and would succeed in their mission remarkably well in an era of intense partisanship.[13]

Since nearly all the states had abolished property qualifications for white men to vote, and were well on the way to having the popular vote determine the electoral vote, the results of the presidential election of 1824 appeared to make a mockery of democracy. That the person receiving the largest number of votes did not become president seemed a travesty. The decision by the delegates to the Constitution to create the Electoral College had only exacerbated a partisan rancor that none of them would have welcomed. Future presidents (or their supporters) who believed they had also had been robbed would repeat Jackson's cries of a "stolen election."

King Andrew I

Exacerbating both the social and partisan conflict was the background of John Quincy Adams, who was born in 1767, the same year as Andrew Jackson, in Quincy, Massachusetts, to a famous family in comfortable circumstances. As a boy, he had gone with his father, John Adams (who had assisted Thomas Jefferson with the Declaration of Independence and was the second President of the United States), on diplomatic missions to France and the Netherlands. At age fourteen, John Quincy had accompanied Francis Dana as private secretary on a diplomatic assignment to Russia. While in Europe, the young Adams studied in Paris, Amsterdam, Leyden, and The Hague and became fluent in French and Dutch, while becoming somewhat familiar with German and other European languages. After returning to the United States, he entered Harvard College, where he earned a Bachelor of Arts degree and later held the chair of rhetoric and oratory at his alma mater. Adams became a superb prose writer as well as a decent poet. He was the very personification of the upper-class easterner whom the populist Jacksonians despised.

Specifically, Jackson excoriated Adams's proposal for a naval academy as a "vast source of patronage," which would undermine democratic virtues while promoting the further rise of an educated upper class. A prominent Jackson supporter added that a naval academy would only "produce degeneracy and corruption of the public morality, and change our simple Republican habits." Adams's proposal for a national university and for federal subsidies to undertake geographical explorations and scientific research met with similar derision.[14] The Jacksonian sabotage of the Adams agenda, combined with Jackson's great popularity, gave him a huge victory against Adams when they faced off against each other again in the presidential election of 1828. This time Jackson won decisively with 56.4 percent of the popular vote and with 178 to 83 in the Electoral College. He would go on to claim a plebiscitary mandate that he believed justified his defying both Congress and the Supreme Court.

For those who disliked him, Jackson's limited formal education, especially in comparison to Adams, along with his frontier manners, more than disqualified him for the presidency. However, his admirers saw a man who had succeeded despite numerous odds. Yet the reality was in some ways very different: Jackson's marriage to Rachel Donelson had connected him with one of the most powerful and socially connected families in Tennessee. And by the time he became president, Jackson was an extremely rich man. He would not be the last wealthy president who could nevertheless appeal to those less well off—individuals who wished to associate vicariously with his wealthy lifestyle, while at the same time seeing him as one of their own.[15] In one sense, the contradiction was not entirely irrational if common men could admire Jackson for his rise and see him as an image of how they too could aspire to wealth and success, even though the odds of reaching anywhere near Old Hickory's heights of fame and fortune were extremely unlikely.

Divided reactions to Jackson's inauguration on March 4, 1829, also demonstrated conflicting views of the new president. Admirers marveled at the estimated 20,000 people who assembled on the grounds of the Capitol to see their hero take the oath of office. Opponents, however, pointed to the crowd that followed Jackson to the President's House (again, not yet called the White House), who smashed delicate furniture and ruined carpets with muddy boots and overturned pails of liquor. To protect Jackson from the crush of people, aides had to rescue and escort him through the back of the building. Detractors saw the new president's admirers pushing and shoving into the mansion as a mob representing the sorts of uncouth men who had voted for Jackson.

Biographer Jon Meacham writes that Jackson, in his struggles against his enemies, liked to compare himself to the biblical hero David, whose story he knew well from all those childhood Sundays in church. David had slain the giant Goliath, who had tried to rob the people of their liberty and went on to become Israel's greatest king. In President Jackson's case, the giant was the Second Bank of the United States, which he denounced as "the Monster of Chestnut Street" because of its street location in Philadelphia.

President of the bank Nicholas Biddle was another personification for Jackson of the oppressive eastern elite. Born in Philadelphia, Biddle could trace his American ancestry back to the earliest days of colonial Pennsylvania. He graduated from Princeton, where he was valedictorian, and afterwards went on a multi-year "grand tour" of Europe, a luxury that only young men from the wealthiest families could afford.[16] While abroad, he became especially enamored of all things Greek, which was responsible for his decision to have the exterior of the Second Bank building in Philadelphia modeled after the Parthenon in Athens. Biddle was exactly the kind of person born to privilege whom Jackson had always despised.

Jackson's self-righteous opposition to compromise and determination to get revenge led to an unnecessarily destructive battle against the Second Bank of the United States, the second of the country's central banks, hence its name. The very concept of a central bank had been the subject of much controversy during its two iterations. Congress had established the First Bank in 1791 at the urging of then Secretary of the Treasury Alexander Hamilton as a depository for federal tax revenues and as a mechanism for managing the public debt and stabilizing the money supply. Many southerners opposed the First Bank, charging that it would unduly benefit northern mercantile and manufacturing interests. In addition, led by the pronouncements of then Secretary of State Thomas Jefferson, they charged that the Constitution had not specifically authorized the bank and that it was therefore unconstitutional. Prevailing against this position was Hamilton's argument that the "implied powers" of the Constitution, as set forth in the "Necessary and Proper" clause (Article I, Section 8), did allow for such a bank. Chartered for twenty years, Congress needed to reauthorize the bank in 1811. With the Jeffersonian Republicans now in charge of Congress, the bill to re-charter was narrowly defeated. However, the financial strains of the War of 1812 led Congress and the Madison administration to support the creation of a new central bank, the Second Bank of the United States, established in 1816 with a charter likewise for twenty years.[17] The headquarters of both banks were in Philadelphia, the nation's capital as well as its financial center when the initial bank had been established.

Jackson turned against the Second Bank early in his presidency when he heard unsubstantiated rumors that officers of various branches of the bank had been hostile to his 1828 candidacy. In addition, Jackson had long been wary of banks since nearly being ruined a generation earlier from speculation in promissory notes. He also viewed the Second Bank as an institution of privilege that benefited wealthier members of society who could afford to buy its stock, in addition to objections that foreign investors could and did buy stock in the bank. Of course, it did not help that the president of the bank was the handsome, aristocratic Nicholas Biddle of Philadelphia.

Biddle himself was not above playing politics with the bank when he asked Congress to renew the institution's charter in 1832, four years before it was set to expire. This was an election year, and Biddle believed Jackson would not risk his reelection prospects by vetoing the recharter bill. Sponsored in part by the hated Henry Clay, the legislation passed the Senate by a vote of twenty-eight to twenty, and in the House by 107 to eighty-five. In response, Jackson reportedly declared to Martin Van Buren, who had just returned from being the American Minister to Great Britain, "The bank is trying to kill me, . . . *but I will kill it!*" Kill the bank he did, with a veto accompanied by a hard-hitting veto message.

Jackson admitted that the Supreme Court back in 1819 had declared the Second Bank to be constitutional in the case of *McCulloch v. Maryland*, but that was irrelevant to him, since he believed he had as much authority to determine what was constitutional as the court did. Nor did Congress have the last word, he charged, over what the president deemed to be right and proper. As Jackson wrote in the veto message, "The opinion of the judges has no more authority over Congress than the opinion of Congress has over the judges, and on that point the President is independent of both." Jackson added, "The authority of the Supreme Court must not, therefore, be permitted to control the Congress or the Executive when acting in their legislative capacities, but to have only such influence as the force of their reasoning may deserve."[18] In other words, the executive branch was preeminent and the president did not have to respect the opinions of either the legislative or judicial branches of government, surely the sentiments of a would-be autocrat.

Elsewhere in the veto message, Jackson listed his specific objections to the bank: The federal government owned only one-fifth of its stock and thereby appointed only five of its twenty-five directors. Foreign nationals also held some of the stock, meaning, according to Jackson, that, "The American Republic proposes virtually to give [these foreigners] a present of some millions of dollars." Back home in the United States, Jackson charged that the bank granted special privileges to a select few: "Distinctions in society will always exist under every just government," he admitted, "but when laws undertake to add to these natural and just advantages artificial distinctions, . . . the humble members of society . . . have a right to complain of the injustice of their government."[19]

Jackson was not all wrong in his criticisms of the bank, which was largely a private corporation with a Congressional charter. It benefited immensely from the prestige of having such a national charter, along with being the sole depository for federal tax revenues. However, a better solution than vetoing the bank bill would have been for Jackson to use his considerable power and influence to broker a compromise to eliminate the bank's shortcomings. Instead, he vetoed the bank bill and then went on to destroy "Monster of Chestnut Street." Despite his veto of the bank legislation, the bank's 1816 charter did not expire for another four years—that is until 1836. To cripple the bank during this intervening period, Jackson as head of a "unitary executive," issued an executive order in September 1833 that all government revenues must be deposited in certain, select state-chartered banks—or "pet banks," as opposition newspapers dubbed them. The Senate passed a resolution by a vote of twenty-six to twenty "condemning Jackson" for the removal of funds, but with no effect on the president's decision, save to make him angrier and more determined to destroy the bank. Nor had the bank fight hurt him when he ran for reelection in 1832, handily defeating his old foe, Henry Clay.

Biddle retaliated by greatly cutting back on loans, thereby constricting the currency and bringing on what was then called an "economic panic." A year later, Jackson pushed through an act of Congress that banned most paper money from circulation (known as the "Specie Circular"), which made gold or silver coins for the most part the only medium of exchange in circulation. Biddle and Jackson thereby plunged the country into a severe economic depression. As the Second Bank passed into oblivion, the United States would not have a central bank until the creation of the Federal Reserve Bank eighty-seven years later in 1913. During those intervening years, the American people had no financial mechanism that could attempt to tame the economy. A more even-tempered president would have stood a good chance of working out a compromise to both reform and retain the bank, but Andrew Jackson was not such a president. Exacting revenge was far more important to him than making sound decisions for the public good.

Jackson defied the Supreme Court opinion more directly in 1832 over the case of *Worcester v. Georgia*, which upheld the right of the Cherokee tribe to remain on their treaty lands in Georgia, and which led to the tragic removal of the tribe to Oklahoma in the winter of 1838–39. Approximately 4,000 of the 16,000 Cherokee died on what is known as the "Trail of Tears." Citing the mandate of the American people who had elected him, another example of the "plebiscitary presidency," Jackson again believed he had as much right to interpret the Constitution as the Supreme Court.[20] Upon learning of the decision, Jackson said to his friend John Coffee, "The decision of the

Supreme Court has fell [sic.] still born, and they find they cannot coerce Georgia to yield to its mandate."[21] Only Jackson could enforce it, and he was not about to go against the wishes of the white people in Georgia who saw him as their champion, a prime example of what would later be called "white nationalism."

It was because of Jackson's uncompromising behavior and claims of executive supremacy that opponents began to call him "King Andrew I," depicted in a cartoon showing Jackson sitting on a throne and clothed in royal regalia, including a crown and scepter, while trampling the Constitution beneath his feet. Opponents began to talk of impeaching Jackson, but Clay discouraged them because he believed the president's great popularity would prevent Congress from acting on it. Then in March 1834, with the Clay wing in control, the Senate voted to censure Jackson for sabotaging the Second Bank, but when Jackson's supporters regained majority control of the Senate, they voted to expunge the censure.[22] This experience, along with the decision not to bring up impeachment in the House, indicated very early on that it was nearly impossible to hold a very popular president accountable no matter how much he violated the hoped-for Constitutional balance of powers and reasonable restraint.

To enhance his image, Jackson sat for innumerable artists. These portraits were widely displayed in urban areas, and they gave the public a sense of how their adored hero appeared late in life—as a prosperous, well-dressed patriarch. Pro-Jackson newspapers also printed woodcut images of the president. Future presidents with the means of mass-producing and widely disseminating photographs of themselves would find it far easier to make themselves into celebrities and/or to create cults of personality.

Angry and resentful to the end of his presidency, Andrew Jackson constantly battled his enemies, whom he believed were also the foes of the common people who twice elected him. His opponents might call him King Andrew, but he preferred to compare himself to the biblical King David, who strove to free his people from the Goliath of special privilege. As his opponents had discovered, it was and would continue to be nearly impossible to rein in this immensely popular president.

The Making of Abraham Lincoln

Democratic processes in Congress had failed to restrain Andrew Jackson's abuses of presidential power. Democratic methods also failed for different reasons to keep the Union from falling apart a generation later, when the southern states refused to accept Abraham Lincoln as the winner of the 1860 presidential election and started a Civil War rather than abide by the results of an election. Throughout his presidency, southerners denounced Lincoln as a dictator and tyrant. Even in the North, a substantial minority of people objected to Lincoln's assertion of emergency powers that in peacetime would have been completely unconstitutional.

Like Andrew Jackson, the formation of Lincoln's character is essential to understanding his craving for high political office and the purposes for which he used it. Lincoln was born in a frontier area of Kentucky, and he spent his earliest years there.

There were few close neighbors, and virtually no one who lived nearby had enslaved laborers in a state that permitted slavery. The Lincolns may have been poor, but they were no worse off than most everyone else in the area. In addition, Lincoln's father Thomas opposed slavery, as did the Primitive Baptist Church the family attended.

In 1816, when Lincoln was seven, his family moved to southwest Indiana, where Abraham would spend the remainder of his childhood and youth. Just two years after their move, when the boy was nine and a half, his mother, Nancy Hanks Lincoln, died. Andrew Jackson had lost both parents by the time he was fourteen and found himself bereft of parental love. However, Lincoln was not forced to live with relatives, as in the case of Andrew Jackson, who had been none too pleased to have him. Indeed, soon after losing his wife, Tom Lincoln went back to Kentucky to find a new spouse. She was Sarah Bush Johnson, and she turned out to be a godsend to Abraham. His stepmother later said of him, "He was the best boy I ever saw. . . . Abe never gave me a cross word or look and never refused in fact, or Even [sic] in appearance to do any thing [sic] I requested him. . . . His mind and mine—what little I had seemed to run together—moved in the same channel."[23] Sarah encouraged Abraham's love of books, and he took enthusiastic advantage of the few volumes she had brought with her, including the Bible, John Bunyan's *Pilgrim's Progress*, *Aesop's Fables*, and William Scott's *Lessons on Elocution*, which probably gave him his first taste of Shakespeare.

Lincoln's formal education was even sketchier than Jackson's schooling. He went sporadically to a series of log cabin schools for only a month or so at a time, which he later confessed did not amount to more than a year when added together. Lincoln would look back on these crude schools with scorn: "No qualification was ever required of a teacher," he reminisced, "beyond 'readin, writin, and ciphern. . . . If a straggler supposed to understand latin [sic], happened to sojourn in the neighborhood, he was looked upon as a wizard."[24]

The Lincoln family moved to Illinois in 1830 when Abraham was twenty-one. He stayed for a year to help clear the land and then set out on his own, determined not to follow in the footsteps of his father. Leaving home, he settled in the village of New Salem, Illinois, where he befriended the local schoolmaster who coached him on the finer points of English grammar. During his five years in that community, he also came to know several well-educated men who introduced him to Thomas Paine and Constantin de Volney, the latter of whom deepened his religious skepticism. Lincoln had never been baptized since the family's Baptist church in Kentucky did not believe in infant baptism, leaving the choice up to Lincoln as an adult, an option that he never took. He never joined a church and apparently never took the sacrament of Holy Communion. At New Salem, friends and acquaintances heard him ridicule such central Christian beliefs as miracles, eternal damnation, the Virgin birth, and the divinity of Christ. Lincoln sometimes carried a Bible around the village from which he read passages aloud and questioned them, and even dared to put his doubts in writing. One fellow skeptic found the composition so extreme and so potentially damaging to Lincoln's reputation that he reportedly threw it into the fire. His learned acquaintances at New Salem also deepened his exposure to Shakespeare. In time, he would become one of the most eloquent masters of the English language, in striking contrast to Andrew Jackson.

Yet like Jackson, Lincoln chose to become a lawyer. While at New Salem, however, Lincoln "read law" on his own from borrowed books rather than with an attorney. He then passed the bar exam at the nearby state Capitol of Springfield, where he settled and eventually built a lucrative career as a lawyer and used his success as an attorney to launch a political career.

Lincoln's father was a devoted Democrat and a strong supporter of Andrew Jackson, like almost everyone else who lived in southern Indiana and Illinois. They admired Jackson's frontier background, including the duels, brawls, and military exploits, along with his opposition to federal spending on transportation improvements and his undying hatred of the eastern banking establishment as represented by the Second Bank of the United States. Tellingly, Lincoln became a strong supporter of the opposition Whig Party, which had come into being to oppose the pretensions of "King Andrew I." Lincoln also agreed with the Whigs in deploring the crude persona of Andrew Jackson, claiming to represent the higher culture and interests of the better-off classes, which Lincoln aspired to join. The shame that Lincoln felt about his father's illiteracy and rough ways, combined with a strong desire to leave his frontier childhood behind and to join Springfield's upper-middle class, doubtless added to his distaste for Jackson and Jackson's Democratic Party.

Lincoln entered politics in 1832 while still living in New Salem, when he ran for a seat in the lower house of the Illinois state legislature. He spoke in favor of a national bank and protective tariffs, both of which would become mainstays of the Whig Party. He lost this first bid for elective office, but he was more successful two years later and went on to win additional terms in 1836, 1838, and 1840.

Six weeks after Lincoln passed the Illinois bar in March 1837, he moved to the state capital at Springfield, where he set out to become a successful attorney. Like Jackson, Lincoln also married well when he chose Mary Todd to be his wife, at least from the standpoint of social and political connections. For Jackson, these benefits accrued from his wife's Donelson family and their connections. In Mary Todd's case, similar advantages came through her brother-in-law, Ninian W. Edwards, who was wealthy, socially prominent, and a leader of the Whig Party in Springfield.

A little less than a year later, in early 1838, young lawyer Lincoln gave a speech to the Young Men's Lyceum in Springfield. His title was "The Perpetuation of Our Political Institutions." In it, he denounced the mobs "who substitute [their] wild and furious passions, in lieu of the sober judgement of Courts."[25] Accordingly, he called on his audience and all Americans to swear never to break the law. In the speech, he also warned his audience to beware of men of great ambition who might try to become an American Napoleon, Caesar, or Alexander the Great. "Some man possessed of the loftiest genus, coupled with ambition, sufficient to push it to its utmost stretch," he feared, "will at some time, spring up among us." Tellingly, he thought the question of slavery might offer a perfect opening for such a person to grasp such power, "whether at the expense of emancipating slaves, or enslaving freemen."[26] Most importantly, he perceived that it might be possible in the future for someone to manipulate certain controversial issues to overthrow American democracy and make himself into something of an emperor or king.

However, most immediately vindicating Lincoln's fears was President James K. Polk's starting an unnecessary and unjust war with Mexico. Lincoln's platform for making such a claim was the single term he served as a member of the House of Representatives. In early December of 1847, he joined several other Whig Congressmen to declare that Polk had made false representations in calling for armed hostilities against Mexico. Although the president insisted that Mexican troops had invaded the United States and had spilled blood on American soil, the Mexicans in fact had moved into a disputed area between the Rio Grande and Nueces rivers that both countries claimed. Lincoln accordingly introduced a resolution in the House. It required the president to give to Congress, "A full knowledge of all the facts which go to establish whether the particular spot of soil on which the blood of our *citizens* was so shed, was, or was not, on *our own soil* at that time."[27] The Whig caucus to which Lincoln belonged voted to support the resolution. Then, on January 12 of the new year, Lincoln delivered a blistering speech on the House floor against Polk, calling special attention to the many gaps in the president's evidence and logic, as if the chief executive were on trial and Lincoln were the prosecuting attorney. Polk ignored both the speech and the so-called "Spot Resolution," which the House neither debated nor submitted for a vote.

Democratic Party newspapers back home in Illinois predictably castigated Lincoln, and some of the Whig newspapers even found fault with him. He also received critical letters from Illinois Whigs, including one from his law partner William Herndon. Lincoln shot back at Herndon, accusing Polk of abusing power and acting like a monarch. "Allow the president to invade a neighboring nation whenever *he* shall deem it necessary to repel an invasion," he wrote, "and you allow him to do so *whenever he may choose to say* he deems it necessary for such purpose—and you allow him to make war at pleasure, . . . and [place] our President where kings have always stood."[28] Certainly, Polk's behavior would have alarmed the delegates to the Constitutional Convention, who had feared presidents might abuse their war powers.

One of the other reasons why Lincoln and his Whig allies had challenged Polk over the war was their fear that any new territory won from Mexico would result in the spread of slavery. Indeed, the annexations resulting from the Mexican War, which included the future states of New Mexico, Arizona, Utah, Colorado, Nevada, and California, ignited furious arguments between the slave states of the South and the free states of the North over whether slavery should be allowed in the new territories. Slaveholders insisted they had a perfect right to take their enslaved workers, which they defined as property, into the newly conquered lands. Southerners also thought it essential to carve out additional slave states lest the North take control of the federal government. The more populous North already controlled the House of Representatives, leaving the Senate, in which every state had two senators regardless of population, as the South's one remaining bastion of protection. It was this heated issue that would eventually lead to civil war. It was another example of how the makers of the Constitution did not foresee that their composition of the Senate, as a representative body of the states, could contribute to disaster.

Because the Illinois Whigs had committed themselves to the principle of rotation in office, Lincoln had pledged to serve only one term in the House of Representatives.

He thus headed home in the spring of 1849, where he worked hard at an increasingly successful and lucrative law practice with William Herndon. Just as Jackson had used his time riding the judicial circuit to make political friendships and alliances, lawyer Lincoln had ridden the circuit in central Illinois to both try and defend cases, and in the same way forged contacts that would help his rise politically. He continued to yearn for higher public office and the chance to make a big name for himself, but the seeming lack of a road ahead often left him feeling depressed: "Oh how hard it is," he exclaimed to Herndon, "to die and leave one's country no better off than if one had never lived for it."[29] Herndon later wrote of his law partner's driving ambition: "That man who thinks Lincoln calmly sat down and gathered his robes about him, waiting for people to call him, has a very erroneous knowledge of Lincoln. He was always calculating and planning ahead. His ambition was a little engine that knew no rest."[30]

Lifting Lincoln's prospects for re-entering national politics was the Kansas-Nebraska Act of May 1854, whose principal author was Democrat and US Senator Stephen A. Douglas of Illinois. Douglas's main goal was to organize the middle portion of the Louisiana Territory, which the Jefferson administration had purchased from France back in 1803, so the nation's first transcontinental railroad could go through it, thereby linking the newly admitted state of California with the eastern half of the country. Douglas stood to profit personally from a central route for the rail line, since he was a director of the Illinois Central Railroad as well as an ambitious land speculator in and around Chicago, the eastern terminus of the line. The proposed transcontinental route would run through the yet unorganized Kansas and Nebraska Territories, which lay north of the parallel 36 degrees, 30 minutes, where the Missouri Compromise passed by Congress in 1820 had forbidden slavery. Southern legislators wanted the transcontinental line to take a southern route. Douglas sought to pacify them by agreeing to have the Missouri Compromise repealed as part of the Kansas-Nebraska Act and to deal with the question of slavery in the new territories in accordance with the principle of "popular sovereignty," which would allow the residents of the territory to decide whether they would allow slaveholding.

The repeal of the Missouri Compromise unleashed a maelstrom of protest in the North, causing many of those who had heretofore taken a moderate stance on slavery to denounce the Kansas-Nebraska Act. Lincoln did not issue a protest immediately, but in August of 1854, he joined the fray by campaigning for fellow Whigs. Then in the spring of 1856, he decided to join the new Republican Party, which was an amalgam of several groups, including northern Whigs and the Free-Soil Party, the latter founded to oppose the spread of slavery into the territories. Although most Republicans stood for keeping slavery bottled up where it already existed, the party also attracted abolitionists who wanted to end slavery everywhere in the United States. Lincoln understandably sided with the first group, since he continued to believe that the Constitution had upheld slavery and that there was no way to end this nefarious institution where it already existed, however much he disapproved of it personally. Two years later, he became the party's nominee to oppose Stephen Douglas's bid for reelection to the US Senate.

It was in a speech on July 10 in Chicago where Lincoln referenced the Declaration of Independence and its well-known line, "All men are created equal." If this passage did not apply to "the Negro," Lincoln argued, it was an easy step to saying that it did not apply to other groups of people. Several days later, lest he be misunderstood, he backed away somewhat from claiming full equality for blacks: "Certainly the negro [sic.] is not our equal in color—perhaps not in many other respects; still, in the right to put into his mouth the bread that his own hands have earned, he is the equal of every other man, white or black."[31] Yet at this point, Lincoln did not say anything about the contradiction between the assertion of equality in the Declaration of Independence and the Constitution's protection of the right to hold others in bondage.

Then came the series of seven debates with Douglas, held between August 21 and October 21 at different Illinois towns and known ever since as the Lincoln-Douglas debates. Major newspapers throughout the United States published all or part of the debates. Douglas already had a countrywide reputation, but their exchanges thrust Lincoln into the national limelight as nothing else could have. He had performed very well in the debates and had frequently put Douglas on the defensive, but the Democrats who controlled the Illinois legislature at a time when the state legislators still chose US Senators, selected Douglas for a third term in Washington.

The loss was devastating for Lincoln, prompting him to write to a doctor friend, "I now slink out of view and shall be forgotten."[32] To another correspondent, he wrote, "I write to let you know that I am neither dead nor dying."[33] However, a year later, he was back in the game, giving speeches by invitation in Ohio for local elections during the fall of 1859. His performances so impressed Ohio Republicans that they asked to publish the Lincoln-Douglas debates in book form. The book appeared in the spring of 1860 and quickly became a national bestseller.

Lincoln was now a serious contender for the presidency and received the Republican nomination that May. Playing on the common-man theme that Andrew Jackson had made a mainstay of his public persona, Lincoln's supporters dubbed him the "Rail Splitter" because of all the wooden rails that he had once split from logs to fence the family farm. In truth, Lincoln had always despised farm work and would rather point to his career as a successful, upper-middle-class lawyer. Yet as an astute politician, he played along with the image, knowing that it would appeal to rural voters, as well as those in towns and cities who also had risen from humble circumstances or who were striving to do so.

Lincoln also used the relatively new technology of photography to present a different and more refined image of himself. By 1860, when he was running for president, the so-called "*carte de visite*" craze was in full swing. These cards (i.e., *cartes*) had been invented by a French photographer several years before and were mass-produced photo duplicates of a person or small group of individuals pasted onto a piece of stiff cardboard that measured two and a half by four inches. Families often placed these cards, which included the photographic portraits of famous persons like Abraham Lincoln, into albums they would show off to visitors—hence the French name, *carte de visite*. Lincoln had thousands of these photographs duplicated and passed out among voters. Before they left the photographer's studio, the negatives were "retouched" to remove the deep lines in Lincoln's face and thus make him appear more attractive.

Although there were several such photographic cards of Lincoln posing alone, more compelling was one that would be taken in 1864, which shows him sitting in a chair with his son Tad standing beside him as they both, fittingly, look at *a carte de visite* album spread open in the president's lap. In the words of Andrea L. Volpe, a writer and researcher about visual culture, this image of Lincoln and his son in "a private moment on public display helped seal a bond between the nation and the viewer called upon to endure personal sacrifices on behalf of the Union. . . . The portrait evokes comfort and protection, not from a president consumed with war and politics, but from a tender patriarch."[34] Both Lincoln and Tad are well dressed in the latest styles, marking them as members of the country's prosperous upper middle class, to which Lincoln had always aspired. This was a view of himself that the president much preferred to the image his campaign publicists had conveyed of him as the backwoods rail-splitter born in a humble log cabin. The ability to produce photographic images from negatives in large quantities certainly beat Andrew Jackson's strategy of having numerous portraits painted of himself and woodcuts printed in newspapers, but it was only the beginning of presidents and presidential contenders using photographic and later more advanced images of themselves to cultivate followers.

Another comparison between the two men was the breakdown of political systems when they ran for president. At the time of Jackson's first presidential contest in 1824, the political parties were in disarray. They were again falling apart when Lincoln ran for president three and a half decades later. Fortunately for him, the Democrats split over their nomination, with the southern faction putting up John Breckinridge of Kentucky, who was then serving as vice president under James Buchanan, leaving Stephen Douglas as the nominee for the northern Democrats. Potentially dividing the presidential vote even further was the emergence of the Constitutional Union Party, which nominated John Bell and promised to honor the Constitution and all national laws. This promise included the Fugitive Slave Act and the repeal of the Missouri Compromise, which had opened the territories to slavery so long as locals approved of it (the principle of popular sovereignty). These political fragmentations virtually guaranteed victory for the newly formed Republican Party and their presidential candidate, Abraham Lincoln. That fall Lincoln received 180 of 303 electoral votes, with seventy-two for Breckinridge, nineteen for Bell, and twelve for Douglas. However, Lincoln received a little less than 40 percent of the popular vote.

Savior or Tyrant

Leading Southerners had warned that their section would secede from the Union if Lincoln were elected, even though he and the Republicans had repeatedly said they would not interfere with slavery where it already existed. However, for secessionists, the election of Lincoln signaled that forces inimical to their interests had taken over the federal government. Beginning with South Carolina at the end of December 1860, seven states had seceded by the time Lincoln took his oath of office on March 4, 1861.

Not quite a month earlier, these states had met in Montgomery, Alabama, to establish the Confederate States of America.

On the day of his inauguration and fearful that more states were contemplating secession, Lincoln was careful in his address to reiterate that he had "no purpose, directly or indirectly, to interfere with the institution of slavery in the states where it exists."[35] He also promised not to interfere with the enforcement of the Fugitive Slave laws passed as part of the Compromise of 1850 and backed up by the Fugitive Slave clause of the Constitution. Turning to the subject of secession, he declared that the Union was perpetual, since it was "safe to assert that no government proper, ever had a provision in its organic law for its own termination."[36] In addition, he promised to do whatever was necessary to hold and occupy federal property in the seceded states, but there would be no shedding of blood "unless forced upon the national authority." Thus if war came, it would be because of aggression by the seceded states: "In your *hands*, my dissatisfied countrymen, and not in *mine*, is the momentous issues of civil war."[37] He closed by remembering the many sacrifices that had given birth to the nation: "The mystic chords of memory, stretching from every battle-field and patriot grave, to every living heart and hearthstone, all over this broad land, will yet swell the chorus of the Union, when again touched, as surely they will be, by the better angels of our nature."[38]

Upon becoming president, Lincoln concluded that he had no alternative but to hold property belonging to the federal government under his authority, as promised in his oath of office, to "execute the Office of President of the United States." Thus, he refused to surrender Fort Sumter, located on an island just outside Charleston Harbor. When he learned the fort was running short of supplies, he notified South Carolina authorities that he was sending a supply flotilla instead of warships, which would emphasize his pledge not to initiate hostilities. Nevertheless, South Carolina, on April 12, 1861, opened fire on the fort. Commander Robert Anderson surrendered the facility the following day, allowing Lincoln to place the blame for starting the war on the Confederacy.

On April 15, Lincoln responded under his authority as commander-in-chief by calling for 75,000 volunteers to suppress the rebellion, and by proclamation on April 19, he ordered a naval blockade of ports in the seceded states. He also called Congress into a special session, which would meet symbolically on July 4. In the meantime, he gave himself space to continue making extraordinary use of executive authority without having to consult the legislative branch.

Among these unilateral and unprecedented actions was the president's suspension of the writ of *habeas corpus*.[39] The writ is a protection against arbitrary arrest and unlawful imprisonment, which has its origins in English common law as far back as the twelfth century. In operation, the writ is a court order that challenges the reasons for a person's arrest. If the petition is granted and a writ is issued, the confined person must be brought before the court for an examination into the reasons for confinement. On April 27, Lincoln authorized the Commanding General of the Army to suspend the writ of *habeas corpus* "at any point or in the vicinity of any military line which is now or which shall be used between the city of Philadelphia and the city of Washington."[40] On July 2, he extended this authority to an area between New York City and Washington—

all before Congress met in emergency session on July 4. The initial reason for doing so was to keep lines of communication and transportation open to the capital, especially after the immediately bordering state of Virginia seceded on April 21. It was now more critical than ever to keep Maryland, which abutted Washington to the north, from leaving the Union, for in that case, the capital would be an island surrounded by two seceded states.

The president also expanded the army and navy beyond what Congress had authorized, called out state militias, requested volunteers to serve in the army for three years, spent money without Congressional approval, and declared a naval blockade of the Confederacy on his own volition. All these actions demonstrated that a president could claim to have the authority, on his own volition, to summon enormous military actions in response to what he deemed a national emergency. As authority to do so, Lincoln invoked the Insurrection Act, passed by Congress in 1792. He was responding to a genuine national crisis, but future presidents might be tempted to declare false national emergencies and invoke the Insurrection Act to keep themselves in power.

On May 25, federal troops arrested John Merryman of Maryland for assembling and training a group of men for service in the Confederate army. Merryman's attorney then petitioned Chief Justice Roger B. Taney for a writ of *habeas corpus*. Taney granted the writ and when the military officer in charge refused service on it, he ruled in *Ex Parte Merriman* that Lincoln did not have the authority to suspend the writ in the first place. The chief justice did admit, quoting the Constitution, that "the writ of *habeas corpus* shall not be suspended, unless when in cases of rebellion or invasion the public safety shall require it."[41] However, he argued that since the prohibition appears in Article I of the Constitution, which deals with the legislative branch of the government, the president who heads the executive branch could not suspend a writ over which Congress has the sole authority.[42] Taney went on to remind the president that his oath required him to "take care that the laws be faith fully executed," adding that if such executive usurpation were to continue, "the people of the United States [would] no longer [be] living under a government of laws." The president quietly ignored the decision, unlike Andrew Jackson, who reveled in denouncing the Supreme Court when it ruled against him.

Lincoln sent a special message to Congress when it finally met in emergency session (very symbolically) on July 4, in which he claimed that the authority to suspend *habeas corpus* could rest with either the president or the legislature and left it up to Congress to decide the question. Congress dithered over the matter for nearly two years, when on March 3, 1863, it authorized the president to suspend the writ under certain conditions, but Lincoln cleverly did not refer to the authorization when suspending the writ thereafter as a way of asserting that he, *as president*, had the power to act without Congressional permission.

Elsewhere in his July 4 message, Lincoln explained why he thought his use of emergency powers should be accepted by Congress: "These measures, whether strictly legal or not," he declared, "were ventured upon what appeared to be a popular demand and a public necessity, trusting then, as now that Congress would readily ratify them."[43] The government, he went on to assert, had the absolute power of self-defense which devolves on the president as chief executive officer and commander-in-chief of the military—even if it means violating the laws and the Constitution. Lincoln put this argument in the form of questions: "Are all the laws but one to go unexecuted, and the Government itself go to pieces lest that one be violated? Even in such a case, would not the official [presidential] oath be broken if the Government be overthrown when it was believed that disregarding a single law would tend to preserve it?"[44] Here Lincoln was channeling, no doubt unconsciously, the words of President Jefferson half a century earlier when his predecessor had claimed that there were "extreme cases where the laws become inadequate to their own preservation and where the universal recourse is a dictator, or martial law."[45]

Lincoln could not ask Congress for a declaration of war against the Confederacy, since such a declaration would be tantamount to admitting that it was a separate country. In the absence of a war measure, the president believed that he had the obligation to wage hostilities against the South based on his oath of office, wherein he had sworn to "preserve, protect, and defend the Constitution of the United States." Included in this obligation under Article II, Section 3 of the Constitution, was to "take care the laws be faithfully executed," the same phrase, ironically, that Chief Justice Taney had used to chastise Lincoln for suspending *habeas corpus*.

The president also assumed authority to clamp down on subversive activities in the North. On September 24, 1862, he imposed martial law in any area of the northern states where disorder and treason threatened, such as in southern Indiana, southern Ohio, and Missouri. Only rarely, however, were those arrested tried before military tribunals. In most cases, they were imprisoned and later released without trial. The aim of these measures was to warn others who might contemplate disloyal actions. Nor did the government take severe measures during the war to block freedom of speech or press.

In 1863, the Supreme Court affirmed the president's extraordinary use of his war powers in the *Prize Cases*. At question was whether Lincoln's blockade of southern ports was constitutional. In making their decision, the justices bowed to presidential prerogative: "Whether the President in fulfilling his duties as Commander-in-Chief, in suppressing an insurrection . . . is a question to be decided *by him*, and this Court must be governed by the decisions and acts of the political department of the Government to which this power was entrusted. . . . He must determine what degree of force the crisis demands." Neither the Supreme Court nor Congress was going to stand in the way of Lincoln's assumptions of vast wartime powers.

The authority Lincoln cited for freeing enslaved people likewise flowed from the application of his powers as commander-in-chief. Congress had passed a Second Confiscation Act on July 17, 1862, authorizing the military to confiscate enslaved persons as contraband of war, since their owners were using their labor to support the rebellion. However, in his Emancipation Proclamation, which took effect on January 1, 1863, Lincoln does not cite Congressional authority from the Second Confiscation Act. Rather, he begins the document by citing "the power in me vested as Commander-in-Chief of the Army and Navy" and ends the document as "warranted by the Constitution upon military necessity."[46] Fearing that the proclamation might face court challenges, Lincoln later supported a Thirteenth Amendment to the Constitution that would forever outlaw slavery in the United States, though he would not live to see its ratification in December 1865.

According to Noah Feldman, in his book, *The Broken Constitution*, Lincoln's assertion of his powers as commander-in-chief led directly to the Thirteenth Amendment and to voiding the Constitution's compromise with slavery. Given his desire to bring about a quick reconstruction with the South and his call for "malice toward none" and "charity for all," it can never be known if Lincoln would have supported, in such rapid succession, the Fourteenth Amendment, which began the process of extending equal rights to all citizens. Nor could it be known if he would have advocated the Fifteenth Amendment, which initiated the right of all citizens to vote. In any case, Lincoln had issued an executive order of possibly dubious constitutionality—the Emancipation Proclamation—which nevertheless began the process of creating a new social contract for the American people. That contract would not always be honored and would require additional constitutional amendments, as well as an ongoing civil rights movement along with several other rights movements, in attempts to complete what Lincoln had launched and that, if fully realized, would go well beyond what he might have imagined.[47]

As commander-in-chief, Lincoln had also taken complete control of prosecuting the war. He hired and fired commanding generals until he found Ulysses S. Grant, who would fight without ceasing. He also read books from the Library of Congress on tactics so he could learn how to execute the war and made suggestions to his generals about specific strategies. He visited battlefields in the eastern theater of war, and several times, out of sheer frustration with certain generals' inaction or incompetence, contemplated going to the front himself and taking command but thought better of it.

With the war raging and with southern Democrats now absent, Lincoln's Republican Party was in control of Congress. The legislators enacted, and the president signed, several landmark pieces of legislation very much in line with ideas that John Quincy Adams had put forth and that the Jacksonians had blocked a generation earlier. There was the first of several Transcontinental Railroad Acts beginning in 1862 that assisted private companies through the sale of government bonds as well as land grants to the railroad companies to connect the east and west coasts by rail—a massive internal improvement project about which Adams could have only dreamed. Congress did not create a national university along the lines Adams had envisioned, but the Morrill Land Grant College Act of 1862 established a series of agricultural and mechanical (i.e., engineering) institutions of higher learning with grants to the states from the sale of federal lands. Although Congress did not create a new Bank of the United States, which Adams had supported, it did pass National Banking Acts in 1862 and 1863 that established nationally chartered banks and a uniform national currency, along with federal supervision of these national banks. Such laws extended the scope of federal initiative that would only grow in the future.

As the war dragged on into 1864 and the casualties mounted ever higher, Lincoln feared that he might well lose the presidential election in the fall, but it never occurred to him to try to call off or delay going to the polls. Doing so would destroy the very government, "of, by, and for the people," that he believed he was defending. Fortunately, General William Tecumseh Sherman took Atlanta, Georgia, in September of that year, and Lincoln won a second term. Despite his assumption of extraordinary executive authority and the very realistic fear that he might lose his bid for reelection, he had no desire to make himself into an American Caesar or Napoleon. Nor would Lincoln have refused to accept defeat in his bid for a second term, using the extreme crisis of the Civil War as justification.

Power Unleashed

Andrew Jackson and Abraham Lincoln were among the most powerful presidents at any time in the nation's history. Both used pictorial imagery to enhance public recognition. Jackson sat for innumerable oil portraits, and Lincoln used the latest breakthroughs in photography to disseminate thousands of photographs of himself. These actions anticipated even more seductive pictorial imagery that presidents would use in the future to attract and hold voters. Both had also risen from humble backgrounds to the highest office in the land. However, Jackson, rather than Lincoln, was bitter over his background and turned that bitterness against elites, Native Americans, and partisan foes to achieve and hold political power. Such bitterness would characterize several future presidencies, including those of Andrew Johnson, Richard Nixon, and Donald Trump.

Lincoln used questionable executive powers to fight the Civil War. He also used his power as commander-in-chief to free enslaved people, declare martial law, and defy the Supreme Court. In contrast, Jackson had defied the Supreme Court in peacetime and asserted that the president had just as much right to determine what was constitutional as the high court. During the Civil War, Lincoln also set the stage for federal intervention in higher education and transportation by supporting the Land Grant College Act and the Transcontinental Railroad Act.

During his lifetime—both before and during his presidency—there was no cult of personality surrounding Lincoln as there had been with Jackson. Indeed, there were many who hated him and thought he was not qualified to be president. Lincoln was certainly ambitious and wanted to make a name for himself, but he was more likely to engage in a pose of self-deprecation than to boast about himself, perhaps as a way of associating with common folk. Even after his death, there was not so much a personality cult surrounding Lincoln as a mystique—that is, a sense of mystery and awe that has elevated him above other presidents and even above mere mortals in the minds of some.

It was death from an assassin's bullet at the very moment of his triumph, just days after Robert E. Lee's surrender at Appomattox Court House, which no doubt sealed Lincoln's outsized place in the nation's history. The shooting on Good Friday 1865 and Lincoln's death the following morning led thousands of religious leaders to compare him that Easter Sunday to the martyred Christ who, for Christians, had also died to make men free. Before the year was out, a print from a now unknown artist entitled "Apotheosis of Washington & Lincoln" depicted Washington greeting the fallen president in heaven with a laurel wreath. Significantly, this image appears to be the only artistic deification of a man who was never as widely lauded during his presidency as Washington had been. Besides, Lincoln himself, who doubted the divinity of Christ, surely would have recoiled at the thought of his own apotheosis. However, historians have showered this Civil War president with numerous secular laurels and have invariably placed him first or second (only after Washington) in the ranks of the country's greatest presidents.

Jackson's opponents called him "King Andrew I," and Lincoln's harshest critics said he was a dictator. Though Congress might reassert itself from time to time after their presidencies, Abraham Lincoln and Andrew Jackson left legacies of greatly enhanced presidential authority that their successors could and did renew—and use for both good and ill. Significantly, Donald Trump would later become a great admirer of Jackson and would make a pilgrimage to the Hermitage, Old Hickory's plantation in Tennessee. As president, he would hang a portrait of Jackson beside his desk in the Oval Office.

Notes

1 The names of these cases were, respectively, *Worcester v. Georgia* (1832) and *Ex Parte Merriman* (1861).
2 James David Barber, *The Presidential Character: Predicting Presidential Character in the White House* (New York: Routledge, 2020). This book was originally published in 1971 and is now in its fifth edition.
3 Ibid., 7.
4 In writing about Jackson, I am indebted to H. W. Brands, *Andrew Jackson: His Life and Times* (New York: Harper and Row, 2006); James C. Curtis, *Andrew Jackson and the Search for Vindication* (Boston: Little, Brown and Company, 1976); Jon Mecham, *American Lion: Andrew Jackson in the White House* (New York: Random House, 2009); and Robert V. Remini, *Andrew Jackson* (New York: Harper and Row, 1999).
5 Quoted in Meacham, *American Lion*, 9.
6 Quoted in James Parton, *Life of Andrew Jackson* (New York: Mason Brothers, 1863), 40.
7 Quoted in Remini, *Andrew Jackson*, 91.
8 Ibid., 91–2.
9 Quoted in Brands, *Andrew Jackson*, 163.
10 Roseboom, *Presidential Elections*, 83.
11 Mary H. M. Hargreaves, *The Presidency of John Quincy Adams* (Lawrence: University Press of Kansas, 1985), 43–7; Meacham, *American Lion*, 44–5.
12 Quoted in Meacham, *American Lion*, 44.
13 For my understanding of John Quincy Adams, I am indebted to Hargreaves, *The Presidency of John Quincy Adams*, as cited above, in addition to Robert V. Remini, *John Quincy Adams* (New York: Times Books, 2002) and Fred Kaplan, *John Quincy Adams: American Visionary* (New York: Harper Perennials, 2015).

14 Quoted in Hargreaves, *Presidency of John Quincy Adams*, 167.
15 For more on the complexities of Jackson's background, wealth, and social standing, see Edward Pessen, *The Log Cabin Myth: The Social Backgrounds of the Presidents* (New Haven: Yale University Press, 1984), 3, 17–18, 81–2, 163–4.
16 See R. A. McNeal, "Nicholas Biddle, Anacharis, and the Grand Tour," *Pennsylvania Magazine of History and Biography* (July 1996), 217–47.
17 Michael Coblenz, "The Fight Goes on Forever: Limited Government and the First Bank of the United States," *Southern Illinois University Law Review* (2015).
18 President Jackson's Veto Message Regarding the Bank of the United States, July 10, 1832, The Avalon Project, http://avalon.yale.edu/19thcetury/ajveto01.asp.
19 Ibid.
20 In his book, *The Imperial Presidency* historian Arthur Schlesinger, Jr. would use the term "Plebiscitary Presidency" to describe Richard Nixon's belief that winning by a landslide in the popular vote allowed him to do virtually anything as president and that the only check on presidential power was an overwhelming popular vote against the behavior and policies of a chief executive. See especially page 377 of Schlesinger.
21 Quoted in Mecham, *American Lion*, 204.
22 Meacham, *American Lion*, 188–9, 278–9, 286–8.
23 Sarah Bush Johnson, interview by William H. Herndon, September 8, 1865, in *Herdon's Informants: Letters, Interviews, and Statements about Abraham Lincoln*, ed. Douglas L. Wilson and Rdney O. David (Urbana: University of Illinois Press, 1998), 107–8.
24 *Collected Works of Abraham Lincoln*, ed. Roy P. Basler et al. (New Brunswick: Rutgers University Press, 1953), 3:511.
25 Lincoln, "Address Before the Young Men's Lyceum of Springfield, Illinois" (January 27, 1838), *Collected Works*, 1:109.
26 Ibid.
27 Lincoln, "'Spot Resolutions' in the United States House of Representatives" (December 22, 1847), *Collected Works*, 1:421.
28 Lincoln to William H. Herdon, *Collected Works*, 1:451–2.
29 Quoted in David Herbert Donald, *Lincoln* (New York: Quadrangle Books, 1995), 162.
30 William Herndon, *Herndon's Life of Lincoln* (New York: Da Capo Press, 1983), 304. This book was originally published in 1888.
31 Lincoln, Speech at Chicago, Illinois (July 10, 1858), *Collected Works*, 2:250.
32 Lincoln to Anson G. Henry, November 19, 1858, *Collected Works*, 3:339.
33 Lincoln to Alexander Sympson, December 12, 1858, *Collected Works*, 3:346.
34 Andrea L. Volpe, "The Carte de Visite Craze," *New York Times*, August 6, 2013.
35 Lincoln, "First Inaugural Address" (March 4, 1861), *Collected Works*, 4:250.
36 Ibid., 252.
37 Ibid., 271.
38 Ibid.
39 On Lincoln and habeas corpus, see James A. Dueholm, "Lincoln's Suspension of Habeas Corpus: An Historical and Constitutional Analysis," *Journal of the Abraham Lincoln Association* 29 (Summer 2008): 47–66. An earlier but very insightful discussion of this matter is Clinton L. Rossiter, *Constitutional Dictatorship: Crisis Government in the Modern Democracies* (Princeton: Princeton University Press, 1948), 226–30.

40 Rossiter, *Constitutional Dictatorship*, 227.
41 Article I, Section 9, Clause 2.
42 *Ex Parte Merryman* 17 F. Cas. 144 (C.C.D. Md. 1861) (No. 9487).
43 Quoted in Rossiter, *Constitutional Dictatorship*, 229.
44 Quoted in ibid.
45 Jefferson to W. C. Claiborne, February 3, 1807; to James Brown, October 27, 1808; to J. B. Colvin, September 20, 1810, in Jefferson, *Writings*, 11:151, 12:183, 418.
46 The Emancipation Proclamation | National Archives, https://www.archives.gov/.../emancipation-proclamation.
47 Noah Feldman, *The Broken Constitution* (New York: Farrer, Straus, and Giroux, 2021).

4

Power and Reform

The Progressive Presidency

I bid you pay no heed to any other authority, no heed to a writ from a judge, or anything else, excepting my commands.

Theodore Roosevelt, instructions to General John M. Schofield, October 13, 1902

If [a president] rightly interpret[s] the national thought and boldly insist[s] upon it, he is irresistible; and the country never feels the zest of action so much as when the President is of such insight and caliber. . . . [He] is at liberty, both in law and conscience, to be as big a man as he can.

Woodrow Wilson, *Constitutional Government*, 1908

The early newsreels and ubiquitous photographs in newspapers all over the country appear to reduce the new president to a drooping mustache, big toothy smile, and pince-nez glasses. What the public cannot see is their president's body in perpetual motion. Nor can they hear his uproarious laughter and avalanche of words, sometimes in conversation but more often in streams of monologue. Four years after he leaves office, a sober-looking but eloquent former professor and college president, who has long studied and taught about the American presidency, calls on the nation to tackle the economic inequalities that beset the country at a time of uneven progress. Woodrow Wilson and Theodore Roosevelt greatly elevate the powers of the presidential office in the name of social reform and economic justice, while Wilson commands the American people to fight a war to champion democracy and in the process becomes the most powerful president since Abraham Lincoln.

At age forty-two, Theodore Roosevelt (1901–1909) remains the youngest president in US history and the first chief executive of the twentieth century. The new century may have already begun on the calendar, but Roosevelt invented the modern presidency. Fittingly, his entry into the White House was as dramatic as it was tragic. On September 6, 1901, then President William McKinley had traveled to Buffalo, New York, to visit the Pan-American Exposition, a world's fair dedicated to showing off the progress of the Western Hemisphere. Although exhibits of the latest manufactured goods and cultural displays from various nations drew visitors' attention, what truly dazzled them was the nighttime illumination of the fair accomplished by thousands of light bulbs tracing the outlines and exterior features of every building. The electricity for this glittering show came from an electrical current generated twenty-five miles away at Niagara Falls, where the churning waters of the Niagara River propelled the massive generators. A new century, lighted and powered by electricity, was on its way.

On the afternoon of the sixth, McKinley positioned himself in the fair's Temple of Music, where he could shake hands with anyone who cared to come by, attracting a long queue of well-wishers. In line was anarchist Leon Czolgosz, who carried a pistol concealed beneath a handkerchief wrapped around his right hand. As McKinley reached out to shake hands, Czolgosz shot the president at point-blank range. One of the bullets tore through McKinley's stomach, injuring both his liver and pancreas before lodging in his back. Vice President Theodore Roosevelt was in Vermont that afternoon getting ready to attend a reception hosted by the Vermont Fish and Game League. He immediately rushed to Buffalo, where surgeons had reportedly saved the president's life. On the tenth, when it looked as though McKinley was out of danger, Roosevelt left town and joined his wife and children at a camp in the Adirondacks. Three days later, on September 13, the president began to sink as a gathering gangrenous infection overwhelmed him. Antibiotics that might have subdued the infection were more than a generation into the future.

Frantic messages went out to Roosevelt, who had joined some friends to climb Mount Mercy, the highest mountain in the Adirondack range. On the way down, a runner intercepted the vice president with the news that McKinley was dying. Roosevelt rode at breakneck speed in a horse-drawn buckboard some forty miles to the nearest railhead. He jumped onto a special train that tore non-stop across New York State to Buffalo, where he arrived early on the afternoon of the fourteenth, a little less than eleven hours after McKinley had breathed his last.

Roosevelt's tumbling down a mountain and roaring across New York State, where he took the oath of office just an hour and a half after arriving, was somehow fitting for a man who had gloried in what he liked to call "the strenuous life." He had chased outlaws in the Badlands of South Dakota and later charged at the head of his Rough Riders up San Juan Hill in Cuba during the Spanish-American War. He would now unleash his colossal energy on many issues facing the United States—and the world at large—at times showing little regard for either precedent or the Constitution.

Conservative members of the Republican Party were more than worried about having Theodore Roosevelt at the nation's helm. During his two terms as governor of New York, he had fought an unrelenting campaign against political corruption. To get rid of him, leaders of the state's Republican Party had decided to "kick him upstairs" into the vice presidency, a position of very little influence at the time from which he could supposedly do no harm. Upon Roosevelt's nomination for vice president, chairman of the Republican Committee Mark Hanna had warned, "Don't any of you know that there's only one life between that madman and the White House."[1]

Roosevelt was no madman, despite his bumptious personality and sometimes daredevil pursuits. However, he sincerely believed that his country needed strong reforms in the wake of widespread transformations. Many of these transformations were unnerving: Rapid urbanization and all its ills, the disquieting disappearance of familiar landmarks, the widening separation between producers and consumers, the rise of irresponsible monopolies, the wasteful exploitation of natural resources, and dangerous working conditions in factories and mines. What historians later called the progressive era of reform had been gestating for several years, and Roosevelt was delighted to wield the cudgel of change. In the process, he and the reformers who came after him would continue to stretch the limits of presidential power far beyond what the framers of the Constitution could have imagined.

Reclaiming Presidential Power

An energetic reform leader, Roosevelt's administration stood in stark contrast to the relatively weak presidencies of the previous three decades. Part of this decline had stemmed from a reassertion of Congressional authority after the Civil War. Another reason for this retreat in executive authority had been the lack of political consensus, as political parties seldom managed to control the presidency and both houses of Congress at the same time. It is therefore no mystery that Presidents Hayes, Garfield, Arthur, Harrison, and Cleveland, all of them serving in the late nineteenth century, were largely unknown to the American public in later decades. McKinley, whom some historians credit with a reawakening of presidential authority, has also largely been consigned to popular oblivion.

It is not surprising that Roosevelt and other progressives looked back to the extraordinarily powerful Lincoln presidency for inspiration. Tellingly, at his inauguration in 1905, after his election as president in his own right, Roosevelt wore a gold ring on his hand, which his secretary of state John Hay had lent him for the occasion. Encased within the ring were several strands of Lincoln's hair. As was the habit in Victorian times, one of the doctors at Lincoln's deathbed had cut half a dozen strands from the dead president's head. Hay later purchased two of them and had them put into a ring. Equally symbolic, Hay was a living link between the two presidents: Having worked closely with Lincoln as one of his two private secretaries, he was now a key member of Roosevelt's administration. In addition, Roosevelt hung an oil portrait of Lincoln above the mantel in his White House office that he could glimpse every time he lifted his eyes from his desk.

Like Lincoln, Roosevelt was not above using—or threatening to use—power not authorized by the Constitution. An early exertion of such authority came when nearly 150,000 miners in the anthracite coalfields of Pennsylvania, led by the United Mine Workers (UMW), struck in May 1902. They demanded a pay increase of 20 percent, a reduction in working hours from ten to nine hours a day, and recognition of the union. UMW president John Mitchell offered to negotiate, but the mine operators refused. George F. Baer, head of the Philadelphia and Reading Railroad, declared that the miners' interests would best be served, "Not by the labor agitators, but by the Christian men to whom God, in his infinite wisdom, has given control of the property interests of the country."[2]

Such talk enraged Roosevelt, who feared that the oppression of workers might touch off class warfare unless something took place to curb the worst abuses of capitalism. Besides, coal was still "king" at a time when industry, rail transportation, and home heating all depended on this resource. As summer turned to autumn and winter beckoned, the desperate president threatened to send the army in to reopen the mines. Advised by Attorney General Philander Knox that he did not have authority under the Constitution to take such an action, Roosevelt admitted to Knox that he indeed had "no legal or constitutional right in the matter." James E. Watson, the Republican whip in the House of Representatives, also objected to sending in troops, asking the president, "What about the Constitution of the United States? What about seizing private property without due process of law?" The president responded by grabbing Wilson on the shoulder and shouting, "The Constitution was made for the people and not the people for the Constitution."[3] In his *Autobiography*, published half a dozen years later, Roosevelt expanded on this assertion of executive authority: "My belief was that it was not only [the president's] right but his duty to do anything that the needs of the Nation demanded unless such action was forbidden by the Constitution or by the laws."[4]

In the end, Roosevelt got both sides to agree to a commission to arbitrate the dispute, in part because he made no secret of his threat to take over the mines. Miners agreed to go back to work while the commissioners deliberated. They won a nine-hour workday and a pay increase of 10 percent, but not recognition of the union. The president was serious about sending in federal troops and had directed Secretary of War Elihu Root to put a force of ten thousand regulars on alert to go into the coalfields at half an hour's notice. Roosevelt handpicked General John M. Schofield, who had restored order during the Pullman strike back in 1894, to command the troops. The president was adamant that Schofield follow only the president's orders: "I bid you pay no heed to any other authority, no heed to a writ from a judge, or anything else, excepting my commands."[5] One can only wonder what Roosevelt would have done if a federal court had issued an injunction against such action on the grounds that it was unconstitutional. Would he have defied the court as Andrew Jackson had done over Native American removal or as Abraham Lincoln had done when the chief justice declared his revocation of *habeas corpus* to be unconstitutional?

When it came to enforcing the Sherman Anti-Trust Act, Roosevelt did find support from the highest court in the land. Both the public and press were constantly denouncing "the trusts," while the president received piles of mail demanding action against them. A prime case involved the Northern Securities Company, a trust established in 1902 and put together by financier J. P. Morgan along with railroad magnates James K. Hill and E. H. Harriman. Their aim was to gain control of two major east-west railroads, the Great Northern and the Union Pacific, as well as to gain ownership of the Burlington Railroad, which would give them access to Chicago. Up to that time, the Sherman Act had been employed most successfully against labor unions, which the courts held, using language from the Sherman Act, to be "conspiracies in restraint of trade."

Roosevelt did not believe all large business combinations were problematic, distinguishing between what he called "good trusts and bad trusts." However, he had no doubt that the Northern Securities Company was one of the bad trusts and directed Attorney General Knox to file suit in federal court against the company. Morgan, who had brokered the combination, was thunderstruck. He met the president at the White House on the morning of February 22 and asked Roosevelt why he had not asked him personally to correct any problems with the new trust. "If we have done anything wrong," Morgan said to the president, "send your man to my man and they can fix it up." "That can't be done," Roosevelt responded. Attorney General Knox then added, "We don't want to fix it up, we want to stop it." Morgan then asked, "Are you going to attack my other interests, the steel trust and others?" "Certainly not," Roosevelt assured him, "unless we find out that in any case they have done something that we regard as wrong."[6] The president stood firm against the most powerful financier in the country. At the same time, Roosevelt, ever the moralist, assured Morgan that he distinguished between right and wrong behavior when it came to the trusts.

Knox could not be certain that the Supreme Court would rule in favor of the government in the *Northern Securities* case, given a high court decision back in 1895, just seven years earlier in *United States v. E. C. Knight* (1895).[7] That case concerned the so-called Sugar Trust, which was attempting to control 98 percent of the sugar refining capacity in the United States. Nevertheless, the court decided that the trust did not fall under the Sherman Act, since the manufacture of a product like refined sugar took place at distinct locations and therefore did not involve interstate commerce per se, which was the only type of commerce that fell under federal control in accordance with the Interstate Commerce Clause of the Constitution. However, in a five-to-four decision, the court ruled in 1904 against the Northern Securities Company, in part because, as a railroad crossing state lines, it clearly was engaged in interstate commerce. Over the next seven years, Roosevelt's Justice Department launched forty-four more successful anti-trust suits.[8]

In other areas of progressive reform activity, Roosevelt also gained cooperation with Congress to pass several regulatory laws, including the Hepburn Act, which gave the Interstate Commerce Commission the power to set maximum railroad rates. At his urging, Congress also passed the Pure Food and Drugs Act and the Meat Inspection Act. In addition, Roosevelt put his power and prestige behind the conservation movement, establishing the US Forest Service, securing five new National Parks, and obtaining the Antiquities Act. The Antiquities Act allowed him and future presidents to use executive proclamations to create National Monuments to protect natural, cultural, and scientific features. Altogether, Roosevelt quadrupled the size of federal lands from forty-two to 172 million acres and established 150 new national forests as well as fifty-one wildlife refuges. He accomplished most of this conservation with a stroke of the pen by issuing executive orders under what he considered the "inherent power"—or prerogative—of the presidency. Altogether, Roosevelt issued 1,081 executive orders, which amounted to ten times the number put forth by any predecessor—not all of them regarding conservation. This was the presidential prerogative in hyper action, a situation that would have alarmed the authors of the Constitution, who had specifically opposed such an executive prerogative, though they had done nothing specifically to prohibit such actions.

Roosevelt's Big Stick

Roosevelt was extremely forceful in the realm of foreign affairs, with or without consent of Congress or constitutional authorization, in the wake of his country's new status as a world power following the Spanish-American War and the conquest of the Philippines. His watchword was "speak softly and carry and big stick; you will go far," a phrase that he attributed to a West African proverb. However, researchers have never been able to confirm the source, leading to the conjecture that Roosevelt himself made it up. He had employed the phrase as early as 1900 when he was still governor of New York. While president, he used it to assert that the country needed to practice patient diplomacy to back up foreign policy, but, when necessary, to use armed force. During this era, force meant a powerful navy, as advocated by Alfred Thayer Mahan in his seminal book, *The Influence of Sea Power Upon History* (1890), a work that Roosevelt read and revered. Pursuant to Mahan's main thesis that world power had always depended on control of the seas, Roosevelt successfully petitioned Congress to embark on an ambitious modern shipbuilding program that resulted in the United States going from the fourth to the second most powerful navy in the world, behind only Great Britain.

Well before this build-up was complete, Roosevelt, under his authority as commander-in-chief, ordered a naval show of force in Cuban waters when British and German ships blockaded the coast of Venezuela in December 1902 when that country failed to pay its debts to each of the countries. Roosevelt was afraid the creditor nations would go even further and occupy Venezuela in defiance of the nearly eighty-year-old Monroe Doctrine, believing that only "power and the willingness to use it" would make the two European powers back down.[9]

A crisis over threats by European powers to use force to collect debts from Santo Domingo led Roosevelt in May 1904 to proclaim in unequivocal terms that the United States, not outside powers, would discipline errant Latin American nations. This statement became the Roosevelt Corollary to the Monroe Doctrine. Secretary of State Elihu Root made the corollary public when he read it in the form of a letter from the president to the Cuba Society of New York. The most pertinent line from the letter declared, "If a nation shows that it knows how to act with decency in industrial and political matters, if it keeps order and pays its obligations, then it need fear no interference from the United States." Acting otherwise, however, could "finally require intervention by some civilized nation, and in the Western Hemisphere the United States cannot ignore this duty."[10]

Roosevelt, as the country's chief foreign policy officer, had put forth this policy without consulting Congress, even though acting on it might involve the nation in endless interventions throughout Latin America. The original Monroe Doctrine, announced by President James Monroe back in 1823, also had been issued without Congressional approbation.[11] Rather, it had warned European powers that attempts to regain any territories in the Americas that had become independent would be considered "the manifestation of an unfriendly disposition toward the United States." However, unlike Roosevelt's later corollary, it had not asserted a right of the United

States to intervene in Latin America. Rather, Monroe correctly assumed that it would be enforced by Great Britain, which had originally proposed a joint statement with the United States warning against any attempts to reinstate European colonialism in the Americas.

Roosevelt's actions in securing the rights to a canal across Panama likewise involved unilateral action on his part. The conquest of the Philippines in the wake of the Spanish-American War had necessitated a two-ocean navy for the United States that could operate in both Atlantic and Pacific waters. However, the only way to send ships from one ocean to the other then was by a long and dangerous route around the southern tip of South America. Thus, the decades-long dream of a canal through the narrow isthmus between North and South America became essential as far as Roosevelt was concerned.

Once the Senate approved the concept of a canal across the Isthmus of Panama in June 1902, the United States commenced negotiations with the Colombian government, since Panama was then a Colombian province. Negotiations dragged on for months until Secretary of State Hay threatened to reconsider an earlier idea of building the canal through Nicaragua, with the result that Colombia agreed to allow the United States to build the canal across Panama with an initial payment of $10 million and an annual rent of $250,000. Just days after the Colombian representative signed the agreement, the Colombia government disavowed it and held out for more money. Roosevelt, who wanted to begin construction before his bid for reelection in 1904, was livid and declared he would not allow those "Bogota jack rabbits" to "bar one of the future highways of civilization."[12] Indeed, the president believed the canal was a moral imperative and was righteous in his determination to push it through.

What Roosevelt did was encourage the Panamanians to stage a revolt for independence against Colombia, something they had attempted to do without success many times before. Now Roosevelt arranged for the US Navy gunboat *Nashville* to be stationed off the port city of Colon on the Atlantic Ocean side of Panama to keep Colombia from landing troops to put down the rebellion. The revolt succeeded and the Panamanians declared their independence, which the United States recognized within hours. The new government signed a treaty that gave the United States the right to build an inter-ocean canal on similar terms originally negotiated with Colombia, but now with a ten-mile-wide canal zone to be administered and guarded by US forces. Roosevelt had acted under his authority as commander-in-chief to aid the Panamanian coup without thought of Congressional approval. Thus, when it came to foreign affairs, Roosevelt often acted on his own authority, much like monarchs of old.

As a show of force well before the completion of the Panama Canal, Roosevelt conceived of a plan to send a large naval force, as a "practice cruise," from the Atlantic to the Pacific Ocean by sending it around the southern tip of South America. Making up the fleet were sixteen battleships, painted white to proclaim the peaceful nature of their undertaking. Congress protested because the president had not consulted them, the Senate Naval Affairs Committee declaring that it would not approve funds for the voyage. Knowing that he had enough money to send the fleet to the West Coast, Roosevelt defied the legislators, figuring they would find the money to bring the ships back. In fact, his plan all along was to send the flotilla around the world as a way of showing that US naval strength was second only to that of Great Britain. The fleet left in December 1907 and returned in late February of 1909 after traveling some 46,000 miles without suffering a mishap. The ships and their crews received a friendly reception everywhere they went. Roosevelt was delighted to welcome them back, later writing, "In my own judgement the most important service that I rendered to peace was the voyage of the battle fleet around the world."[13]

In this action, as in his other foreign policy initiatives, the president enjoyed powerful support among some senators. During a 1906 debate, Senator J. C. Spooner of Wisconsin argued that except for the Senate's refusal to ratify a treaty, presidents had "absolute and uncontrolled and uncontrollable authority over foreign affairs."[14] In the area of international relations, according to this argument, presidents had an authority similar to absolute monarchs.

Roosevelt could get away with defying or ignoring Congress as well as threatening to act unconstitutionally (as during the Anthracite Strike) in large part because of his extreme popularity, as registered in his smashing victory in 1904, when he was elected to the presidency in his own right. He won the popular vote by 56 percent to 37.6 percent against Democratic candidate Alton B. Parker and in the Electoral College by 336 to 140. Thereby, Roosevelt could claim to govern by a plebiscitary mandate, meaning that he could and did claim a source of power and legitimacy for a period of four years that was independent of Congress, and during which his authority was very unlikely to be challenged by the Senate, which was also in Republican hands. So much, then, for the operation of effective checks and balances if the president's party was in control of Congress.

The "Bully Pulpit"

Roosevelt also used large gestures at home, such as placing a personal stamp on the president's residence to cement his popularity and authority. Although the executive mansion had long been called the White House in common usage, Roosevelt made the name official by having the name printed on the president's official stationery. He also obtained substantial funds from Congress to remodel and extend the building, with his wife Edith proposing that they engage the firm of McKim, Mead & White, renowned architects of the rich and famous, to design the work. As part of the renovation, Roosevelt moved his office from the second-story residence to a new West Wing. Both the new wing and the renovations in the rest of the White House were in the then very popular Colonial Revival style, which in part reflected a nostalgia for the time when Anglo Americans dominated all aspects of life. Roosevelt had clearly put his stamp on the White House, the presidency, and the Republican Party.

Roosevelt also viewed his presidency as what he liked to call a "Bully Pulpit" from which to advocate his many agendas. Whenever addressing a crowd, he spoke with his whole body—flailing his arms, flashing his big toothy smile, and laughing uproariously.

Newspaper cartoonists delighted in depicting him. He also cultivated good relations with selected newspaper reporters who were welcome to stop by the White House in the late afternoons while the president was going over his outgoing correspondence. He forbade reporters to quote him, speaking only on background, and in this way got his views across to the press. Reporters were happy to cooperate since they had access to the most important political source in the land.

Like Jackson and Lincoln before him, Roosevelt was a master at using imagery, now including moving pictures, to spread his image around the country—as well as around the world. Seeing photographs of a president—or still better, moving images of a president—made (and still makes) the country's chief executive *seem* increasingly real and even something of a friend, about whose life the public wants to know as much as possible. Hence, there develops an insatiable thirst to see and know about White House pets, about what the president does on vacation, or about the First Lady's clothing and hairstyles.

One can even imagine being with a president at a faraway event from seeing the chief executive in a photograph or on film. The more people who see images of another person, in this case presidents or first ladies, the greater public status the public will attribute to them. The same phenomenon applies to multiple images of accomplished athletes or movie stars, whose fans want to know everything about them and come to view them almost as friends—what psychologists call "parasocial relations," a phenomenon to be explored at greater depth in a later chapter.[15]

During Roosevelt's presidency and after, he made good use of newsreels, those short news films that were increasingly part of the movie going experience.[16] None was a candid shot, with each one carefully staged with input from Roosevelt himself. In 1912, Pathe News made the trek to Roosevelt's home at Sagamore Hill, New York. He refused to let them film him while playing tennis, fearing that some people would find the sport both "elite" and "effeminate." However, he gave permission to film him jumping his horse and vigorously chopping down a tree, activities that would show him as a rugged outdoorsman.[17] A 1910 film depicts Roosevelt (after his presidency) taking a ride in an early airplane, which makes several steep dips with its famous passenger on board and who afterwards, as written on the screen, exclaims "Bully!" In 1916, with Europe in a death grip during First World War, Roosevelt appears on film giving a preparedness speech from his porch at Sagamore Hill, New York. Carrying a riding crop, he periodically whips it through the air to emphasize salient points. Of course, it is a silent movie and viewers could only get a gist of what the former president (who continued to have aspirations to return to the White House) was saying by reading a bit of text projected on the screen at various intervals.[18]

Given the growing but still limited audience for newsreels, Roosevelt also made good use of still photography to convey images of himself as an active and adventurous president with numerous causes he wished to promote. Because a photogravure process was now available for printing photographs in newspapers and magazines, Roosevelt's image could appear millions of times before the reading public. There were photos of him sitting in the cab of a giant steam shovel used to dig the Panama Canal and of him posing beside naturalist John Muir with the dramatic falls at Yosemite in the background to emphasize his support for conservation and the National Parks. Photographs taken during his big game hunting trip in Africa and later in the Amazon, where he nearly lost his life, drove home the dual themes of explorer and intrepid hunter. Roosevelt also liked to pose with his brood of six children, marking him as a family man and perhaps pointing, ever so politely and silently, to his virility. Well before he left office, the president had created a cult of personality for himself that an adoring public embraced.

Given his immense popularity, Roosevelt could have easily won another term as president in 1908, in effect a third term (as he himself viewed it), since he had served for three and a half years following McKinley's assassination. He had also been elected in his own right in 1904. However, Roosevelt made the mistake after his triumph in 1904 when he promised not to run again four years later. As 1908 rolled around, he designated his Secretary of War, William Howard Taft, as his successor.

Despite his success and promoting himself through pictorial images, Roosevelt was most at home with print and became the most prolific writer of any American president. He published articles and books in a steady stream, partly to get his ideas across, partly to reinforce a manly view of himself, and partly as a way of supplementing his income. Typical of these publications, in addition to the African hunting saga, were *The Strenuous Life* (1899), *The Rough Riders* (1899,) *Ranch Life and the Hunting Trail* (1902), *Stories of the Great West* (1909), and *Through the Brazilian Wilderness* (1914).

Although Roosevelt had declared that he would not run for president again, he became disenchanted with President Taft while he was away, finding his successor insufficiently progressive. Perhaps more importantly, Roosevelt simply could not endure being out of the political arena and decided to seek the Republican presidential nomination for 1912. When he failed to obtain the nomination because the Taft forces were in control of the party, he bolted to the Progressive Party, with this "third party" being re-christened as the Bull Moose Party when Roosevelt declared that he was as fit as a Bull Moose to make another run for the White House. (Roosevelt just could not face being out of power.) The Republicans nominated incumbent President Taft, while the Democrats chose Woodrow Wilson.

During his presidency, Roosevelt had described his domestic program as the "Square Deal," which featured the conservation of natural resources, the reining in of corporations, and the protection of consumers. During his run in 1912, he changed the name of his program to the "New Nationalism," which would emphasize heavy federal regulation of the economy. Wilson, whom Roosevelt saw as his main opponent, took the term "New Freedom" for his election slogan, which called for the breaking up of powerful economic interests and the restoration of competition. Between them, Wilson and Roosevelt launched a tradition of slogans that presidents would embrace throughout the twentieth century and beyond as a way of attracting voters and giving the media a succinct handle for describing their agendas, and in the process exalting the presidency even more above the legislative branch of government.

Roosevelt's apostasy in 1912 split the Republican vote and handed the election to the Democrats. Had the Republican Party not been divided, it is conceivable that the immensely popular Roosevelt, who continued to crave power, could have won a third and even a fourth term in office at a time when there were no term limits for the presidency. (His distant cousin Franklin would win four presidential elections a generation later.) Given Theodore's cult of personality, craving for power, vast use of executive orders, temptation to ignore the Constitution, and his command over everything that piqued his interest both at home and abroad, it is no surprise that Roosevelt's most prominent modern biographer, Edmund Morris entitled his volume about the Roosevelt presidency, *Theodore Rex—rex* being the Latin word for king.

A Scholar President

Woodrow Wilson (1913–1921), who had been a professor of history and politics at Princeton and then president of the university, is second only to Roosevelt among American presidents in the number of books he published. He is also the only president to hold an earned doctorate, a Ph.D. in political science from Johns Hopkins University. As might be expected, his writings were very different from Roosevelt's accounts of the strenuous life. Virtually all of them fall into the category of political history and include *Congressional Government* (1885), *The State and Federal Government* (1889), *Division and Reunion* (1895), *George Washington* (1896), and *Constitutional Government in the United States* (1911).

There are hundreds of photographs of Wilson in office, but these are typically photographic portraits or scenes of him at some official activity, such as sitting at a desk signing bills, giving speeches, or standing and talking to advisors, politicians, or foreign dignitaries. There are far fewer informal photos of Wilson, such as riding in a horse-drawn carriage or automobile, or throwing out the "first ball" at the beginning of the baseball season in Washington. There are also occasional pictures of the president enjoying golf, a game he played frequently but never very well, or of him reading on the front porch of a summer getaway cottage. Nowhere are there images of strenuous activity. Not surprisingly, newsreels featuring Wilson are also tame in comparison to those of Theodore Roosevelt. Like his still photographs, Wilson's appearances in newsreels show him conducting official comings and goings.

For the most part, Wilson was content to rely mainly on the spoken word in a style that was clear, dramatic, and at times bordering on the emotional. However, in some respects, his speeches were like academic lectures but sometimes interlarded with the cadences of a sermon, which he was always careful to tailor to a more general audience. From an earlier age, at the suggestion of his Presbyterian minister father, he had practiced oratory from his father's pulpit in an empty church. Reverend Wilson had hoped his son might become a clergyman but held that a life in public service was also a religious calling for which his son would need to speak effectively. As it turned out, Wilson had many opportunities to hone his speaking abilities—as a professor, as president of Princeton (where he had earned an undergraduate degree), as a popular public speaker, and during his brief term as governor of New Jersey, which presaged his presidency. Even as president, he wrote his own speeches, the last occupant of the White House to do so.

Wilson's first inaugural address on March 4, 1913, is a prime example of his talents as a speaker, especially the passage where he addressed the contradictions of the nation's economic progress:

> We have been proud of our industrial achievements, but we have not hitherto stopped thoughtfully enough to count the human cost, the cost of lives snuffed out, of energies overtaxed and broken, the fearful physical and spiritual cost to the men and women and children upon whom the dead weight and burden of it all has fallen pitilessly the years through. The groans and agony of it all had not yet reached our ears, the solemn, moving undertone of our life, coming up out of the mines and factories, and out of every home where the struggle had its intimate and familiar seat. With the great Government went many deep secret things which we too long delayed to look into and scrutinize with candid, fearless eyes. The great Government we loved has too often been made use of for private and selfish purposes, and those who used it had forgotten the people.[19]

In early December 1913, Wilson overturned a precedent established by Thomas Jefferson when he delivered his State of the Union message in person before a joint session of Congress, as opposed to sending a written text for reading aloud to the legislators, as every president since Jefferson had done. However, he did not confine his speaking appearances before Congress to the State of the Union message but went before the legislators whenever he wanted to roll out a new policy or comment on a pressing matter. It helped greatly that his Democratic Party enjoyed substantial majorities in both the House and Senate, which allowed him to claim that he and his party had a mandate to govern. "There has been a change of government," he proclaimed in the opening line of his inaugural address. "No one can mistake the purpose for which the Nation now seeks to use the Democratic Party," he continued. "It seeks to use it to interpret a change in its own plans and point of view. . . . We have been refreshed by an insight into our own life."[20]

Wilson's statement about the public's expectations for the Democratic Party spoke directly to his conceptions of government in general, and of the presidency in particular. Ever since he had been an undergraduate student at Princeton, Wilson had been thinking and writing about the American political system. Vexed over what he believed were the weak presidencies of the post-Civil War period, he blamed the problem on committee control of both the Senate and House of Representatives. Each committee, he charged, represented a venal fiefdom that had little insight into or concern about broad national issues and problems. Under these circumstances, Wilson believed that "the President can seldom make himself recognized as a leader." Rather, "he is merely the executor of the sovereign legislative will; his Cabinet officers are little more than chief clerks . . . in the Executive Departments . . ."[21] Of course, he wrote these words long before the presidency of Theodore Roosevelt.

Wilson's alternative had been what he called "Cabinet Government," the topic of an article he published as a senior at Princeton, which he amplified in his book, *Congressional Government*, written while a graduate student at Johns Hopkins.[22]

Greatly influencing Wilson at the time and for many years thereafter was the English journalist and political analyst Walter Bagehot's seminal work, *The English Constitution*, published in 1867. Bagehot pointed to the overwhelming influence ministers wielded as senior members of the majority party in Parliament, leading to what Bagehot called "the nearly complete fusion of the executive and legislative powers" that resulted in a unified system of government.[23]

In the United States, by contrast, Wilson believed the Constitutional separation of powers was applied so rigorously that the separation had resulted in the nearly complete isolation of the executive and legislative branches and in the near impossibility of coordination between them. In Wilson's words, the separation was "so complete as to amount to isolation."[24] As Wilson continued, "The Executive is in constant need of legislative cooperation," while "the legislative must be aided by an Executive who is in a position intelligently and vigorously to execute its acts."[25] An additional advantage of a parliamentary system was that the House of Commons could depose prime ministers as well as put them into power. This method stood in stark contrast to the American system, where "nothing short of a well-nigh impossible impeachment can unmake a President, except four successions of the seasons."[26] Thus, "a Prime Minister must keep himself in favor with the majority," while "a President only need keep alive."[27]

Wilson knew that the United States was not about to shift to a complete parliamentary form of government, but his solution for creating a system very much like a parliamentary system was to have presidents appoint cabinet members who were also members of the House of Representatives. In that way, there could be close coordination between the presidency and Congress in an arrangement that resembled in certain ways a parliamentary form of government. Significantly, Wilson had earlier praised the caucus method of nominating presidential candidates that had prevailed during the early decades of the nineteenth century. Back then, members of Congress had caucused with those in their respective political parties to agree on a presidential nominee. Under such an arrangement, the person elected president would owe allegiance to the Congressional caucus that had nominated him and would likely work closely with these Congressmen from his party to pass an agenda.[28] This, in fact, was an arrangement that had worked well for Jefferson, Madison, and Monroe.

Wilson abandoned his proposal for a cabinet-style arrangement in later editions of *Congressional Government*, but not the idea that there needed to be closer cooperation between the president and the legislative branch. His alternative solution was party discipline, with the president as head of the party that elected him, hopefully along with a substantial majority of legislators in both houses who belonged to the president's party. An example for Wilson was Theodore Roosevelt's effective mastery of the Republican Party and the legislative successes it brought to him, even though he often found Roosevelt's behavior undignified. Not only should the president be the leader of his party, but he should also have "the only voice in national affairs." Whereas members of the House of Representatives were answerable solely to their individual and often narrow constituencies, the president gained office from a nationwide election and was responsible to all the people.

Wilson, like Theodore Roosevelt before him, was describing a "plebiscitary presidency," with the result that the president could claim a mandate to lead that was independent of the legislative branch. In fact, Wilson had never wanted a real parliamentary system in which the president, as a sort of prime minister, would have to go before parliament regularly to answer questions and be responsible to members of parliament who could remove him through a vote of "no confidence" or by calling new elections. What Wilson really had in mind was a pseudo-parliamentary system that would enhance the powers of the presidency.

In addition, Wilson attributed presidential weakness in recent decades to there being so few men in that high office who demonstrated "commanding character, of acknowledged ability, and thorough political training," in contrast to the earliest holders of the executive office. Such a person could weaken the separation and balance of powers, which had been so celebrated by James Madison at the Constitutional Convention, to enhance the power of the presidency, an arrangement Wilson deemed necessary for governing in a new age of economic complexity. With a large dose of exaggeration and wishful thinking, he wrote in this regard, "If [a president] rightly interpret[s] the national thought and boldly insist[s] upon it, he is irresistible; and the country never feels the zest of action so much as when the President is of such insight and caliber." Such a president, he added, "is at liberty, both in law and conscience, to be as big a man as he can."[29] And as a historian, Wilson drew inspiration from strong presidents in the past. Washington had become a symbol of national unity, Jefferson had shown the way for a president to be a strong party leader, Jackson had exemplified the president as tribune of all the people, and Lincoln had demonstrated the power of moral leadership. He was not concerned that any of them had threatened the constitutional balance of powers.

Wilson believed that his own presidential leadership depended heavily on his ability to shape public opinion, as he wrote, "[It] is the great and only coordinating force in our system." He therefore worked diligently to galvanize public opinion in support of his initiatives to put pressure on Congress to act. Indeed, just eleven days after his inauguration, Wilson held his first official press conference at the White House, inviting any reporter who wished to attend. These events took place in the large and impressive East Room of the White House. Wilson was comfortable speaking informally, giving responses to reporters that were brief and straightforward, never admitting more than he needed to, and sometimes declining to speak about certain issues altogether. He could also be witty in his interactions with reporters, who often laughed in sympathy with him. Wilson thus came across to members of the press, in the words of the *Washington Post*, "as so unaffected and honest about his way of talking . . . that it won everybody . . ."[30] These excellent relations with the "fourth estate" went a long way to the president's receiving a sympathetic hearing in the press for his policies and proposals.

Wilson also thought of himself as a man of destiny. Since childhood, growing up in his father's Presbyterian manse (or home), he had been a deeply religious man, and in at least one instance, he claimed that God himself had placed him in the White House. To his campaign chairman following his victory in 1912, he reportedly declared, "God ordained that I should be the next president of the United States. Neither you nor any other mortal could have prevented that."[31] This personal self-righteousness could give him great confidence but also make him averse to compromise, to the detriment of the country and the world. In addition, this allusion to ruling by divine right—if he really believed that—was as troublesome as it was dangerous to American democracy in echoing the claims of traditional European monarchs.

For the first eighteen months of his presidency, Wilson's strategies with the legislature seemed to work wonders. He called a special session of Congress on April 8, 1913, slightly more than a month after his inauguration, which was still on March 4, and convinced them to pass the Underwood Tariff Act, which represented the first major tariff reduction in decades. Democrats had long held that the high protective tariffs enacted by one Republican Congress after another amounted to a tax on consumers (with the cost of importing these taxes passed on to consumers) as well as a boon to big businesses, which would not have to worry about foreign competition. The Federal Reserve Act, passed in late 1913, went after what Wilson and others called "the money trust," composed mainly of a few large New York banks that controlled the nation's money supply. As directed by the Federal Reserve Act, a decentralized system of twelve regional Federal Reserve banks could regulate the supply of money. (During the New Deal of the 1930s, the Federal Reserve System would become more centralized.)

In 1914, Wilson continued his onslaught against economic concentration by securing passage of the Clayton Anti-Trust Act that more clearly defined behavior representing "conspiracies in restraint of trade." The Federal Trade Commission Act that same year allowed the government to go after corporations that violated antitrust legislation but permitted the accused to enter into a consent agreement without admitting guilt and thereby avoiding drawn-out court battles. Wilson also supported the Adamson Act of September 1916. This legislation headed off a railroad strike by granting an eight-hour day and a pay raise to four major railroad unions, representing the first example of federal law regulating the working hours of private companies. Although Wilson had used the umbrella term of the "New Freedom" in supposed contrast to Roosevelt's "New Nationalism" in his unsuccessful campaign for a third term in 1912, his program nevertheless had the effect of greatly expanding the power of the executive branch.

Making the World "Safe for Democracy"

Nowhere was this power more evident than in the president's sway over matters of war and foreign policy. As Wilson had written in his 1907 book, *Constitutional Government*, "The initiative in foreign affairs, which the President possesses without any restriction whatsoever, is virtually the power to control them absolutely."[32] Although admitting that he needed the Senate's ratification of any treaty, he believed he could shape every stage in diplomatic negotiations in a manner that left the Senate with no choice but to ratify.

The outbreak of First World War in Europe in the later summer of 1914 allowed Wilson a wide scope to wield his powers over both foreign and domestic affairs.

Initially, however, Wilson and most Americans were aghast at the war. The Europeans had seemingly lost their minds, and Wilson, as well as his fellow citizens, vowed to remain above the senseless slaughter. On August 18, he addressed a joint session of Congress, where he delivered his famous pronouncement of neutrality: "We must be impartial in thought, as well as action, must put a curb upon our sentiments, as well as upon every transaction that might be construed as a preference of one party to the struggle before another."[33]

The war in Europe soon settled into a stalemate on the western front, marked by a zigzag line of trenches that stretched from the English Channel to the Swiss border. Each side flung its armies across "no-man's land" into the barrels of blazing banks of machine guns which massive artillery barrages had failed to "soften up" before the charge, and which turned the landscape into a cratered charnel house. The year that Wilson ran for reelection, 1916, was the bloodiest year of the war so far, and Wilson ran on the slogan, "He kept us out of war." The hope that he could keep the country out of the European conflict was most likely the reason Wilson eked out a narrow Electoral College victory. His eloquent speeches and refusal to talk down to his listeners also attracted voters.

With the election behind him, Wilson decided he could act as an impartial arbiter with the warring parties, and he drew up a "peace note" that he sent on December 18 to all the combatants. He asked them to respond by stating their specific war aims as preliminary to a peace conference over which he would preside. When the responses came back as ambivalent or dismissive from all sides, Wilson's next step was to make a speech before Congress on January 22, 1917, in which he outlined what he considered reasonable peace terms that anticipated his later "Fourteen Points." He also made his famous plea for "peace without victory." The speech, like the peace note, was of no avail.

Just a little over a week later, on January 31, the Germans declared "unrestricted" submarine warfare in waters around the British Isles, believing they could force Britain to sue for peace by cutting off their maritime lifeline for importing foodstuffs and war material, the bulk of it from the United States. Germany began sinking American merchant ships in British waters, hoping they could bring Britain to its knees before the United States could intervene to save them from defeat. In addition, the British intercepted and published a telegram from the German Foreign Secretary Arthur Zimmerman to Mexico proposing an alliance with Germany. In the event of a German victory, it promised to restore Texas, Arizona, and New Mexico to Mexico, territory that they had lost in the United States-Mexican War.

On April 2, Wilson stood before Congress and asked for a declaration of war. The war resolution passed two days later, and the president signed it on April 7. Wilson had very reluctantly made his decision to go to war but attempted to salve his conscience by insisting that American participation would make it a "war to end all wars" and a war "to make the world safe for democracy." He believed the key to both goals was his Fourteen Points, which he had earlier outlined in a speech before Congress. Wilson based these points on what he believed had caused the war in Europe and on what he thought could remove these causes. Since the fourteen items were somewhat redundant, one can distill them into five principles: Freedom of the seas, disarmament, national self-determination, open covenants, and establishment of a League of Nations. Believing that he was right—and that the right must prevail—Wilson was attempting to set himself up as the savior of Europe.

Wilson was aware of considerable opposition to his country's involvement in the war, and during the conflict, he determined to suppress all expression of this opposition by any means possible. He also did everything he could to mobilize the nation to fight the war. One could argue that such actions were practical measures for winning, but Wilson had always believed his decisions were righteous and would brook no defiance or dissent. In the process, with or without official authorization from Congress, he assumed nearly unlimited authority, making him the most powerful American president since Abraham Lincoln during the Civil War. For example, he acted without Congressional authorization to set up various war agencies, such as the War Industries Board, the War Labor Board, and the Committee on Public Information. In addition, he seized private property and armed American merchant ships. Nevertheless, Congress delegated other unprecedented powers to the president, such as nationalization of most of the country's railroads and operating them under joint control.

One of the most disturbing actions taken by Wilson during the war was to vastly restrict freedom of speech and try to silence all criticisms of the war and its management. He supported the passage of the Espionage Act of June 1917, which imposed a maximum penalty of $10,000 and twenty years in prison for anyone who encouraged disloyalty and empowered the postmaster general to deny use of the postal system to send any material considered seditious. The Sedition Act of May 1918 extended these penalties to anyone who would "willfully utter, print, write, or publish any disloyal, profane, scurrilous, or abusive language about the form of government of the United States, or the Constitution of the United States, or the military or naval forces of the United States . . ., or advocate any curtailment of production of anything necessary to the prosecution of the war."[34]

Wilson unfortunately did not act to curb the worst excesses of either his postmaster general or attorney general, with the result that the government came down hard against even legitimate criticism. The federal government censored newspapers and banned socialist publications from the mails. Socialist Party leader Eugene V. Debs received a twenty-year prison sentence for supposedly speaking out against the draft, a charge that was never proven. Victor L. Berger, the editor of the *Milwaukee Leader*, a founding member of the Socialist Party of America and the first Socialist elected to Congress, also received twenty years, in his case for writing editorials claiming the war was a capitalist conspiracy. Other prosecutions appear downright ludicrous, as when a film producer received a ten-year sentence for making a film called *The Spirit of Seventy-Six* because it would supposedly cause anti-British sentiment. Then there was a Vermont clergyman's fifteen-year sentence for refusing to decorate his church in red, white, and blue for "Liberty Loan Sunday" as a way of encouraging congregants to buy war bonds. Wilson never should have tolerated these unnecessary curbs on free speech and free expression.

The arrival of some 2 million American troops in France by the late summer of 1918 was enough to turn the tide for the western allies, and on November 11, the Germans agreed to an armistice to end the fighting. Wilson now believed the time had come to forge a peace grounded in his Fourteen Points, which would promote democracy and end the scourge of war in Europe. He set off for Paris to superintend the peace negotiations in person. Several advisors warned him against going, fearing he would bear personal responsibility for any failure if he went in person to head up the American delegation, but whenever Wilson thought he was right, it had always been impossible to stop him.

Wherever Wilson went, huge crowds greeted him and hailed him as a savior. For a time, he was the most admired individual in the world. However, the Allied leaders insisted on exacting revenge from Germany, and the Fourteen Points were effectively set aside in whole or in part. The president did manage to salvage the League of Nations but made the mistake of enfolding it into the 1919 Treaty of Versailles, the peace treaty with Germany. He also failed to include any leading Republicans in the American delegation in Paris, which turned out to be a serious error.

Unfortunately for Wilson, the Republicans had won control of the Senate, as well as the House of Representatives. Some analysts have blamed this partisan situation in part on a speech that Wilson gave during the 1918 campaign, in which he called for "a solemn referendum" on his peace plans by asking voters to return Democratic majorities to Congress. Perhaps he was still thinking of a pseudo-parliamentary system in which voters could be persuaded to return the chief executive's party to the legislative branch in the aftermath of a successful war. If so, he was very mistaken since the Republicans continued to be the majority party in the United States, as they had been since the late nineteenth century. Wilson had won the presidency in 1912 because the Republican vote was split between Taft and Roosevelt, and he won a narrow victory in 1916 under the slogan, "He kept us out of war."

Republican Senators, led by Chairman of the Foreign Relations Committee Henry Cabot Lodge, insisted on adding "reservations" to the treaty so the United States would not be required to go to war in cases where the League of Nations called for military force to keep the peace. However, raw partisan politics also motivated the Republicans to oppose the treaty as a way of discrediting Wilson in case he decided to run for a third term in 1920 when there was not yet a Constitutional prohibition against doing so. Although public opinion as well as a majority in the Senate approved of ratifying the treaty with the reservations included, Wilson refused to compromise. In a defiant, self-righteous speech delivered in Boston on February 19, 1919, just after returning briefly to the United States as the treaty discussions continued in Paris, he threw down the gauntlet: "Any man who resists the present tides that run the world will find himself thrown upon a shore so high and barren that it will seem as if he had been separated from his human kind forever."[35] Such talk only stiffened Republican resolve to oppose the president and his treaty.

As summer came and then waned and treaty passage remained in doubt, Wilson decided to mobilize public opinion as a way of pressuring the Senate to give in. His personal physician, Rear Adm. Cary Grayson, warned the president, now a man of sixty, that he must consider his health. "I know that I am at the end of my tether," Wilson answered, "but my friends on the Hill say that the trip is necessary to save the Treaty, and I am willing to make whatever sacrifice is required . . ."[36] He set off by train on September 2, often giving two speeches a day, each lasting for an hour or more. Then on September 25 in Pueblo, Colorado, Wilson collapsed and returned immediately to Washington, where he suffered a severe stroke that nearly killed him and left him weak and debilitated for the rest of his term.

Wilson had always been a stubborn man when he thought he was right, but the stroke may have made him even more obdurate. Although two-thirds of the Senate were prepared to vote in favor of the treaty, with the League embedded in it, Wilson would not accept the so-called Lodge Reservations, named for the Chairman of the Senate Foreign Relations Committee, Henry Cabot Lodge. What had been both Wilson's greatest strength and greatest weakness—his iron will and firm belief in the rightness of his actions and beliefs—defeated him in the end. Yet however one might evaluate the Wilson presidency overall, he left office with the executive power greatly enhanced. He again demonstrated the awesome power of a wartime president; he used his speech-making gifts with great effect, at least until his campaign for the League of Nations; and he showed how presidents could mobilize public opinion by holding effective press conferences. However, a self-righteous streak, leavened perhaps with the belief that he was a man of divine destiny, along with reckless disregard for his health, all helped to defeat him in the end.

Although they were very different in temperament and belonged to different political parties, Woodrow Wilson and Theodore Roosevelt showed how a powerful president could obtain numerous overdue domestic reforms. They also demonstrated again the tremendous and virtually unchallenged powers that presidents wielded in foreign affairs. It remained to be seen if future presidents would abuse such powers or use them responsibly.

Notes

1 William McKinley and Mark Hanna (livejournal.com). See also Edmund Morris, *Theodore Rex* (New York: Random House, 2001), 30.
2 Quoted in Jonathan Grossman, *The Coal Strike of 1902: Turning Point in U.S. Policy* , U.S. Department of Labor (dol.gov).
3 Morris, *Theodore Rex* (New York: Random House, 2002), 165.
4 Theodore Roosevelt, *An Autobiography* (New York: Charles Scribner's Sons, 1913), 357.
5 Quoted in ibid.
6 Quoted in Nathan Miller, *Theodore Roosevelt: A Life* (New York: William Morrow and Company, 1992), 369.
7 *United States v. E. C. Knight Co.* (1895).
8 *Northern Securities Co. v. United States* (1904).
9 Quoted in Morris, *Theodore Rex*, 184.

10 Quoted in ibid., 326.
11 The term Monroe Doctrine did not appear until the 1850s in reference to Monroe's declaration.
12 The Panama Canal, Bill of Rights Institute.
13 Quoted in Miller, *Theodore Roosevelt*, 482.
14 Quoted in E. S. Corwin, *President's Control of Foreign Relations* (Princeton: Princeton University Press, 1917), 172.
15 For psychological explanations of the power of images, see Charlotte J. S. De Backer, "Blinded by Starlight: An Evolutionary Framework for Studying Celebrity Culture and Fandom," *Review of General Psychology* 16, no. 2 (2012): 144–51.
16 On this medium see Erik Barnouw, *Documentary: A History of the Non-Fiction Film* (Oxford: Oxford University Press, 1993) and Raymond Fielding, *The American Newsreel: A Complete History, 1911–1967* (Jefferson: McFarland, 2011).
17 Kathleen Dalton, *Theodore Roosevelt: A Strenuous Life* (New York: Vintage Books, 2004), 393.
18 These films can also be viewed online from the Library of Congress Collection at https://www.loc.gov/collections/theodore-roosevelt-films/about...
19 Woodrow Wilson, First Inaugural Address, March 4, 1913, https://www.bartleby.com/124/pres44.html.
20 Ibid.
21 Woodrow Wilson, "Cabinet Government in the United States," *International Review* 4 (August 1879): 36.
22 Ibid., 146–63.
23 Walter Bagehot, *The English Constitution* (London: Chapman & Hall, 1867), 12.
24 Woodrow Wilson, *Constitutional Government in the United States* (New York: Columbia University Press, 1908), 25.
25 Wilson, "Cabinet Government," 41.
26 Woodrow Wilson, *Congressional Government* (Boston: Houghton Mifflin Co., 1885), 249.
27 Ibid., 41.
28 Ibid., 247–8.
29 Wilson, *Constitutional Government*, 67, 70.
30 Quoted in *Slate Magazine*, March 14, 2013.
31 Quoted in A. Scott Berg, *Wilson* (New York: G. P. Putnam's Sons, 2013), 252.
32 Wilson, *Constitutional Government*, 77.
33 Woodrow Wilson, Message to Congress, 63rd Cong, 2nd Sess. Senate Doc. No. 566 (Washington, 1914), 3–4.
34 United States Sedition Act of 1918, enacted by Congress, May 16, 1918.
35 Quoted in August Heckscher, *Woodrow Wilson: A Biography* (New York: Charles Scribner's Sons, 1991), 358.
36 Berg, *Wilson*, 619.

5

Fighting Depression and War

From New Deal to World Primacy

I shall ask for the one remaining instrument to meet the crisis—broad Executive power to wage a war against the emergency, as great as the power that would be given to me if we were in fact invaded by a foreign foe.

Franklin D. Roosevelt, Inaugural Address, March 4, 1933

The three presidents who follow Wilson—Warren G. Harding, Calvin Coolidge, and Herbert Hoover—preside over what can be called a period of reaction—reaction against the sort of internationalism practiced by Theodore Roosevelt and Woodrow Wilson, as well as reaction against the domestic reform agenda of these two presidents.

It would be Wilson's Assistant Secretary of the Navy, Franklin D. Roosevelt, who revived the reform traditions of his old boss—and of his distant cousin Theodore Roosevelt. Like Theodore, Franklin belonged to the American upper-upper class and inherited an ingrained sense of noblesse oblige, a belief that those who were better off had a duty to help others who were less fortunate. And like Wilson, he felt called to public service. While Wilson had answered this call from his clergyman father, Roosevelt took inspiration from the teachings of the Reverend Endicott Peabody, the founder and longtime headmaster of the elite Groton School in Groton, Massachusetts. Peabody had attended a boarding school in England, the goal of which was to prepare gentlemen to take their rightful place in governing the country, a goal that he hoped to instill in his American students at Groton.

Both Roosevelt and Wilson were deeply religious men, but Wilson was a more devout believer while Roosevelt approached religion with a somewhat lighter touch. Although a lifelong Episcopalian, Roosevelt did not place great store in denominational lines. When asked once if his Dutch ancestors had been Jewish, given the original spelling of the family name as Rosenvelt, he gave a telling answer: "In the dim past they may have been Jews or Catholics or Protestants—what I am more interested in is whether they were good citizens and believers in God—I hope they were both."[1]

Franklin Roosevelt, like Woodrow Wilson, had a strong sense of American Exceptionalism, believing that his country's democratic experiment, with its many freedoms and unparalleled prosperity (despite its shortcomings), could provide a model for the rest of the world. The two men were superb speakers, but Franklin Roosevelt's language was less formal than Wilson's. Roosevelt's irresistible smile and constant *joie de vivre* also contrasted with Wilson's often more serious visage. He was also markedly charming and known for a habit of throwing back his head and filling the room with laughter. Roosevelt's approach to governing was also less doctrinaire than Wilson's. In addition, the two had entered politics from different directions: Wilson was a scholar who taught and wrote about politics, while Roosevelt learned politics by plunging into the arena and gaining on-the-job experience. Furthermore, he was the consummate pragmatist and was far more willing to compromise than Wilson had been.

Triumph Over Adversity

In campaigning for political office, it did not hurt that Roosevelt carried a famous name. In fact, many voters believed that he and Theodore Roosevelt were more closely related than they were—perhaps even father and son. Franklin had been a student at Harvard when Theodore became president and although he and his immediate family were Democrats, he voted for his distant relative when he ran for a second term in 1904. Then when Franklin married Theodore's niece Eleanor, his fifth cousin once removed, Theodore became "Uncle Ted." Franklin also consciously sought to imitate Theodore's steps to the presidency, though not in the same order or always with the same success: Both Roosevelts served in the New York State legislature, and both became assistant secretaries of the navy. Each ran for the vice presidency, Theodore successfully and Franklin unsuccessfully, but both served as governors of New York.

Although Franklin lost his bid to become vice president as the running mate of James M. Cox in 1920, he attracted much favorable attention, and the Democrats began touting him as their presidential candidate for 1924. Then tragedy struck in the summer of 1921 when Roosevelt became severely crippled with polio. He never regained the use of his legs. Yet, by grasping someone's arm, wearing heavy braces, and swinging his legs forward with his torso and hips, he managed to give the impression that he was walking. Yet if he had not come down with polio and had run for president in 1924, he surely would have lost during this decade of Republican ascendency and probably never would have become president.

After being stricken with polio, Franklin's wife Eleanor gave addresses at various Democratic Party functions. She also made numerous forays around New York State and beyond and reported back to her husband what she had seen and heard, a role she would play throughout his presidency. In part because of her help, Roosevelt agreed to run for governor of New York in 1928. He believed winning was a long shot, at a time when the nation's economy was booming and when the Republican Party continued to enjoy substantial majority support among the public at large, including New York State. Still, leaders of the Democratic Party believed the Roosevelt name might work a bit of magic. Vigorous campaigning in the northern part of the state, which was a Republican stronghold, also helped to dispel beliefs that polio had made him unfit for such high office. In the end, he squeaked through with a majority of just 25,000 votes, or one-half percent of the total. Tellingly, he won 100,000 more votes in the state than fellow New Yorker and former Democratic Governor Al Smith, who ran unsuccessfully for president that year against Herbert Hoover.

Roosevelt won a second, two-year term in 1930, by over 700,000 votes this time, as the Great Depression was creating massive unemployment in the Empire State and around the country. At first, Governor Roosevelt hesitated to engage in deficit spending to launch massive public works projects or to give monetary relief to the unemployed, but he relented in the summer of 1931 when there seemed to be no alternative. These actions, along with his tax cuts for farmers and advocating for cheap electric power, along with his famous name in the then most populous state in the union, made him an obvious Democratic nominee for president in 1932.

Meanwhile, President Hoover had become one of the most despised persons in the United States, at least among those who were suffering from the economic ravages of the Depression, giving Roosevelt an excellent chance to win the White House in November. With no fixed philosophy of government, it is not surprising that his campaign statements were all over the map. He had imbibed progressive views from the examples of Theodore Roosevelt and Woodrow Wilson, but he also harbored conservative ideas about deficit spending, as he had shown while governor of New York. In addition, he did not want to be too specific about his proposals, which would give ammunition to Hoover and the Republicans. In any event, he won a momentous victory on election day: He received 57.4 percent of the popular vote against Hoover's 39.7 percent, with an electoral college victory of 472 to 59.

A New Deal

Like the progressive presidents before him, who had chosen slogans for their reform programs, the second Roosevelt president very early (and inadvertently) supplied a label for his domestic agenda. He had broken precedent by taking a very bumpy commercial flight to the Democratic National Convention in Chicago to accept his nomination in person rather than waiting for a party delegation to come to him and receive his acceptance, as had been the tradition. In what became the most memorable line in his speech at the convention, he said, "I pledge you, I pledge myself, to a new deal for the American people."[2] Roosevelt's speechwriter had not consciously chosen the phrase for a domestic agenda, but it resonated with the media, including a newspaper cartoon showing a farmer looking up in the sky at an airplane with the words "New Deal" written on its side.

The catchy phrase would help Roosevelt to galvanize public opinion and even to organize large Democratic majorities on Capitol Hill. But on his inauguration day of March 4, 1933, he was prepared to ask the legislators for what amounted to dictatorial powers to cope with the worst economic crisis in the nation's history, at a time when one-quarter to one-third of the workforce was unemployed and the banking system was near collapse. He promised in his inaugural address, broadcast coast to coast over radio, to recommend "the measures that a stricken nation in the midst of a stricken world may require." In the event that Congress did not act, he would go much further and ask, "For the one remaining instrument to meet the crisis—broad Executive power to wage a war against the emergency, as great as the power that would be given to me if we were in fact invaded by a foreign foe."[3] Fortunately for the country, Roosevelt was not scheming to use the economic crisis to become an American dictator.

Tellingly, like Theodore Roosevelt before him, this second Roosevelt president often referred to the extraordinary powers that Abraham Lincoln had commanded during the emergency of the Civil War. Although the Republican Party had sought to monopolize the Lincoln heritage in politics, Franklin Roosevelt made it a point to go to the Lincoln Memorial every February 12 when he was in Washington to lay a wreath in honor of Lincoln's birthday. He admired the Civil War president's vigorous use of executive authority as well as his pragmatism that would become a hallmark of his New Deal programs to attack the Great Depression. In a speech that he would give at Gettysburg, Pennsylvania, in 1938 on the seventy-fifth anniversary of the battle, he sought to weave together these themes of practical action, as a none-too-transparent comparison between himself and Lincoln: "A statesman deals with concrete difficulties—with things which must be done from day to day," he said. Now the nation faced "another conflict, as fundamental as Lincoln's fought not with glint of steel but with appeals to reason and justice on a thousand fronts—seeking to save for our common country opportunity and security for its citizens in a free society. . . . May we live by the wisdom and humanity at the heart of Abraham Lincoln."[4]

Roosevelt did not have to ask for the extraordinary powers of a President Lincoln—or that he had threatened to wield in his inaugural address—in part because he was successful in carrying out an unparalleled campaign of public persuasion. During his four years as governor of New York, he had mastered the art of talking to the American people over the radio, realizing that stentorian performances, which had long characterized political addresses, simply would not work when speaking to listeners in their homes. Fortunately, he had a well-modulated, rich tenor voice and the ability to come across both informally and sincerely, even though he prepared his broadcast remarks with great care. While president, he continued to make such radio talks, which became known as the famous "Fireside Chats." Roosevelt did not actually sit by a fireside while speaking—nor did most of his listeners—but the term was perfect for the cozy, intimate image he wanted to put forward.

Roosevelt gave the first of these fireside chats on March 12, just eight days after his inauguration. It was also three days since Congress had passed the Emergency Banking Act, enacted to save the nation's financial system, which Roosevelt had closed temporarily to stop depositors from making panicked withdrawals from their accounts and damaging the banks further. He began by saying in his best conversational tone, "I want to talk for a few minutes with the people of the United States about banking . . . [,] particularly with the overwhelming majority who use banks for the making of deposits and the drawing of checks." After explaining that the recently enacted National Banking Act would rescue both their banks and their deposits, he assured listeners that "It is safer to keep your money in a reopened bank than under the mattress," an image that anyone could understand. In closing, he asked the American people for their help: "Let us unite in banishing fear. We have provided the machinery to restore our financial system; it is up to you to support and make it work. It is your problem no less than it is mine. Together we cannot fail."[5]

Despite Roosevelt's warm tone, his upper-class, Hudson Valley accent was far removed from the speech patterns and intonations that most listeners were used to hearing. Yet far from being put off by Roosevelt's manner of speech, which could sound a bit British at times, audiences sensed an air of confident assurance, such that millions who heard him that evening believed what he said, and the next day bank deposits far exceeded withdrawals. Roosevelt would give thirty-one fireside chats in all between 1933 and 1944, or an average of about three per year, knowing that giving them too often would undermine their effectiveness through undue familiarity.

Like Wilson and the first Roosevelt president, Franklin Roosevelt worked hard to cultivate good relations with the press to gain public support for his policies and indirectly pressure Congress to go along with his proposals. Each week he invited a selected group of reporters to crowd into his Oval Office, where he spoke to them and answered questions, but only on background, with no direct quoting allowed. There was usually much banter back and forth as the president and reporters traded jokes. Sometimes Roosevelt played poker with a group of them who stood directly in front of his desk. In so doing, he gained a reservoir of affection from reporters covering the White House, even if their wealthy publishers may have opposed the president's policies. Not surprisingly, the newsreels carried something about Roosevelt virtually every week during his twelve years in office at a time when millions attended the movies on a regular basis.

Roosevelt's mastery of the new media of the day, radio and film, and his cultivation of the press made him a master at public relations, and they were key elements in getting what he liked to call "action now." In the three months after his inauguration, known ever since as the "Hundred Days," virtually every piece of legislation that he recommended to Congress became law, often with Republican support. There was the Federal Emergency Relief Act (FERA), which authorized immediate relief to the unemployed, providing some 500 million dollars for such items as soup kitchens, blankets, nursery schools, and various employment projects. The Civilian Conservation Corps (CCC) enlisted young men to engage in various types of conservation work all over the country. They lived in camps and received $30 a month, with $25 sent home to help their families. The Agricultural Adjustment Act (AAA) endeavored to raise farm income by setting quotas to reduce production and thereby raise agricultural prices. The Public Works Administration (PWA) came out as part of the National Industrial Recovery Act and provided grants to the states for large public infrastructure projects, such as roads, airports, and schools, along with the construction jobs that accompanied them. The same act also created the National Recovery Administration (NRA), which allowed businesses to create trade associations of fair practices without fear of violating antitrust laws. Labor received the right to engage in collective bargaining. Then there was legislation that created the Tennessee Valley Authority, which built dams and generated cheap electric power in several economically depressed southern states.

Later Roosevelt got Congress to authorize other recovery measures. Chief among them was the massive Emergency Relief Appropriations Act of January 1935. With funds from this legislation, the president created by executive order the Works Projects Administration, later renamed the Works Progress Administration (WPA). The agency undertook numerous construction projects through grants to states and municipalities. In addition to providing jobs for construction workers, both skilled and unskilled, the WPA gave work to unemployed writers, musicians, actors, artists, and photographers. Their efforts included published guides to cities, states, and various points of interest, traveling symphony orchestras and dramatic productions, murals in public buildings, and photographic records of the ravages of the Great Depression.

Other New Deal legislation aimed to ward off financial disasters in the future. The Federal Deposit Insurance Corporation (FDIC), part of the Banking Act of June 1933, insured bank deposits in amounts that have increased over time, with premiums paid by member banks. The idea was to allay fears that depositors would lose money because of bank failures and thereby prevent runs on banks as during the winter of 1933. The Banking Act of 1935 centralized control of the Federal Reserve system under a board of governors in Washington and, in the process, shifted a great deal of power away from the Federal Reserve District Banks, as had been authorized in the more decentralized system established back in 1913. Through greater centralization, the Federal Reserve was equipped to act nationally on monetary policy.

There was the National Labor Relations Act of 1935, which became necessary after the Supreme Court declared the NRA unconstitutional and swept away labor's right to collective bargaining. The new act guaranteed the right to form unions and to bargain collectively and established the National Labor Relations Board (NLRB) to supervise union elections. A major goal of this act was to give labor leverage to obtain wage increases, giving them more purchasing power and thereby increasing economic activity. The Wages and Hours Act of 1938 pursued a similar goal by establishing minimum wages for those who worked for interstate businesses and industries, along with time-and-a-half wages for work over forty hours a week. The law also had the effect of establishing a forty-hour workweek since employers would want to avoid paying overtime and, in theory, hire more employees.

Perhaps the most far-reaching piece of legislation of the entire New Deal was the Social Security Act of 1935. Although it is best known for the retirement benefits and assistance to children and the disabled, its provision for unemployment compensation provided income for those out of work who would still have some money to spend that helped to limit declines in consumer demand. Roosevelt had also wanted to include national health insurance as part of the Social Security Act but refrained, fearing that the legislation might be defeated.

The various New Deal programs did make inroads against unemployment. It fell from approximately 25 percent in 1933 to about 17 percent in 1936, when Roosevelt ran for a second term. By then, the so-called Roosevelt coalition had resulted in substantial majority support for the Democratic Party. The coalition consisted of voters in large cities where unemployment had been the worst, farmers grateful for government assistance, African Americans whose unemployment rate was probably twice that of the general population, and the southern states which had been a mainstay of the Democrats since the Civil War. Many intellectuals and opinion makers also supported the New Deal. Not surprisingly, Roosevelt defeated Republican Alfred M. Landon by a landslide. He won 60.8 percent of the popular vote and in the electoral college his lead was 523 to eight, failing to carry only Maine and Vermont.

Roosevelt's huge mandate led him to conclude that he could accomplish virtually anything he wanted, including a "court packing" scheme and proposals for reorganizing the office of the president. His attempts to add justices to the Supreme Court more sympathetic to the New Deal came in reaction to the court's declaring several pieces of New Deal legislation to be unconstitutional. Cases included *Schecter v. US* (1935), which ruled against the National Industrial Recovery Act, and *US v. Butler* (1936), which turned thumbs down on the Agricultural Adjustment Act. There had not yet been any vacancies on the nine-member high court during Roosevelt's presidency, with the result that it was dominated by conservatives who had been put on the bench under the Republican administrations of the 1920s. Roosevelt feared the court was about to rule against more recent New Deal programs such as the National Labor Relations Act and the Social Security Act.

There was nothing illegal or unconstitutional about the president's plan to enlarge the court, allowing him to appoint more liberal justices, since the Constitution had left it to Congress to determine the number of members on the high bench. At various times in the past, there had been as few as five and as many as ten justices on the court. Since the 1936 election had swept huge Democratic majorities into Congress, amounting to three-fourths of the membership in both the House and Senate, Roosevelt believed he would have no problem getting the legislators to pass a Court Reorganization bill increasing the number of justices. But instead of being forthright about his motives, he formulated a scheme that fooled no one: Claiming that the six justices over seventy years of age needed help with the court's caseload, he asked Congress to expand its ranks from nine to fifteen members.

Roosevelt was so confident of his power and influence after his huge reelection victory that he did not even bother to take congressional leaders into his confidence before springing his court plan. Republicans were enraged, but Conservative Democrats were also appalled. Some liberals also opposed what had come to be called the court packing bill because they saw the court as the ultimate protector of American liberties at a time when fascist dictators had taken power in Europe. The time might come, they worried, when some future president might try to seize power in part by reshaping the court to his liking. If that were not enough, most public opinion was squarely against packing the court. In the end, Congress let Roosevelt's court proposal die.

Then while the court packing debate was raging, the Supreme Court began upholding New Deal legislation by five-to-four majorities, including both the National Labor Relations Act in *NLRB v. Jones and Laughlin Steel* (1937) and the Social Security Act in *Helvering v. Davis* (1937). The court's motive has never been entirely clear. Some historians have argued that the threat to the court caused a majority to begin approving New Deal legislation to undermine support for adding justices, thereby saving its honor and independence. Then over the next few years, five justices stepped down and allowed Roosevelt to nominate sympathetic replacements. However, his attempt to transgress the separation of powers in the minds of many greatly damaged him politically, contributing to a large defeat for the Democrats in the off-year elections of 1938. They lost seventy seats in the House and seven places in the Senate.

Also raising the ire of many conservatives in Congress was Roosevelt's request to streamline the executive branch to bring it in line with modern administrative practice. The president had initially wanted to pair administrative reform with his reform of the judiciary, but Congressional outrage over court reorganization had forced him to postpone the reorganization of the executive office. He then returned to the subject with a plan worked out by three of the leading experts in the nation on public administration. The president's main concern was the plethora of federal agencies that had come into existence over the years and that were largely answerable to Congress, which had created them, rather than to the president, in part because they were not under any of the cabinet departments. In his ineffable way, Roosevelt described his aim to the editors of a religious journal by saying that the White House's administrative machinery was "awfully old fashioned and sort of grew up like Topsy." What he wanted to do was "to put it on the same kind of efficient basis that we would run an industrial plant or a private charity or even the financial end of a church."[6]

What sounded so mild and even innocuous from this interview caused some members of Congress to claim that the president was trying to engineer a naked power grab not unlike Hitler, Mussolini, or Franco. Hurt that he was being accused of wanting to be a dictator, Roosevelt declared, "I have no inclination to be a dictator," which only inflamed passions. He then withdrew demands to subordinate all federal bureaus under the various department heads and in April 1939 was able to sign a Reorganization Act. Among other things, it gave the White House control over the Bureau of the Budget as well as the authority to hire full-time executive assistants. Despite withdrawing his demands to place federal bureaus under the auspices of cabinet departments, he went ahead and placed most federal agencies under cabinet-level departments anyway. In the process, Roosevelt greatly enhanced both the concept and substance of a unitary executive to which he could issue executive orders through a presidential prerogative that the delegates to the Constitutional Convention had specifically opposed.

As to the New Deal itself, there was little or no prospect of obtaining additional legislation by the spring of 1939. The court packing plan and Congressional suspicion over the proposals for administrative reform had caused Roosevelt to lose significant support on Capitol Hill, even among Democrats. His reputation had also suffered from his decision before the 1936 election to cut back domestic spending, which resulted in a new spurt of unemployment. He had never been comfortable with running large deficits and wanted to undercut Republican criticism of New Deal spending. However, what resulted from these budgetary economies was something critics called the "Roosevelt Recession." By June 1938, unemployment had jumped to 19 percent. Although Congress did approve increased spending, which began to bring the numbers of unemployed down, it was rearmament and then American participation in Second World War that ended the Great Depression for good and demonstrated conclusively that massive deficit spending could vanquish unemployment. The outbreak of war in

Europe in September 1939 also gave an opening for Roosevelt to seek a third term in 1940; and once the United States joined the war, he became without a doubt the most powerful person in the world—the first American president to wield such power.

Commander-in-Chief

For several years, Roosevelt had been concerned about ominous signs coming from Europe: Hitler reoccupied the Rhineland in 1936, absorbed Austria in 1938 (the Anschluss), and annexed Czechoslovakia in 1938–39. However, Roosevelt recognized that public opinion in the United States was overwhelmingly against involvement in another European war, and that pushing Americans too hard into recognizing the danger posed by Germany might risk his reelection in 1940.

It also did not help that the Republican candidate Wendel Willkie was a moderate who approved of most New Deal programs, claiming only that he and his party could administer them more efficiently and economically. Moreover, Willkie did not initially attack Roosevelt over his foreign policy, but when it became clear that he was flagging in the polls, he and fellow Republicans began to charge that Roosevelt was a warmonger. When this tactic appeared to gain traction, the president made firm promises that he might not be able to keep. In New York City at the end of the campaign, he told the crowd, "I have said this before, but I shall say it again and again and again: Your boys are not going to be sent into any foreign wars."[7] When one of his advisors pointed out that he had not added his usual disclaimer, "except in case of attack," Roosevelt cynically responded, "Of course. . . . If somebody attacks us, then it isn't a foreign war, is it?"[8]

This disingenuous promise may indeed have helped Roosevelt to win in 1940, although Willkie received more popular votes than either of Roosevelt's opponents in 1932 or 1936 (44.9 percent to the president's 54.7 percent). However, the electoral vote was not even close, at eighty-two for Willkie and 449 for Roosevelt. The fact that the president won handily in the twelve largest cities, whose states had large numbers of electoral votes and whose populations had been strong supporters of the New Deal, certainly helped him to carry the day.[9]

Well before the election, Roosevelt had been wearing his commander-in-chief hat to bring about military readiness. He succeeded in bypassing Congressional opposition by using still valid First World War statutes to establish defense agencies by executive order, such as organizing the production of military supplies in the name of defending the Western Hemisphere and aiding potential European allies. Congress's recent permission to reorganize the executive office greatly assisted this endeavor.

The president continued to grow alarmed about the aggressive behavior of Hitler's Germany, as well as Japan's invasion of China and atrocious human rights abuses there and elsewhere, even as the American public remained adamantly opposed to being drawn into another war. The Japanese bombing of the US Pacific fleet at Pearl Harbor on December 7, 1941, gave him no choice but to ask Congress for a declaration of war against Japan on December 8. Three days later, Germany declared war on the

United States, presenting the country with a daunting two-front war. Critics would fault Roosevelt for insufficient preparation, but given the strong isolationist sentiment in the country, there was little more that he could have done. As late as August 1941, polls showed that 75 percent of the American people wanted nothing to do with war against either Germany or Japan.

Following the declaration of war, Roosevelt could invoke his vast powers as commander-in-chief. In a memorandum that he posted on December 11, the day Germany declared war, Roosevelt declared that as "Commander-in-Chief," he was "the final arbiter in all departments and agencies of the Government."[10] From then until the end of the war in the late summer of 1945, he and his successor Harry S. Truman controlled every lever of weapons production, military mobilization, and overall combat strategy. It was Roosevelt, for instance, who agreed with the British on the plan to concentrate on defeating Germany first, to build an atomic bomb, and to demand unconditional surrender of enemy nations. He also set policies to regulate the civilian economy, including measures to ration scarce goods and to take other steps to dampen wartime inflation. Meanwhile, Roosevelt became the senior partner of his British allies despite their heroic struggle alone against the Germans because the United States, as the war progressed, commanded far superior wealth, human power, and productive capacities.

Unlike during First World War, the government did not clamp down on free speech, in part because there was widespread support for the war after Pearl Harbor. Yet Roosevelt's act of racial discrimination against Japanese Americans living on the West Coast of the United States will forever remain a blot on his reputation as president. In response to public hysteria, born of fears that Japanese Americans would be disloyal, Roosevelt signed an executive order to remove all such individuals, 117,000 in total, from the Pacific Coast to relocation centers in remote parts of the country. There they lived in primitive conditions behind barbed wire and were watched over by armed guards. It did not matter that two-thirds of them were citizens born in the United States, or that there was no evidence then or later that any Japanese Americans had acted in any way to support Japan or to engage in any sort of sabotage or disloyal behavior. However, the Supreme Court, in *Korematsu v. the United States* (1944), upheld the president's authority to have issued the order and thereby upheld the virtually unlimited powers of a president in wartime.

The United States was still at war in the election year of 1944, and Roosevelt decided he would run for an unprecedented fourth term. His stated purpose was to preside over a peace that would not result in his country turning its back on world order as it had done after First World War. But it is probable that he simply did not want to relinquish the sort of power he had wielded already for a dozen years, plus his belief that he had become indispensable. In November, he managed to win against Republican Thomas E. Dewey by 53.5 percent of the popular vote, the lowest margin of his four victories, though the electoral tally was more lopsided at 432 to ninety-nine. One of the issues in the campaign had been Roosevelt's health, if only because of his alarming appearance in the months leading up to the election. In truth, he was suffering from dangerously high blood pressure and died a little less than three months into his final term. His four terms seemed to justify the fears of some delegates to the Constitutional Convention that a popular president during extraordinary times could make himself into a president for life, which, in fact, Roosevelt had done.

Big and Bigger

Liberals and progressives would look back and applaud Franklin Roosevelt, along with Theodore Roosevelt and Woodrow Wilson, for expanding the effective power of the presidency, believing that only a powerful presidency could bring about needed reforms and central direction at a time when the United States had become an industrial giant and world power. It concerned them less that all three presidents bridled at the checks and balances the framers had established through a separation of powers. Theodore Roosevelt threatened to use the army to take over the anthracite mines during a coal strike, knowing that his action would very likely be unconstitutional. He also issued a corollary to the Monroe Doctrine without consulting Congress, which would lead the country to use armed force in Latin America on numerous occasions. Frustrated with the pace of obtaining rights to build an inter-ocean canal across Panama, he acted on his own authority to support a Panamanian revolt against Colombia.

Before his presidency, Woodrow Wilson had advocated what might be called a pseudo-parliamentary system for the United States that would go far in breaking down the separation between the legislative and executive branches. In the name of national security during Second World War, he lashed out against all dissent, and his possible sense of divine destiny and ill health kept him from compromising with Congress on the peace.

Franklin Roosevelt sought to pack the Supreme Court and thereby undermine its judicial independence, and his creation of the Executive Office of the President greatly enhanced the concept and reality of the "unitary executive," even as it brought about greater efficiency to the presidency. In one of the worst examples of executive overreach, Roosevelt ordered Japanese Americans resettled in remote areas of the country under armed guard. Believing that he needed to hold onto power for the good of the nation, Roosevelt defied the no-third term precedent established by George Washington and went on to win a third and then a fourth term.

Theodore Roosevelt also had a difficult time giving up power and attempted a failed bid to win what was essentially a third term in 1912. He was being urged by Republicans to run again in 1920, but his death the year before precluded that possibility. There were some predictions that Wilson would try for a third term in 1920, at least before his stroke in 1919 removed him from the running. Whether Wilson would have wanted another term is unknown, but his passion for persuading his country to join the League of Nations may well have been a powerful motivator for him to run again, as would his stubbornness and sense of personal destiny.

All three of these powerful presidents used new forms of media—published photographs, moving pictures, and then radio under the second Roosevelt—to form powerful bonds with the American people against which Congress or rivals for the presidency found it very difficult to compete. They were also very successful in cultivating the print media of their day by conducting highly successful press conferences.

The presidency was becoming big—and bigger—and presidents during the decades after Second World War would rely on the increasing powers of the executive branch that had grown up earlier in the century to realize their programs. One could argue that such powers remain essential for any successful action on social, economic, and foreign policy issues. At the same time, they would be there for any unscrupulous president in the future to abuse in ways that could damage the nation and even threaten American democracy itself.

Notes

1 Roosevelt to Philip Slomovitz, March 7, 1936.
2 Franklin D. Roosevelt Library and Museum, https://www.fdrlibrary.org/dnc-curriculum-hub.
3 Franklin D. Roosevelt, First Inaugural Address, March 4, 1933, https://avalon.law.yale.edu/20th_century/froos1.asp.
4 Franklin D. Roosevelt, July 4, 1938, quoted in Merrill D. Peterson, *Lincoln in American Memory* (New York: Oxford University Press, 1994), 321.
5 Franklin D. Roosevelt, March 12, 1933: Fireside Chat 1: On the Banking Crisis, National Archives.
6 Quoted in Frank Friedel, *Franklin D. Roosevelt: A Rendezvous with Destiny* (Boston: Little, Brown and Company, 1990), 274.
7 Franklin D. Roosevelt on Reorganization of Cabinet Departments, Millercenter.org/president/speeches/detail/3310.
8 Quoted in Friedel, *Roosevelt*, 355.
9 See Samuel Lubell, *Future of American Politics* (New York: Doubleday and Company, 1951), 51–7.
10 Quoted in Friedel, *Roosevelt*, 409.

6

Social and Racial Justice

Reaching for the Promises of American Life

We shall not, however, finally achieve the ideals for which this Nation was founded so long as any American suffers discrimination as a result of his race, or religion, or color, or the land of origin of his forefathers.

President Harry Truman, Special Message to Congress on Civil Rights, February 2, 1948

As the train rolls slowly along the rails in mid-April 1945, bringing the remains of President Franklin Roosevelt from Warm Springs, Georgia, back to Washington, thousands line the tracks to pay their last respects. For many, he is the only president they can remember. For those who have loved or admired Roosevelt, having Harry Truman in the White House is a shock, and for some, nearly unbearable. Gone is the smooth voice with its aristocratic accent, replaced by the new president's Missouri twang. Unlike his predecessor, who had visited Europe numerous times before becoming president, Truman's only time abroad was as captain of an artillery unit in France during the First World War. His formal education ended with high school graduation, while Roosevelt went to Harvard and then to Columbia University Law School. It is not for lack of either intelligence or ambition that Truman did not attend college, but because the family needed his labor on their farm outside Independence, Missouri.

The three presidents who succeeded Truman—Dwight D. Eisenhower, John F. Kennedy, and Lyndon Johnson—all attended institutions of higher learning. Yet two of them—Eisenhower and Johnson—came from humble backgrounds not unlike Truman's. The outlier was Kennedy, born to great wealth and the privileges that came with it. However, only Johnson mustered enough power to move Congress to enact domestic reforms that promised greater social, economic, and racial justice for the American people. His startling successes would lead liberals and reformers to continue insisting that a powerful presidency was essential to provide needed reforms for the American people, as they had since the time of Theodore Roosevelt, Woodrow Wilson, and Franklin Roosevelt. In the process, Johnson would vastly expand the real and the potential powers of the presidency. In the domestic area, this expansion won him many plaudits, but his abuse of war powers would later lead to widespread condemnations.

"Give 'Em Hell Harry"

After returning home from First World War, Truman became the co-owner of a men's clothing store in Kansas City, Missouri, only to have the business collapse in the steep recession of 1923. The failure of this venture led Truman to enter politics to secure a job and support his family. Drawing on the popularity and respect he had gained among the men he commanded during the war as the captain of an artillery unit, he won a spot as county judge (equivalent to county commissioner in other states). He secured election to the US Senate in 1934 and reelection in 1940. Although he had risen with the support of Kansas City's corrupt Pendergast machine, Truman was personally honest and came to public attention during the Second World War when presiding over a Senate committee that investigated wartime waste, fraud, and corruption in defense industries and suppliers. The Democrats tapped Truman for vice president in 1944 as a replacement for Henry Wallace, who had served as vice president during Roosevelt's third term but who was thought too liberal for the times.

Republicans, determined to recapture the presidency in 1948, showed open disdain for Truman. "I'm just mild about Truman," was often heard among detractors. A joke making the rounds began with a question: "Have you heard about the new Truman doll?"—to which the questioner responded, "You wind it up and it puts its foot in its mouth," a reference to the president's tendency to speak sometimes without thinking. The wife of Republican Senator Robert A. Taft reportedly launched the line, "To err is Truman." Nor did it help that the new president had to confront a wave of labor strikes and rising prices just after the war. As the presidential election of 1948 drew near, pollsters, pundits, and most of the major newspapers predicted an electoral slaughter if Truman decided to run.

Instead of playing it safe by shying away from controversial campaign issues, Truman decided to run on a slate of issues that he announced during his State of the Union Address on January 7, 1948, and that many political analysts believed would doom him in November. He asked Congress to pass legislation for national health insurance and for federal aid to education, along with an increase in the minimum wage. He also advocated increases in farm price supports and large appropriations for housing. Most controversial of all was an announcement that he would soon send a special message about civil rights to Capitol Hill.

Just two weeks later, and based on the report entitled *To Secure These Rights,* composed by the Civil Rights Commission he had appointed, Truman forwarded his recommendations for comprehensive action against racial discrimination. They read in part:

> We believe that all men are created equal and that they have the right to equal justice under law. . . . Today, the American people enjoy more freedom and opportunity than ever before. Never in our history has there been better reason to hope for the complete realization of the ideals of liberty and equality. We shall not, however, finally achieve the ideals for which this Nation was founded so long as

> any American suffers discrimination as a result of his race, or religion, or color, or the land of origin of his forefathers.[1]

Truman went on to call for protection by federal statute of the right to vote throughout the country, in addition to legislation abolishing poll taxes, a device used in southern states to disenfranchise African Americans. He also wanted Congress to establish a Fair Employment Practices Commission to forbid discrimination by both employers and labor unions and to outlaw discrimination in all forms of public interstate travel, whether by rail, bus, or air. Finally, Truman asked Congress to examine claims of injustice from Japanese Americans who had been forced out of their homes and confined in relocation centers during the Second World War "solely because of their racial origin."[2] For a man born and raised in the border state of Missouri where southern attitudes on race prevailed, Truman's requests were as bold as they were sincere.

Truman pressed forward with his civil rights agenda at the Democratic National Convention in Philadelphia in July, where he sought his party's nomination for a run in his own right for president. He received support at the convention from the liberal Americans for Democratic Action (ADA) under the leadership of Hubert Humphrey, who personally and successfully insisted that the party platform include a strong and detailed statement on civil rights. In his acceptance speech, Truman called for federal aid to education, national health insurance, a hike in the minimum wage, wider Social Security coverage and increased benefits, public generation of electrical power, which would lower costs for consumers, and greater price supports for farmers.[3] He also set a populist tone for the campaign: "The people know that the Democratic Party is the people's party," he declared, "and the Republican Party is the party of special interest, and it always has been and always will be."[4]

Southern Democrats were enraged at the party's plank on civil rights and bolted rather than accept such goals. They gathered in Birmingham, Alabama, as a group of states' rights Democrats, or "Dixiecrats," as they were dubbed, nominating then-Governor Strom Thurmond of South Carolina as their presidential nominee. Truman would also face opposition from the left in the person of Henry Wallace, who received the Progressive Party nomination. As noted earlier, Wallace had been Roosevelt's vice president during his third term but had been rejected in favor of Truman in Roosevelt's successful fourth White House run. Wallace and his party favored accommodation with the Soviet Union and opposed Truman's hardline policies against Communism. While the Dixiecrats posed a threat because they might carry large swaths of the South, Wallace's Progressive Party was not a serious cause for worry by the Democrats at a time when the overwhelming majority of Americans were hostile to both Communism and the Soviet Union, thus making Wallace a very unattractive candidate.

Still, with his Democratic Party now split and with all the leading opinion polls showing Republican presidential candidate Thomas E. Dewey firmly in the lead, it looked to most everyone but Truman himself that he had no chance of winning in the fall. However, Truman was not about to give up and adopted the clever strategy of running against the Republican Congress, which had taken control of both houses in the "off-year" elections of 1946 for the first time since the early 1930s. Not only that, but he would also accuse this Eightieth Congress of hypocrisy for claiming to support civil rights, aid to education, and relief for a postwar housing shortage, while at the same time doing nothing to deal with these issues through appropriate legislation.

To call their bluff, Truman had announced in his acceptance speech at the Democratic Convention that he would call a special session of Congress to meet for two weeks beginning on July 26, which out in Missouri, he explained, was "Turnip Day," when farmers put their turnip seeds in the ground. Angry Republicans charged that the special session was nothing but pure politics. It was indeed; and in the end, the move would pay off handsomely for the president, especially since Truman knew the Republican leadership on Capitol Hill would do nothing to enact his proposals. On July 26, the same day Congress reconvened for its short summer session, Truman directed the Secretary of Defense to desegregate the US military and to do whatever else was necessary to stop discrimination among the armed forces.

The president then took his campaign to the people with a preliminary rail trip in June, officially to give the commencement address at the University of California, Berkeley. He could have flown directly to the West Coast, but he instead took a meandering route by train with numerous stops to try out his campaign strategy. Truman and his close advisors realized that the president's set speeches from a written text usually resulted in a wooden delivery and awkward hand gestures that somehow had the effect of emphasizing his Missouri twang. Instead, he would speak extemporaneously at formal gatherings in the larger cities and make brief off-the-cuff remarks at small railroad stations or road crossings dubbed "whistle stops," where trains were required to blow their whistles as they approached.

More than satisfied with his foray in June, what has come to be known as Truman's famous whistle-stop campaign began in earnest that fall. Truman and his wife Bess, along with their daughter Margaret, left Washington's Union Station on September 27 aboard the *Ferdinand Magellan*, a bulletproof Pullman car to carry the presidential party that had been outfitted in 1942 for wartime travel by President Roosevelt. By the time the tour ended on October 31, Truman would cover just under 22,000 miles and deliver over 300 addresses of varying lengths, averaging some ten speeches a day. That the Gallup and Roper polls showed Dewey well ahead by double digits did not faze him, but only fired his determination to fight to the finish.[5]

At each whistle stop, someone in the crowd would invariably yell, "Give 'em Hell Harry," a battle cry first heard at the Democratic Party convention. This was the signal for the president to oblige with gusto. He would then rip into the Republicans and especially into what he relished calling "that, no good, do nothing 80th Congress," which had refused to enact any of the legislation he had recommended for the special session. Furthermore, he charged that the Republicans were plotting to take away popular New Deal programs and again turn the economy over to the same Wall Street folks and various special interests that had brought them the Great Depression.

In places where the whistle stop coincided with a track-side station, there was often a high school band waiting to welcome the president with music to excite the crowds. The band would send him off ten minutes later, accompanied by one or more state or local politicians who boarded the train and rode down the line with the president to the next few stations. A feature of each stop was Truman's introduction of the First Lady, whom he sometimes referred to as "the boss," a phrase that came to rankle her so much that she threatened to stay inside their train car if he kept it up. Then he would introduce their daughter Miss Margaret, who appeared with a bouquet of roses in her arms, several of which she would detach and throw into the crowd. Neither of the Truman women said anything but stood with the president, who beamed with pride over his small family, and in this way identified with the other families who had come out to see the "Three Traveling Trumans."[6] First hundreds, and then thousands, showed up to see the First Family and hear their president speak. However, the largest crowds were at urban venues such as Oklahoma City, where 100,000 came out to see the Democratic candidate. In Boston toward the end of the tour, a quarter of a million cheering people lined Truman's parade route. The next day, one and a quarter million fans lined his six-mile motorcade route through New York City.

Anyone expecting to hear elegant, political oratory would have been disappointed, especially at whistle stops. As Truman put it in his *Memoirs*, "There were no special 'gimmicks' or oratorical devices. I refused to be 'coached.' I simply told the people in my own language that they had better wake up to the fact that it was their fight."[7] The crowds loved his plain speaking and lack of pretense. Many of his presentations in rural areas from the rear platform of the *Ferdinand Magellan* understandably appealed to the farm vote, which would be essential for his reelection, such as when he referred to a not-too-distant past that he and his older listeners could well remember. When asked if it was true that he had been known for plowing the straightest furrows in Missouri, he said it was true but only according to his mother. However, it *was true*, he added, when people remarked that he never left a "skip place" when sowing a field of wheat. "My father always used to raise so much fuss," he remembered, "about a skip place."[8]

In many respects, the whistle-stop campaign was a throwback to an earlier type of campaigning, very much in the style of populist Democrat William Jennings Bryan's 1896 campaign by rail. However, by the time of the 1948 campaign nearly fifty years later, television was making an appearance on the American scene, especially in larger American cities on the two coasts. The networks had provided "gavel-to-gavel" coverage of both parties' conventions that summer, televising them to eighteen stations in nine cities, though the viewership was tiny at a time when most areas of the country did not have television reception and when there were only 345,000 television sets in the entire United States. Even those who could have watched Truman give his acceptance speech were unlikely to have stayed tuned until 2:00 a.m., when he finally mounted the rostrum. However, the newsreel cameras were there, and moviegoers could later catch a glimpse and hear the high points of Truman's acceptance speech.[9]

As the campaign went on and the crowds and excitement built, some newspaper reporters began to speculate that Truman's bid for reelection might not be impossible after all. On the Dewey team, there was a creeping sense of alarm, though they remained outwardly confident of winning. Then on November 2, Truman pulled off a victory that had seemed impossible at the start of the campaign, winning the popular tally by 2.1 million votes over Dewey and taking the Electoral College by 303 to 189. Stopping in St. Louis on his way back to Washington from his Missouri home, where he had spent election day and night, Truman stepped out on the train's rear platform holding up a copy of the *Chicago Tribune,* which carried the bold headline, "DEWEY DEFEATS TRUMAN." Pollsters had been so confident that Dewey would win that they stopped sampling during the last weeks of the campaign, and the Chicago newspaper had not bothered to wait for the election returns to compose its headline.

The Democrats also won back control of Congress, with 263 seats to 171 in the House and fifty-four to forty-two in the Senate. But his party's legislative victory would not help the president advance his domestic reform agenda when a coalition of conservative Republicans and southern Democrats refused to budge and blocked his legislative agenda.

Although Truman had condemned the Eightieth Congress for not considering his domestic legislation, he had not run hard on the Democrats' then controversial platforms of civil rights, national health insurance, and federal aid to education. Instead, he tended to look backward in charging that Republicans would attempt to take away the benefits voters had received from the New Deal. This strategy made sense in the aftermath of two decades of crises and emergency—first the Great Depression, then Second World War, and most recently, an escalating Cold War. Under the circumstances, most Americans had little appetite for more dramatic changes in their lives. Thus, even though Truman and his party won in 1948, it was not the time for bold domestic reform. The country simply was not in the mood for it. For a variety of reasons, then, Truman could not wield the power to leave a significant legacy of domestic reform, though his proposals would help to call attention to the need for such reforms that would grow over time and become reality a generation later.

Truman was constitutionally entitled to run again in 1952 because the Twenty-Second Amendment, ratified in 1951, did not apply to him retroactively. However, the grind of the Korean War, which Truman had decided to wage without a Congressional declaration, and, ironically, relentless criticism from Republicans that he was not tough enough in combating Communism led to the lowest presidential approval rating ever measured by public opinion polls—a dismal 22 percent according to Gallup in February 1952. Under the circumstances, Truman decided not to run that fall.

"I Like Ike"

By 1952, the Republican Party was desperate to take back the White House after twenty years of Democratic rule, and they did not want to make the mistake of selecting a candidate like the very conservative Senator Robert Taft of Ohio, who believed he deserved the prize. Thus, the party dispatched Senator Henry Cabot Lodge to go to Paris, where Dwight D. Eisenhower was NATO commander, and persuaded him to come back and vie for the GOP nomination. Without a Republican win, which Lodge believed Eisenhower could deliver, party leaders warned the two-party system itself would be in danger of collapsing. Eisenhower's greatest strength, Lodge and fellow Republicans believed, was his having served as "Supreme Allied Commander in

Europe" during the Second World War and, as such, was rightfully credited with leading the final defeat of Nazi Germany. With all the fears and uncertainties unleashed by the Cold War, voters would hopefully see Eisenhower as a strong protector of the nation. Ironically, Truman himself had suggested on at least three occasions that Eisenhower seek the Democratic nomination for president in 1948 and that he would assist him in that quest, but each time he foreswore any interest in the job.[10] In fact, Eisenhower's party preferences were then unknown.

Many personal factors besides his military triumphs recommended Eisenhower to American voters. Like Truman, he hailed from the center of the country—in his case from Abilene, Kansas—and his family background was not all that different from Truman's. His father worked at a local creamery, and they made ends meet by growing much of their food on a three-acre plot surrounding a small house. "Ike," as friends and family knew him, was soft-spoken. He also had a broad Midwestern accent that linguists have long considered standard American pronunciation, so that it was difficult for many voters to trace his speaking patterns to a particular part of the country. He had a wide, friendly smile, and at sixty-two, when he ran, could seem fatherly—or even grandfatherly, depending on one's age.

By 1952, in comparison to just four years earlier, television was nearly as ubiquitous as radio once had been, and not surprisingly, the Eisenhower campaign turned to the new medium to promote their candidate, especially through brief advertisements as opposed to longer presentations featuring the candidate himself. One thirty-second television ad begins by referring to Eisenhower's humble, small-town origins. Entitled "The Man from Abilene," viewers hear the narrator say, "Out of the heartland, out of a small frame house in Abilene, Kansas came a man, Dwight D. Eisenhower." Appearing on the screen as the narrator speaks is the photo of the candidate's birthplace superimposed in the middle of a map of the United States. Next, there are newsreel images of D-Day and victorious American troops marching down the Champs Elysees in Paris, as a reminder that "General Eisenhower," as Supreme Allied Commander in Europe, had led the victorious defeat of Nazi Germany. A few seconds later, Eisenhower himself appears as if in a brief interview about national security, allowing the television audience to hear the flat intonations of the heartland candidate's voice.[11] Thus Eisenhower, like Truman, Lincoln, and Jackson before him, was appealing to the "common man" theme.

Other short television ads emphasize the candidate's likability. Among these was a cartoon segment made by Disney Studios and presented as an imaginary political parade led by Uncle Sam. Following Uncle Sam is a large elephant with the drawing of a smiling Eisenhower on a banner attached to its side. Then come marching cartoon figures of Americans from every walk of life who sing a jingle over and over:

> You like Ike; I like Ike.
> Everybody likes Ike for president.[12]

The "I like Ike" mantra, which played on the fact that "Ike," Eisenhower's nickname, rhymed perfectly with the word "like," appeared everywhere during the campaign—

from buttons to flyers, placards, and billboards, invariably with Eisenhower's smiling face that appeared to be liking voters back. However famous and admired Eisenhower was and would remain, there would be no cult of personality surrounding him, as there had been with the two earlier war hero presidents—George Washington and Andrew Jackson. He was temperamentally incapable of either creating or accepting such a cult.

The Democrats that year nominated Adlai Stevenson, then serving as a popular governor of Illinois.[13] His grandfather, also named Adlai Stevenson, had been vice president from 1893 to 1897 during Grover Cleveland's second presidential term. During the campaign, Stevenson became known for his frank and straightforward assessments of problems facing the nation, often interlarded with wit and wisdom. His acceptance speech for the nomination set the tone: "The ordeal of the twentieth century, the bloodiest, most turbulent era of the Christian age," he declared, "is far from over." Continuing in this vein, he warned the delegates, "Sacrifice, patience, understanding and implacable purpose may be our lot for years to come." Thus, he added, "Let's talk sense to the American people. Let's tell them the truth." There would be no "easy decisions, . . . but a long, patient, costly struggle which alone can assure triumph over the great enemies of man—war poverty and tyranny—and the assaults upon human dignity which are the most grievous consequences of each."[14]

Stevenson's speeches would later be collected and published as a bestseller. Indeed, he remained a man who valued political rhetoric and the printed word; and at a time when television was sweeping the nation, Stevenson did not even own a TV set and consequently did not wholly appreciate the power of the new medium as a campaign instrument. The number of households owning sets was now 17 million, some fifty times greater than during the most recent presidential campaign in 1948. Nor could he compete on an equal footing with a war hero like Eisenhower at a time when so many Americans were terrified about the seemingly unstoppable march of Communism around the world, especially given the not-so-subtle but false charges from Republicans that Stevenson was soft on Communism. The Republicans' vice-presidential candidate Richard Nixon became notorious for such accusations. One of his favorite lines during the campaign was to say again and again, "Stevenson holds a Ph.D. degree from [Secretary of State Dean] Acheson's College of Cowardly Containment." Nixon considered the Doctrine of Containment, as a way of combating Communism, to be a shameful sell-out. Furthermore, he used the word "College," as an anti-intellectual smear at Stevenson's graduation from an Ivy League university, in his case Princeton, and at Stevenson's often thoughtful and nuanced positions on foreign affairs.

A Middle Way

Nixon aside and to no one's surprise, Eisenhower won handily in November, with 55.2 percent of the popular vote to Stevenson's 44.2 percent. The electoral vote was more lopsided at 442 to 89. During the campaign, Eisenhower had not announced any bold new initiatives if he captured the White House. Rather, he would pursue "a middle way" that would not attempt to dismantle the principal achievements of the New Deal, as some conservative Republicans had been demanding. For instance, he checked the expansion of public power generation but did not privatize the vast system of dams and electrical generating plants already operated by the Tennessee Valley Authority that had been created during Franklin Roosevelt's New Deal. When it came to Social Security, another major New Deal program, Eisenhower expanded its coverage to millions of white-collar workers who had not been included in the original system.

Revolutionary in its impact, however, was the Interstate Highway Act of 1956, which Eisenhower proposed and strongly supported, and which he was able to get through a Congress controlled by the Democrats at a time when partisan gridlock was not the ruling passion of the day, in contrast to later decades. The act led to the construction of 41,000 miles of expressways that linked the country together by automobile as never before. Although not intended as such, many segments of these new highways became commuter roads, giving a huge boost to suburban sprawl with its automobile culture and the pollution of air and water with all the climate change forces that would come with them. The interstates also sped up the decline of cities, with the erosion of urban tax bases and an abandonment of passenger rail service in many parts of the United States as further unintended consequences of the act.

Unlike Truman and in line with his emphasis on what he called his middle way, Eisenhower did not push vigorously for civil rights reform. He was not personally a racist, but he had lived in a segregated world all his life, beginning in his native Kansas and then while an officer in the segregated US Army. Nor did he have any close associations with African Americans. Consequently, he did not fully appreciate the great humiliation and many social and economic disadvantages that segregation imposed on African Americans.

Following the Supreme Court's unanimous 1954 ruling in *Brown v. Board of Education* that racial segregation in the public schools was unconstitutional, Eisenhower declined to comment publicly on the decision, stating that doing so would violate the separation of powers between the executive and judicial branches. A follow-up case, commonly known commonly as *Brown II*, left decisions to community school boards to desegregate "with all deliberate speed." Eisenhower thus felt comfortable leaving the matter to local authorities. Critics at the time and later have charged that his silence on the school desegregation issue may well have emboldened protesters in Little Rock, Arkansas, in September 1957 to block the admission of nine African American students to the city's Central High School as ordered by a federal court. The situation became so dangerous that Eisenhower had to federalize the Arkansas National Guard as well as send in units from the 101st Airborne Division to clear away huge groups of angry, and in some cases violent, protesters.

When Eisenhower gave a nationwide television address from the White House on September 21, he did not speak of racial injustice but of his need to enforce federal court decisions: "The very basis of our individual rights and freedoms depends on the certainty that the president will enforce the decisions of the courts. . . . A foundation of our American way of life is our national respect for the law."[15]

At the time he left office, Eisenhower was the oldest person, at age seventy, to serve as president. He had suffered a serious heart attack in 1955 and continued to have a weak heart. Democrats did not attempt to exploit the president's health. However, a sharp but brief recession in 1958 allowed them to question his economic leadership. Liberals also criticized what they saw as Eisenhower's weak record on civil rights and his failure to address the problem of decaying urban areas.

A New Frontier

Eisenhower was the last president born in the nineteenth century, while his successor, Democrat John F. Kennedy, became the first president born in the twentieth century. At age forty-three, Kennedy was the youngest person ever elected president (though Theodore Roosevelt had become president at age forty-two as the result of McKinley's assassination). Kennedy's youthfulness allowed the Democrats to play indirectly on the age of the outgoing incumbent by repeating that it was time to "get this country moving again." Kennedy's Republican opponent Richard Nixon, at age forty-six, was hardly an old man, but he put himself forth as an "elder statesman" whose experience as vice president made him the obvious choice for Republicans to contest the 1960 election.

Although Kennedy had not served in an executive capacity, he had been in national politics as long as Nixon had. Both had been elected to the House of Representatives for the first time in 1946, and both went on to win seats in the Senate, Nixon in 1950 and Kennedy in 1952. While Nixon won the vice-presidency that same year, Kennedy remained in the Senate. Both had also served in the Navy during the Second World War. In other respects, their backgrounds were very different. Nixon hailed from California, and Kennedy from Massachusetts on the opposite side of the country. Whereas Kennedy had grown up in an increasingly wealthy family, Nixon's family had struggled to maintain a middle-class lifestyle.

As the fall campaign got underway, the opinion polls showed the candidates neck and neck, with neither seemingly able to pull into the lead, in part because the two men differed very little on the issues. As it turned out, the election results would turn more on matters of personal appearance and mannerisms than on ideas of substance, as their televised debates, discussed in the next chapter, would reveal. Indeed, Kennedy's appearance and likability may well have made the difference in November, given that his victory in the popular vote was razor thin. When the returns came in, Kennedy won by just 113,000 popular votes, though the electoral count was more convincing at 303 to 219. Still, with his slim margin in the popular tally, he would have a hard time claiming a strong mandate to govern.

From the time of his nomination, Kennedy wanted to present himself as a new kind of president who would preside over a new era in American life. Such was the soaring theme of his address in accepting the Democratic Party nomination at the Los Angeles Coliseum on July 15, 1960. "Today our concern must be with the future. For the world is changing. The old era is ending. The old ways will not do." Here was a string of phrases contrasting past and future that some commentators thought amounted to a not too veiled reference to Eisenhower's age, and with it, the out-of-date policies of the Republican Party. In contrast, he looked to a future that would be nothing short of "revolutionary." Roosevelt's New Deal and Truman's Fair Deal had been "bold measures for their generation," Kennedy said, but they were entering a new era. He admitted that the presumptive Republican nominee Richard Nixon, whom he did not name in the speech, was also "a young man." However, he charged that "his approach is as old as McKinley. His party is the party of the past. His speeches are generalities from Poor Richard's Almanac." In contrast, Kennedy and the Democrats would not ignore the problem of overcrowded schools, urban slums, and racial discrimination.

In that spirit, his administration would launch a "New Frontier." This latest chapter, he told them, was "not a set of promises—it is a set of challenges. . . . Kennedy offered no details about what he and his party would do to address these domestic issues, instead reminding the crowd of the intrepid pioneers who had trekked west and made a new country. We stand today on the edge of a New Frontier—the frontier of the 1960s—a frontier of unknown opportunities and perils—a frontier of unfulfilled hopes and threats."[16] Exactly what Kennedy had in mind was unclear—perhaps purposely so—but the tag "New Frontier" caught on and would become a colorful shorthand for the Kennedy presidency.

Kennedy's inaugural address six months later, on January 20, 1961, stressed even more the novel challenges that he and his fellow Americans faced, again beckoning the future. "The world is very different now," he declared. "For man holds in his mortal hands the power to abolish all forms of human poverty and all forms of human life." However, beyond mentioning the power to combat poverty and a fleeting reference to poverty several lines later, the remainder of his address focused on the challenges of the ongoing contest with Communism and the threat of nuclear war. "Let every nation know," he intoned, "whether it wishes us well or ill, that we shall pay any price, bear any burden, meet any hardship, support any friend, oppose any foe to assure the survival and the success of liberty. This much we pledge—and more." The task would not be easy: "The torch has been passed to a new generation of Americans"—Kennedy's generation—"born in this century, tempered by war, disciplined by a hard and bitter peace, proud of our ancient heritage—and unwilling to witness or permit the slow undoing of those human rights to which this nation has always been committed, and to which we are committed today at home and around the world." At the end of the address came the famous line calling on his fellow citizens, "ask not what your country can do for you—ask what you can do for your country."[17]

At just 1,335 words, Kennedy's inaugural address was one of the shortest of all time— about half the historical average. The address was well received by both the media and the public and is still rated as one of the most memorable inauguration speeches. In retrospect, its call for struggle and sacrifice without any explanation about just what had to be done appears vague and incomplete. However, Kennedy's goal was to bestir the American people from what he saw as a lethargy that had befallen over the country during the past decade of self-satisfaction and a complacency that had elicited a number of critical books about American life in the mid-twentieth century. Although Kennedy did not mention any by name, included in any list at the time would have been David Riesman's *Lonely Crowd*, William White's *Organization Man*, and John Keats' *The Crack in the Picture Window*.

Still, as his inaugural address revealed, Kennedy believed his most important task was to galvanize the nation to face the threat posed by the Communist Soviet Union, and like other twentieth-century presidents, he had the utmost freedom to act alone in the realm of foreign affairs. As such, he also had abundant freedom to make mistakes. In asking his fellow citizens "to pay any price," Kennedy surely did not intend to bring on the real possibility of nuclear war, but a decision he made just three months after his inauguration very nearly led to a nuclear holocaust over Cuba.

While running for office in 1960, Kennedy had unfairly accused the Eisenhower administration of having "lost Cuba" to Communism because of Fidel Castro's successful revolution on the island, which had occurred on Eisenhower's watch, as if there were something Eisenhower could have done to stop the Cuban revolution. Partly to further demonstrate his credentials as a cold warrior, Kennedy in April 1961 approved a plan concocted by the CIA to land a group of Cuban emigres at the Bay of Pigs. The CIA had operated on the misguided belief that vast numbers of the Cuban people would join with these landing emigres to overthrow Castro, who appeared to be in league with the Soviets. Several of Kennedy's advisors, especially Arthur Schlesinger, Jr., warned the president that the hoped-for uprising might well not occur, and that the invasion would turn into a fiasco. J. William Fulbright, who had been briefed about the plan as Chairman of the Senate Foreign Relations Committee, was also adamantly opposed; but for the sake of maintaining secrecy, the president made no request for Congress to approve the operation. In any case, Kennedy feared that if he did not go through with the Bay of Pigs operation, Republicans would attack him for being a Communist appeaser.

As predicted in various quarters, the invasion was a dismal failure. Soon thereafter, Castro turned to the Soviet Union for assistance, and the Soviets sent medium-range missiles to the island that could easily hit targets in the United States. Kennedy rejected the proposals of military advisors to bomb and invade Cuba, fearing that such actions would touch off a nuclear war and kill millions on both sides. Instead, the president declared a naval quarantine around Cuba, which was in effect a blockade and, as such a risky move that could have been considered an act of war by the Soviets.

Fortunately, Soviet leader Nikita Khrushchev stepped back from the brink of disaster and decided to work with Kennedy to defuse the crisis. The Soviets agreed to remove their missiles from Cuba in exchange for an American promise to remove their missiles from Turkey, though there was not to be any admission of a quid pro quo on the part of the United States. Kennedy also promised not to invade Cuba. The consensus among historians in both the United States and Russia following the break-up of the Soviet Union holds that the world came closer to a devastating nuclear exchange than at any time before or since. On the American side, Kennedy held the fate of the planet in his hands, demonstrating the awesome unilateral power of a president as commander-in-chief.[18] Many Americans also came to understand for the first time that their presidents acting alone had the power to destroy most life on earth, but, unfortunately, it is not a power that most voters consider when voting for president.

Meanwhile, what was being called "the space race" continued, as both sides sought to demonstrate to the world that its technology was superior. The Soviet Union's successful launch of the first human into Earth orbit in April 1961 appeared to be an alarming setback to the American space program, prompting Kennedy to announce in February 1962 that the United States would land a person on the moon by the end of the decade. For Kennedy, the moon challenge was indeed a new frontier and perfectly echoed the theme of his nomination acceptance speech in the summer of 1960. Although the moon program would require massive appropriations from Congress, it began with a presidential pronouncement.

Another presidential initiative, established by executive order and designed to demonstrate the goodwill of the United States in underdeveloped areas of the globe, was the Peace Corps, an idea that had originated with Senator Hubert Humphrey of Minnesota. Largely young Americans would go abroad "to help foreign countries to meet their urgent needs of skilled manpower."[19] Peace Corps volunteers would receive no salaries but only basic living allowances. Kennedy insisted that the corps, to be headed by his brother-in-law Sargent Shriver, would not be an instrument of American propaganda or ideology, but a real-life example of the nation's idealistic commitment to assist development in third-world countries. The Soviets saw it as nothing more than a propaganda ploy, and, in truth, Kennedy himself hoped that the corps would cause emerging nations to favor an American model of development in preference to Communism.

While Kennedy enjoyed a largely free hand when it came to foreign affairs, he needed legislative action on all his major domestic programs, and in this arena, his successes were meager. During his presidential campaign in 1960, he had been wary of pushing a civil rights program for Black Americans. He knew that he needed a strong turnout from African American voters if he were to win the election in November, but he also feared losing votes from Southern Democrats who were intent on maintaining racial segregation. Kennedy sincerely believed that the mistreatment of Blacks was a moral stain on the nation, but with little personal exposure to African Americans (not unlike Eisenhower before him), it was difficult for him to know how deeply painful racism was to persons who lived it every day. However, when during the presidential campaign the Reverend Doctor Martin Luther King was jailed in Birmingham, Alabama, for attempting to integrate a restaurant in a local department store, Kennedy felt genuine sympathy and called King's wife to express his concern. Knowledge of the call spread widely in the Black community and may have helped Kennedy to bring out the African American vote.

The partisan balance in Congress when the new session began would on the surface seem propitious for passing civil rights legislation, with the Democrats winning 262 House seats to the Republicans' 173. Yet 101 of the Democratic members hailed from the Old South and were very likely to vote with conservative Republicans against any significant domestic legislation, especially civil rights. The Democrats also controlled the Senate with sixty-four to thirty-six seats, but there, too, southern Democrats in tandem with conservative Republicans were in a good position to block any domestic reforms. This conservative phalanx in the national legislature had been in place since the late 1930s and had blocked any furtherance of the New Deal and then of Truman's Fair Deal. As a result, Kennedy's "high priority" legislative proposals to Congress for a tax cut to stimulate the economy, federal aid to education, and health insurance for the elderly (later to be called Medicare) were not even reported out of the requisite committees.

The president especially faced ongoing frustration over civil rights reform. He concluded early on that waging a fight with Congress over civil rights would be a futile gesture in which he would lose and, in the process squander much of his political capital. Nor would he issue an Executive Order to desegregate housing financed by the federal government for fear of enraging southern Democrats. Instead, he issued a less controversial executive order that established a Committee on Equal Employment Opportunity (CEEO). Its purpose was to stop discrimination in hiring federal employees and to withhold federal contracts from businesses that denied equal employment opportunities to blacks. He used yet another order to extend the life of the Civil Rights Commission to assess the state of civil rights throughout the nation.

Even Kennedy's desire to secure federal aid to education foundered on the rocks of racial politics, since southern legislators feared such aid would be a stalking horse to force school desegregation by withholding aid to any public schools that did not integrate. Indeed, even the most remote possibility of federal intrusion into education raised the opposition of house members and senators from the South who saw it as a way of trying to make them alter race relations.

Yet events forced Kennedy to continue addressing racial justice. In May 1961, some thirteen members of the Congress of Racial Equality (CORE), including both black and white individuals, traveled by bus from Washington, DC, on "Freedom Rides" into the deep South as a way of protesting segregation in interstate transportation. Mobs met and severely beat them at bus stations. The president's brother, Robert Kennedy, whom he had appointed as his attorney general, threatened to send federal forces into Montgomery, Alabama, which effectively compelled the state's governor to protect the Freedom Riders who made it safely to Montgomery. Then, in September 1962, Kennedy had to send National Guard units into Oxford, Mississippi, to protect James Meredith, whose enrollment in the heretofore all-white University of Mississippi had been ordered by a federal court.

In the late spring of 1963, the president decided to send a civil rights bill to Congress that would outlaw racial discrimination in public accommodations. To dramatize the need for such legislation, Martin Luther King and other black leaders planned a massive "March on Washington" for August 28 of that year. Kennedy at first tried to dissuade the marchers but eventually gave up and used his influence to arrange a sizable participation in the march by white citizens from various unions and churches. King's speech electrified the crowd of over a quarter of a million attendees, but the march did nothing immediately to secure passage of a civil rights act, which remained bottled up in committee, as did Kennedy's renewed pitch for a tax cut. A bill to create health care for the elderly fared no better, as opponents continued to denounce it as "socialized medicine."

Hoping to "mend fences" in the South, Kennedy traveled to Dallas, Texas on November 22, 1963, where he was fatally shot while riding in a motorcade in an open convertible. The nation was thrown into deep mourning as the life of their young, handsome, and charismatic leader had been torn away from them. Sixty-two years before, McKinley's murder had placed Theodore Roosevelt, another young president, into the White House, whose subsequent years in office launched a powerful set of reforms. However, there was no reason to believe that Kennedy's successor Lyndon B. Johnson would preside over a burst of domestic reforms like Theodore Roosevelt.

The Great Society

Historian Eric Goldman, who served as a special advisor to Johnson, began his book about the Johnson presidency with a backward glance at the Kennedy years, partly as a way of contrasting it with his successor's time in office. Goldman's assessment of Kennedy was one that few members of the public would have recognized in 1969 when the book was published—or even half a century later, when many Americans, some not even alive at the time of the assassination, continue to view him as one of the country's best presidents. Reflecting on the assassination, Goldman wrote, "President Kennedy was passing from life, to apotheosis with no interval of critical evaluation." Goldman continued, "By some measurements, the brief thirty-five months of the Kennedy Presidency had scarcely been a conspicuous success." To buttress his assertion, Goldman listed a number of shortcomings: There had been the Bay of Pigs fiasco and Kennedy's inability to find a solution for the mounting problem with Vietnam, along with his failure to get Congress to pass his "big four legislative proposals—civil rights, tax reduction, Medicare and federal aid to education."[20] This assessment was no anti-Kennedy screed by a Johnson loyalist, for Goldman would also take his own boss to task over what he considered some serious lapses in judgment.

At the same time, Goldman was impressed by Johnson's unparalleled success at shepherding major domestic legislation through Congress, including those bills that Kennedy had failed to get through. These victories, Goldman believed, resulted from a startling similarity between Johnson and Woodrow Wilson, a person Johnson often had dismissed as a cold, intellectual prig. Their great similarity was how they viewed their relationship with the legislative branch. According to Goldman, "It was Woodrow Wilson who made his academic reputation arguing that the president should be, as much as the American system permitted, a prime minister, and it was Lyndon Johnson who, more than any other president including Woodrow Wilson, was proceeding to function in that manner."[21] In other words, Johnson worked assiduously and effectively with his majority party in Congress to obtain legislation.

Of course, there was no way Johnson would have wanted a genuine parliamentary system that could subject him to constant grilling. Johnson's approach to Congress was also experiential rather than a formally thought-out philosophy of government as in Wilson's case. His consummate experience had begun as a member of the House of Representatives from 1937 to 1949. He had gone on to win a seat in the United States Senate, where he became Minority Leader in 1953 and Majority Leader in 1955, holding the later position until becoming vice president in 1961. When Johnson assumed the presidency following Kennedy's death in November 1963, he had been out of the Senate for less than three years and continued to have many friends and acquaintances on Capitol Hill.

Johnson was also fortunate to be president at a time when the partisan divide was not as rigid as it would become a generation later. There were conservative and liberal Democrats, as well as conservative, moderate, and even liberal Republicans, which made bipartisan lawmaking, especially when leavened by compromise, a realistic possibility. Given the chance of forming coalitions among these groups, and because Johnson respected legislators regardless of their affiliations, he did not resort to demonizing the opposition. In addition, many Senators and Representatives then lived in Washington with their families, instead of flying back home weekly to their home districts (in this age before commercial jet air transportation was ubiquitous). Under these older traditions, members of both parties socialized together, went to the same entertainments and sporting events, and sent their children to the same schools, which engendered cordial relations and even friendships "across the aisle." In addition, because the Republicans seemed to be in a permanent legislative minority, their only possibility of influencing legislation was through collaborating with the Democrats.

Johnson's intimate knowledge of House and Senate rules and traditions also gave him great advantages in working with Capitol Hill. In Goldman's words, "He knew where every wire of power ran, whose influence was waxing or waning [along with] the rules and habits of the committees . . ." Goldman added that Johnson had a "consummate sense of 'timing' in dealing with the House and Senate. It came not only from the facts he had learned but [also] from the moods he sensed."[22] Then there was his tenacity, hard work, and refusal to take no for an answer, combined with his shameless flattery and artful bestowal of favors—or withholding of the same. Another strategy was to gain support for legislation from various pressure groups to make it easier for a representative to vote for a bill the president wanted passed. As a last resort, he could be physically intimidating, as when the muscular, six-foot-three Johnson rose from his chair, "peering intently into the other man's eyes, literally grasping a lapel, a shoulder or an arm."[23]

Johnson also called on the memory of John Kennedy to urge passage of the bills that the fallen president had been unable to get through Congress. In his speech to a joint session of both houses on November 27, 1963, just five days after the assassination, he declared, "no memorial oration or eulogy could more eloquently honor President Kennedy's memory than the earliest possible passage of the civil rights bill for which he fought so long. We have talked long enough in this country about equal rights. We have talked for one hundred years or more. It is time now to write the next chapter, and to write it in the books of law."[24]

The civil rights bill was the most important of the "big four" pieces of legislation that Kennedy had wanted passed and that Johnson was determined to push through. The other three were federal aid to education, Medicare, and a tax cut. The first of these enacted was the tax bill on February 26, 1964. The Civil Rights Act passed a little over four months later, on July 2, with considerable support from Republicans that helped to neutralize southern resistance in Congress. This landmark act outlawed segregation in public accommodations and banned discrimination in employment because of race, color, religion, sex, or national origin. However, the Civil Rights Act did nothing to remedy continuing roadblocks in the South to keep blacks from voting through such devices as poll taxes and unfairly administered literacy tests, along with various forms of intimidation, including outright violence or threats of violence. The Voting Rights Act of 1965 sought to address this injustice by authorizing federal registrars to oversee voter registration in states where fewer than 50 percent of adults residing there had voted in the 1964 election. Over the next several years, black voter registration rose dramatically. Unfortunately, backlash over the civil rights acts, combined with opposition to other social and cultural changes, would be used to create severe political polarization in the future that would threaten American democracy itself.

The remaining two initiatives, Medicare and federal aid to education, had to await the results of the 1964 elections, which would decide whether Johnson could secure the presidency in his own right. He was fortunate in facing Republican candidate Senator Barry Goldwater of Arizona, whom even many members of his own party considered too conservative and too far out of the mainstream of American politics. Goldwater liked to see himself as the personification of the rugged individualism that had flourished in the Old West and that had been threatened by the growing power of the federal government, and especially by what he and other conservatives liked to call the welfare state. Goldwater had also voted against the Civil Rights Act in the name of states' rights.

Goldwater often appeared back home in Arizona wearing western-style shirts, boots, and bolo ties, and liked to talk to supporters about what he called a "he-man" approach to solving the nation's problems. "The trouble with the so-called liberal today," he would exclaim, "is that he doesn't understand straightforward simplicity. The answers to America's problems are simple."[25] And throughout the campaign, Goldwater made statements and took positions that alarmed many voters. Before his nomination, he had proposed making Social Security voluntary, which would have wrecked the system, and during the campaign said that Social Security needed "drastic revision," which also worried many. He also undermined his chances by making statements in various parts of the country, which were sure to put off voters. In Charleston, West Virginia, a city surrounded by some of the worst poverty in the nation, he ripped into federal anti-poverty programs. In Memphis, Tennessee, the world's cotton center, he lambasted cotton subsidies that he said Washington had forced onto cotton farmers; and in Knoxville, where the Tennessee Valley Authority, created under Roosevelt's New Deal, had been immensely popular, he insisted that the operation should be sold to private power companies. If that were not enough, he terrified many citizens around the country by casually saying with a sort of cowboy bravado that he was not afraid to use nuclear weapons against America's enemies. In accepting the Republican nomination in July, he had promised not to hold back in confronting the nation's foes, declaring, "Extremism in the defense of liberty is no vice, . . . moderation in the pursuit of justice is no virtue."[26]

At first, Johnson confined his campaign to saying, "the president [is] in Washington doing the country's business," with an occasional foray out of town to dedicate some new public work or to visit the site of a natural disaster. In the fall, at a time when campaigns still started in earnest after Labor Day, he put most of his emphasis on domestic affairs. This strategy made sense since he was running against an opponent who constantly bashed the gains from Johnson's beloved Franklin Roosevelt and Roosevelt's New Deal. However, he would not do as Roosevelt had done in 1936 when he invited the hatred of the "economic royalists," or as Truman had done on the stump in excoriating that "No good, do nothing Eightieth Congress." Rather, Johnson believed there was now a consensus of support for the accomplishments of the New Deal, and he proposed to move ahead with social and economic programs in that same spirit. He also believed that most Americans supported continuing efforts to find a workable means of coexistence with communist powers.

During this autumn phase of the campaign, Johnson flew over 60,000 miles, four times the distance of Harry Truman on his whistle-stop tour, without, of course, covering as much physical ground as Truman, with his many stops along the tracks. Also, unlike Truman, whom Johnson liked very much personally, he refrained for the most part from attacking the opposition. Much like Truman, he enjoyed the folksy touch with his audiences. He wanted the crowds to know he was just a friendly "guy" who enjoyed talking to friendly faces. "Don't y'all say anything ugly," he would say. "Let's keep our shirts on and be nice." By the end of the campaign, he was painting a picture of a nation that echoed many of the teachings on which he and many in his audiences had been brought up: "It's the time when man gains full dominion under God over his destiny. It's a time of peace on earth and good will among men." "Love thy neighbor as thyself," he said, "[and] do unto others as you would have them do unto you." "Let's keep a smile on our face, let's keep hope in our vision."[27]

By the time election day rolled around, Johnson was very optimistic about his chances, and for good reason as it turned out: He won a historic victory, with an all-time high of 61.6 percent of the popular vote, which exceeded even the 60.8 percent that Roosevelt had won for a second term in 1936. His equally impressive electoral vote of 486 to fifty-two was second only to Roosevelt's 1936 tally. Johnson was elated. No longer an "accidental" president, he had triumphed in his own right.

There could be no doubt Johnson had secured a historic mandate that included overwhelming control of both houses of Congress by his party. House Democrats won an additional thirty-six seats that gave them a commanding majority of 295 to 140. In the Senate, they maintained a two-thirds majority. As a student of political history, however, Johnson remembered Roosevelt had become too cocksure after his 1936 victory, taking Congress for granted and making the blunder of trying to pack the Supreme Court. To avoid a similar fate, he would continue to pay Congress due respect. He also knew that his mandate would not last forever. He would have to get as much legislation passed as possible before his welcome wore out on Capitol Hill.

As it turned out, Johnson's successes with legislation in 1965 were unprecedented. There was the Medicare Act that established health insurance for the elderly, as well as the Medicaid Act that created a health insurance program for the poor. The same year,

Congress passed the Elementary and Secondary School Act, which provided money for professional development and instructional materials, and the Higher Education Act, which established federal aid to colleges and universities, along with student scholarships and low-interest loans.

This aid to education was part of Johnson's larger "War on Poverty," which he had announced as part of his first State of the Union Message in January 1964. "This administration today, here and now," he said, "declares unconditional war on poverty in America. I urge this Congress and all Americans to join with me in that effort." He added, "It will not be a short or easy struggle; no single weapon or strategy will suffice, but we shall not rest until that war is won. The richest nation on earth can afford to win it. We cannot afford to lose it."[28] A little more than four months later, Johnson connected the war on poverty with what he called "The Great Society" during a commencement speech at the University of Michigan on May 22. It would be a society, "Where the city of man serves not only the needs of the body and the demands of commerce but the desire for beauty and the hunger for community." Above all, Americans did not have to accept the world as they found it, insisting, "We have the power to shape the world that we want."[29]

On August 20, Johnson signed into law the Economic Opportunity Act of 1964 as the first onslaught against poverty. Then, administered through the Office of Economic Opportunity, the Johnson White House launched Head Start, a program to prepare children from low-income families to enter school on a more equal academic and social footing. The Upward Bound program aimed at preparing teens from similar backgrounds for success in college. Job Corps provided job training for young men and women, while Vista was established as a sort of domestic Peace Corps that sent volunteers to assist people in economically depressed areas of the country. A Community Action program hired community organizers to rally residents to press for government programs to help them.

Very much in line with the War on Poverty was the Appalachian Redevelopment Act of 1965, which aimed to stimulate economic growth in depressed mountainous areas that stretched from Western Pennsylvania into Northern Alabama. The act provided $1.1 billion for highways, health centers, and resource development. To assist depressed urban areas, Congress passed the Urban Development Act that appropriated funds for metropolitan planning, thousands of new housing units, housing repairs, and rent subsidies, along with neighborhood health and recreation centers. The Model Cities Act of 1966 provided funds for the rehabilitation of blighted areas and the upgrading of mass transit.

As if this were not enough, Johnson steered through Congress a Traffic Safely Act (1966) and a Consumer Protection Act (1966). Then there was a spate of environmental legislation: The National Wildlife Protection Act (1964); The Land Conservation Fund (1965); The Solid Waste Disposal Act (1965); and the Clean Water Restoration Act (1966).

Such legislative action did indeed give Johnson significant authority to try to shape the world he wanted for his fellow citizens. Of course, some opponents believed that Johnson's vision of the Great Society was more of a nightmare. Still, he could bask in the knowledge that no other president, save possibly his hero Franklin Roosevelt, had accomplished so much landmark legislation in such a short time. From that perspective, he seemed well on his way to securing a place in the first rank of American presidents. Unlike Truman and Kennedy before him, he had combined his own considerable experiences and skills with wider forces and events to promote new levels of social and economic justice for millions of Americans. Johnson was also able to work with Republicans at a time when bipartisanship was possible.

The record amount of social legislation that Johnson had been able to push through Congress reinforced reformers' belief that a powerful presidency, as under predecessors such as Wilson and the two Roosevelts, was essential to accomplish a social agenda. Yet by then he had already exercised his powers as commander-in-chief to undermine his historical legacy when he decided to escalate an unnecessary and disastrous war in Vietnam. That is a story that needs to be told within the context of a series of needless wars started by various presidents during nearly a century and three-quarters.

Notes

1 Harry S. Truman, *Special Message to the Congress on Civil Rights*, February 2, 1948, https://glc.yale.edu/special-message-congress-civil-rights.
2 Ibid.
3 Harry S. Truman, *Memoirs, Volume 2, Years of Trial and Hope* (Garden City: Doubleday, 1956), 207–8.
4 Harry S. Truman, quoted in Steven R. Goldzwig, *Truman's Whistle-Stop Campaign* (College Station: Texas A&M University Press, 2008), 43.
5 On this epic campaign by rail, see Goldzwig, *Truman's Whistle-Stop Campaign*. Truman, *Years of Trial and Hope*, 208–12, 219–20; and David McCullough, *Truman* (New York: Simon & Schuster, 1992), 653–719.
6 McCullough, *Truman*, 664.
7 Truman, *Memoirs*, 2:211.
8 McCullough, *Truman*, 660.
9 See the retrospective account by Frank Reuven, "1948: Live from Philadelphia . . . It's the National Conventions," *New York Times*, April 18, 1988.
10 McCullough, *Truman*, 399, 431, 584.
11 "The Man from Abilene," Youtube.
12 "I like Ike" 1952 Presidential Commercial: Roy Disney, YouTube.
13 On Stevenson, see Porter McKeever, *Adlai Stevenson: His Life and His Legacy* (New York: William Morrow and Company, 1989); Jean Harvey Baker, *The Stevensons* (Woodstock: Foul Play Press, 1997).
14 Adlai Stevenson, Accepting the Democratic Nomination, July 26, 1952, https://www.americanrhetoric.com/speeches/adlaistevenson1952dnc.html.
15 Dwight D. Eisenhower, Address to the Nation, September 21, 1957, quoted in Jean Edward Smith, *Eisenhower in War and Peace* (New York: Random House, 2012), 724.
16 Address of Senator John F. Kennedy Accepting the Democratic Party Nomination for the Presidency of the United States, Los Angeles, CA, July 15, 1960, https://www

.jfklibrary.org/archives/other-resources/john-f-kennedy-speeches/democratic-party-nomination-19600715.

17 John F. Kennedy, Inaugural Address, January 20, 1961, https://www.jfklibrary.org/learn/about-jfk/historic-speeches/inaugural-address.

18 A highly readable and insightful account of the Bay of Pigs and the Cuban Missile Crisis may be found in Robert Dallek, *An Unfinished Life: John F. Kennedy, 1917–1963* (Boston: Little, Brown and Company, 2003), 535–75.

19 Quoted in ibid., 338.

20 Eric F. Goldman, *The Tragedy of Lyndon Johnson* (New York: Alfred A. Knopf, 1969), 13.

21 Ibid., 57.

22 Ibid., 59.

23 Ibid., 63.

24 President Lyndon B. Johnson's Address to a Joint Session of Congress, November 27, 1963, https://www.archives.gov/legislative/features/civil-rights-1964/lbj-address.html.

25 Barry Goldwater, quoted in Goldman, *Tragedy of Lyndon Johnson*, 210.

26 Speech of Barry Goldwater, 1964 Republican National Convention, quoted in *National Review*, August 4, 1964; *New York Times*, July 17, 1964.

27 Goldman, *Tragedy of Lyndon Johnson*, 246, 253.

28 Lyndon Baines Johnson, First State of the Union Adddress, January 8, 1964, https://www.americanrhetoric.com/speeches/lbj1964stateoftheunion.htm.

29 Lyndon Baines Johnson, The Great Society, May 22, 1964, Ann Arbor, https://www.americanrhetoric.com/speeches/lbjthegreatsociety.htm.

7

Deception and War

America's Needless Wars

I am not going to lose Vietnam. I am not going to be the president who saw Southeast Asia go the way China went.

Lyndon Johnson, as told to Henry Cabot Lodge, Jr.

On March 17, 2003, the United Nations Security Council declined to support the American resolution to use force against Iraq. The UN inspectors had not found any weapons of mass destruction (WMD) in Iraq. In addition, allegations of ties between Saddam and al-Qaeda terrorists had proven groundless. Nevertheless, President George W. Bush was determined to have his war against Iraq. Facts simply did not seem to matter to the president, who now switched to emphasizing the benefits of implanting democracy in Iraq and hoping that it would spread from there throughout the region. Bush was going to war no matter what.

Of all the powers given to the chief executive, the framers of the Constitution most feared the authority that presidents could wield as commander-in-chief. They understood there had to be a unitary command of the military with the president at its head. However, they were also keenly aware of the many times European monarchs had used their command of military forces to launch and fight unnecessary as well as disastrous wars. To prevent American presidents from taking similar actions, the framers assigned to Congress the sole right and responsibility for declaring war. They also believed that Congress's exclusive role in authorizing taxes and expenditures ("the power of the purse") could constrain presidents from launching needless conflicts, since money would always be required to launch and fight a war. Yet over the years, presidents would find numerous ways to manipulate or circumvent these constraints.

A satisfactory way to define a needless war is to review briefly what has long been called "just war theory," a set of well-established principles that began some sixteen centuries ago with the writings of Saint Augustine of Hippo. Recent concepts of just war have become part of international law, as in the United Nations Charter and the various Geneva conventions. At the crux of all these understandings are the requirements of "necessity" and "last resort." Michael Walzer in his book, *Just and Unjust Wars*, adds that a just war must be in response to some "supreme emergency"—that is, an imminent danger to the country "of an unusual and horrifying kind."[1]

At least five wars fought by the United States during the past two centuries would appear to be needless conflicts that do not fit the definition of a just war. These are the war against Mexico in the 1840s, the Spanish-American War in 1898, the American conquest of the Philippines at the turn of the twentieth century, the Vietnam War that mainly took place during the 1960s and early 1970s, and the Iraq War beginning in 2003.[2] All these conflicts involved some degree of deception or even outright lies by presidents in power at the time.

Mexico and Manifest Destiny

Presiding over the first of these needless wars was James K. Polk, a young protégé of Andrew Jackson, who insisted that Polk vie for the Democratic presidential nomination in 1844. A relative unknown (or "dark horse" in the political slang of the day), Polk managed to win the nomination with Jackson's unyielding support, with campaign literature hailing Polk as "Young Hickory." Once in office, Polk spared no effort to make himself as powerful a president as Jackson had been.

Polk was an ardent expansionist and a firm believer in what many Americans were calling "Manifest Destiny." This concept meant, among other things, that the United States was clearly destined to expand all the way to the Pacific Ocean, and maybe, one day, to own all of North America. Not a few believed that this destiny had been ordained by God. In fulfillment of this goal, Polk decided to provoke a war with Mexico, which would give the United States an excuse for seizing the entire Southwest, then still part of Mexico. The American annexation of Texas in 1845 had enraged Mexico, which had never recognized Texan independence that had resulted from the 1836 revolt of US migrants who had settled in Texas, originally at the invitation of Mexico. Even if Mexico were to acquiesce in Texas statehood, there was strong disagreement about the boundary. Mexico claimed the border was along the Nueces River, which appeared to be justified by older maps of the area, while Texans claimed it was further south along the Rio Grande.

In the summer of 1845, Polk ordered General Zachary Taylor to move his troops "as near the boundary line, the Rio Grande, as prudence will dictate."[3] He later added that Taylor should regard any crossing of the Rio Grande by Mexican troops into the disputed territory as an act of war. Furthermore, the president authorized Taylor to make a preemptive advance across the river and not wait for an attack. On April 12, 1846, Mexican military authorities on the south bank of the Rio Grande demanded that Taylor and his men retreat north of the Nueces River. Then on the twenty-fifth, an American patrol skirmished with a unit of Mexican troops who had crossed to the north side of the Rio Grande, which was considered by both Texans and President Polk to be the proper boundary—but not by Mexico.

Even before Polk received any knowledge of the skirmish, he was preparing to ask Congress for a declaration of war as soon as he could find an excuse. Then, on May 9, dispatches arrived informing him of the encounter on the Rio Grande. In his subsequent war message to Congress, Polk recited Mexican refusals to accept Texas annexation or to recognize the Rio Grande as the boundary. As such, he insisted, "The cup of forbearance had been exhausted even before the recent information from the frontier . . ." adding, "Mexico has passed the boundary of the United States, has invaded our territory and shed American blood upon American soil."[4]

At first, few in Congress dared to dispute the president's claims. As in subsequent presidential decisions to go to war, most legislators as well as most citizens assumed that the president was telling the truth and that there was no alternative but armed conflict. Polk also let it be known that anyone who questioned him would be marked as a coward. Back in 1812, President Madison had simply reported the facts to Congress and let them decide whether to declare hostilities against Great Britain. In contrast, Polk demanded that Congress declare war. According to biographer Walter R. Borneman, "Polk made the president the decision-maker, subject only to Congress's coerced acquiescence. . . . Polk's strong executive leadership was the click that sent the pendulum of the war-making power swinging away from Congress and toward the executive branch."[5] Thereafter, it would be virtually impossible to stop a president bent on war, in effect making the legislative branch's check on the executive virtually worthless in this crucial area of the nation's life.

Former President John Quincy Adams, now a member of the House of Representatives, was one of the few to vote against the war measure. He believed the annexation of Texas, followed by American expansion into the Southwest, would permit the spread of slavery and thereby give the slave-owning southern states even more sway in Washington. As the war went on, members of the new Whig Party, formed in 1834 in opposition to what they considered "King" Andrew Jackson's imperious ways, began to question the need for war with Mexico. They consciously took their name from the English Whig party that had successfully led the resistance in the late seventeenth century to the then unchecked authority of the British monarch.[6]

As reported in an earlier chapter, Whig Congressman Abraham Lincoln was among Polk's critics and, as such introduced the so-called "Spot Resolutions" in the House. In them, he and the others in his group posed eight specific questions for the president, including one demanding that Polk specify "whether the spot on which the blood of our citizens was so shed was or was not at that time *our own soil*."[7] Like Adams, Lincoln was adamantly opposed to the spread of slavery into new territories and saw the war against Mexico as part of a southern plot to carve out more slave states. He also believed that Polk was dangerously expanding executive authority. To repeat, Lincoln wrote to his law partner William Herndon back in Illinois, "Allow the President to invade a neighboring nation, whenever he shall deem it necessary for such purpose—and you allow him to make war at pleasure." Furthermore, according to Lincoln, if Congress did not stand up against the president's assertions of war-making power, he would stand "where kings have always stood."[8]

Attempting to defend himself, Polk flat out lied when he said in his Second Annual Message, "The existing war with Mexico was neither desired nor provoked by the United States. On the contrary, all honorable means were resorted to avert it." He was also untruthful later in the address when he claimed, "This war has not been waged with a view to conquest."[9] In reality, Polk had schemed to start a war with Mexico with the goal of conquering what became the entire Southwest of the United States. Although the Whigs continued to castigate Polk for his perfidy, most of them voted funds to fight the war, fearing they would be accused of abandoning the troops on the field of battle, a dilemma that war opponents would face in future conflicts.

Despite his protestations of innocence, Polk knew that growing criticism meant he had to bring the war to an end as soon as possible. American forces invaded the Mexican seaport of Veracruz and marched overland to Mexico City, which fell on September 14, 1847. Mexico had no choice but to negotiate a peace. The resulting Treaty of Guadalupe Hidalgo, signed on February 1, 1848, recognized the Rio Grande as the southern boundary of Texas, and Mexico ceded to the United States what became the State of California. It also granted to the United States all of what became the Southwest (save for a piece of land below the future states of New Mexico and Arizona that would later be purchased).[10]

The United States paid Mexico $18 million for what was known as the Mexican Cession. The war cost 13,283 American lives and perhaps as many Mexicans. Some historians have argued in retrospect that the war with Mexico, besides being perpetrated through presidential mendacity, was entirely unnecessary: Texas had already been annexed by the United States in 1845, and Mexico was not powerful enough to take it back. As for California, the Americans who had moved there had revolted against Mexico even before the US military took possession of it. The same year the Mexican-American War ended, gold was discovered in California, touching off the famous gold rush that brought tens of thousands of Americans to the territory, so many that they would have easily overwhelmed the sparsely settled Mexican settlements and their very weak and essentially defenseless government in California. It would only be a matter of time until the rest of the southwest, very sparsely populated by Mexico, fell inexorably into the hands of the United States.[11]

In any case, the consequences of the Mexican-American War were far-reaching: Impassioned arguments over whether slavery should be allowed in the territories won from Mexico would become one of the principal causes of the far costlier Civil War a decade and a half later. As for the future of the presidency, Polk created a model for the manipulation and abuse of the war power that his successors could use to their advantage.

War and Empire

The Spanish-American War of 1898 and the associated American war of conquest in the Philippines also qualify as unnecessary conflicts that turned on presidential decision-making. The war with Spain had stemmed from a Cuban revolt that began in 1896 against their Spanish colonial masters. Then Democratic President Grover Cleveland refused to become involved in the conflict. Successor William McKinley, who took office in early 1897, inherited the problem, which was inflamed by expansionists in his own party and pro-war newspapers whose publishers found pro-intervention demands and lurid tales of Spanish cruelty to be very good for circulation.

Two events occurred in February 1898 that gave the press splendid opportunities for sensational reporting and the arousal of war fever. One was a private letter by the Spanish minister to Washington, Enrique Dupuy de Lome. Commenting on McKinley's recent Annual Message to Congress, de Lome wrote, "McKinley's message I regard as bad. . . . It shows once more what McKinley is: weak and catering to the rabble, and, besides, a low politician, who desires to leave a door open and to stand well with the jingoes of his party."[12] There was some truth to de Lome's comments: McKinley was truly in a tight spot. He sincerely wanted to avoid war but was being pelted by the press and wide segments of the public to use force. The rebels managed to steal the de Lome letter and send it to the New *York Journal*, which published it on February 9. In a huge headline, the rival *New York World* cried that the de Lome letter was the "WORST INSULT TO THE UNITED STATES IN ITS HISTORY." The revelation triggered widespread public fury as well as anger among many in the government.

Just six days later, on February 15, with outrage over the de Lome letter still fresh, the USS Battleship *Maine* exploded in Havana Harbor with the loss of 262 American lives. The ship had been sent to Havana to protect and, if necessary, to evacuate Americans in Cuba. The newspapers and the public immediately blamed the explosion on a Spanish torpedo. Assistant Secretary of the Navy Theodore Roosevelt insisted to Congress that the *Maine* was sunk by "an act of dirty treachery on the part of the Spaniards . . ."[13] All over the country, people chanted the phrase, "Remember the Maine, the Hell with Spain." Desperate to avoid war, Spain removed de Lome from his post. Spanish authorities in Cuba had in fact begged the United States not to send the *Maine* to Havana, fearing that some incident might result. They helped to rescue and care for those injured in the *Maine* explosion, and they allowed an American naval team to come down to Havana to investigate. The results were inconclusive: The court of inquiry held that the ship had been deliberately sunk by a submerged mine, but they could not assign any blame for it. Common sense would have suggested that the Spanish, who did not want a war with the United States, which they knew they would lose, would not have blown up the ship. If any agents were responsible, it was more likely the rebels, who wanted American help in winning their independence. Most naval experts today believe the explosion resulted from a fire in one of the coal bunkers that ignited the ship's powder magazine and set off a massive internal explosion. In fact, this was the conclusion drawn by Spanish authorities, who had undertaken an independent investigation of the disaster.

Also doubting Spanish culpability at the time was Philip Alger, the leading authority on explosive naval ordnance and a professor at the US Naval Academy. The day after the *Maine* sinking, Alger shared his doubts with the *Washington Star* newspaper: "No torpedo such as is known in modern warfare," he told the newspaper, "can of itself cause an explosion as powerful as that which destroyed the *Maine*." He added, "We know of no instances where the explosion of a torpedo or mine under a ship's bottom has exploded the [gunpowder] magazine within." Alger believed the most plausible cause of the sinking was a spontaneous fire in the coal bunker of the ship, which directly abutted the powder magazine and was separated from it only by a steel bulkhead, a hazard that was well known from other ships of similar design.[14] Tellingly, Alger was not selected to serve on the court of inquiry established to investigate the *Maine*.

Theodore Roosevelt, based on knowledge gained as Assistant Secretary of the Navy, also knew about the design flaw in ships that had placed coal bunkers next to power magazines and the danger this arrangement posed for internal explosions.[15] However, Roosevelt was determined to have a war and was not about to disseminate any information that would dampen cries for revenge against Spain.

In contrast, McKinley, who still hoped for peace, refrained from speaking out about the *Maine*. Just a week after the sinking, he gave a Washington's Birthday speech at the University of Pennsylvania in Philadelphia. In it, he recalled Washington's cautious advice in dealings with other countries: "Observe good faith and justice toward all nations; cultivate peace and harmony with all."[16] Roosevelt was furious that the president had not denounced Spain and called for war in the speech.

On March 25, McKinley reluctantly sent Spain an ultimatum demanding an immediate armistice and the granting of Cuban independence. Even after the ultimatum, McKinley still hoped to avoid war. "I have been through one war," he said in reference to his service in the Civil War as a staff officer: "I have seen the dead piled up, and I do not want to see another."[17] However, political pressure and ridicule from the press put him into a difficult position. Roosevelt declared that the president invited national humiliation by refusing to fight and complained in a private letter that the president had "no more backbone than a chocolate éclair."[18] The *Washington Post* questioned McKinley's manhood, adding that "a weak or vacillating policy would mean the overwhelming defeat of the Republican party and everlasting repudiation of the administration."[19] Hearst's *New York Journal* printed a cartoon showing the president as a woman wearing a bonnet and apron, and the *Chicago Tribune* featured a cartoon of him as a coward holding out the white feather of surrender. Republican strategists worried that the Democrats would soon be campaigning under the slogan "Cuba Libre" as a means of discrediting McKinley and his party.[20]

Demands for a war against Spain were also grounded in the negative views of Spain and of the Spanish people held by most Americans, who had imbibed these prejudices from various sources but especially in school. Textbooks invariably presented the Spanish as greedy and cruel, which allegedly stemmed from the basic Spanish character, and condemned the way Spain had treated indigenous peoples in South and Central America—while conveniently ignoring the cruelty of English settlers toward Native Americans, actions that continued under the government of the United States in the decades after independence. The Spanish, it was also claimed, had no capacity for good government, and Spanish culture was rooted in the "superstitions" of medieval Catholicism (channeling a longstanding anti-Catholicism among many Americans). Such widespread views of Spain made it easy, indeed automatic, for Americans to assume that Spanish authorities in Cuba had purposely, with malice aforethought, blown up the *Maine*.[21]

Given McKinley's great popularity, he arguably could have mounted a campaign for patience while continuing to pursue a diplomatic solution. To be successful, he would have had to build a public case during the past year against going to war with Spain. However, throughout his public life, McKinley had been a very willing political compromiser. Another path for the president could have been to give strong support to powerful members of the Senate, such as Nelson W. Aldrich, William B. Allison, Mark Hanna, George F. Hoar, Orville H. Platt, and John C. Spooner, all of whom had acted earlier to block resolutions recognizing the Cuban rebels or giving them the status of belligerents. The president could have also allied himself with the powerful Speaker of the House, Thomas B. Reed, who was adamantly opposed to a war with Spain. Yet McKinley failed to take any of these men into his confidence and thereby stiffen the legislators' resolve to stand against war.

Instead, McKinley's method of avoiding war had been to say as little as possible about the Cuban situation. He said nothing about Cuba in any of his public addresses and remained silent when the *Maine* exploded and sank. Not wanting to buck public opinion, he became paralyzed to act and allowed himself to slide into a war he dreaded. Later he confided to a former private secretary, "[The] declaration of war against Spain was an act which has been and always will be the greatest grief of my life. I never wanted to go to war with Spain. Had I been let [alone] I could have prevented [it]. All I wanted was more time."[22]

As the cries for war mounted, the president had to take drugs to sleep, dark circles appeared around his eyes, and he aged noticeably. A friend who went to see McKinley reported that the president "broke down and cried like a boy of thirteen."[23] Finally bowing to pressure from legislators, the newspapers, the Republican Party, and public opinion, he asked Congress for a declaration of war, "in the name of humanity, in the name of civilization, [and] in behalf of endangered American interests."[24] Congress obliged and declared war on April 25. The vote was overwhelming for war in the House of Representatives by a vote of 311 to six. In the Senate, it was closer at forty-two to thirty-five. According to the resolution, the war would be fought, "For the recognition of the independence of the people of Cuba, demanding that the Government of Spain relinquish its authority and Government in the island of Cuba and withdraw its land and naval forces from Cuba and Cuban waters, and directing the President of the United States to use the land and naval forces of the United States to carry these resolutions into effect."[25]

At the last moment, Spain, bowing to the request of Pope Leo XIII, pledged that it would declare a unilateral armistice in Cuba. By then it was too late. The United States was determined to fight. In addition, the question remains whether armed American intervention was necessary to secure Cuban independence. By the time war was declared, some 50,000 Cuban rebels had occupied most of the island, and it may have been only a matter of time until they prevailed without armed intervention by the United States. A more watchful and resolute William McKinley might have prevented a conflict that he did not want.[26]

The great majority of American soldiers who died in the war over Cuba did not lose their lives as warriors on the battlefield. Although 345 of them perished in combat, 5,462 died of sickness due to lax sanitation practices, tropical diseases, and an almost total lack of sufficient medical facilities and care. Spanish losses are very unclear, especially since they had been fighting the Cuban rebels before the US entry into the conflict.

Even before the declaration of war against Spain on April 25, 1898, the United States laid the basis for the possibility of a war in the Philippines. Following orders, the commander of the US Asian fleet, Admiral George Dewey, prepared to attack Spanish naval forces in Manila Bay as part of an all-out move on Spanish assets. Dewey followed through immediately after the war declaration and easily demolished the decrepit Spanish fleet in Manila Bay on May 1, with only one American death. An English historian later described the battle as "a military execution rather than a real contest."[27]

Having achieved his objective, Dewey was unsure what to do next. His only orders had been to destroy the Spanish fleet but he assumed that he should go ahead to capture the City of Manila itself. The American fleet could not stay off Manila indefinitely without re-supplying, and all the ports in Asia were closed to him under international law. He could have steamed back to the United States, which would have seemed a repudiation of his victory, and faced an outraged public that had exulted over his success, with no real understanding of the serious, long-term consequences. Realizing that a land force would be needed to take Manila, Dewey cabled Washington for troops.

President McKinley now found himself in a quandary over what to do about the Philippines. Taking the islands had never been part of the initial war aims, either in McKinley's reluctant statements about the need to fight Spain or in Congress's declaration of war, which had called only for liberating Cuba. After agonizing for weeks, the president decided that the Filipinos were not fit for self-government and therefore could not be allowed their independence. While giving them back to Spain, he declared, would be cowardly and dishonorable. He added that it would also make no sense to turn the islands over to commercial rivals such as Britain, France, or Germany. Besides, the American people would be outraged if the United States failed to keep the Philippines as a trophy of war. Moreover, a desire to increase trade with China led to claims that an American presence in the Philippines would put the country in a better position to assert its trading rights in China, even though most Chinese were desperately poor by western standards and in no position at the time to purchase many American goods.

On June 12, 1898, the leader of the Philippine rebels, Emilio Aguinaldo, announced a declaration of independence from Spain. Then reaching out for American support, Aguinaldo sent an associate named Felipe Agoncillo as his personal representative to Washington to see McKinley and solicit his support for Philippine independence. Agoncillo met with the president on October 1, but went away empty-handed. He then journeyed to Paris, where the peace talks between the United States and Spain were taking place and where both sides ignored him. He then wrote a memorandum to the US State Department setting forth the case for Philippine independence. It, too, fell on deaf ears.

McKinley wired the American peace commissioners in Paris on October 28 that they should demand the annexation of the Philippines. The rationale put forward was the "right of conquest," but this was a weak claim in international law since the United States had not yet occupied Manila, the capital of the Philippines, when Spain had sued for peace in July. To overcome this objection, the United States agreed to pay Spain $20 million to help defray its debt in the islands. By then, there were several thousand American troops in the Philippines who had been sent to secure the islands. An uneasy standoff ensued between the American occupiers and the Filipino revolutionaries until early February 1899, when General Elwell Otis, the US commander, ordered his troops to advance to the Filipino lines just outside Manila. On the night of February 4, an American sentry fired on and killed three Filipino soldiers, which touched off fierce fighting the next day. Aguinaldo had not wanted to open hostilities with the Americans and even sent a man out under a flag of truce to report that the fighting had commenced without his orders and offered to set up a neutral zone between the two sides. Otis refused the offer and insisted that the fighting had to go on to "the grim end."[28]

The orders from Otis for troops to move toward the Filipino lines were obviously provocative. Contrary to what had taken place on February 4, the McKinley administration reported to the press that the Filipino insurgents had attacked Manila, when in truth they had stationed themselves outside the city. As with the situation on the Rio Grande fifty years before, McKinley, like Polk, insisted falsely that the United States had been attacked without provocation. Regardless of the evidence, the United States was hell-bent on waging war. All told, the McKinley administration sent some 75,000 troops to the Philippines. Congress could have stopped any escalation of American military action in the Philippines through its power of the purse (i.e., by refusing to authorize the necessary expenditures), but the Republicans controlled both houses of the national legislature and they were not about to withdraw support from a Republican president, which would have meant questioning whether McKinley had told the truth about the incident that had ignited the fighting. And any dubious Democrats at the time did not want to be accused of lacking in patriotism.

Ironically, given its own revolutionary heritage, the United States had decided to make war against forces that were fighting for independence and self-determination in a place located halfway around the world. In the process, the American military under Commander-in-Chief McKinley committed unspeakable atrocities against the Filipino people. They wiped out entire villages because they suspected the inhabitants were harboring rebels or supporting them in some way. They also herded people into filthy camps that were much like those set up by Spain as a tactic for breaking the rebellion in Cuba, which had only a few years earlier been cited as reasons for American intervention there. Americans also used waterboarding and other forms of torture to extract information from rebels.

Predictably, those who criticized the war were accused of both cowardice and a lack of patriotism. In his Memorial Day address in 1902, President Theodore Roosevelt, who had become president following McKinley's assassination the previous September, excoriated what he called "the councils of unmanly weakness." Americans in the Philippines, he insisted, were undertaking "a great work for civilization. . . . All honor to them; and shame, thrice shame, to us if we fail to uphold their hands."[29] (Imperial powers claiming that they were mainly interested in civilizing supposedly backward peoples was a standard excuse at the time.)

Before the conflict in the Philippines ended officially in 1902, it claimed 4,234 American lives. Estimates are that about 34,000 "rebels" were killed and that as many as 200,000 Filipino civilians lost their lives from direct and indirect causes. According to some Filipino sources, civilian deaths were over 1 million. President McKinley did not have to order troops to put down the Filipino freedom fighters, especially once Aguinaldo had reached out a hand of friendship to the United States and asked for recognition of Philippine independence. Instead, the United States could have offered encouragement and support for Philippine independence and could have warded off other imperial powers.

Vietnam Hubris

Unfortunately, future presidents would learn little or nothing from the unnecessary wars against Mexico, Spain, and the Philippines. This failure was nowhere more evident than in the protracted and devastating War in Vietnam, to which the United States began committing itself as early as 1946 and which lasted for nearly three decades. This conflict was part of the larger Cold War, a simmering contention between the Soviet Union and the United States and their respective allies.

According to historian and Kennedy advisor Arthur Schlesinger, Jr., it was the Cold War that resulted in the belief that the United States had "the duty and the right to intervene swiftly in every part of the world." This view, Schlesinger added, resulted in an ever greater "centralization of war and peace in the Presidency." With it came "an unprecedented exclusion of the rest of the executive branch, of Congress, of the press and of public opinion in general from these decisions," and "at the expense of the Constitutional order."[30]

As Second World War was ending, President Franklin Roosevelt had announced himself against the resumption of European imperialism. However, Roosevelt died on April 12, 1945, less than a month before the German surrender in Europe and some four months before Japan's capitulation ended the war in the Pacific, which represented the official end of Second World War. Whether he could have followed through on his opposition to a return to European imperialism can never be known.

Succeeding Roosevelt and guiding American foreign policy during the first years of the Cold War was his vice president, Harry S. Truman. Although Truman had been a US Senator before becoming vice president, he had not dealt extensively with foreign affairs while a member of the Senate. Furthermore, during his short tenure as vice president, he had talked to President Roosevelt only twice and had not been made privy to the president's plans for a postwar world.

Immediately after the end of Second World War, Truman initiated the American involvement in Vietnam, which would result almost entirely in a presidential war based all too often on deception, misrepresentation, and outright lies. Vietnam had been part of a French colony known as Indochina, made up of Vietnam, Laos, and Cambodia. In September 1940, the Japanese invaded and took over Vietnam a little more than three months after the Germans had defeated and occupied France. Then at the end of Second World War, Japan was forced to relinquish Vietnam, along with other areas it had conquered over the years.

On September 2, 1945, the day of Japan's formal surrender to the United States, Ho Chi Minh, who had led the Vietnamese resistance to its Japanese occupiers, proclaimed Vietnamese independence with himself as head of the independence movement. During the ceremony, Ho partly quoted from the American Declaration of Independence of 1776: "All men are created equal, endowed by their creator with inalienable rights: Among these are life, liberty, and the pursuit of Happiness." Afterwards, at a gala celebration in Hanoi, he referred to the recently drafted charter of the United Nations, which called for national self-determination, also a principle of the Declaration of Independence that both Woodrow Wilson and Franklin Roosevelt had embraced as centerpieces of their international politics. Ho even had the band play the US National Anthem. He clearly hoped for American recognition, believing that the other great powers would follow suit. He added that if the French attempted to return, the Vietnamese people would "fight to the bitter end."[31]

Between October 1945 and February 1946, Ho wrote eight letters addressed to Truman or to his Secretary of State James Byrnes, asking for American support, appealing to them as "guardians and champions of world justice," and hoping to open a dialogue with the president.[32]Neither Truman nor anyone in his administration answered these missives, assuming they could not trust Ho or any other Communist leader. Instead, Truman supported France's return to its Vietnamese colony. The president had come to believe he needed French support in blocking the spread of Communism in Europe, and in return, the French argued that Communism had to be thwarted everywhere. Thus, in late 1946, Truman arranged a $160 million line of credit for military aid to France, knowing that it would be used against the rebels in Vietnam. He did so even though the French themselves believed they faced an uphill battle to re-conquer the country. But after being humiliated by Germany in Second World War, which included four years of German occupation, France was determined to reassert itself as a great power, and this reassertion meant regaining its colonies. Rather than make the sort of raw imperial claims that would have been acceptable in another age, they used the cover of crusading against Communism. The existence of Truman's monetary support to the French, along with Ho Chi Minh's letters seeking American support, remained unknown to the public for another quarter of a century, which meant there would be no questioning of the president's actions by Congress, the press, or the public.

In reality, there was little possibility that either Ho or the Vietnamese people would become lackeys to China or the Soviet Union, given their fervent nationalism and fierce desire for independence. They had fought off the Chinese for centuries, after which they had resisted the French and then the Japanese, a reality that Truman apparently did not appreciate at the time. In any case, as journalist and historian Marvin Kalb has written, "Truman did not have to take this step [in Vietnam]. He could have chosen to fight the Republicans at home and support the French in Europe but not in Vietnam."[33] Instead, he prepared the ground for an ongoing American commitment to Vietnam that would end in disaster for the United States.[34]

In addition to pressure from the French, Truman felt pressure on Vietnam from growing criticisms by Republicans who were bitter over losing the presidency five times in a row (1932, 1936, 1940, 1944, and 1948). As a strategy for fighting back and hopefully regaining the White House, Republicans increasingly accused Truman and the Democrats of being "soft on Communism"—that is, of not combating the Communist menace with sufficient vigor. The victory in the long-running Chinese Civil War of Mao Zedong's (Mao Tse-tung's) Communists over Nationalist Chiang Kai-shek (Jiang Jieshi) in October 1949 especially proved a godsend to those who wanted to heap abuse on the Truman administration.

In late 1945, Truman had sent General George Marshall, who was Army Chief of Staff during Second World War and who would later become Secretary of State and Secretary of Defense, on a fact-finding mission to China. At the end of his China visit in early 1947, Marshall concluded that Chiang was his own worst enemy. His rule was corrupt, incompetent, and tyrannical, and he could not attract the support of the Chinese people, who increasingly sided with Mao and the Communists. Marshall added that Chiang could not win the Chinese civil war without massive American assistance, including huge numbers of ground troops and massive air strikes. He warned Truman that the United States would virtually have "to take over the Chinese government" and remain there indefinitely in the face of fierce and continued Communist resistance.

Senator Joseph R. McCarthy, who soon became notorious for his wild accusations of disloyalty in the federal government, accused Marshall of being a Communist appeaser. Republican Senator Robert Hale of Maine and Congressman Walter Judd of Minnesota joined McCarthy in excoriating Truman for supposedly betraying China and pursuing policies that favored the Communists. Another leading spokesperson of the China Lobby was Henry Luce, the son of Presbyterian missionaries, who had grown up in China and was the publisher of the very influential *Time* and *Life* magazines. All too often, Truman reacted to such unjust criticism by making unwise decisions to prove he was not soft on Communism, including his continuing commitment to the French in Vietnam. The outbreak of the Korean War in 1950, when the Communist North Koreans invaded South Korea and the United States committed itself to using armed force to throw back the invasion, also meant that Truman would have to stay the course in Vietnam.

The Republicans finally won the White House again in 1952 with Dwight D. Eisenhower, who now inherited the American policy in Vietnam. In 1954, Eisenhower surreptitiously diverted some $300 million in supplies earmarked for Korea to be added to the $800 million already allotted for Vietnam that year. When it was clear in the spring of 1954 that the French were going to be defeated in Vietnam at the Battle of Diem Bien Phu, Eisenhower sent forty B-26 bombers, along with a number of air force technicians, with the idea of bombing Viet Minh positions as they tightened their ring around the French. The strikes never occurred because of strenuous objections from the Congressional leadership, but, unfortunately, such legislative objections would not be sustained in the long run.[35]

In the wake of the French defeat at Diem Bien Phu, Eisenhower privately expressed his disgust at the way they had allowed the enemy to occupy the high ground and then to defeat them. He never had any intention of sending American troops to bail out the French. Nor did he have any patience with the chairman of his Joint Chiefs of Staff, Admiral Arthur Radford, who advocated using nuclear weapons against the Vietnamese Communists. At the same time, Eisenhower did not want to be attacked by conservative members of his own Republican Party for "losing Vietnam," in the same way they had castigated Truman for "losing China." Yet given his great prestige and popularity, he probably could have gotten away with honestly explaining to the American people why a continuing American commitment in Vietnam was a great mistake.

At a peace conference in Geneva, Switzerland, which ended in the so-called Geneva Accords of 1954, the participants agreed to divide Vietnam "temporarily" along the seventeenth parallel, with the Communists in charge of the northern part and a non-Communist regime in charge of the southern part. Popular elections in 1956 would then allow the people of Vietnam to decide what kind of government they wanted in a united Vietnam. The United States sent an observer to Geneva but did not sign the accords. Still, the United States pledged that it would respect the agreements on Vietnam and would do nothing to interfere with their implementation. Within a year, the United States broke its word when it became apparent that even the freest elections in Vietnam would deliver an overwhelming victory to Ho Chi Minh and the Communists in both North and South Vietnam. Claiming the United States was not bound by the provisions of the Geneva Accords, since it had not signed them, Eisenhower backed the South Vietnamese government in its refusal to hold elections in their part of the country.[36] Eisenhower also approved military aid for South Vietnam, and by the time he left office, the United States had some 1,700 military advisors in the country. The Eisenhower administration claimed it would create a stable, non-Communist government in South Vietnam and succeed where the French had failed. Tens of thousands of Americans and hundreds of thousands of Vietnamese would pay with their lives for this hubris.

After winning the 1960 presidential election, John F. Kennedy had to cope with Vietnam. As a young senator, he had thought the French should clear out of Indochina, that its peoples should be free to chart their own course, and that the United States should not interfere. However, now that he was president, some of his advisors urged him to intervene militarily in Laos against the Communist Pathet Lao. On the contrary, Kennedy thought such intervention was a bad idea for several reasons, including uncertainty over how the Soviets would react.

General Charles de Gaulle, then President of France and a man who knew something about the futility of fighting an insurgency in Southeast Asia, advised Kennedy not to send troops to Laos. Instead, Kennedy decided to broker an agreement with the Soviets, the Chinese, and other interested parties, including Britain and France, for neutrality in Laos. According to the agreement hammered out at a conference in Geneva from May 1961 to July 1962, a coalition government would be assembled in Laos, and foreign troops as well as foreign military bases would be forbidden in the country. Kennedy—and most everyone else who understood the situation—realized that such a coalition government would sooner or later lead to a Communist victory, but the arrangement had the virtue of buying time and giving the president a good excuse for not committing troops. In fact, both the United States and the Soviet Union were soon violating the agreement by sending arms and supplies into Laos, but neither side objected and, "officially," the agreement held.

Neutrality might have been a solution for Vietnam, but Kennedy worried that if he did not take a stand somewhere in Indochina he would be accused of weakness on Communism. He still did not want to commit combat forces and even solicited the advice of retired General Douglas MacArthur, who said it "would be foolish to fight on the Asian continent and that the future of Southeast Asia should be determined at the diplomatic table." The general added that "there was no end to Asia," and that even if the United States "poured a million American infantry soldiers into that continent, we would still find ourselves outnumbered on every side."[37] This prediction would be tragically borne out by future events. Kennedy fell back to sending more military advisors to assist the South Vietnamese in standing up to the enemy and continued to give millions of dollars in aid to the Saigon regime but did not commit American combat units.

Among all the other problems in Vietnam was the fact that the conflict was a genuine civil war. It was not just a case of aggression by the North Vietnamese (known as the Viet Minh) against South Vietnam, but internecine fighting in the South between Communist supporters (the Viet Cong) and the non-Communist government in Saigon. If that were not enough, the South Vietnamese government, headed by President Ngo Dinh Diem, was corrupt and dictatorial.

To buy time, Kennedy sent Secretary of Defense Robert McNamara and General Maxwell Taylor on another fact-finding mission to Vietnam. As so often in the past with such missions, the advice they offered the president was contradictory. However, they presented a rosy picture to the media of South Vietnamese military successes, along with the prediction that most American troops could be withdrawn from Vietnam by the end of 1965. In the meantime, Kennedy continued to send American military advisors to Vietnam, some 17,000 in all by the end of his presidency. Although the American commitment to the war was growing, Kennedy, like Truman and Eisenhower before him, did not solicit official approval from Congress and did not level with the public about the progress of the war.

By late 1963, Republicans were criticizing Kennedy for being indecisive on Vietnam. One of his aides, Kenneth O'Donnell, reported Kennedy as saying that "he'd be damned everywhere as a communist appeaser" if he got out of Vietnam before the election, adding, "But I can do it after I'm reelected."[38] Historians have debated over the years whether Kennedy would have ended the American commitment to Vietnam if elected for a second term. The doubters have said that Kennedy never would have done so and thereby handed the Republicans ammunition to use against him and his party. Kennedy's assassination on November 22, 1963, meant the question would never be answered.

It would now be up to Kennedy's vice president and successor Lyndon B. Johnson to take hold of an increasingly slippery Vietnam imbroglio. Johnson worried sincerely about the Communist threat and was painfully aware of how Democrats under Truman had been falsely accused of "losing China." "I am not going to lose Vietnam," he told the American ambassador to Saigon. "I am not going to be the president who saw Southeast Asia go the way China went."[39]

However, Johnson did not want to escalate the war until after the 1964 presidential election. At the same time, he had to show himself to be tough on Communism during a campaign in which he faced Republican nominee Senator Barry Goldwater, who called for a stronger stand against Communism and charged that Johnson was not up to the task. Johnson and his team countered by saying Goldwater was a trigger-happy extremist who well might get into a nuclear war with the Soviet Union. Throughout the campaign, Johnson vowed, "We are not about to send American boys nine or ten thousand miles to do what Asian boys ought to be doing for themselves."[40] Soon, Johnson would do exactly that.

Giving Johnson an opening to send combat troops to Vietnam were two allegedly unprovoked attacks on American naval destroyers operating in the Tonkin Gulf off the coast of North Vietnam. The first occurred on the night of August 2, 1964, when North Vietnamese PT boats began firing at the *USS Maddox*, which was engaged in a spying mission from waters off North Vietnam. The American ship was not harmed, and no American sailors were killed, while US aircraft in the vicinity sank one of the PT boats. Two days later, another US destroyer, the *Turner Joy*, reported during a tropical storm that it was picking up odd radar signals and assumed that it was about to be attacked. The skipper was taking no chances and opened fire.

It is now known that Johnson and his White House advisors realized there was no attack that second night. In the words of Undersecretary of State George Ball, Johnson had told him, "I just think those dumb soldiers were shooting at flying fish. I don't think there was any, any attack."[41] Nevertheless, the president went on television to tell the American people there had been hostile actions against the United States in the Tonkin Gulf and that he had ordered US military forces to take retaliatory action. The president followed through by asking Congress for a resolution allowing him to counter Communist aggression in Vietnam. On August 6, Secretary of Defense McNamara testified before a joint meeting of the Senate Foreign Relations and Armed Services committees. He reported less than truthfully that the *Maddox* had only been "carrying out a routine mission of the type we carry out all over the world at all times." When asked, he denied that the United States had played any part in South Vietnamese patrol boat raids on the offshore islands of Hon. Me and Hon. Nieu on the nights of July 30 and July 31. In fact, these raids had been carried out by US-trained South Vietnamese commandos under the control of an American special operations unit.

On August 10, both the House and Senate passed the so-called Tonkin Gulf Resolution by overwhelming majorities. As with both Polk's war message about Mexico and McKinley's statements about Cuba and the Philippines, the legislators had not been told the whole truth. However, members did not insist on holding their own investigations into what had happened in the Tonkin Gulf. Nor did the legislators know that the administration had written the resolution weeks before in anticipation of the need to use it. In many ways, the administration's claims before Congress were reminiscent of the assertions that President Polk had made back in 1846 when he claimed that Mexican troops had attacked American forces in Texas, or that President McKinley had made in 1899 when he asserted that Filipino rebels had assaulted American troops outside Manila. It is also chilling to realize that both Johnson and Polk had drafted justifications for war in advance of finding supposedly justifiable incidents to put before Congress and had them ready when any excuse should arise, no matter how dubious.

The Tonkin Gulf Resolution gave the administration authority "to take all necessary measures to repel an armed attack against the United States and to prevent further aggression."[42] The resolution did not specify that these measures were valid only for Vietnam, and thus it could be argued that they applied anywhere in the world. Johnson might have asked Congress for a specific declaration of war against North Vietnam. As he explained later, he feared that such a declaration might touch off war with China or the Soviet Union in case either of these countries had mutual defense treaties with North Vietnam that would require them to defend the North in a war with the United States.

With the Tonkin Gulf Resolution in his pocket and his reelection to the presidency accomplished in November, Johnson unabashedly did what he accused Goldwater of wanting to do: He began escalating the war. By the spring of 1965, the South Vietnamese army was on the verge of collapse. The president reacted by increasing American troop strength in Vietnam and authorizing them to move from providing base security and military advice to carrying out combat missions against communist forces in the South. Over the next three years, Johnson sent more and more troops to Vietnam, until there were over 500,000 fighting both the Vietcong (communists in South Vietnam) and the Vietminh (communist forces from the North). And once "American boys" were coming home in body bags, Johnson could not and would not consider backing out, for that could mean the Americans who died there had died in vain, the same trap in which McKinley and Theodore Roosevelt had found themselves ensnared in the Philippines.

In public, and especially in televised addresses and news conferences, Johnson falsely insisted that the United States was winning the war. Then in January 1968 came the Lunar New Year's Tet Offensive. North Vietnamese troops attacked more than 100 cities and villages and entered Saigon itself, where they briefly occupied the grounds of the US embassy. American forces beat them back and, in the end, the offensive failed. Yet the fact that the "enemy" was able to pull off these attacks gave the lie to what the administration was saying about the war. More than ever before, what was called the "credibility gap" was widening—the difference between administration claims and realities on the ground in Vietnam.

In the aftermath of Tet, it became clear to Johnson and his advisors that the United States had no plausible military strategy for either winning the war or for getting out of Vietnam without complete humiliation. There was serious talk among the president's national security advisors of using nuclear weapons against North Vietnam, even if it meant having to take on China and the Soviet Union. Meanwhile, anti-war protests grew increasingly massive. Outside the White House, protesters chanted, "Hey, hey, LBJ, how many kids did you kill today?" At that point, about 300 American soldiers were losing their lives every week. Johnson denounced the protesters for being unpatriotic and accused them of giving aid and comfort to the enemy. Then, concluding that he could not win another term as president, Johnson announced on March 31, 1968, in a nationally televised address, that he would not seek the Democratic Party's nomination.

Just two weeks before Johnson's announcement, US Senator Robert Kennedy, brother of slain President John Kennedy, entered the race for the Democratic nomination as an outspoken critic of the Vietnam War, who promised that, if elected, he would end American participation in that conflict. Johnson gave the nod to Vice President Hubert Humphrey, who was handicapped by his association with what many had come to call "Johnson's war." By early June, after he had won the California primary, Kennedy seemed well on his way to capturing the Democratic nomination and seemed poised to end the war if he won the presidency. Following his victory celebration in California, Kennedy was shot and killed at the Ambassador Hotel in Los Angeles as he was making his way through the hotel's kitchen en route to a press conference elsewhere in the building. With Kennedy dead, Humphrey was a cinch for the nomination.

The Democrats' convention held in Chicago in late August turned out to be a disaster for the party. Outside the convention hall, Chicago police and the Illinois National Guard attacked protesters, resulting in what many called a police riot. Millions of Americans saw the violent melee on television, and many viewers, through guilt by association, blamed the Democrats for the rioting. The violence outside the convention floor provided a perfect campaign theme for Richard Nixon, who received the Republican nomination. Nixon promised to restore law and order in the country and, realizing the great unpopularity of the war, said he had a "secret plan" for ending it. Leading Humphrey in the early polls, Nixon's numbers began to slip after Humphrey distanced himself from Johnson and the war. Some analysts believed that if the campaign had lasted another ten days or so, Humphrey would have won. Unknown for nearly half century, Nixon also secretly dissuaded the South Vietnamese government through intermediaries from cooperating with peace negotiations that Johnson had proposed after deciding not to run again, fearing that peace talks would benefit the Democratic candidate.[43] Nixon's approach to the Vietnamese while a "civilian" was clearly against the Logan Act passed by Congress in 1799. The act makes it a crime for an unauthorized American citizen to attempt to negotiate a dispute between the United States and a foreign government, punishable by up to three years in prison.[44]

As it turned out, Nixon won 43.42 percent of the popular vote to Humphrey's 42.72 percent. Third-party candidate George Wallace won 8.6 percent of the popular tally. In the Electoral College, Nixon led Humphrey 301 to 191, with Wallace at forty-six electoral votes. The so-called secret plan to end the war, as well as the illegal sabotaging of peace talks, probably had much to do with Nixon's victory. If Robert Kennedy, with his famous name and star power, had not been killed, it is very likely that Nixon never would have made it into the White House and equally likely that Kennedy would have pulled out of Vietnam. The American people were already paying a high price for Richard Nixon, but this was only the beginning.

Nixon Goes to China

Nixon knew very well when he took office that the Vietnam War was unwinnable.

National Security Advisor Henry Kissinger also knew it, and Nixon did genuinely wish to get out of Vietnam. However, he did not want to be seen as losing a war, and he did not want the United States to leave Vietnam in ignominious defeat, which is why he constantly talked about "peace with honor." Unfortunately, like Johnson, Kennedy, Eisenhower, and Truman before him, Nixon failed to understand Ho Chi Minh and his determination to fight on no matter what. Nor did he appreciate that Ho would demand both a military and a political settlement that required the United States to withdraw all its troops and that would clear the way for him to take over all of Vietnam. Because Nixon would not agree to these terms, the killing continued for the entire five and a half years of his presidency.

Nixon astounded many on both the right and left when he announced plans for a visit to the People's Republic of China (i.e., Communist China) in February 1972. Over the years, he had been a leading anti-Communist and had vehemently opposed any move to recognize "Red China." Nixon's talks with Mao Zedong (Mao Tse-tung) and foreign minister Zhou Enlai (Chou En-lai) did not lead immediately to diplomatic recognition, but the United States promised to withdraw its forces from Taiwan and to accept, in principle, that Taiwan was part of China. The talks led to further dialogue between the two countries, and in 1978, the United States extended full diplomatic recognition to the People's Republic, nearly three decades after Mao's victory over Chinese Nationalist Chiang Kai-shek. Nixon realized full well that no Democrat could have made this move toward China, but with impeccable credentials as an anti-Communist, he would be above suspicion and reproach. As Nixon himself put it, "Those on the right can do what those on the left can only talk about."[45] In fact, if a Democratic president had even mentioned such a mission to China, Nixon himself would have surely ripped into him for being soft on Communism—or worse.

There were concerns that the Soviet Union would take the Chinese trip as a calculated slight, which, in fact, Nixon wanted them to do. Consequently, the Soviets invited Nixon to come to Moscow for a summit in May 1972, with the main goal of agreeing to a Strategic Arms Limitation Treaty (SALT). Nixon and Soviet Premier Leonid Brezhnev agreed to recognize the status quo in Berlin that for a quarter century had been a flashpoint, opening the way for the East and West German governments to sign treaties recognizing each other and formally assenting to the division of Germany. The diplomatic establishment as well as the news media used the term détente to label these better relations between East and West.

Nixon's visit to China and his agreements with the Soviet Union in 1972 were extraordinary achievements that would, less than two decades later, contribute to ending the Cold War. But Nixon's triangulation did not immediately help to stop the Vietnam conflict. The war went on, and as more and more American troops were pulled out and it looked increasingly likely that the Communists were winning, Nixon responded with savage bombing of North Vietnam, the destruction of dams, and the mining of Haiphong Harbor. Nixon wanted the Chinese, the Soviets, and the North Vietnamese to think that he had gone crazy and would stop at nothing to win the war. Journalist Marvin Kalb recalls that senior State Department officials were purposely telling reporters such things as, "Nixon has gone mad." "No one can control him anymore—he's nuts."[46]

Meanwhile the peace talks, which had been initiated by Johnson, initially sabotaged by Nixon, and commencing once Nixon became president, were dragging on in Paris. Nixon hoped his hard line would force the North Vietnamese negotiators to see reason, but they demanded a unilateral withdrawal of American troops and the destruction of the South Vietnamese regime as a precondition for serious talks. Nixon refused these demands from what he called that "little shit ass country."[47] In March 1969, he ordered the bombing of Communist supply lines in neighboring Cambodia. Realizing that these air raids would provoke a new wave of antiwar demonstrations, Nixon ordered the operations to take place in secret. In April 1970, he again ordered attacks on Communist forces in Cambodia with American and South Vietnamese ground forces. This time he announced his decision over nationwide television, unleashing campus protests from one end of the country to another. At Kent State University in Ohio, panicky National Guard troops fired their weapons into a group of rock-throwing students, killing four and seriously wounding nine others. Several days later, students were shot and killed at Mississippi's Jackson State University. Students across the nation reacted in fury, occupying administration buildings, boycotting classes, and demonstrating wherever they could. Many colleges simply closed for the balance of the semester to avoid further violence and upheaval.

There was also widespread and growing opposition in Congress. Legislators responded by requiring American troops to withdraw from Cambodia within thirty days, the first formal move by Congress to limit American participation in the Southeast Asia war. Despite Congress's clear opposition to widening the conflict, Nixon defiantly ordered American air support for a South Vietnamese invasion of Laos in February 1971. However, he continued to remove American troops from South Vietnam. Then in October 1972, the North Vietnamese, acting under pressure from the Soviets, signaled their willingness to resume serious talks. Negotiators in Paris agreed that the remaining 60,000 American troops would leave Vietnam, with Communist forces maintaining their current positions in the field, while South Vietnamese President Thieu would remain in power for the time being. Thieu rejected the peace plan, and Nixon resumed heavy bombing over Christmas 1972. In January 1973, both sides finally accepted an agreement that was little different from the one proposed in October, and American participation in the Vietnam War finally ended. Over 58,000 Americans had died and more than 300,000 were wounded in the nation's longest war. About a million Vietnamese were killed and millions made homeless.

It was only a matter of time until the Communists triumphed in South Vietnam, a foregone conclusion for many years. In April 1974, Saigon fell to North Vietnamese and Vietcong forces. The United States had clearly lost a war that had been unwinnable from the beginning and that it never should have fought. The fate of Vietnam had nothing to do with American security or with genuine American national interests. From beginning to end, it was a very political war, since none of the presidents in power during the Vietnam years, including President Eisenhower, wanted to be accused of "losing Vietnam." The Democrats especially feared it would be political suicide to pull out and face a firestorm of accusations from the Republicans.

Confirming the suspicions of anti-war groups was the publication by the *New York Times* and the *Washington Post* in 1971 of the Pentagon Papers. Its official title was *United States—Vietnam Relations, 1945–1967: A Study Prepared by the Department of Defense*. The most damning observation was that four presidential administrations—those of Truman, Eisenhower, Kennedy, and Johnson—had misled the public about their intentions in Vietnam and had painted falsely optimistic pictures about the progress of the war. These deceptions included schemes to provoke North Vietnam into launching a major military strike that would justify widespread retaliation by the United States. The papers also recounted that the Johnson administration justified the war as necessary for "containing" China and stopping it from organizing "all Asia against the United States." It did not seem to matter that Ho Chi Minh would no more tolerate Chinese domination than he would domination by the United States—and before that, domination by France or Japan. Perhaps most devastating of all was proof that four administrations in a row had misled, dissembled, and outright lied in their efforts to sell the war to Congress and the American people. Richard Nixon's reaction to the Pentagon Papers, discussed later, would ultimately force him to resign as president.

The unnecessary Vietnam War no doubt contributed to the continuation of the Cold War and to the very real danger of a nuclear holocaust. Although the threat of Communism was real, the United States was never in danger of being taken over by Communism from either domestic or foreign entities. Maintaining a strong defense, containing Communism in Europe, trusting in the best of what America represented, and being willing earlier to explore possibilities of understanding with China and the Soviet Union would have been a far better approach. Unfortunately, partisan warriors too often ruled the day and put American foreign policy in a straitjacket from which it could not escape.

9/11 and Iraq Falsehoods

Large majorities both in and outside of government were determined in the aftermath of Vietnam that the United States would not again make the mistake of fighting an unnecessary war anywhere on the globe. Yet only a generation after the end of the Vietnam conflict, the country launched a disastrous war in Iraq decided entirely by President George W. Bush. He had lost the popular vote against Albert Gore, Jr. in the 2000 election, and having lost the popular vote, Bush could not legitimately claim a strong mandate to govern. Yet he soon acted as if he did enjoy the overwhelming approval and support of the American people. His vice president, Richard "Dick" Cheney, insisted they take on the mantle of a mandate, and in that way force the Washington establishment, the media, and the American people to respect and support the administration.

There has been much debate about Cheney's role in the administration. Some critics have contended that Cheney was the real president and that the inexperienced Bush was a mere puppet in the vice president's hands. Such claims were and are an exaggeration, but during his first term, Bush did lean heavily on Cheney for advice and direction, especially in foreign affairs. Cheney had served for over ten years in the United States House of Representatives, was White House Chief of Staff for two years under President Gerald Ford, and was Secretary of Defense under Bush's father, President George H. W. Bush. As a member of these earlier administrations, Cheney had not stood out as an extreme conservative, which led some observers to suppose that he had somehow changed in the years since then. Colin Powell, the younger Bush's secretary of state, disagreed with this assessment. He contended that Cheney, much younger and much less experienced than Ford or the first president Bush, had been contained by these earlier presidents. In the words of journalist and historian Peter Baker, Cheney had been "surrounded by other adults in the room with experience and gravitas."[48]

Cheney and several key advisors belonged to a loosely knit group known as neo-conservatives (neo-cons for short). These included Cheney's assistant for National Security Affairs I. Lewis "Scooter" Libby, Secretary of Defense Donald Rumsfeld, Deputy Secretary of Defense Paul Wolfowitz, Chairman of the Defense Policy Advisory Board Richard Perle, and Undersecretary for Defense Policy Douglas Feith.

The neo-cons had their roots in the Cold War and the strong consensus of American liberals at that time about the need to combat Communism. When many liberals turned against the war in Vietnam, those who believed the country should continue to oppose Communism by force established the neo-conservative movement. Once the Cold War ended, they wanted to use America's position as the only remaining superpower to shape the world to their liking. Thus, they turned their attention to spreading democracy in authoritarian countries, even if it meant using military force, with the belief that democratic governments were less likely to go to war with each other and would be more sympathetic to the United States. While it may be true that democratic governments are not as likely to go to war with each other, implanting democracy by force in countries where there was no tradition of it would prove to be a very difficult and dangerous enterprise, as well as often impossible to implement.

Surprisingly, given what would transpire, Bush had called for restraint in foreign policy during the 2000 presidential campaign: "I'm not so sure the role of the United States is to go around the world and say, 'This is the way it's got to be.' I just don't think it's the role of the United States to walk into a country and say, we do it this way, so should you. I think the United States must be humble and must be proud and confident of our values, but humble in how we treat nations that are figuring out how to chart their own course." He also warned against American arrogance: "If we're an arrogant nation, they'll resent us. If we're a humble nation, but strong, they'll welcome us. Our nation stands alone right now in the world in terms of power. And that's why we've got to be humble and yet project strength in a way that promotes freedom. We're a freedom-loving nation. If we're an arrogant nation, they'll view us that way, but if we're humble nation, they'll respect us."[49]

Bush's philosophy of foreign policy, as presented during the debates, was both impressive and commendable, representing the best possible approach in dealing with other nations: Remain strong, show a good example to the rest of the world, and refrain from using military power unless it is absolutely necessary. Regrettably, Bush did not practice what he preached when he dragged the United States into one of the most disastrous wars in its history.

Bush wanted to win acclaim as a great president, and the terrorist attacks on the United States on September 11, 2001, offered him such an opportunity. Tellingly, at the meeting of the National Security Council held at the White House on January 30, 2001, just ten days after Bush's inauguration and more than eight months before the September 11 attacks, the group took up the subject of Iraq. Since the end of the Persian Gulf War of 1991, the United States had continued to enforce "no-fly zones" in both the northern and southern parts of Iraq, areas where the Iraqi air force was forbidden to operate. Economic sanctions had also been in place against Iraq, but the Iraqis had found ways to get around them. Secretary of State Colin Powell suggested at the meeting that sanctions be tightened and better enforced. Secretary of Defense Rumsfeld responded by asking, "Why are we even bothering with sanctions?"[50] Far more important to Rumsfeld was locating and destroying weapons of mass destruction (WMD) that he believed were still in Iraq. The president asked Powell to look into tightening sanctions and directed Rumsfeld to examine the military options for addressing the Iraqi situation.

The events of 9/11 are well known, including the two planes that were flown into the World Trade Center in New York City, a third plane that was flown into the Pentagon, and the crash of a fourth aircraft, United Airlines Flight ninety-three, which was en route to Washington for an attack on the nation's capital. In total, nearly 3,000 Americans were killed that day. Following these terrifying events, the neo-cons gained tremendous influence in the administration.

On the evening of September 11, Bush addressed the nation over live television. He proclaimed, "We are at war against terror." But going to war against an amorphous idea was difficult to grasp, which may partly explain why the president added, "We will make no distinction between the terrorists who committed these acts and those who harbored them."[51] Nine days later during a speech to a joint session of Congress on September 20, 2001, the president repeated his declaration of a "war on terror." Not everyone was happy about Bush's use of the word "war." Democrat and US Senate Majority Leader Tom Daschle objected to it at a White House meeting the next day, saying that war was "a very powerful word," adding "this war is so vastly different [from more conventional conflicts]."[52] Besides, it might not result in any tangible victory, which would put both the president and the nation in a very difficult situation wherein failure to achieve an all-out victory could look like defeat.

Bush went further during his State of the Union message the following January 29 to denounce what he called an "axis of evil," whose members were Iran, Iraq, and North Korea. Bush accused all three of aiding terrorists and seeking "weapons of mass destruction." The president's speechwriter Michael Gerson may have used the word axis very consciously as a way of comparing the nation's current enemies to the Axis powers of Second World War, namely Germany, Japan, and Italy. An administration spokesman later tried to qualify the phrase by saying the president had not intended to say that Iran, Iraq, and North Korea were actually collaborating with one another, but that they were all doing the same evil things independently.

The Axis of Evil speech likely would not have been made were it not for the 9/11 attacks. Nor would the neo-cons in the administration have been able to insist on a war in Iraq to topple Saddam Hussein. One of their main arguments in favor of the war was what might be called a "reverse domino theory": During the Cold War against Communism, the principal architects of American foreign policy had insisted that Communism was bound to spread from one country to the next like a row of falling dominos. Thus, it was argued that opposing attempted Communist takeovers, such as in Vietnam, was essential for protecting countries around and beyond it. Some even had gone so far as to insist that Americans had to fight Communism in Southeast Asia so they did not have to fight Communism at home. Now, so the argument went, the United States would implant democracy in Iraq, and it would spread from there throughout the Middle East—a hoped for example of the reverse domino theory.

Bush, Cheney, and the other neo-cons in the administration should have known better than to make this argument, since anyone who has taken a good, basic political science or history course should realize that political systems are extremely difficult or well-nigh impossible to impose from the outside. Instead, political systems evolve slowly out of the culture, traditions, and experiences of a people. Such had been true of the American system of government whose roots went well back into the colonial period when there had been a degree of representative government through the colonial legislatures. American political ideas and practices were also rooted in the centuries-old English common law and various documents of British history, such as the Magna Carta and the English Bill of Rights.

But the democracy argument was not the main assertion initially in the Bush administration's campaign to convince Congress and the American people that an invasion of Iraq was necessary. First, they alleged that Iraq and its leader Saddam Hussein were closely linked to the 9/11 attacks; and, second, that Iraq possessed "weapons of mass destruction" that had to be seized. The day after Bush gave his September 20 address to Congress, he wandered into the office of Richard Clark, his counterterrorism chief. Clark remembered being astounded when the president said, "I want you, as soon as you can, to go back over everything, everything. See if Saddam Hussein did this. See if he's linked in any way." When Clark responded that the culprit was al-Qaeda, the president answered, "I know, I know, but see if Saddam was involved. Just look, I want to know any shred."[53] As it turned out, Saddam Hussein had nothing to do with the 9/11 attacks and he did not possess weapons of mass destruction, but the administration did everything it could to promote these false claims.

During his speech to Congress on September 20, Bush also demanded that the Taliban who controlled Afghanistan must turn over to the United States the leaders of al-Qaeda and shut down their training camps. The demands were not open to discussion, and if they were not met, the Taliban would share the same fate as al-Qaeda. Congress responded by authorizing the president "to use all necessary and appropriate force [and to] preempt any related future acts of terrorism of aggression against the United States." Some critics believed the statement was far too broad and that it would allow the president to do almost anything as commander-in-chief, not unlike the virtually unlimited authority the Tonkin Gulf Resolution had given to President Johnson regarding Vietnam. In any case, Bush held a meeting with his defense team the day after the speech to plan an attack on Afghanistan.

The following day, September 22, Bush held a cabinet meeting at the presidential retreat at Camp David in Maryland. Early on, Assistant Secretary of Defense and outspoken neo-con Paul Wolfowitz began asserting the need to go to war against Iraq and Saddam Hussein. He declared that Afghanistan, the headquarters of al-Qaeda and the hideout of its leader Osama Bin Laden, would not be an especially attractive place for a war since there were so few important targets in this primitive country. Iraq, in contrast, would have plenty of targets to hit. Secretary of State Powell and National Security Advisor Condoleezza Rice were both irritated by Wolfowitz's suggestion. Voicing his dissent, Powell insisted that, "No one will understand or support us doing anything but going after those who attacked us," adding that launching a military campaign against Iraq would shatter the anti-al-Qaeda coalition that the administration was trying to assemble. Rumsfeld retorted that maybe it was "not a coalition worth having." When Wolfowitz persisted in his campaign for an attack against Iraq, the president broke in and said, "How many times do I have to tell you we are *not going* after Iraq right this minute?"[54] Later that day Powell persisted in arguing that Afghanistan should be the target: "Whatever problem Iraq is," he said, "it is not the cause of what happened [on 9/11]."[55]

In any case, the Afghan campaign was extraordinarily successful during the first few months, and by November 2001, the Taliban offered to surrender in exchange for amnesty. However, the Bush administration refused the offer, believing that it could go on to crush the Taliban. Once again, as with the Filipino insurrectionists in 1898 and the Vietnamese independence movement in 1946,[56] the United States, with self-destructive hubris, rejected out of hand serious peace overtures that led to prolonged and costly fighting that cost hundreds of thousands of lives and the unnecessary expenditure of trillions of dollars. Although any surrender deal with the Taliban may have ultimately fallen apart, the United States should have pursued it.

Although Bush did not think the time was right for a war in Iraq, he clearly did not rule it out. Meanwhile, Vice President Cheney began searching for evidence that would justify an invasion of Iraq. When CIA analysts could not come up with the evidence that he wanted—because the facts were either lacking altogether or were very uncertain—Cheney went personally to CIA headquarters and pushed analysts to find the "proofs" he desired. The vice president had already come to his conclusions and wanted to find data to back them up, as opposed to how CIA analysts typically worked by carefully gathering data, verifying it with as many trustworthy sources as possible, and only then drawing conclusions.

Distrustful of the CIA and not satisfied with what they were giving him about Iraq, Cheney's office demanded to be given raw, unconfirmed information from the agency. In particular, Cheney's National Assistant for Security Affairs, Scooter Libby, demanded such raw data from the CIA, believing that he and others could comb it for nuggets of damning information that the agency had missed or was somehow unwilling to take seriously. For instance, Cheney's office used this unverified data and other questionable sources to insist that the Iraqis had tried to purchase "yellowcake" uranium from Niger with which to make nuclear weapons. They also charged that the Iraqis were purchasing aluminum tubes for use in nuclear centrifuges and had built mobile chemical weapons labs. None of these allegations were true: The Iraqis had not tried to purchase yellowcake uranium, the aluminum tubes had been acquired to house conventional artillery shells, and there were no mobile labs. Even after the CIA told the administration that the Niger yellowcake uranium story was very doubtful, the president and others continued to use it in speeches and various other presentations. They also refused to let go of the incorrect tube charges.

The administration's continuing claims that Iraq was linked to 9/11 were likewise false. Their main piece of evidence was a supposed meeting in Prague during April 2001 between Mohamed Atta, the lead 9/11 hijacker, and an Iraqi intelligence agent. Both the CIA and the FBI concluded that such a meeting had never taken place. Reason alone should have also led Cheney and his office to conclude that Saddam and the Iraqis had nothing to gain from any cooperation with al-Qaeda or from any other Islamic terrorist groups. Saddam and his regime were members of the secular Baath Party, the greatest threat to which was Islamic militants such as al-Qaeda.

In trying somehow to blame Iraq for 9/11, the administration was also playing on public credulity. Why would the United States be preparing to go to war in Iraq, many citizens wondered, unless Iraq was responsible in a large way for 9/11? In addition, it was hard for most people to believe such an attack had been possible without state support. Indeed, the Bush administration failed to adjust to the idea that terrorism was largely a stateless phenomenon—or that it could be used as a weapon to destabilize states from the inside.

President Bush never precisely and directly blamed Iraq for the 9/11 attacks, but he continued to drop strong hints to this effect, which caused many to believe that the Iraqis were culpable. For instance, in his 2003 State of the Union address he said, "Imagine those nineteen hijackers with other weapons and other plans—this time armed by Saddam Hussein. It would take one vial, one canister, one crate slipped into this country to bring a day of horror like none we have ever known."[57] On March 16 of that year, Cheney appeared on NBC's *Meet the Press* and declared that Saddam had had "a long-standing relationship with al-Qaeda."[58] This assertion was untrue, but the American people had no way of knowing it was false.

Statements by respected members of the administration also convinced many in the public that a war against Iraq was both necessary and justified. These included

Condoleezza Rice, who was Bush's National Security Advisor from 2001 to 2005, and then Secretary of State from 2005 to 2009. Although not a neo-con herself, Rice supported "transformational diplomacy," which would engender democracy in Middle Eastern countries. On CNN she declared that there was "increasing evidence that [Saddam] continues his march toward weapons of mass destruction." The only evidence she cited was the aluminum tubes, which she insisted were "only really suited for nuclear weapons programs."[59] It is unclear if she believed this claim at the time, but in fact, it was false. On September 25, 2002, she insisted on the PBS *News Hour* that the Iraqi dictator was providing "training to al-Qaeda in chemical weapons development."[60] This assertion was likewise untrue. On January 10, 2003, she did an interview with CNN's Wolf Blitzer and said, "The problem here is that there will always be some uncertainty about how quickly he [Saddam] can acquire nuclear weapons. But we don't want the smoking gun to be a mushroom cloud."[61]

Meanwhile Colin Powell remained dubious. During dinner with Bush on August 5, 2002, Powell warned the president that attacking Iraq would mean the United States would be responsible for a shattered country. "You break it, you are going to own it," he told Bush. "It isn't getting to Bagdad. It is what happens after you get to Bagdad. And it ain't going to be easy."[62] Ten days later, on October 15, a devastating op-ed piece appeared in the *New York Times*. Its author was Brent Scowcroft, who had served as the first President Bush's National Security Advisor. Under the headline, "Don't Attack Iraq" Scowcroft wrote that a war in Iraq could prove a distraction from the larger war on terrorism. It would not be the "cakewalk," he added, that some in the administration wanted to believe. The consequences would be costly in blood and treasure and "could well destabilize Arab regimes in the region" and require "a large scale, long-term military occupation."[63] The president was furious over the Scowcroft article, fearing that many would believe he was speaking for his father, which is exactly what many readers did conclude.

The administration also made dubious claims to Congress as part of a campaign to convince them to authorize the use of force against Iraq. In response to constant claims by the president and those around him that Saddam was making and stockpiling weapons of mass destruction, the Senate Intelligence Committee asked the CIA to prepare a National Intelligence Estimate (NIE). The agency rushed to put the estimate together. The resulting ninety-five-page document, delivered to Capitol Hill on October 1, repeated all the familiar charges that had been made and the bases for them, but it also contained many caveats and dissents, especially in the appendices. Unfortunately, when the document was made available to members of the House and Senate, the vast majority of them did not bother to read it. By their own admissions, neither President Bush nor Condoleezza Rice read the document, an appalling dereliction of duty for leaders about to take their country to war.[64]

Although Democrats in particular were dubious about the president's request to authorize force, they did not want to be accused of being soft on either Iraq or terrorism—equivalent to charging someone with being soft on Communism during the Cold War or of lacking in patriotism during the Mexican War and the brutal American conquest of the Philippines. The war authorization vote came on October

10, 2003. The House passed the resolution 293 to 133, and the Senate seventy-seven to twenty-three. It gave Bush the power to use military force, "as he determines to be necessary and appropriate to defend the national security of the United States against the continuing threat posed by Iraq," as well as to enforce all relevant UN Security Council resolutions relating to Iraq. Some dubious members of both houses comforted themselves by concluding that they had only voted to authorize war as a last resort. They may have also been comforted by the president's prediction that the war would be all over in six months (the same prediction made by many countries at the beginning of the First World War).

Even the august *New York Times* bought the official story line. For instance, *Times* reporter Judith Miller wrote a story in September 2002 claiming that Iraq was buying aluminum tubes for its nuclear centrifuges. When Miller was informed that most scientists doubted the story, she and a fellow reporter admitted that there had been some debate among intelligence experts, but that it was nevertheless "the intelligence agencies' unanimous view that the types of tubes that Iraq has been seeking are used to make such centrifuges."[65] Cheney and Rice then went on the Sunday talk shows and cited the article as proof of the aluminum tubes story, as if the *Times* article were an independent source. In a series of articles that followed, Miller continued to convey the administration's line about WMD without questioning it in any way. Later, after no WMD were found, the *Times* editors apologized, saying, "We wish we had been more aggressive in re-examining the claims as new evidence emerged—or failed to emerge."[66] By then the damage had been done. Such unquestioning stories in the *Times* and the other mainstream media, including radio and television, helped to convince 69 percent of the public to believe, falsely, that Saddam Hussein had been personally involved in the attacks on 9/11, and 57 percent to believe, also falsely, that Iraq was a key supporter of al-Qaeda. As late as 2008, 48 percent of voters believed incorrectly that Saddam had played a large role in the attacks.

Bush and Chaney had originally opposed going through the United Nations, but Powell insisted the United States needed the organization's backing and approval. British Prime Minister Tony Blair also wanted authorization from the UN as cover for his support of the United States in the face of tremendous opposition in the United Kingdom against his country's participation in an Iraq war.

In November 2002, the United States convinced the Security Council to vote unanimously that Iraq was in "material breach" of earlier resolutions concerning weapons of mass destruction. It declared that Baghdad must allow enhanced weapons inspections or face "serious consequences." A team of UN inspectors led by Hans Blix entered Iraq late that month to begin operations. At the same time, Defense Secretary Rumsfeld began moving military units into the Persian Gulf area.

On December 7, the Iraqis submitted a long document to the UN, as required by the resolution, stating that they had no unconventional weapons stockpiles and no program for building nuclear weapons. The Bush administration insisted that the Iraqis were lying because they did not own up to trying to purchase yellowcake uranium from Niger and buying aluminum tubes for supposed use in a nuclear centrifuge, even though the CIA had already dismissed the Niger story. The US Department of Energy had also concluded that the tubes, which the Iraqis had been buying on the open market, were not suitable for centrifuges. What is more, over the next few months, the UN inspectors found nothing on the ground in Iraq in the way of weapons violations.

Secretary Powell continued to hope for a peaceful resolution in Iraq. Powell was one of the most admired and respected men in American public life and was not a neo-con. He had served as Chairman of the Joint Chiefs of Staff during the Persian Gulf War, was a retired four-star general, and the first African American Secretary of State. In order to avoid a war with Iraq, Powell wanted to keep the inspections going as long as possible while building up American forces and pressuring the UN to threaten military force if Saddam did not come clean. Powell hoped these actions might lead to an internal coup against the Iraqi dictator.

Whatever his misgivings, Powell was a good soldier and he had promised President Bush he would support his policies toward Iraq. However, Powell did not want to go before the UN Security Council and ask for a declaration to use military force unless he had an "airtight" argument to make against Iraq. Scooter Libby, Vice President Cheney's assistant for National Security Affairs, wrote a draft speech for Powell to use at the UN. After hours of fact-checking, Powell's team at the department concluded that Libby had "cherry-picked" anything and everything that might make a case. They tossed out the Libby document and began working on their own draft based on the National Intelligence Report, which had been submitted to Congress but concluded that even many of its assertions were unsubstantiated or questionable.

Although Powell himself rejected numerous claims in the National Intelligence Report, he went ahead with his speech to the Security Council, delivered February 5, 2003. Unsurprisingly, many of his assertions were already in doubt or would soon be proven false. For instance, he insisted that the Iraqis had not accounted for all the WMD they had possessed a dozen years before at the end of the Persian Gulf War, adding, "We know . . . of the existence of mobile production facilities used to make biological agents."[67] The source for this story was an unreliable witness then living in Germany, whom the CIA had not been allowed to question. Powell mentioned the aluminum tubes but took care to state that, although some doubts about their purpose had surfaced, he claimed incorrectly that most experts believed they were for use in nuclear centrifuges. He went on to insist that there was a sinister network between Iraq and al-Qaeda terrorists. Days earlier, the CIA had discounted such a network, revealing that it had been based on an account from an individual who was not in any position to know about such alleged connections between Iraq and al-Qaeda. In any case, Powell's presentation was not enough to persuade either France or Russia, which as permanent members of the Security Council held a veto over its decisions. Both announced on March 17 that they would not support the resolution to use force against Iraq.

Despite the fact that the UN inspectors had not found any WMD in Iraq, despite the fact that the yellow cake uranium and aluminum tube assertions turned out to be false, and despite the fact that allegations of ties between Saddam and al-Qaeda terrorists had proven groundless, President Bush was determined to have his war against Iraq. Facts simply did not seem to matter to the president, who now switched to emphasizing the benefits of implanting democracy in Iraq and having it spread from there throughout the region—the reverse domino theory. At the end of February 2003, he spoke before the American Enterprise Institute in Washington, where he told the crowd of 1,500 people, "The world has a clear interest in the spread of democratic values. . . . A new regime in Iraq would serve as a dramatic and inspiring example of freedom for other nations in the region."[68]

In effect, Bush was going to war no matter what. This attitude caused the Republican House Majority Leader Dick Armey to say that Bush and administration officials were in the grip of a "he-man psychosis where they felt they needed to go out and shoot somebody to show they're the tough guy on the block."[69]

Despite the administration's dissembling, lies, and exaggerations, Bush finally got his war. In a televised address from the White House on March 17, 2003, he gave Saddam Hussein an ultimatum: He and his sons would have to leave Iraq within forty-eight hours or there would be war. Despite not receiving the "imprimatur" of the UN, he had managed to persuade several countries—most importantly the United Kingdom—to join in an invasion of Iraq, which began three days later on March 20, 2003. At first, the war went well as Iraqi forces collapsed and then melted away. Very soon, however, widespread looting broke out, US and allied forces were attacked by a variety of armed groups in Iraq, and a full-scale civil war gripped the country. Democracy did not triumph in Iraq, and there was no spread of democracy throughout the region. Some 4,400 Americans lost their lives, and 32,000 were wounded. Estimates put the number of Iraqi dead, most of them civilians, at close to 200,000, with many more civilians seriously injured. The conflict would cost the American people as much as $3 to $4 trillion if one figures in the cost of interest payments on the money borrowed to pay for fighting and the funds required over the next several decades to cover veterans' health care and other benefits.

(The War Powers Act of 1973, which Congress passed over President Nixon's veto as the war in Vietnam was winding down, has also proved ineffective. The Act required presidents to notify Congress within forty-eight hours of introducing military forces "into hostilities or into situations where imminent involvement in hostilities is clearly indicated by the circumstances." It also required presidents to end foreign military actions after sixty days unless Congress declares war or authorizes the action to continue, which did not occur in the case of the Iraq war.[70] However, the federal courts have refused to declare presidents in violation of the War Powers Act, making the legislation essentially worthless in curbing presidents when it comes to initiating military actions.[71])

Presidential Wars

Whenever presidents have asked Congress to declare or otherwise to authorize war, there was little likelihood that legislators would refuse to go along. In asking Congress for authority to use force against Mexico or to wage war against Spain and the freedom fighters in the Philippines, President Polk and President McKinley both used various degrees of deception and even downright lies to maintain that war was unavoidable. The war in Vietnam, which was eventually authorized by the Tonkin Gulf Resolution, involved and would continue to involve a series of false claims by five presidents over nearly three decades. President Bush's requests to Congress to use military force in Iraq also depended on numerous falsehoods and misrepresentations. The authors of the Constitution feared just such outcomes. However, the separation of powers and concomitant checks and balances have not proved strong enough to curb presidents who opted for wars whether they were necessary or just. A precedent had long been set that allowed presidents to drag the country into needless wars for lack of better barriers to prevent them from doing so. Americans have long wanted to believe that only rulers in other countries have started foolish, devastating, and unnecessary wars, but the United States is far from immune to such behavior by its presidents.

Notes

1 Michael Waltzer, *Just and Unjust Wars*, 4th ed. (New York: Basic Books, 2007), 251–3.
2 I have written more extensively about all these conflicts, with the exception of the Mexican War, in an earlier book. See David R. Contosta, *America's Needless Wars* (Amherst: Prometheus Books, 2017).
3 James K. Polk, quoted in Walter Borneman, *Polk: The Man Who Transformed the Presidency and America* (New York: Random House, 2008), 191.
4 Polk, quoted in ibid., 205.
5 Ibid., 210.
6 See Daniel Walker Howe, *The Political Culture of the American Whigs* (Chicago: University of Chicago Press, 1979).
7 Lincoln's Spot Resolutions, December 22, 1847, National Archives, https://www.archives/gov/edcation/lessons/lincoln-resolutions.
8 Lincoln to Herndon, February 15, 1848, in *Abraham Lincoln: Speeches and Writings, 1832–1858* (New York: Library of America, 1989), 175–6.
9 Polk, Second Annual Message, December 8, 1846, The American Presidency Project, www.pesidency.uscb.edu/ws/?pid=29487.
10 This was the Gadsden Purchase of 1853/54, through which the United States acquired some 30,000 square miles below the future states of New Mexico and Arizona. The reason for acquiring the territory was that it provided a more level terrain to construct a southern route for a transcontinental railroad.
11 For an excellent example of this idea, see Walter McDougall, *Throes of Democracy: The American Civil War Era, 1829–1877* (New York: Harper Perennials, 2009), 229–30, 278–80, 285–6, 297.
12 De Lome Letter, The Spanish-American War Centennial Website, http://www.spanamwar.com/Delome.htm.
13 Roosevelt to Benjamin Harrison Diblee, February 16, 1898, Etling B. Morrison, ed., *Letters of Theodore Roosevelt*, 6 vols. (Cambridge, MA: Harvard University Press, 1951–1954), 1:783–4.

14 These quotations are from Evan Thomas, *The War Lovers: Roosevelt, Lodge, Hearst and the Rush to Empire* (Boston: Little, Brown and Company, 2010), 210–11.
15 Ibid., 213–14.
16 William McKinley, *Speeches and Addresses of William McKinley* (New York: Doubleday & McClure, 1900), 67–8.
17 Quoted in Hermann Hagedorn, *Leonard Wood: A Biography*, 2 vols. (New York: Harper & Brothers, 1931), 1:141.
18 Quoted in Edmund Morris, *The Rise of Theodore Roosevelt* (New York: Coward, McCann & Geoghegan, 1969), 610.
19 Quote in Dalton, *Theodore Roosevelt*, 170.
20 Ibid., 171.
21 Ruth Miller Elson, *American Schoolbooks in the Nineteenth Century* (Lincoln: University of Nebraska Press, 1964).
22 James Boyle, quoted in the *New York Times*, September 1, 1912.
23 H. H. Kohlsaat, *From McKinley to Harding: Personal Recollections of Our Presidents* (New York: Scribner's, 1923), 67.
24 William McKinley, "Message to Congress Requesting a Declaration of War with Spain," The American Presidency Project, April 11, 1898, http://www.pesidency.ucsb.edu.
25 American Declaration of War, April 25, 1898, http://www.spanamwar.com/mckinleywardec.htm.
26 Dalton, *Theodore Roosevelt*, 171.
27 Quoted in T. Harry Williams, *The History of American Wars from 1745 to 1918* (Baton Rouge: Louisiana State University Press, 1981), 331.
28 Quoted in Marcel P. Lichuaco and Moorefield Story, *The Conquest of the Philippines by the United States, 1898–1925* (New York: G.P. Putnam's Sons, 1926), 120.
29 Address of Theodore Roosevelt at Arlington Memorial Day, May 30, 1902, in Alfred Henry Lewis, ed., *A Compilation of Messages and Speeches of Theodore Roosevelt, 1901–1905* (New York: Bureau of National Literature and Art, 1906), 28–34.
30 Schlesinger, *The Imperial Presidency*, 208.
31 Quoted in Marvin Kalb, *The Road to War: Presidential Commitments Honored and Betrayed* (Washington, DC: Brookings Institution Press, 2013), 29.
32 Quoted in Alexander Kendrick, *The Wound Within: American in the Vietnam Years, 1945–1974* (Boston: Little, Brown and Company, 1974), 38.
33 Kalb, *The Road to War*, 34.
34 These facts became public with the publication of the Pentagon Papers in 1971.
35 Kendrick, *Wound Within*, 61–5.
36 Ibid., 92–3; George Donelson Moss, *Vietnam: An American Ordeal* (Upper Saddle River: Prentice Hall, 2002), 68.
37 Quoted in Kalb, *Road to War*, 61.
38 Quoted in ibid., 79.
39 Quoted in ibid., 77.
40 Quoted in ibid., 86.
41 Quoted in ibid., 85.
42 Tonkin Gulf Resolution, National Archives Foundation, Tonkin Gulf Resolution (archivesfoundation.org).
43 Peter Baker, *New York Times*, January 2, 2017. This *Times* reporting was based on the notes of former White House Chief of Staff H. R. Haldeman, which had been

deposited in the Nixon Presidential Library and Museum. For a circumstantial discussion of this interference, written before the revelation in the *Times*, see Evan Thomas, *Being Nixon: A Man Divided* (New York: Random House, 2016).

44 Michael V. Seitzinger, "Conducting Foreign Relations Without Authority: The Logan Act" (PDF). Congressional Research Service, Congress and the Scope of the President's Article II Foreign Policy Authorities | Congress.gov | Library of Congress. February 1, 2006. accessed April 9, 2007.

45 Quoted in Kalb, *Road to War*, 150.

46 Quoted in ibid., 153.

47 Foreign Relations of the United States, 1969–1976, https://history.state.gov/historicaldocuments/frus1969-76v14/d126.

48 Peter Baker, *Days of Fire: Bush and Cheney in the White House* (New York: Doubleday, 2013), 230–1.

49 George W. Bush, The Second Gore-Bush Debate, Debate Transcript, October 11, 2000.

50 Quoted in Baker, *Days of Fire*, 91.

51 Ibid., 130, 131.

52 Ibid., 135.

53 Quoted in ibid., 135.

54 Ibid., 144.

55 Ibid., 145.

56 *New York Times*, August 23, 2021.

57 Quoted in Michael Isikoff and David Corn, *Hubris* (New York: Crown Publishers, 2007), 173.

58 Ibid., 208.

59 Ibid., 41.

60 Ibid., 119.

61 Wolf Blitzer, "Search for the 'Smoking Gun,'" CNN, January 10, 2003. accessed November 3, 2008.

62 Baker, *Days of Fire*, 208.

63 Ibid., 209.

64 Isikoff and Corn, *Hubris*, 137, 296, 414.

65 Quoted in ibid., 60.

66 The *New York Times*, May 26, 2004.

67 Isakoff and Corn, *Hubris*, 186.

68 Ibid., 191.

69 Ibid., 25.

70 50 U.S. Code Chapter 33—WAR POWERS RESOLUTION.

71 See *New York Times*, June 21, 2011. In the D.C. Circuit case of *Campbell v. Clinton* (2000), in which a member of Congress claimed that President Bill Clinton's bombing of Kosivo violated the War Powers Act, the court ruled that the petitioner had no standing over what was deemed a political matter.

8

Image and Celebrity

"It's What People Think You Are"

We shall assume that what each man does is based not on direct and certain knowledge, but on pictures [i.e., images] made by himself or given to him.

Walter Lippmann, *Public Opinion*, 1922

"Jack is the greatest attraction in the country. . . . You advertise the fact that he will be at a dinner and you will break all records for attendance. He can draw more people to a fund-raising dinner than Cary Grant or Jimmy Stewart."[1] For Joseph P. Kennedy, his son Jack, running for president in 1960, is a commodity: "We'll sell him like soap flakes," he declares.[2] Fourteen years earlier, in 1946, as Jack is declaring his first run for Congress, his sister Eunice wonders if her "frail and sickly brother," just home from the war, has the stamina to enter politics. To that, their father remarks, "You must remember—it's not what you are that counts, but what people think you are."[3]

Joseph P. Kennedy knew all about creating images, since for many years he had been a highly successful movie producer and financier of film studios and liked to predict that America's future aristocracy would not consist of old, wealthy families but of film celebrities.[4]

It is no wonder his son Jack grew up fascinated with Hollywood and managed to meet many leading actors through his father's connections in Tinseltown. In the fall of 1940, while a student at Stanford University's business school, he took a jaunt down to Hollywood, where he attended a party and talked easily to blockbuster stars Spencer Tracy and Clark Gable, and may well have gone back to campus with a sense of how to make himself look and act like a film celebrity.[5]

Image extended well beyond Hollywood for Jack's father, who had long been furious over their Irish Catholic family's social ostracism by Boston's old Protestant families, fittingly known as Boston Brahmans after India's highest caste. Putting one of his sons in the White House would force open those long-closed doors. Initially, the oldest boy, Joe, Jr., would carry the torch, but he was shot down and killed as a bomber pilot in the Second World War. Now the baton passed to Jack, who would raise the family image to irrefutable heights. Despite his shaky health and despite the Republicans' taking control of both the House and Senate for the first time since 1930,

Kennedy won his House seat in a personal landslide in November 1946. Even here, Hollywood played a role when his father used film industry connections to get Pathe News to shoot Jack campaigning, and then arranged to have the newsreel shown in movie theaters throughout the Boston area a few days before voters went to the polls. Jack won reelection to the House in 1948 and 1950, but far sweeter was his narrow defeat of Henry Cabot Lodge, the very personification of the Boston blue blood, for a seat in the United States Senate in 1952, which put him on the front page of the *New York Times* and landed him a feature story in *Time* magazine.

As Walter Lippmann had written in his 1922 book, *Public Opinion*, "We shall assume that what each man does is based not on direct and certain knowledge, but on pictures [i.e., images] made by himself or given to him."[6] Lippmann's insight had been true when the Constitution was being debated and put into effect, but the framers as well as the general population then lived in a world "of print," where politicians and the public alike had to depend on the written word to disseminate their ideas, arguments, and platforms. This domination of print had begun with the invention of the printing press in the West during the mid-fifteenth century and had lasted well into the twentieth century. However, the mental images made available by print were of a far different order than the pictorial images that came later.

Sorting Fact from Fiction

Just a year after the 1960 presidential election, which John F. Kennedy narrowly won, historian Daniel J. Boorstin published a book called *The Image* that has become a classic analysis of media and advertising. Especially prophetic for what would increasingly take place in campaigning for the American presidency was his discussion of "celebrity."[7] As defined by Boorstin, a celebrity is "a famous or well-publicized person—a person who is known for his [or her] well-knownness." Over the next six decades, being a celebrity of one sort or another became increasingly important to anyone seeking to become president—until celebrity alone could become the key to winning the White House.

In 1985, author Neil Postman offered a penetrating study of television and its connection to celebrity and showmanship in a book he aptly entitled *Amusing Ourselves to Death*, which included an explanation of how the world of print had earlier formed distinct habits of thought and expression.[8] Postman writes, "To engage the written word means to follow a line of thought, which requires considerable powers of classifying, inference-making and reasoning." Furthermore, to read and understand "means to uncover lies, confusions, and over-generalizations, to detect abuses of logic and common sense." In the process, the reader also must "weigh ideas, to compare and contrast assertions, to connect one generalization with another."[9] Reading thus means wrestling actively with the text, deciding whether one agrees or disagrees with what the writer is asserting, and making mental responses to what has been read. Reading for understanding also requires a preexisting stock of knowledge, including information about what went before—or a good sense of history—since increasing knowledge is largely a linear proposition that builds on other authors and ideas.

Sentence by sentence, paragraph by paragraph, page by page, and chapter by chapter, the theses, arguments, examples, and conclusions of a text build and require readers to keep track of what has been read. After finishing the text, readers hopefully would have armed themselves with topics to discuss or dispute with others. For these reasons, a high degree of literacy, which existed even in early colonial America, was essential for any sort of communal debate and consensus building, and for many decades lay at the heart of creating and sustaining a democracy. According to Postman, "Here was argument and counterargument, claim and counter claim, criticism of relevant texts, [and] the most careful scrutiny of the previously uttered sentences of one's opponent." As oratory based on the printed word, it had "semantic, paraphrasable, propositional content."[10] Democracy thus depended on sorting out fact from fiction and, at best, endeavoring to use the facts to investigate problems and make policy.

Campaigns for office in later generations relying heavily on pictorial images were very different experiences that engaged very different mental processes. Gone was the more intellectually challenging content, the elaborate thrusts and counterthrusts that must be weighed and judged against each other, including the ability to pick up obvious contradictions, deceptions, and downright lies. Of course, one could still form images of a candidate—or of a sitting president—from reading speeches or other written messages. But words were later at a great disadvantage when competing with visual images, since even in everyday life, one comes to "truly know" a person by seeing him or her, as opposed to merely hearing or reading about the individual. Indeed, people will go to great lengths to meet a person with whom they have only communicated through some sort of written communication—or failing that, to seek photographic images of the other person. Thus, it is often said that "seeing is believing."

In her 2012 article, "Blinded by Starlight," communications scholar Charlotte J. S. De Backer discusses the importance of "recognition" in creating celebrity. "The more people recognize an individual," she writes, "the more fame can be attributed to that person and the bigger star that person becomes." Humans, she adds, "have a natural tendency to attribute higher status to people and objects they recognize compared to people and objects they do not recognize." The duration of recognition is another important factor: "An individual should be well-known for a sufficient amount of time," not for some fleeting notice.[11]

Witnessing numerous photographs of a president or presidential candidate—or still better, seeing numerous moving pictures or television images of that person—makes him or her seem increasingly intimate, about whose life one wants to know as much as possible. To again quote the prescient Walter Lippmann, "Photographs have the kind of authority over imagination to-day, which the printed word had yesterday. . . . They seem utterly real. They come, we imagine, directly to us without human meddling, and they are the most effortless food for the mind conceivable."[12] Lippmann proposes that watching a moving picture requires even less cognitive effort: "On the screen the whole process of observing, describing, reporting, and then imagining, has been accomplished for you without more trouble than is needed to stay awake . . ."[13]

Thus, with little demand for critical thought, presidential aspirants, or those already in office, make themselves celebrities by using pictorial images—both still and moving—to acquire heightened recognition and status. If successful, there also develops an insatiable thirst to see a president's pets, to view presidents on vacation, or to have a look at First Ladies' clothing and hairstyles. One can even imagine being present at a far-away event with the president from seeing it in a photograph, on film, or on TV, which becomes a ubiquitous source of moving images in the mid-twentieth century. This same phenomenon applies to multiple and repetitive images of accomplished athletes, movie stars, or pop singers whose fans want to know everything about them and come to view them almost as members of the family or best friends—what, as mentioned before, psychologists call "parasocial relations."[14]

There is no reason to believe that John F. Kennedy knew the term parasocial relations, but he took especially good care with his personal appearance for a 1960 presidential debate against Richard Nixon, the first televised presidential debate in the nation's history. Perhaps primed by the family's knowledge of Hollywood production techniques, his campaign sent scouts ahead to report back on the color of the backdrop to be used in the studio. It turned out to be a light shade of gray. Kennedy accordingly showed up in a crisp dark blue suit, which made him stand out against the background, even though the broadcast was in black and white. Nixon wore a light gray suit that blended visually into the background. Nixon also looked haggard and tired, the result of a staphylococcal infection. Nixon had also refused to wear makeup, which could have softened his distinct jawline that had a tendency to make him look angry. Of the two, however, Kennedy was in much poorer general health than Nixon, since he had been suffering for years from Addison's disease, a disorder of the adrenal glands that he had kept at bay with cortisol steroids. He also suffered from several other chronic ailments, including a very painful back.[15]

Critical reaction to the televised debate was devastating. One British diplomat wrote back to his Foreign Office, "[Nixon] seems in the last few weeks to have aged and shriveled, and the way in which his tongue kept darting in and out of his lips [during the debate] was positively reptilian." Veteran newspaper columnist Joseph Alsop thought Nixon "looked like a suspect who is being questioned . . . in connection with a statutory rape case." And Chicago Mayor Richard Daley quipped that Nixon looked as if he had been embalmed.[16]

The debate appalled Daniel Boorstin for other reasons. He described it as a pseudo, contrived event that was modeled after the TV quiz shows of the time in which contestants were asked questions that had not been given to them beforehand and were expected to come up with a cogent answer with little thought. As he put it, "A man's ability, while standing under klieg lights, without notes, to answer in two and a half minutes a question kept secret until that moment, had only the most dubious relevance—if any at all—to his real qualifications to make deliberate Presidential decisions on long-standing, public questions after being instructed by a corps of advisors."[17]

In any case, Nixon was no match for the polished and photogenic Kennedy whose performance in that debate confirmed his star quality. Crowds now mobbed him at campaign events and once tore off his cufflinks, leaving his forearms scratched and bleeding. Kennedy was also careful to avoid photographs of himself in awkward situations, such as wearing odd hats or eating in public to project an image of being above the ordinary.[18]

All the glamour aside, Kennedy had a problem that candidates from wealthy families often faced—the charge that they were using family money and connections to win the election and that they could not possibly relate to the common voter. Both Theodore and Franklin Roosevelt had come from wealthy families, but their wealth paled in comparison to the Kennedys, considering that the candidate's father was worth over $4 billion in the values of half a century later, making Joseph P. Kennedy one of the wealthiest individuals in the United States at the time of the campaign.[19]

One way to make Kennedy seem more like a "regular guy" was to show photographs of him playing "touch football" with his brothers and friends at the family compound at Hyannis Port, Massachusetts. The other and perhaps more effective antidote to neutralizing the rich kid image was to remind the public of Kennedy's heroic rescue of his crew on the night of August 1, 1943, when a Japanese destroyer rammed the patrol boat, PT 109, that he commanded in the Solomon Islands. Kennedy had towed the boat's badly burned engineer to safety by swimming while clinching the straps of the injured man's life vest between his teeth. War correspondents in the area picked up the story and hailed Kennedy as a hero, the saga appearing on the front pages of many metropolitan newspapers. *The New Yorker* and *Reader's Digest* also published the story. Part of the reason for this extensive coverage was that Lieutenant Kennedy had come from a wealthy and well-known family, his father having served only a few years earlier as the US Ambassador to London. However, according to biographer Robert Dallek, Kennedy's heroic actions also provided a "unifying example of American egalitarianism." It was not just ordinary G. I. s who were fighting for their country, "but also the privileged son of a wealthy, influential father who had voluntarily placed himself in harm's way . . ."[20]

The PT 109 saga had been used to great effect during Kennedy's first campaign for the House of Representatives in 1946, his father having 100,000 copies of the *Reader's Digest* story printed and distributed throughout the district. And Jack had opened every campaign speech that year by reciting the tale. When he ran for the Senate four years later, the campaign distributed millions of copies of a tabloid-sized, eight-page account of the story, complete with dramatic drawings of Kennedy leading his crew to safety. A decade later, during the critical 1960 West Virginia primary election, his main opponent, Senator Hubert Humphrey, put himself forward as a populist being outspent by the wealthy Kennedys. But Jack fought back with a television ad that featured a recital of his wartime heroics narrated over the image of the wake of a speeding PT boat.[21]

Kennedy's election by no means ended references to the naval saga. In June of 1963, two and a half years into Kennedy's presidency and nearly twenty years after the event, Warner Brothers released a feature movie called *PT 109*. The movie was based on a bestselling book of the same name written by Robert J. Donovan and first published in January 1961, thereby coinciding with Kennedy's inauguration.[22] His father used his Hollywood connections to negotiate film rights to the book with Warner Brothers. The

White House had complete approval over the casting and other details of the movie. After considering several actors to play the young naval officer, Cliff Robertson got the role. It became the first commercial film made about a sitting US president. The film appeared more than a year before Kennedy would face reelection in 1964, and it is unclear if it was calculated to help boost his popularity for that event. The contest did not take place, of course, because of Kennedy's assassination in November 1963, though Kennedy saw the film at a special screening in the White House just before it was released to the public.[23]

Throughout his presidency, Kennedy was a big "hit" with his televised press conferences. Advisor and historian Arthur Schlesinger, Jr. later wrote that these conferences "offered a showcase for a number of [Kennedy's] most characteristic qualities—the intellectual speed and vivacity, the remarkable mastery of the data of government, the terse, self-mocking wit, the exhilarating personal command."[24] Not only did Kennedy charm TV viewers, but he also gained a powerful means of speaking directly to the country without the filter of the news media. He also showed himself enjoying the presidency immensely, much like Franklin Roosevelt a generation before, and in the process cemented his celebrity image. Being a celebrity also helped to deflect attention from the deficits of his administration, such as the Bay of Pigs fiasco and his inability to get major legislation through Congress. No doubt his celebrity status would have put him in an excellent position to win a second term in 1964. Like Franklin Roosevelt before him, he had set a standard for popularity that future presidents have been hard-pressed to emulate.

Kennedy's successor, Lyndon Johnson (1963–1969), had none of the star power of his predecessor. He had tried for the Democratic nomination in 1960 but had little chance against the youthful, polished, and charming Kennedy. For one, Johnson's speech was halting as well as leavened by a deep, rural Texas drawl. Nor had he ever been as handsome as Jack Kennedy. Far from it. But Johnson, who had served in the House of Representatives and then in the Senate, was a master politician who knew how to move legislation on Capitol Hill better than anyone in recent memory. Kennedy, in comparison, had garnered a less than impressive record in Congress, having sponsored little or no important legislation. Save for Kennedy's assassination, it is unlikely that Johnson ever would have become president. Once in office, though, he would use his consummate legislative skills to move an astounding array of landmark laws through Congress. In many ways, he seemed an affirmation of Boorstin's belief that a candidate's television performance, "had only the most dubious relevance—if any at all—to his real qualifications to make deliberate Presidential decisions on long-standing public questions . . ."[25]

Selling the President

Despite his epochal legislative successes while president and his Electoral College sweep against Barry Goldwater in 1964, Johnson's popularity was in tatters by 1968 because of the growing unpopularity of the Vietnam War. That year, Republicans nominated Richard Nixon, who had made a dramatic comeback after his defeat in the presidential election of 1960 and his even more humiliating defeat when he ran for governor of California in 1962. But Nixon continued to have image problems. His smiles often seemed forced and insincere. In addition, he had gained the reputation of an underhanded campaigner because of the way he had smeared Helen Gahagan Douglas, his Democratic opponent for Congress in 1950, by hinting strongly as well as falsely that she was a Communist by branding her as "The Pink Lady" in campaign literature. A Democratic ad responded by calling Nixon "Tricky Dick," a moniker that would follow him for the rest of his public life.[26] Detractors also ridiculed Nixon for his Checkers Speech, to be discussed in a subsequent chapter.

Following a 1968 Nixon appearance on the *Mike Douglas Show*, then a very popular afternoon TV talk venue, the show's young producer, Roger Ailes, who later became Chairman and CEO of Fox News, told Nixon he needed a media advisor and offered himself for the job. With Ailes on board, the Nixon team set out to remake their candidate's image—what came to be called the "New Nixon." In his book, *The Selling of the President 1968*, author Joe McGinnis related in detail the story of what the Nixon team attempted to do.[27] They faced a daunting task, since, as McGinnis wrote, "Television demands gentle wit, irony [and] understatement. . . . He must engage in intimate conversation. . . . Nonchalance is the key word. Carefully studied nonchalance." Their candidate fulfilled none of these characteristics: "Into this milieu came Richard Nixon: grumpy, cold, and aloof."[28] In order to overcome these deficits, the campaign's advertising crew worked out a two-pronged strategy. The first was a series of televised "citizens forums" called *Man in the Arena*, taken from the title of a speech that Theodore Roosevelt (a Nixon hero) had given in 1910. These events were supposed to show Nixon at his spontaneous best, answering questions from members of the audience. In fact, the attendees were carefully picked by local Republican operatives, as were the questioners. Most of these programs came off relatively well; even so, Nixon was sometimes thrown off by certain questions and had a hard time thinking on his feet and thereby seeming spontaneous. The second approach involved spot advertisements in which Nixon's image did not appear—only his voice narrating a set of still photographs that flashed on the screen to illustrate his message. In this way, Nixon's awkward body language and unpleasant facial expressions were in no danger of appearing on TV screens and putting off viewers.

One member of the advertising team had said, "Without television, Richard Nixon would not have a chance. He would not have a prayer of being elected because the press would not let him get through to the people."[29] The trouble was that Nixon hated the very medium said to be his salvation. So, according to McGinnis, the campaign had to resort to the "con game" of advertising and sell Nixon as if he were any other commodity for sale, which is what John F. Kennedy's father had said earlier when he compared selling political candidates to selling soap. According to McGinnis, with some exaggeration, presidents as commodities must be "measured against an ideal that's a combination of leading man, God, father, hero, pope, [and] king . . ."[30] It remained to be seen if carefully staged images of Nixon could create a real "New Nixon," or if they would succeed in causing citizens to vote for someone whose television persona had only slight resemblances to the real person.

In the end, Nixon nearly lost the 1968 election to Democrat Hubert Humphrey, who was Johnson's vice president. Early in the campaign, Humphrey had refrained out of loyalty from breaking with Johnson over the war in Vietnam. But when he did so in October, his numbers began to rise in the opinion polls. Humphrey also came across as more cheerful, more spontaneous, and far more genuine than Nixon. If the campaign had gone on another ten days or two weeks, some historians have concluded, Humphrey may well have won the presidency. As it turned out, Nixon won by just half a million popular votes out of the nearly 63 million cast. There was no "New Nixon," as the Watergate scandals of his administration would later show. In any case, it was very unlikely that the fifty-five-year-old Nixon, who had been in politics for a generation, was really going to change his mode of operation.

Celebrity Deficit

Neither of Nixon's two immediate successors, Gerald Ford (1974–1977) or "Jimmy" Carter (1977–1981) even tried to be celebrities. In fact, Ford, who had been plucked from the House of Representatives when Nixon's vice president, Spiro Agnew, was forced to resign in disgrace, made it a point to emphasize his plain, middle-class, Midwestern roots, joking that he was "a Ford, not a Lincoln."[31] His supporters considered this low-key, matter-of-fact way of speaking a virtue, especially in the dramatic aftermath of Nixon and Watergate. But Ford, who was the House minority leader before becoming vice president, had never hankered to become president; rather, his greatest ambition had been to serve as Speaker of the House if the Republicans ever reclaimed a majority in that body. That he became president was an accident of history.

Carter, who hailed from tiny Plains, Georgia, and had served most recently as governor of his state, played up his lack of Washington experience at a time when many Americans were still reeling from the Watergate scandals. Far from seeking any sort of celebrity, he billed himself as a farmer, when in fact he and his family were the prosperous owners of a large peanut warehouse. He also insisted on being called "Jimmy" rather than his full name of James Earl Carter, a common touch that helped to cast him as a "common man" in the White House. Instead of wearing traditional formal attire to his inauguration, he donned a plain business suit for the swearing in, and immediately after the event, he, his wife and daughter walked the mile and a half from Capitol Hill to the White House.

Once in office, Carter dispensed with much of the pomp and circumstance that had surrounded the Nixon presidency, sold the presidential yacht, and got rid of the gold-braided uniforms for the White House police that Nixon had both instituted and savored. He also appeared on TV dressed in a sweater and slacks, in part to dramatize the importance of lowering thermostats and saving fuel, which many viewers found undignified. Carter's as well as his staff's lack of knowledge about Washington ways limited his effectiveness with Congress. Yet, he did decide to rid himself of his pronounced rural southern accent by taking elocution lessons from a Georgia radio broadcaster that would leave him with a more refined southern tone and a smoother cadence.[32] Like Ford, he came across as something of an anti-celebrity. Although neither has gone down as a president who presided over significant changes, both succeeded in restoring a sense of normality in the office and have been respected for doing so as a historical consensus has emerged about them.

"The Acting President"

There could be no mistaking the fact that the next president, Ronald Reagan (1981–1989), who defeated Carter in his bid for reelection, emerged out of the celebrity culture of Hollywood. The idea that a Hollywood actor could become president would have seemed preposterous at any other time in the past, since both stage and screen actors were traditionally considered less than genuine because they had the ability to pretend to be someone else. For this reason, Hollywood was dubbed "Tinseltown"—that is a place that created the flashy, the fake, and the fleeting. Indeed, some actors were so successful playing certain roles that both the moviegoing public and television audiences could easily come to confuse the actor with the character played.

Before going to Hollywood, Reagan had a successful career as a radio broadcaster in Des Moines, Iowa. He became famous locally as a play-by-play announcer in the 1930s for the Chicago Cubs baseball team, even though he was hundreds of miles away in his Des Moines studio. As was standard practice in those days, he received bare-bones reports over the telegraph but was extremely adept at imagining colorful details for his listeners, making them feel they were present at the field in Chicago.

A big break came for Reagan when he took a Hollywood screen test in 1937 while traveling with the Cubs team in California. The country was still suffering from the Depression, and in Europe, the threat of Hitler was becoming more menacing. During this time of turmoil, the movie industry made great efforts to emphasize traditional norms and "feel good" movies. In the words of film historian Robert Sklar, "Hollywood's contribution to American culture was essentially one of affirmation." Films were "carefully constructed to stay within the bounds of essential American cultural and political myths."[33]

Reagan was perfect for acting out this Hollywood mission. He was extraordinarily handsome, as well as tall with an athletic build and an easy, friendly smile that reflected his genial personality. Even though he was taking on the role of a particular character in each film, he was not stepping entirely out of his own persona and as such did not strike voters later as a superstar completely beyond reach, but as someone they might have known as the boy down the street or a favorite schoolmate.

When Reagan began his career in films, the studios cranked out one "grade-B" movie after another to fill the bill for thousands of theaters around the country that typically played two new sets of double features every few days. These films were usually shot in just four or five weeks. Although Reagan typically appeared in supporting roles, he became a familiar and encouraging presence to moviegoers.

Several decades later, the wholesome roles that Reagan had played in the movies reminded older voters of what they liked to think were better, more moral, and less complicated times — before what they considered to be the alarming counterculture of the 1960s. When Reagan's movie career subsided in the 1950s, he turned increasingly to television. For ten seasons (1953–1962) he was the genial host of the *General Electric Theater*, which featured a series of weekly plays. He also served briefly as the host (1964–1965) of a weekly television program known as *Death Valley Days*, which presented stories about the Old West that were loosely based on real events. Reagan himself acted in twenty-one of the episodes. By acting in these "westerns" and by riding horseback over his own ranch in California, Reagan amplified his image as a rugged outdoorsman, as did a 1980 campaign poster showing him wearing a cowboy hat, with a caption below spelling out, "America: Reagan Country."

Reagan did not go straight to the White House from movies and television, having served two terms as Governor of California (1967–1975). Both as governor and president, however, Reagan preferred to delegate much of the work to various aides and assistants, which, according to some critics, allowed him to play the role of governor and president—that is, to look like a statesman and to give stirring speeches that drew on his early radio career and later acting experiences. Partly in admiration and partly in criticism, CBS News' Chief Washington Correspondent Bob Schieffer teamed up with CBS features reporter Paul Gates to do a book that they called *The Acting President*. They write, "Indeed, the roots of Ronald Reagan's extraordinary success [in politics] can be found in the skills and personality he [had] first unveiled to the public as a professional actor."[34] As such, the presidency became the greatest role of his life.

Throughout his presidency, Reagan liked to tell stories about his years in Hollywood, sometimes to amuse but sometimes thinking they would help him make a point about some issue. He also tended to make up facts and stories as easily as he had invented colorful details of the play-by-play when announcing Cubs games back in the Des Moines studio. In their book, Schieffer and Gates chronicle a number of these inventions: When asked on the *Today* TV show about his age, sixty-nine, soon after announcing his decision to run for president, he claimed that, if elected, he would be the youngest head of state with whom he would be dealing on the world stage, the only exception being Margaret Thatcher. In fact, there were several other leaders who were younger than Reagan. He also invented quotes that he attributed to famous men in history such as Winston Churchill who, according to Reagan, had once said, "The idea that a nation can tax itself into prosperity is one of the crudest delusions which has ever befuddled the human mind"—a line that no librarian or archivist could manage to find with reference to Churchill. When the president referred to a non-existent British law to argue against gun control, Press Secretary Larry Speaks dismissed criticism by saying, "It made the point, didn't it?"[35]

Then there were stories from movies that Reagan came to believe had really happened. One involved a 1944 film called *Wing and a Prayer* which featured the pilot of a B-17 holding the hand of a wounded turret gunner who could not bail out and thereby went down in the plane with him. Reagan ended the story by saying, "Congressional Medal of Honor, posthumously awarded." The trouble was that there was no record of a medal being awarded for such an action. When he met with a group of Israelis in 1983, he declared that he was especially sympathetic to them since he had personally witnessed the liberation of concentration camps at the end of the Second World War. In fact, Reagan was never out of the United States during the Second World War. Although a member of the US Army, he had spent the war years in Burbank, California, making training films, having been rejected for active service because of poor eyesight. What the president had meant to say, the White House tried to explain, was that Reagan had viewed Army films of the liberation and had been very moved by them.[36]

In 1983, authors Mark Green and Gail MacColl published a little book called *There He Goes Again: Ronald Reagan's Reign of Error*, which listed some 300 misstatements by the president. Members of the media, who questioned the president's fictitious stories and various claims, did nothing to dent his great popularity. Consequently, they began calling Reagan the "Teflon president" in reference to a popular brand at the time of "no stick" cooking pans. In addition, according to an article in *Newsweek* by Robert Perry, the press "seemed a little fearful that if it wrote stories that were perceived as tough on this President, the public would not like them."[37]

It appeared that nothing could shake wide public confidence in Reagan. Not even his disastrous televised debate performance on October 7, 1984, against second term challenger Fritz Mondale made a dent in his Teflon armor. That evening, Reagan was obviously tripped up while reciting some statistics, and at one point in the debate said the format was confusing, with the result that he came off sounding like a "befuddled old man." The White House did damage control by saying the president had been "over briefed" for the debate and therefore became confused. During the second debate, held on October 21, Reagan again looked "lost" when Mondale threw a barrage of facts and figures at him. Then one of the journalists on the panel inadvertently threw out a lifeline when he stated that Reagan was the oldest person to ever serve as president and asked if he would have the strength to cope with a crisis as challenging as the Cuban Missile Crisis during the Kennedy administration. Regan hit back with what has become a famous zinger: "Not at all, and I want you to know that I also will not make age an issue in this campaign. I am not going to exploit for political purposes, my opponent's youth and inexperience." For those who loved Ronald Reagan and wanted him to be reelected, the quip was all the reassurance they needed that their candidate was not a senile old man.[38]

Also contributing to what turned out to be a historic landslide reelection, with Reagan winning the electoral votes of every state but Mondale's Minnesota, was clever image making through a set of television ads. The most well-known of these opens with the words, "It's morning again in America," accompanied by uplifting visuals of citizens from all walks of life going off to work. That afternoon, the narrator adds, some 6,500 young Americans will get married, and with jobs and lower inflation, they will be able to make a good start on family life. "So why would we want to return to where we were four years ago?" the voice intones at the end. Reagan also promised to "Make America Great Again" in both 1980 and 1984, a phrase that would become the centerpiece of Donald Trump's campaigns three and four decades later.[39]

Another advertisement gives a more frightening view of the future—frightening that is, unless President Reagan remains in office. The ad shows a large grizzly bear roaming over hills, with the narrator saying, "There is a bear in the woods. For some people the bear is easy to see. Others do not see it at all. Some people say the bear is tame. Others say it is vicious and dangerous. Since no one can be sure who really is right, isn't it smart to be as strong as the bear, if there is a bear?" It takes no stretch of the imagination to suppose that the bear represents the Soviet Union and that President Reagan would protect the American people from this wild beast.[40] When critics charged that such ads and other campaign claims ignored the complexity of issues facing the United States, one Reagan advisor bluntly responded, "We are not here to educate America. We are here to re-elect Ronald Reagan."[41] Whether the advisor knew it or not, he encapsulated in just a few words the desperate shortcomings of political communication in the age of television.

Reagan's detachment from details and his penchant for delegating decisions probably contributed to the so-called Iran-Contra scandal (1985–1987), which nearly wrecked his second term. The scandal had its origins in the president's deep concern over seven Americans held hostage in Lebanon by Hezbollah, a paramilitary group closely associated with Iran. Reagan approved a plan to sell arms to Iran in exchange for their intervening with Hezbollah to release the hostages, even though the United States had embargoed arms sales to Iran. Meanwhile, the CIA had been assisting the Contra rebels in Nicaragua, who were fighting to overthrow the democratically elected Sandinista government of that country due to its Marxist ideology. Because the Contras were short of weapons and cash, the Reagan administration decided to give the Contras the proceeds of three arms sales to Iraq, with Israel acting as an intermediary, despite a specific Congressional prohibition of assistance to the Contras.

In 1986, Reagan went on television and admitted that arms had been sold to Iran but denied the transaction amounted to "arms for hostages," which would have violated the president's frequent and adamant vows never to appease hostage takers. At the end of that year, the president appointed a commission headed by former Republican Senator John Tower to examine the whole matter. When commissioners questioned Reagan in the Oval Office, he said that he could not remember if he had authorized the arms sales and seemed genuinely disoriented. The final Tower report, issued on February 27, 1987, did not specifically hold Reagan accountable for what had taken place but did cite him "for a lax managerial style and aloofness from policy detail."[42] Some critics believed such dereliction was an impeachable offense, given that he had sworn in his inaugural oath, as prescribed in Article II of the Constitution, to "faithfully execute the Office of the President of the United States" and that he had blatantly failed to do so. Even though Democrats controlled both houses of Congress, the charge of dereliction would have been difficult to prove, and for the millions of Americans who continued to love Ronald Reagan, his failure to execute a specific act of Congress was not enough to justify removing him from office. If nothing else, the decision not to sanction Reagan demonstrated once again that a very popular president can weather most any storm.

A Patrician Problem

Succeeding Reagan was his vice president and Republican nominee, George H. W. Bush (1989–1993). No one would have considered him a celebrity, but his impressive record of public service made him one of the best prepared of any recent candidates to become the nation's chief executive. In addition to being vice president for eight years, Bush had been a member of the US House of Representatives, the US Ambassador to the United Nations, the Chief US Liaison to the People's Republic of China where he prepared the ground for full recognition, Director of the CIA, and Chair of the Republican National Committee. In contrast, the Democrats' nominee, Michael Dukakis, had a less varied record, having served several terms in the Massachusetts House of Representatives and then three terms as Governor of Massachusetts.

However, Bush carried several negatives into the campaign, chief among them the charge that he had participated in discussions while vice president about Iran-Contra, a contention that he strenuously denied. He was also bucking a long-standing habit among voters to want a change in the White House after one party has held it for two terms. The only exception in the twentieth century had been when the Democrats won five terms in succession—with Franklin Roosevelt in 1932, 1936, 1940, and 1944 and Truman in 1948. Two back-to-back emergencies, the Great Depression and the Second World War, had allowed Roosevelt to claim four victories in a row, and Truman had prevailed because the Democrats' New Deal coalition had held together sufficiently to elect him, assisted by Truman's own feisty whistle-stop campaign. In 1988, there was no crisis that would appear to justify party continuity in the White House. On the contrary, Iran-Contra plus the final lackluster years of the Reagan presidency seemingly pointed to a need for change.

If these problems were not enough, Bush had to fight against what was being dubbed the "wimp factor"—the belief that he was somehow weak, indecisive, lacking in self-confidence, and even in political courage. This view was so widely discussed when it looked as if Bush would become his party's nominee that *Newsweek* magazine devoted a lengthy cover story to the supposed wimp factor.[43] Some of this perception stemmed from the fact that nearly all the positions Bush had held, with the exception of his four years as a Congressman from Texas, resulted from appointments. Even the vice presidency was essentially appointive, given that Reagan had selected him as his running mate. Then, as Regan's vice-president, Bush had had to jettison many of his own positions, such as opposition to Reagan's tax cuts and his earlier support for the Equal Rights Amendment.

Contributing further to the image of Bush as a wimp was his politeness, calm demeanor, and discomfort with expressing strong emotions in public, which probably stemmed from his patrician New England background. Brought up in wealthy, privileged Greenwich, Connecticut, he had been taught it was improper to praise himself in any way. Competition was a positive trait that his parents encouraged. Yet the competitiveness should never show. It is no wonder, then, that he felt uncomfortable about touting his accomplishments during the presidential campaign. His family was equally reticent to speak about their religious beliefs, prompting the *Newsweek* article to imagine how awkward he would look as an Episcopalian trying to participate in an evangelical revival meeting.

Contradicting the impression that Bush was some sort of weakling was his physical appearance and accomplishments in sports: He was 6 feet 2 inches tall with an athletic build and had excelled at baseball in both school and college. Then there were his harrowing experiences in the Second World War as the youngest pilot in the United States Navy. On September 2, 1944, he and his two-man crew took off from an aircraft carrier to attack and destroy a Japanese radio tower. Although the Japanese hit his plane with rounds of flak, causing it to catch fire, Bush released his bombs as he was going down and managed to damage the tower before guiding the plane out to sea and parachuting into the water. Inflating his life raft, he had to paddle with his hands to keep from being blown back to the Japanese-held island and being captured by the enemy. An American submarine finally rescued him, and someone on board the sub shot a black-and-white "home movie" of him being pulled out of the drink.[44] Bush's campaign advisors urged him to talk about this life-and-death experience, but his inbred modesty stood in the way. Although he had moved to West Texas after leaving the service and thrived in the oil business, it was the New England WASP identity that most defined his background and temperament.

Unlike either Jack Kennedy or Ronald Reagan, who were very much at ease on television, Bush struggled with the medium and turned to working with several television "coaches" to improve his TV persona. One coach advised him, "When you express a thought in politics . . . you have to feel and show some passion, some involvement"—something Bush could never quite do.[45]

Michael Dukakis, Bush's challenger for the presidency in 1988, was also from New England and had likewise gone to an Ivy League college, in his case Harvard as opposed to Bush's Yale. However, born to Greek immigrant parents, he had grown up in a gregarious family and had no difficulty promoting himself on the campaign trail or on television. Under the circumstances, it is not surprising that Bush lagged badly in the opinion polls coming out of the Republican convention.

As a strategy for pulling ahead, a political action committee not directly associated with the Bush campaign painted Dukakis as an extreme liberal who was soft on crime. Their example was a Massachusetts furlough program, established by legislation in 1972, which would allow prisoners to have weekend passes to the outside. In April 1987, a convicted murderer named Willie Horton, who had received such a furlough but had not returned to prison, broke into a home and attacked a young couple—binding and stabbing the man and raping his girlfriend. Horton, who was African American, became the subject of a Republican campaign ad called "Weekend Passes," which played on cable television nearly all of September. Viewers saw a mug shot of a heavily bearded Horton, as the voiceover hailed Bush as tough on crime in contrast to Dukakis, who approves of weekend passes.

Ostensibly, the message was about crime, but the ad featuring a menacing photo of Horton sent another message—that Black men are to be feared and that Bush will protect the nation from them.[46] The Bush campaign tried to distance itself from the Willie Horton ads by declaring to mainstream media that it had nothing to do with them. But on September 1, just before the ads began running, Bush was making a tour of polluted Boston Harbor and declaring that Dukakis could not be trusted on environmental issues. As his boat passed a prison, a reporter called out to Bush, "Are any of those people getting furloughs over there?"—to which Bush replied, "Only one, Willie Horton."[47] So Bush seemed well aware of the Horton issue before the ads began running just a few days later.

Throughout the campaign, the Bush team criticized Dukakis as a far-out liberal and referred to him over and over as a "card-carrying member of the ACLU," which obviously echoed a charge during the McCarthy era that someone under suspicion was a "card-carrying" member of the Communist Party. The Bush campaign also attacked Dukakis for being weak on defense because of his criticisms of various new weapons systems. To counter this impression, Dukakis took a three-day tour of military facilities. At one Michigan base, he rode around in a tank with his head sticking out of the top and wearing a helmet that many associated with what the cartoon character Snoopy the dog wore in his First World War-vintage airplane while fighting the Red Baron. Dukakis became a laughingstock and handed the Republicans an irresistible opportunity to make him appear both ridiculous and incompetent. A Bush campaign ad featured Dukakis in the tank, with words scrolling down the image that listed all the weapon systems he had criticized, with a voice-over concluding at the end, "And now he wants to become our commander-in-chief. We can't afford that risk."[48] In November, Bush won with 426 electoral votes—and 53.4 percent of the popular vote—to Dukakis's 45.6 percent and 111 electoral votes.

Although neither presidential candidate in 1988 could be listed as a celebrity, the television ad campaign against Dukakis demonstrated powerfully Lippmann's quote about political imagery: "We shall assume that what each man does is based not on direct and certain knowledge, but on pictures made by himself or given to him."[49] Just as telling was the admonition from Joseph P. Kennedy when his sickly son Jack decided to run for Congress in 1946: "You must remember—it's not what you are that counts, but what people think you are."[50]

A little less than two years before facing reelection in 1992, Bush scored approval ratings of 89 percent, a record high for any president, after ordering a brief and very successful invasion that forced Iraqi dictator Saddam Hussein out of Kuwait in February 1991. However, various factors soon eroded his popularity. One was the lingering aftermath of the Iran-Contra scandal. Bush had constantly said he had been "out of the loop" on these decisions, but doubt continued to hover over his denial. Subsequent evidence has demonstrated, including entries in his own diary, that he was fully aware of these plans at the time. His decision to pardon five high-ranking members of the Reagan administration for their involvement in Iran-Contra also gave ammunition to the Democrats.

A steep recession that broke out in 1990, with unemployment of 7.8 percent, likewise hurt Bush. His masterful handling of German unification and the collapse of the Soviet Union was impressive, but the public was far more interested in having him address economic problems at home. An incident in February 1992 that occurred while he was attending a convention of the National Grocers Association seemed to emphasize to many how far out of touch their president was with the experiences of everyday Americans. When shown the improvements to equipment for price scanning at grocery checkouts, he expressed amazement that such technology could exist, even though it had been common for more than a decade to anyone who had gone grocery shopping.[51]

Playing it Cool

This story and other accusations of Bush's being out of touch, along with his memory of rigors on the campaign trail, made him less than enthusiastic about hitting the road again. As it turned out, he faced a Democratic challenger in William Jefferson "Bill" Clinton, whose experience in government was far less impressive. Clinton had been a three-term governor of Arkansas, by any definition a small southern state. And at age forty-six, he was a full generation younger than the sixty-eight-year-old Bush, who could rightfully claim to be an accomplished elder statesman. Temperament, however, favored Clinton. Bush had been taught since childhood to keep his feelings in check and never to call undue attention to himself. Clinton, in contrast, was magnetic, exuberant, outgoing, high-spirited, and empathetic.

From a very early age, Clinton loved being at the center of attention. He was always the most popular kid in school and automatically drew others into his orbit. He also loved to perform, whether playing the jazz saxophone, savoring his role as the high school band major, or giving talks to local service clubs while still in school. In fact, performance and showmanship were literally in the air in Hot Springs, Arkansas, to which Clinton's family had moved when he was in second grade from his birthplace of Hope, Arkansas. Besides the springs, their new home was famous for its resort hotels and the glitzy shows they put on for guests.

Clinton got himself elected to "Boys State" and then to "Boys Nation," where he had his photo taken shaking hands with President Kennedy in the Rose Garden at the White House. The picture was reproduced in his senior yearbook, along with approximately thirty other photographs in which he appeared, but it was the one with Kennedy that he proudly signed for friends and teachers in their yearbooks. That he had shaken hands with this president just months before Kennedy had been assassinated made Clinton something of a local celebrity, and this event, however fleeting, became the topic for many of the talks he gave to civic groups around town.[52]

During the 1992 presidential campaign, Clinton was electrifying, much like John F. Kennedy three decades before. He loved to speak before adoring crowds and to work the rope lines where admirers often grabbed his hands and arms and tried to pull him closer, which exhilarated rather than exhausted him. The second presidential debate, held on October 15, featured a town hall format where members of the audience could ask spontaneous questions, probably cinched the election for Clinton. When, toward the end of the debate, an African American woman asked a confusing question about how the national debt affected each candidate, Bush struggled to answer her. But when it was Clinton's turn to respond, he took several steps toward the woman and, empathizing with her, said, "Tell me again how it's affected you." Bush, by contrast, was spotted on television looking down at his watch as if to say, "When is this going to be over?"[53]

Clinton's advertising spots were also far more appealing than Bush's. The best of them played on the name of Hope, Arkansas, where he had been born and lived until the family moved to Hot Springs: The ad opens with a photograph of the train station at Hope, with the name emblazoned on the side. Then in a voiceover, Clinton says, "I was born in a little town called Hope three months after my father died." Viewers learn next that he and his mother went to live with his grandparents, who had very little money. Next, he tells of going to Washington with Boys Nation, where he meets President Kennedy, illustrated with a still photograph of the handshake, along with a short black-and-white movie clip of the same unforgettable experience. Reliving the event for viewers, he takes them back in time: "What a great country this was, I thought, if somebody like me with no money or anything would be given the opportunity to meet the President of the United States." (In fact, his mother was by then a very successful nurse-anesthetist, which was providing the family with a prosperous middle-class lifestyle, but those seeing the ad had no way of knowing that.) Meeting Kennedy, Clinton goes on to say, had inspired him to devote his life to public service and to help people. Then, after working his way through law school, the ad continues, he went home to Arkansas—not because he wanted to make money but because he wanted to make a difference in people's lives by becoming governor. Now, if elected president, he would "bring back hope to the American Dream."[54] (Another huge omission was Clinton's attendance at Oxford University as a Rhodes Scholar, perhaps because it would have seemed too elitist or exotic to many voters.)

Clinton also broke new ground as a candidate by playing his saxophone on the *Arsenio Hall Show*. Wearing sunglasses, he performed a soulful rendition of "Heartbreak Hotel," and the audience went wild—standing, clapping, and swinging their bodies to the tune. "Cool" Clinton, with his boyish good looks, had introduced himself to a new generation of voters who, up to that point, had seen and heard little about him. During an interview with Arsenio Hall several years later, CNN news reporter John King declared that Clinton's performance on the show had changed politics forever by demonstrating that a candidate could go beyond traditional news programming to present himself.

Of course, Clinton's playing the saxophone revealed nothing about his policies or whether he would make a good president—which, of course, was not the point of the appearance on television. Nor could one imagine the more reserved George H. W. Bush doing a similar gig even if he were able to play a musical instrument with equal skill and emotional fervor.[55] In the process, Clinton made himself into what might be called a minor celebrity—not on the level of a John Kennedy or Ronald Reagan, but his example would show the way to other prospective presidents.

Clinton's saxophone performance and his demonstration of empathy during the debates, plus the cleverly written and designed television ad that played on the image of hope no doubt helped him in November. However, Bush had far more going against him than not coming across as cool and emotionally available, as he faced a bad economy and the entrance of third-party candidate Ross Perot, who siphoned more votes away from Bush than from Clinton. The Republicans tried to undermine Clinton because he had arranged several deferments to get out of serving during the Vietnam War, but by then many Americans had soured on the conflict, and Clinton came through the criticism unscathed. In November, Clinton won with 43 percent of the popular vote to Bush's 37.4 percent and Perot's 18.9 percent. Clinton carried the Electoral College 370 to Bush's 168, with no electoral votes for Perot.

That Electoral College

In 2000, the Democrats nominated Albert "Al" Gore, who had been Clinton's vice president. Before that, he had served four terms in the United States House of Representatives and seven years in the United States Senate. He had also been born in Washington and spent most of his childhood and youth in the capital while his father, Albert Gore, Sr., was a senator from Tennessee. More than anyone else who aspired to the presidency in modern times, he knew the capital and its ways "inside out." He had used his knowledge of politics as well as his many contacts in Washington as a basis for the senior thesis he wrote in 1969 as a history major at Harvard University. Its title was "The Impact of Television on the Conduct of the Presidency, 1947–1969." Very perceptively, he wrote in one part of it, "Only television effectively stimulates interpersonal contact. Radio came very close; it conveyed an impression of 'personality,' and increased the importance of the listener's emotional responses, but only one sense was stimulated, and the most important factor in interpersonal contact—visual recognition—was still missing." Gore went on to rate various presidents for their mastery of this visual medium, giving the highest marks to Kennedy: "A large part of the credit for Kennedy's success on television was due to his personality. Not everything can be explained in terms of formats and camera work. . . . President Kennedy was simply better on television than most. He was equipped with an understanding of the medium and its exigencies, and he knew how to use the visual rhetoric."[56]

Unfortunately, when it came to performing on television himself, Gore was not the "natural" that Kennedy or Clinton had been. He often came across as lecturing instead of connecting to his audiences with the sort of effortless emotion and empathy that had become Clinton's trademark. Clinton might have used this skill to help connect Gore to voters, but Gore refused to call on Clinton for fear that the sex scandal involving his old boss and Monica Lewinsky would tarnish him by association. In contrast, Republican nominee George W. Bush, the son of President George H. W. Bush, came across as spontaneously friendly despite numerous verbal gaffes which may have endeared him to as many voters as they put off. Carrying the Bush name certainly helped with voter recognition, and his having grown up in Texas, with a real Texas accent, allowed him to claim he was a Washington outsider, an identity that continued to attract those with a jaded view of anyone like Al Gore who had spent almost his entire life in the Capitol City. Also attractive was the fact that Bush was a two-term governor of Texas rather than a member of Congress. Of the two candidates, polls showed that more people would rather have a beer with Bush than with Gore, even though Bush, who had been a serious alcoholic, had quit drinking years before.

Nevertheless, Gore was favored to win going into election day.[57] In the end, he defeated Bush by nearly half a million popular votes—48.4 percent to 47.9 percent. However, Green Party nominee Ralph Nader received 3 percent of the popular vote overall and in the process probably deprived Gore of popular vote victories in Minnesota, Oregon, and Florida, since exit polls indicated that many more Nader voters would have cast their votes for Gore if Nader had not been on the ballot. In Florida, the Bush-Gore contest resulted in essentially a tie, with Bush ahead by a few hundred votes. This outcome resulted in a recount, which the US Supreme Court halted while it was in progress. With Bush declared as the winner in Florida, he won by 271 to 266 electoral votes (with none for Nader). Although it cannot be measured, Bush's friendlier and folksier profile may have also taken votes from Gore. In any case, this was the fourth time in the nation's history when the person who lost the popular vote became president.

"Audacity of Hope"

The path that Barack Obama took to the presidency eight years later was both common and uncommon: Common because he went to law school and became an Illinois State Senator and then a US Senator, but uncommon because of his rapid rise through the political ranks, with three terms in the Illinois legislature and not quite four years in the US Senate. His background was also unusual, being the first African American candidate for president, with an upbringing that was multi-ethnic and multicultural. Using this background to write a best-selling book and making compelling speeches gave him a celebrity status that propelled him into the White House.

Obama's white mother had been born in Kansas, in the heartland of America. Her family later moved to Hawaii, where she met and married Obama's Kenyan-born father, also named Barack. Born in 1961, young Barack's parents divorced when he was two years old, and the only other time he saw his father was during a visit when he was ten. Young Barack and his mother moved to Jakarta, Indonesia, when he was six to join his Indonesian stepfather (and his mother's second husband). During four years of school in Jakarta, Barack learned to speak the local language. They returned to Hawaii four years later and lived with his mother's parents, remaining there until Barack graduated from high school. After Columbia University, he moved to Chicago and worked there for five years as a community organizer, where he learned "hands-on" about the challenges and complexities of urban poverty and deprivation. Then it was on to Harvard Law School, where he became editor of the *Harvard Law Review* at the end of his freshman year and president of the law review a year later.

As the first African American to become president of Harvard's prestigious law review, Obama received wide publicity. It was this notice that attracted an offer from a publisher to write a book, as Obama described it, in the "belief that the story of my family, and my efforts to understand that story might speak in some way to the fissures of race that have characterized the American experience, as well as the fluid state of identity."[58] Returning to Chicago in 1991, he became a civil rights lawyer while teaching law at the University of Chicago and completed his memoir, *Dreams from My Father* (1995), a conscious effort to make sense of the varied strands of his life.

The years in Hawaii had given Obama a vision of how a multiracial society could operate in harmony. Looking back on their arrival in Hawaii in 1959, he wrote, "It . . . seemed as if the earth itself, weary of stampeding armies and bitter civilization, had forced up this chain of emerald rock where pioneers from across the globe could populate the land with children bronzed by the sun." And the great diversity of its people—Native Hawaiians, Japanese, Chinese, and Caucasians from around the globe, "meant there were too many races, with power among them too diffuse, to impose the [United States] mainland's rigid caste system . . ."[59] In Indonesia, he had easily made friends with local children, running the streets with them "morning and night, hustling odd jobs, catching crickets, [and] battling swift kites with razor-sharp lines . . ."[60] However, it was while they were living in Jakarta that his mother brought home books about the civil rights movement back in the United States, which initially gave him a sense of pride about his heritage. But it was also during that time that he saw photographs in *Life* magazine of a Black man who had used chemicals to peel off his skin. The pictures shocked young Barack, who had been thus far sheltered from the horrors of racism.

Obama's quest took him to Kenya in 1987 where he visited his father's extended family. There he discovered that family members had widely different opinions of the now deceased senior Obama. He also found the same grinding poverty and deprivation in Nairobi he had witnessed as a community organizer in Chicago, though in Kenya there was no social safety net—only appeals for help from kinfolk. Then there were the cleavages of Kenya's forty tribes—leading Obama to try declaring to his Kenyan relatives, "We're all part of one tribe. The black tribe"—and on a larger plane, "the human tribe."[61] Not surprisingly, he ends his narrative by asking himself questions about the essence of community: "What is our community, and how might that community be reconciled with our [individual and group freedoms]? How far do our obligations reach? How do we transform mere power into justice, mere sentiment into love?" His answer was one of hope: "I find myself modestly encouraged, believing that so long as the questions are still being asked, what binds us together might somehow, ultimately, prevail."[62]

Obama described his book sales as "underwhelming," but his writing style and his story were, in fact compelling and suggested he could have staked out a writing career alongside his teaching and legal practice. However, a penchant for practical action led him to run successfully for the Illinois State Senate in 1996, serving there until his election to the United States Senate in 2004. As an up-and-coming young Democrat from a large state, his party tapped him to give a keynote speech at their convention that summer. The speech was electrifying and introduced him to a wide national audience, as well as helping him win his US Senate seat that fall.

Initially, the speech seemed to take its cue from the well-worn theme of how dedication and hard work might allow anyone in America to rise. But then, he delved into the story of his diverse ancestry and experiences as a living example of how Americans could work together to overcome division and solve problems. At this point in the speech, words and phrases poured out as if propelled by some inner necessity:

> There's not a liberal America and a conservative America; there's the United States of America. There's not a black America and white America and Latino America and Asian America; there's the United States of America. . . . We are one people, all of us pledging allegiance to the stars and stripes, all of us defending the United States of America.

For all Americans, there was "the audacity of hope! In the end, that is God's greatest gift to us, the bedrock of this nation; the belief in things not seen; the belief that there are better days ahead."[63]

Of everything Obama said that evening, the phrase "audacity of hope" stood out and became the title for a second book that he published in 2006.[64] It quickly rose to number one on the *New York Times* Best Seller list. Throughout the book, there was his emphasis on a set of ideas that Americans had in common: ". . . At the core of the American experience are a set of ideals that continue to stir our collective conscience, a common set of values that bind us together despite our differences; a running thread of hope that makes our improbable experiment of democracy work." These values and ideals were not limited to what one read on public monuments and in the history books: "They remain alive in the hearts and minds of most Americans—and can inspire us to pride, duty, and sacrifice."[65] The new book, combined with Obama's electrifying speeches, had made him into a national celebrity.

After a hard-fought primary campaign against Senator Hillary Clinton, Obama received the Democratic nomination for president in 2008. Throughout his presidential campaign, he continued to emphasize the need for more cooperation and less partisanship in government. He also stressed the need for a change of party in the White House, given the growing public consensus that President Bush had launched a needless and disastrous war in Iraq. His slogan was "Change We Can Believe In," which elicited the chant from supporters, "Yes We Can."

Obama's challenger for the presidency was John McCain, who at the time had served three terms as Arizona's US Senator and before that, two terms in the United States House of Representatives. McCain had no reservations about speaking his mind and described himself as something of a maverick who was well-equipped to bring about change in Washington. However, as a Republican, it was impossible for him to break with the policies of the Bush administration, especially the Iraq War, which he had voted to authorize in October 2002. McCain's age, at seventy-two, was also an unspoken factor that worked against him, in contrast to Obama, who was then forty-seven and a full generation younger than his opponent. McCain attempted to compensate for the age difference by selecting Alaska Governor Sarah Palin as his running mate. That she was just forty-four was thought to compensate for McCain's age, as well as to attract women voters. As it turned out, Palin was woefully ill-informed on issues, which became obvious during interviews and debates.

In the end, more voters believed that Obama was likely to be an agent of change. He won the popular vote by 53 to 46 percent and the Electoral College by 365 to 173. There could be no question about his celebrity status, as attested by the 240,000 people who gathered in Chicago's Grant Park to hear his acceptance speech and the estimated 1.8 million who attended his inauguration, the largest in US history. For African Americans especially, Obama was both a celebrity and a hopeful deliverer from centuries of racial hatred and discrimination. And around the world for people of color, as well as for many others who had been disgusted by what they saw as the arrogance of the Bush administration and its neocon policies, the new president seemed to promise a new and hopeful beginning. In many ways, Obama built an image for himself that could seem a return to the past, rooted in the written word and in well-crafted speeches that echoed the stentorian speaking styles of nineteenth-century statesmen. At the same time, he seemed propelled into the present and future as the first African American inaugurated by a major party and elected to the highest office in the land.

Pictures Made

Other presidents elected from 1948 to 2012 might be defined, with varying degrees of incompleteness and exaggeration, through Lippmann's "pictures made by himself or given to him": Truman (feisty common man); Eisenhower (smiling, fatherly protector); Kennedy (glamorous celebrity); Johnson (folksy, can-do spirit); Nixon (good family man and "New Nixon"); Ford (unpretentious and honest); Carter (Washington outsider); Reagan (rugged all-American); Bush I (experienced and modest); Clinton (cool and gregarious); Bush II (friendly and accessible); Obama (eloquent and hopeful).

One is tempted to ask if most of these presidential images were helpful guides to voters, or if such images, in varying ways, deflected voters' attention from the important issues of the day while at the same time ignoring the real strengths and weaknesses of candidates. Walter Lippmann, Daniel Boorstin, Neil Postman, and Charlotte De Backer, writing at different points over the past century and discussed earlier in this chapter, would probably agree. But neither they nor any other analysts of the American political system could have imagined that a man named Donald Trump, advertising himself for the presidency as a celebrity deal maker, could be elected president in 2016 (and again in 2024) and become the most powerful man in the world. Trump would also take his place among those presidents whose sense of resentment, forged early in their lives, contributed greatly to their impeachments, attempted impeachments, or threatened impeachments.

Notes

1 Quoted in Peter Collier and David Horowitz, *The Kennedys: An American Drama* (New York: Summit Books, 1984), 235.
2 Quoted in ibid.
3 Quoted ibid., 150.
4 Ibid., 148.
5 Ibid., 121.
6 Walter Lippmann, *Public Opinion* (Middletown: Renaissance Classics, 2002 [1922]), 17.
7 Daniel J. Boorstin, *The Image: A Guide to Pseudo-Events in America* (New York: Vintage Books, 1961), 45.
8 Neil Postman, *Amusing Ourselves to Death: Public Discourse in the Age of Show Business* (New York: Penguin Books, 2005 [1985]).
9 Ibid., 51.
10 Ibid., 49.
11 De Baker, “Blinded by Starlight,” 145.
12 Lippmann, *Public Opinion*, 71.
13 Ibid.
14 De Backer, “Blinded by Starlight,” 148.
15 Still worth reading is Theodore H. White’s account in his *Making of the President 1960* (New York: Harper Perennial, 2009 [1961]), 283–95. White was an accomplished newspaper journalist, whose book about the 1960 election coveys a sense of color and immediacy.
16 Quoted in Evan Thomas, *Being Nixon: A Man Divided* (New York: Random House, 2016), 115.
17 Boorstin, *The Image*, 42.
18 Collier and Horowitz, *The Kennedys*, 245.
19 Ībid., 161.
20 Dallek, *An Unfinished Life*, 98.
21 Theodore S. White, *Making of the President 1964* (New York: Harper Perennial, 2009 [1961]), 108; Collier and Horowitz, *The Kennedys*, 188.
22 Robert J. Donovan, *PT 109: John F. Kennedy in World War II* (New York: McGraw-Hill, 1961).
23 Collier and Horowitz, *The Kennedys*, 285; Dallek, *An Unfinished Life*, 96–9.
24 Arthur Schlesinger, Jr., *A Thousand Days: John F. Kennedy in the White House* (Boston: Houghton Mifflin Company, 1965), 717.
25 Boorstin, *The Image*, 42.
26 See Greg Mitchell, *Tricky Dick and the Pink Lady* (New York: Random House, 1998).
27 Joe McGinnes, *The Selling of the President 1968* (New York: Trident Press, 1969).
28 Ibid., 30, 31.
29 Quoted in ibid., 58.
30 Ibid., 26.

31 Gerald Ford, "Quotations: The words of Gerald Ford," *New York Times,* December 27, 2006.
32 *New York Times,* November 19, 1977.
33 Robert Sklar, *Movie-Made America*(New York: Vintage, 1994), 196–7.
34 Bob Schieffer and Gary Paul Gates, *The Acting President: Ronald Reagan and the Supporting Actors Who Helped Him Create the Illusion That Held American Spellbound* (New York: E.P. Dutton, 1989), 165.
35 Ibid., 176–7, 181.
36 Ibid., 178–9.
37 Quoted in ibid., 179.
38 Both of these debates are available for viewing on YouTube.
39 *The Columbus Dispatch,* November 10, 2016.
40 Both the Morning in America and Bear ads are available on YouTube.
41 Quoted in Schieffer and Gates, *The Acting President,* 189.
42 *The Tower Commission Report: The Full Text of the President's Special Review Board* (New York: Bantam Books/New York Times Books, 1987).
43 Margaret Garrard Warner, "Bush Battles the 'Wimp Factor,'" *Newsweek,* October 19, 1987.
44 Jon Meacham, *Destiny and Power: The American Odyssey of George Herbert Walker Bush* (New York: Random House, 2015), 59–63. This short film can be seen on YouTube under the title, "George Bush Rescued at Sea by the USS Finback," 02 September 1944.
45 Lilyan Wilder, quoted in ibid.
46 See "Willie Horton Political Ad 1988" on YouTube.
47 Quoted in Meacham, *Destiny and Power,* 341.
48 See "Michael Dukakis, The Tank Ad 1988," YouTube.
49 Lippmann, *Public Opinion,* 17. This pioneering study was first published in 1922.
50 Collier and Horowitz, *The Kennedys,* 150.
51 *New York Times,* February 5, 1992.
52 For an account of Clinton's childhood and youth see David Maraniss, *First in His Class: The Biography of Bill Clinton* (New York: Simon & Schuster, 1995), 21–49. Also writing a about Clinton's early years, but from a more explicitly psychological point of view, is John D. Gartner, *In Search of Bill Clinton* (New York: St. Martin's Press, 2008), 1–132.
53 A transcript if this debate appeared in *the New York Times,* October 17, 1992.
54 See YouTube, "Bill Clinton Hope Ad 1992."
55 Clinton's performance and John King's reflections about it can be viewed on YouTube, "Arsenio Hall Recalls Bill Clinton Playing Sax."
56 Albert A. Gore, "The Impact of Television on the Conduct of the Presidency, 1947–1969," Harvard University Senior Thesis, https://www.nytimes.com/.../word-for-word-al-gore-s-senior-thesis-even-college-vice-pr...
57 Robert G. Kaiser, "Academics Say It's Elementary: Gore Wins," *Washington Post,* August 31, 2000.
58 Barack Obama, *Dreams from My Father: A Story of Race and Inheritance,* Preface to the 2004 Edition (New York: Three Rivers Press, 2004), vii. The book was originally published in 1995 and reissued in 2004 following Obama's sensational keynote address to the Democratic National Convention that same year.

59 Ibid., 23.
60 Ibid., 36.
61 Ibid., 348.
62 Ibid., 438.
63 Barack Obama, 2004 Democratic National Convention Keynote Speech, www.americanrhetoric.com/speeches/convention2004/barackobama2004. A video of this speech is also available on YouTube.
64 Barack Obama, *The Audacity of Hope: Thoughts on Restoring the American Dream* (New York: Three Rivers Press, 2006).
65 Ibid., 8.

9

Impeachment and Resentment

Formations of Presidential Character

Bad men will sometimes get in, and with such an immense patronage, make great progress in corrupting the public mind and principles.

Thomas Jefferson to Moses Robinson, March 23, 1801

The secret tape recordings, now made public, contain numerous obscenities along with racial and ethnic slurs, in addition to clear evidence that the president has authorized hush money payments and obstructed justice. On August 7, 1974, a small delegation of leading Republican senators visits the president in the White House. The Judiciary Committee of the House of Representatives has already approved three articles of impeachment, and the senators tell the nation's chief executive that the upper chamber will very likely convict and thereby remove him from office. Two days later, on August 7, Richard Nixon resigns rather than become the first president in history to be expelled from office.

Shortly after the Civil War, the House of Representatives did impeach Andrew Johnson, who escaped conviction in the Senate by just a single vote. A little over a century later came the resignation of Richard Nixon, when faced with an impending impeachment and very probable conviction. Donald Trump would be impeached twice, but he would not be convicted in either instance. In between Nixon and Trump, Bill Clinton was impeached but not convicted for lying under oath about a sexual affair that neither threatened a large group of people nor the nation at large. The Clinton impeachment will therefore not be considered in this chapter even though Clinton's behavior was outrageous to many Americans. (In other respects, Clinton also does not fit the pattern of these other presidents who emerged as angry and resentful from childhoods and youth. Clinton suffered some difficult circumstances early on, having been raised by a single mother and then having to endure a sometimes abusive stepfather, but he was well-loved by his mother and grandparents and grew up self-confident, cheerful, and well-liked. In this sense, one might say Clinton is the exception that proves the rule.)[1]

Here it bears repeating an earlier quotation from political scientist James David Barber: "*Character is the way the President orients himself toward life*—not at the moment, but enduringly." Barber adds, "Character is the person's stance as he confronts experience. . . . The man develops a combination which makes psychological sense for him, a dynamic arrangement of motives, beliefs, and habits in the services of his need for self-esteem."[2] For Barber, the character of a president is the most important predictor of how an individual will behave in office. Accordingly, the best way to predict a president's character, Barber asserts, is to explore its construction during the person's childhood, adolescence, and early adulthood.[3]

One wonders if presidents who were impeached—or were seriously threatened with impeachment—share certain experiences in early life that shaped their characters in ways that could help to explain their abuses of power. Upon examination, it is clear that Johnson, Nixon, and Trump evidenced personal resentments that stemmed from their early lives. These resentments may have allowed them—consciously or unconsciously—to commiserate with voters who had come to resent their own life circumstances, and in the process to employ what has been called the "politics of resentment."[4] Of course, the vagaries of politics and current events would help to channel how these presidents gave vent to the anger and resentments that distorted their views of the world. These distortions contributed to refusals to compromise, to the blunting of inhibitions about breaking presidential norms, and even to violating the law and defying the Constitution.

One should note, however, that some presidents who faced various deprivations in early life nevertheless do not share such patterns of resentment. For instance, Abraham Lincoln grew up in a one-room log cabin in a family with little money; his mother died when he was nine and a half years old, and his father was a hard-driving and often angry man. Yet the Lincolns were no worse off than anyone else in their frontier neighborhood, thus shielding young Lincoln from invidious social and economic comparisons. He was also fortunate in having a stepmother who loved and cherished him and who encouraged his thirst for learning.

The Making of Andrew Johnson

Andrew Johnson (1865–1869) suffered from difficult social and economic circumstances while growing up in Raleigh, North Carolina. He was born in 1808 to parents who were illiterate, unskilled workers who could not afford to send him to school. Although the Johnsons' prosperous neighbors referred to the family as "white trash," they could console themselves in not being at the absolute bottom of the social ladder: They might be poor, but at least they were not black, which would become a mantra for an insecure Johnson for the rest of his life.

Added to the sting of being called white trash, Johnson must have suffered from a sense of abandonment when his mother died and left him under the care of relatives whom he knew would rather not put up with him. In Johnson's case, feelings of abandonment were probably triggered powerfully after his father died. His widowed mother remarried and then apprenticed him to a tailor when Andrew was not quite ten years old.[5] This banishment may well have left him feeling both worthless and unloved.

The master tailor, who now held complete sway over the boy, taught him to read as well as to make fine men's clothing. However, bridling under the master's control, as if he were enslaved, Andrew fled and eventually opened a shop in partnership with another man in the East Tennessee village of Greenville. He was an excellent suit maker, and their business flourished. Meanwhile, he read every book he could get his hands on and joined a local debating society. He also loved to talk politics and was elected in 1829 as a village alderman. Politics now became his path to rise in the world, becoming a state legislator, a member of the US House of Representatives, and then a US Senator. He also bought land and slaves, owning some eight or nine bondsmen at one point. Now, no one would call him white trash.

Over the years, Johnson was blunt, crude, and unapologetic in his remarks about black people. In 1843, he declared, "The black race of Africa [is] inferior to the white man in point of intellect—better calculated in physical structure to undergo drudgery and hardship—standing, as they do, many degrees lower in the scale of gradation that [expresses] the relative relation between God and all that he had created than the white man." While a member of the House of Representatives, he accordingly spoke out against a proposed amendment to a piece of legislation that would remove the word "white" from voting requirements in Alexandria, Virginia. "If the bill passe[s]," Johnson exploded, "it [will] place every splay-footed, bandy-shanked, hump-backed, thick-lipped, flat-nosed, woolly-headed, ebon-colored negro in the country upon an equality with the poor white man."[6] Years later, in a speech delivered at Raleigh, he insisted that enslaved blacks were better off in America than they were in Africa because of the elevating effects of contact with the white race, characterizing them as "an inferior type of man, incapable of advancement in his native country."[7] It takes no imagination to conclude that these vicious pronouncements about the black race made Johnson feel all the more elevated in social standing and allowed him to play out his resentment at being looked down on as a child and youth.

Once Johnson had risen socially, he liked to boast about his advancement from humble origins as a means of connecting to plain folk whom he believed would share his resentments at being disrespected by the social establishment, in what amounted to a recurring populist campaign on Johnson's part. In doing so, Johnson employed a sort of reverse snobbery by contending that farmers and the laborers were the "real" people, in contrast to "would-be aristocrats" such as haughty graduates from West Point and Annapolis, echoing Andrew Jackson's earlier diatribes against the military academies. While a member of the House of Representatives, Johnson referred to West Point officers as an "illegitimate, swaggering, bastard, scrub aristocracy, who assumed to know a good deal," but who were, in actuality, both ignorant and incompetent.[8]

This anti-elitism, comingled with a bitter anti-intellectualism, extended to an almost maniacal hatred of the Smithsonian Institution, founded in 1846 "for the increase and diffusion of knowledge." Johnson vehemently opposed Congressional legislation to accept funds from the estate of James Smithson to establish the institution, and regularly condemned any subsequent appropriations for the Smithsonian. Far more worthwhile to him was his Homestead Bill, which would provide a quarter section of public land (160 acres) to the head of each family applying for the program, provided they would reside on and cultivate the property for a required period. He constantly asserted that government should exist for the good of the people and therefore that it was wrong for the federal government to hoard public land which landless citizens could farm to rise economically, thereby strengthening their stake in democracy.

Being a member of Congress did not quell Johnson's drive for affirmation, and as early as 1852, he set his sights on the presidency. At the beginning of 1860, he persuaded Tennessee Democrats to endorse him as their "favorite son" candidate for president. Later that year, he hoped the national Democratic Convention would turn to him as their presidential nominee when it looked increasingly as if Steven Douglas, their leading contender, could not win in November. Then when Douglas's prospects improved, some of Johnson's supporters suggested he would make the best possible running mate to help defeat Republican candidate Abraham Lincoln in the fall, but this idea went nowhere.

In seeming contradiction to his vehement defense of slavery, Johnson fought to keep his adopted home state of Tennessee from seceding and joining the Confederacy. In many of his pro-Union speeches, he brought up the example of the much-admired Andrew Jackson, who had forced South Carolina to back down from its secession threats over the tariff three decades before. Disunion, to Johnson's way of thinking, would be the surest way to enable abolitionist Republicans to have their way, since the US Constitution had enshrined and protected slavery. Remaining in the Union, therefore, would be the best protection for the owners of enslaved people. Even more telling, Johnson both resented and despised the southern grandees who were leading the secession movement and who would rule the South even more than in the past.[9] However, his campaign against Tennessee's secession failed, and his state voted to leave the Union in early June of 1861.

Obdurate to the end, Johnson remained in the Senate as the only member from a seceded state to do so and received applause from both Republicans and War Democrats in the North. He took advantage of this popularity to urge the Lincoln administration to use military force to liberate Tennessee from the Confederacy. When Union troops made considerable inroads in Tennessee during early 1862, Lincoln appointed Johnson as military governor of the state. Although he had often spoken about his beliefs in the racial inferiority of Black people, he embraced Lincoln's Emancipation Proclamation most probably as a pragmatic decision to remain in the president's good graces, as well as a tactic for winning the war by depriving the South of its workforce. Anticipating that Lincoln would soon move to end slavery, he declared during a speech at Nashville on July 4, 1862, "If you persist in forcing the issue of slavery against the Government, I say in the face of Heaven, 'Give me my Government and let the negroes [sic.] go!'"[10] Having embraced the Emancipation Proclamation, he also supported the Thirteenth Amendment, ratified at the end of 1865, which made human bondage unconstitutional in the United States.

As time would tell, Johnson had not changed his beliefs about the inferiority of African Americans; but in the meantime, his popularity in the North and his support for Lincoln would garner his nomination as Lincoln's vice-presidential running mate in 1864 and his election as vice president on the ticket with Lincoln that November.

In selecting him to be vice president, Lincoln may not have been aware of Johnson's caustic and unrelenting racism, or of his reputation for stubbornness and reflexive fury. In any case, Johnson turned out to be a poor choice indeed.

Six weeks after the inauguration, Lincoln was dead, cut down on April 15 by an assassin's bullet. Six days earlier, Robert E. Lee had surrendered at Appomattox Court House, Virginia, essentially ending the Civil War. Lincoln now proclaimed his wish to heal the nation as during his eloquent Second Inaugural address. He would, "Strive on to finish the work we are in; to bind up the nation's wounds; to care for him who shall have borne the battle, and for his widow and orphan—to do all which may achieve and cherish a just and lasting peace, among ourselves, and with all nations."[11]

During the past three years, Lincoln had given much thought to Reconstruction—about how and under what circumstances the seceded states could come back into the Union. In his Annual Message for 1863, he had proposed his "ten percent plan," which would offer a "full pardon" accompanied by a restitution of all property rights, except for formerly enslaved people, to all who took an oath of future loyalty to the Constitution. They must also pledge to abide by all acts of Congress and presidential orders regarding emancipation. As soon as 10 percent of a state's 1860 voters took the oath, they could reestablish a loyal state government.

Radical Republicans in both the House and Senate grew increasingly wary about the ten percent plan, fearing that the same individuals who had plotted and carried out secession would end up back in power and that the civil rights of those so recently freed would not be advanced or respected. As the Congressional session neared its end in 1864, both chambers passed the Wade-Davis Act, named for its principal sponsors, Senator Benjamin F. Wade of Ohio and Representative Henry Winter Davis of Maryland. It required any reorganized state to accept emancipation and mandated that 50 percent (rather than Lincoln's ten percent proposal) must take the oath of loyalty. Drawing a sharp line over jurisdiction, the bill further declared that Reconstruction was under the "paramount" authority of the legislative branch of the federal government. Lincoln killed the bill with a pocket veto, an unusual strategy at that time, which occurs when a president does not sign a given piece of legislation following a Congressional adjournment. The radicals were furious, and the requirements for Reconstruction remained unsettled when Lincoln began his second term. As it turned out, the contest between the legislative and executive branches over Reconstruction would take place during the Johnson presidency.

Congress Versus the President

Following Lincoln's assassination, the Radical Republicans in Congress believed they had a strong ally in Johnson. He had opposed secession and remained in the Senate after his own state had left the Union. He had also been a member of Congress's Joint Committee on the Conduct of the War. However, he continued to harbor a deep hatred for black people and opposed any attempts to extend equal rights to them. The Radicals were soon disappointed: Despite his support for emancipation, Johnson continued to harbor a deep hatred for black people and opposed any attempts to extend equal rights to them.

Although Congress during that era did not begin its sessions until early December, Lincoln's death and the end of the war would clearly seem to indicate that Johnson should call the lawmakers into special session to pass legislation about Reconstruction. Instead, taking advantage of Congress being out of session much like Lincoln at the beginning of the Civil War, Johnson issued a series of executive orders that set down extremely lenient policies and that did nothing to elevate the lives of freedmen. The *Cincinnati Enquirer* quoted Johnson as writing to Governor Thomas C. Fletcher of Missouri, "This is a country for white men, and by God, as long as I am President, it shall be a government for white men."[12] Under Johnson's Reconstruction plan, small farmers and members of the white working class elected new state governments, which predictably legislated "black codes" depriving the formerly enslaved of virtually all their civil rights.

When Congress finally came back into session, Republicans responded by enacting several pieces of legislation that attempted to take control of Reconstruction from the president. One was a bill passed in February 1866 to continue funding the Freedman's Bureau, founded a year earlier to supply food, clothing, medical care, and education to those emerging from enslavement. Johnson vetoed it, claiming it was an unconstitutional use of the federal government's authority in peacetime. Both houses of Congress mustered the necessary two-thirds vote to override his veto. Then, in April, Congress passed a Civil Rights Act that mandated equal rights for African Americans, declaring them citizens of the United States and entitling them to equal rights under the law. Johnson also vetoed this Civil Rights Act of 1866, and Congress once again overrode his veto.

Congress then moved to keep Johnson from influencing the Supreme Court. When a vacancy opened on the court, Congress abolished the position, and anticipating that another vacancy would soon occur, the legislators voted to abolish that position as well, meaning there would be seven instead of nine members on the high court. Congress was well within its rights to reduce the size of the court, since the Constitution was silent on how many justices there should be on the bench, and from the beginning, the legislative branch had decided the precise number.

Far from being cowed, Johnson went on a speaking tour throughout the North leading up to the 1866 Congressional elections and lashed out against the approval of the Fourteenth Amendment, proposed earlier that year and sent to the states for ratification. The amendment defined all persons born or naturalized in the country as citizens of the United States and of the states wherein they resided, and who were therefore entitled to all the rights, privileges, and legal protections of all other citizens. Throughout the tour, Johnson condemned the Radical Republicans and urged voters to defeat them at the polls. Instead, the Radicals won impressive gains that fall.

With their numbers enhanced, the Radicals moved to take control of Reconstruction from the president through the Military Reconstruction Act, which abolished all state governments in the former Confederacy, replacing them with military districts under army commanders. The president vetoed the act, declaring that it violated his constitutional authority as commander-in-chief, but Congress once more overrode the veto. Congress then acted to take control of all major executive personnel through the Tenure of Office Act, which forbade the president to remove officials approved by the Senate without its consent. The constitutionality of the act was legally dubious, and the Supreme Court many years later declared it unconstitutional.[13]

Having severed his ties with fellow Democrats by running with Lincoln as his vice president and then having alienated Republicans, Johnson found himself largely bereft of effective political support in Washington. He then turned to the public for support in a series of speeches that were especially vitriolic and often heightened by the effects of alcohol. He compared Republican leaders in Congress to Confederate traitors and charged that his opponents wanted to "incite assassination." The tactic backfired as the public resented his attacks on the Congressional leadership at a time when it was still thought unseemly for a president to try to influence opinion through verbal smears against the opposition.

The House of Representatives responded in March 1868 by drawing up eleven articles of impeachment against Johnson. One of them took him to task for his inflammatory political rhetoric, while most of the others involved aspects of his alleged violation of the Tenure of Office Act in dismissing Edmund M. Stanton as Secretary of War. The House acted to impeach the president by a strictly partisan vote of 128–47. In the Senate, the tally to convict was 35–19, one less than the two-thirds necessary to remove a president from office. Saving Johnson was moderate Republican Senator Lyman Trumbull, who reasoned that a conviction would open the way for future Congresses to impeach and remove presidents for purely political reasons and, in the process, dangerously weaken the executive power.

Although Johnson barely survived removal from office, he was determined to redeem himself by seeking election for another term as president. However, neither the Democrats nor the Republicans wanted him as a nominee, and he has carried the stigma of impeachment throughout American political history. In poll after poll of historians and other students of the presidency, Johnson has ranked near the bottom in overall approval. The hatreds and resentments he carried throughout life had kept him from compromising in the face of political reality or from appreciating the desperate needs of those so recently freed from bondage.

The Making of Richard Nixon

At first glance, Richard Nixon (1969–1974) would seem to have nothing in common with Andrew Johnson. Nixon was born in Yorba Linda, California, in 1913, a little more than a century after Johnson came into the world. Yet there was much about Nixon's early years that scarred him for life, resulted in a thirst for revenge, and caused him to project his own resentments onto people whom he thought also felt alienated and left out.[14] In Nixon's case, however, historians know a great deal more about the specifics of his background than about Johnson's early life.

The Nixons were by no means impoverished, and despite having to work very hard to make a decent living, they belonged during Richard's childhood and youth to what might be described as the lower-middle class.[15] His father, Frank Nixon, had left Ohio after working at a variety of unsatisfying jobs and headed to Southern California and the promise of better times. The year of Richard's birth, his father planted some lemon groves on soil so thin that the trees failed to flourish. Giving up, he moved his family about three miles west to the outskirts of Whittier, where he opened a gas station and general store. Richard and his brothers, along with their mother Hanna, had to toil daily in these modest businesses to support the family.

Frank Nixon had dropped out of school in the sixth grade, whereas Richard's mother, Hannah Milhous Nixon, had attended the local, Quaker-affiliated Whittier College for two years. Hannah's Milhous relatives, belonging to a set of well-off Quaker families in the area, believed she had married beneath herself, with the result that the Nixons found themselves shunned by polite society in and around Whittier. Smarting over the snub, Frank always felt awkward at Milhous family gatherings. Richard could not have missed these stains and probably felt that his branch of the family was not as good as his mother's siblings, who had made better marriages. For this and other reasons, Richard tried very hard not to be like his father. While Frank Nixon shouted, the son took pride in being "the coolest man in the room," and while his father did not care about how he was dressed, Richard took great pains with his clothes for the rest of his life.[16]

Richard could remember his father's explosions of anger vividly when writing his memoirs more than half a century later: "It was his temper that impressed me most as a small child. His tempestuous arguments with my brothers Harold and Don, and their shouting could be heard all through the neighborhood."[17] Nor did Frank Nixon hesitate to mete out corporal punishment at the least provocation. Once, when he caught his sons playing in an irrigation ditch, he pulled them out, only to fling them back in again, shouting, "If you want water, I'll give you enough." An aunt witnessing the event cried out, "Frank, you'll kill them, you'll kill them!"[18] Richard tried to avoid his father's wrath, he explained in his memoirs, by following his mother's example "of not crossing him when he was in a bad mood."[19]

Indeed, his devout Quaker mother, whom he would later describe in public as "a saint," never raised her voice against the boys. Instead, she gave them cold looks of disapproval, a silence that could be just as punishing as their father's hand and harsh words. Many years later, Hannah Nixon told a *Los Angeles Times* reporter, "[I believed in] silent punishment—in making a child sit quietly while he thinks through what he has done."[20]

Such silent punishment could seem to a child like a form of abandonment. Richard also suffered two lengthy separations from his mother, which no doubt reinforced his sense of abandonment. When he was fifteen, Hannah left for a tubercular community in Arizona with his older brother Harold, who had come down with TB. She took care of three other bedridden patients at the facility to help pay for Harold's care and was gone for most of two years. Although these circumstances were different from Andrew Johnson's, Richard might also have felt worthless and unloved.

Such emotions may have only exacerbated those from several years earlier when he was twelve. Believing that Richard possessed musical talent, his mother had sent him away for five months to live with an aunt who taught music. Another reason for this banishment was the illness of Richard's younger brother Arthur, who had come down with tubercular meningitis and needed constant care. While still living with the aunt, Richard was called home when Arthur died. The death left him feeling that he must do well in life as a sort of redemption for his dead brother.[21] According to Barber in his study of Nixon, "The conclusion of the Arthur story shows how [Richard] began to sense he had a special destiny and how he began to translate the negative morality of repression into the positive morality of achievement."[22]

Making matters worse, neither of Nixon's parents was the type to hug their children or offer warm words of assurance and praise. Years later, Henry Kissinger, Nixon's national security advisor and then secretary of state, would ask, "Can you imagine what this man would have been like if somebody had loved him?" Answering himself, Kissinger added, "I don't think anybody ever did—not his parents, not his peers."[23] Nixon presidential aide Bruce Harlow would speculate that this dearth of love, along with feelings of abandonment, resulted in a "badly, badly hurt" child, causing him not to trust others and for others not to trust him. According to Harlow, "Richard Nixon went up the walls of life with his claws."[24]

One area where Richard could appease his father and receive some approbation was by discussing politics. Frank Nixon was a devoted Republican with a populist bent, who identified with the "forgotten man," who no matter how hard he worked could never get ahead because of exploitation by greedy employers and elite interests. It was not by accident that his son would later pitch himself as a presidential candidate to the "common man." Yet Nixon was never proud of being the son of a poorly educated grocer, even though he sometimes spoke of pinched circumstances in childhood and youth as a way of appealing to America's "forgotten men."[25]

Another area where Nixon sought to please his father was by sharing his love of the rough and tumble sport of football, going so far as to play football in both high school and college, despite his slight build and lack of coordination, which resulted in real physical punishment on the playing field. The pain of playing the sport may also may have been a way of proving to himself that life was a constant struggle, which he must overcome through challenge and extreme discomfort.

Of course, Richard mostly got along with his father by not defying him and by following the example of his mother in repressing his emotions, often while churning inside with fear. At the same time, the lesson he learned from his father was that the best way to wield power was through fear. As he once told his speechwriter William Safire, "People react to fear, not love—they don't teach that in Sunday School, but it's true."[26] His own escape from fear, as a child and later in life, was by imitating (or sometimes pretending to imitate) his mother's suppression of emotions. As summarized by Barber, "Richard felt the tension around him and learned to deal with it. . . . He would be able to grow, but there would always be that expectation of trouble ahead, that concentration on challenge and suffering."[27] He would constantly alternate between playing out the behaviors of his father and mother and representing these poles of action in himself through constant struggle.

Partly as a way of pleasing his parents and partly as a means of manifesting a sense of destiny, the young Nixon studied hard in school and received excellent grades. At school and then at college, he was a champion debater because he could argue any side of a question with equal fervor and could convincingly talk around controversial issues without addressing them head-on, or by issuing dubious interpretations of the facts that he knew his debate opponents would have a difficult time challenging. In the process, he discovered the power of convincing others through words, eventually coming to believe that he could make a proposition true merely by pronouncing it true.

Impressed by Richard's record in school, a group of local Harvard alums secured a tuition grant for him to attend their alma mater. However, he had to turn down the offer because he could not afford either the travel or living expenses, and because his family needed him to work in the gas station/grocery store. Perhaps one result of this disappointment was a lifelong resentment of Ivy League graduates, who for Nixon represented a cadre of privileged, though often undeserving, upper-class men.

Instead of Harvard, Richard enrolled in the local Whittier College with expenses paid out of a fund his grandfather Milhouse had set aside for his grandchildren. The Quaker institution forbade fraternities, but the college did allow literary societies, which, like fraternities, functioned within a social pecking order. The most selective of these societies at Whittier were the Franklins. Nixon applied to the Franklins but was rejected, no doubt because of his family background as reflected through his father. Nixon was both angry and hurt but dealt with the rejection by founding a rival group called the Orthogonians, which roughly translates as the "Square Shooters," part of a lifelong battle against individuals and groups he resented and considered enemies—a reaction not unlike Andrew Johnson's behavior toward being looked down on.

After graduation from Whittier, Nixon received and accepted a scholarship to Duke University Law School, but again faced disappointment and rejection when he applied for jobs with prestigious Wall Street law firms in New York City, which he concluded were reserved for Ivy Leaguers. Still resenting the snub many years later, he wrote, "I knew that these firms were virtually closed shops, which hired only from the establishment elite of the Ivy League law schools, but I thought it would be worth a try. I must have looked pretty scruffy sitting in those plush mahogany and leather reception rooms in my one good suit."[28]

After law school, Nixon headed west to his hometown of Whittier, where he started his own legal practice and met and married Pat Ryan. Whatever his disappointment over not making it on the New York scene, Whittier turned out to be an excellent location for launching a political career. After his release from the Navy at the end of the Second World War, local Republicans, looking for a promising veteran to run for the House of Representatives, tapped Nixon as their candidate.

Nixon's campaign for Congress in 1946 established his reputation for bitter, no-holds-barred political combat that would culminate three decades later in the Watergate scandals and his forced resignation from the presidency. Directing this early pugilistic approach to winning public office was a seasoned campaign consultant named

Murray Chotiner, whose specialty was character assassination and manipulation of popular discontents, what Gary Wills, in his classic study *Nixon Agonistes,* called "The Denigrative Method."[29] As practiced, the denigrative method directed the candidate to reveal as little about himself as possible while drilling down on a selected negative aspect of the opponent, often based on twisted or even false accusations, which would induce the public to vote *against* rather than *for* the other candidate. Then, the opposing candidate would be on the defensive, backed into a corner and forced to try to explain away the charges.

Incumbent Congressman, Democrat Jerry Voorhis, was a perfect target for Nixon. He came from a wealthy family and was a Yale graduate, just the sort of person Nixon resented. Voorhis had first won election to the House in 1936 as a loyal New Dealer and Roosevelt man. Now, with prosperity restored by the war and millions of working-class Americans enjoying various New Deal economic reforms, Republicans accelerated their criticisms of meddlesome, bureaucratic intrusions from the federal government as a way to attack the Democrats.

Voorhis's Achilles heel, according to Chotiner and Nixon, was his strong support of labor unions, both before and after his time in Congress. Republicans had long opposed the union movement and found ammunition in the fact that some of the more radical unions were found to have connections to the Communist Party. Among them was the Political Action Committee (PAC) of the Congress of Industrial Organizations (CIO), which Voorhis himself had vigorously condemned because of its Communist connections. Nixon lied in claiming that the CIO-PAC had endorsed Voorhis. Rather, it was the distinct National Citizens' PAC, with no Communist ties, that had endorsed Voorhis. By repeating that Voorhis was accepting PAC money, Nixon sewed confusion among voters who did not distinguish between the two organizations. He thereby forced Voorhis into lengthy explanations about the differences between the two PACs rather than landing any punches against Nixon. Not surprisingly, Nixon won handily with 57 percent of the vote and easily won reelection in 1948. He later admitted to a Voorhis aide, "Of course, I knew Jerry Voorhis wasn't a Communist. . . . The important thing is to win. You were just being naïve."[30]

In 1950, the California Republican establishment asked Nixon to run for the US Senate. He would face off against Congresswoman Helen Gahagan Douglas. She was the wife of movie star Melvin Douglas, and she had acted on Broadway and in the movies, as well as having been a light opera singer. Primary election opponents in the Democratic Party had already falsely accused her of Communist sympathies, dubbing her variously as "the Red Queen" and the "Pink Lady." These accusations were a godsend to Nixon and Chotiner, who put out a flyer charging that Douglas had frequently voted the same way as New York Congressman Vito Marcantonio, a well-known Communist sympathizer. The Nixon campaign printed the flyers on pink paper and distributed half a million copies of them, forcing Douglas into the position of arguing that she did not harbor Communist sympathies. The critical East Coast press began referring to Nixon as "Tricky Dick," a label that would follow him for the rest of his political life, and that launched Nixon's perpetual feud with the news media. Tricky Dick or not, he won by twenty percentage points in November and became a US

Senator at age thirty-seven from one of the wealthiest and most populous states in the nation. In the process, he learned that falsehoods about opponents had to be repeated endlessly, followed by denials that he had lied. He believed that most of those who voted for him would accept the denials, since they would not want to think they had backed a morally compromised person, a perfect example of "cognitive dissonance" of the sort that would later benefit Donald Trump.

By whatever means available, Richard Nixon had risen to unimaginable heights from his family's gas station and grocery store at the edge of Whittier, California. Yet he saw and would continue to see his life as a struggle against overwhelming odds, which he chronicled in his 1962 book, *Six Crises*, written with the assistance of a ghostwriter.[31] On one level, the book was a response to John F. Kennedy's *Profiles in Courage* (1955), also written with the help of a ghostwriter, which had helped Kennedy to make himself known to a wider public while still a senator.

Not surprisingly, Nixon viewed the six crises as part of an ongoing personal struggle against great odds and over which he prevailed at great personal cost as a public servant. The six crises were his accusations of Alger Hiss as a Communist spy; the claims in 1952 about his alleged political slush fund and the associated Checkers Speech; President Eisenhower's heart attack; the mob of protesters he confronted in Caracas, Venezuela; his "Kitchen Debate" with Nikita Khrushchev in Moscow; and his 1960 presidential campaign against Kennedy.[32]

In three of the chapters especially, Nixon puts himself across as a "common man" doing battle against privileged foes. These are the chapters about Alger Hiss, the slush fund controversy, and the 1960 election. The combat with Hiss stemmed from young Congressman Nixon's membership on the House Committee on Un-American Activities (HUAC), which heard testimony in August 1948 from Whitaker Chambers, once a member of the Communist Party himself, who accused former State Department official Alger Hiss of having spied for the Soviet Union during the 1930s. When Hiss testified before the committee, he denied the charges and denied ever knowing Chambers. Nixon doubted Hiss's testimony and was able to prove Hiss had in fact known Chambers very well and had lied about it. The statutes of limitations prevented Hiss's prosecution for espionage, but after being tried and found guilty of perjury, he received a sentence of forty-four months in prison. Hiss denied the espionage accusation for the rest of his life, but years later, declassified documents from both US and Soviet archives appeared to prove that he had in fact engaged in espionage.[33]

Initially, Nixon faced an uphill slog, since Hiss was one of the most respected men in Washington. He had served as a high-ranking State Department representative to both the Yalta and Potsdam conferences during the final months of the Second World War, and at the time of the accusations leveled against him, he was president of the prestigious Carnegie Endowment for Peace. Because of Hiss's prestige and his denials under oath, the leadership of HUAC concluded that there was no alternative but to drop its investigation against him.

Although Nixon did not refer to the biblical story per se, his account of what he faced in the Hiss case makes him out to be something like a modern-day David facing a

Communist Goliath (a biblical image that an embattled Andrew Jackson had also liked to use). First, Nixon was just a freshman Congressman going up against a man who had degrees from Johns Hopkins University and Harvard Law School, after which he had clerked for the legendary Supreme Court Justice Oliver Wendell Holmes. Hiss was a man, in Nixon's words, "in education, background, and intelligence, the very best the nation could produce."[34] Not only that, but also much of the eastern press, including the *Washington Post*, came out against the committee, as did President Truman, who called the investigation a "red herring." Thus, Nixon, in his own words, was "opposing the President of the United States and the majority of press corps opinion . . . and against one of the brightest and most respected young men following a public career."[35]

Looking back on the Hiss affair, Nixon expressed his contempt for the Ivy League establishment that he accused of reflexively supporting Hiss, "typical of the people closely associated with Harvard and the other great universities. . . . They had considered the Hiss case as an attack on the whole elite establishment, an attack on the foreign service, . . . and an attack on Roosevelt's foreign policy."[36] In contrast, here was Richard Nixon with his honest, common man roots taking on the entire eastern social establishment, the East Coast press corps, and even the President of the United States. Triumphing over Hiss was indeed sweet, given how the socially prominent Franklin Debating Society at Whittier College had rejected him, and how he had lost out to Ivy League candidates when applying for jobs with prestigious Wall Street law firms.

In recounting the slush fund charges and the associated Checkers speech in *Six Crises*, Nixon again portrayed himself as the "common man" against powerful, establishment forces. Nixon told readers that publicity about the fund had come at a high point in his life. "I thought that no one in the world could have been more fortunate than I," he wrote in reference to having just received the Republican Party's nomination to be Eisenhower's running mate in 1952 and having been treated to a triumphal homecoming rally on the football field at his alma mater, Whittier College. By then, the heckling had begun along the campaign trail as the press picked up the slush fund story and reported it. Responding to one group of hecklers, Nixon blamed the attacks on people who had opposed his anti-Communist investigations. Reprising the scene in his book, he related what he had said to the hostile crowd: "Ever since I have done that [investigative] work, the Communists and the left-wingers have been fighting me with every possible smear. . . . And believe me, you can expect that they will continue to do so. They started it yesterday. They have tried to say that I had taken $16,000 for my personal use."[37]

Neither then, nor later, did Nixon offer any evidence of a Communist conspiracy against him, but the charge allowed him to name additional enemies. The newspapers, he charged, were again out to get him, including the *New York Herald Tribune*, whose opposition especially stung him since it was a mainstay of the East Coast Republican establishment. Nixon then repeated his argument that Communists and left-wingers were out to destroy him. If that were not enough, the old guard leadership, as represented by former presidential nominee Thomas E. Dewey, said he should resign from the ticket once he had given a televised speech, ever after known as the Checkers Speech.

Eisenhower had advised Nixon to go on TV and tell the audience everything he owned and everything he had earned since entering public life. Both he and his wife Pat bridled at this invasion of their privacy. "What we owned and what we owed was our own business and nobody else's," Nixon wrote in *Six Crises*. He also professed embarrassment at revealing how little they owned "in the way of the world's goods."[38]

On the evening of September 23, 1952, Republican vice-presidential candidate Nixon went on TV to defend himself against the charge that he had used a $16,000 campaign "slush fund" for personal, as opposed to genuine campaign expenses. The studio backdrop for the speech looked like a contemporary middle-class living room, with Nixon doing a good part of his talk while seated behind a desk as if working on family accounts while he explains his financial history. Reminiscing about his childhood in California when he and his brothers had to work in the family's grocery store, he declares that such hard work was "the only reason we were able to make it . . ."[39] Later he tells viewers how he worked his way through college and law school, and after practicing law for a few years, entered the Navy during the Second World War. At one point he turns to his wife Pat, who is sitting nearby in an upholstered chair, mentioning that she had done stenographic work for him free of charge (and not on his office payroll at taxpayer's expense). "She's a wonderful stenographer," he adds. Later in the speech, he remarks, "Pat doesn't have a mink coat. But she does have a respectable Republican cloth coat" (a dig at revelations that some low-ranking members of the Truman administration had taken fur coats for their wives in exchange for political favors). Finishing the thought, he says, "and I always tell her she'd look good in anything." Nor did he leave out his parents, who were living in the house he and Pat owned back in Whittier, California, adding that he was dutifully repaying, with interest, a loan from the senior Nixons. Then came the most important part of the speech:

> One other thing I probably should tell you, because if I don't they'll probably be saying this about me, too. We did get something, a gift, after the election. A man down in Texas heard Pat on the radio mention the fact that our two youngsters would like to have a dog. And believe it or not, the day before we left on this campaign trip we got a message from Union Station in Baltimore, saying they had a package for us. We went down to get it. You know what it was? It was a little cocker spaniel dog, in a crate that he had sent all the way from Texas, black and white, spotted, and our little girl Tricia, the six-year-old, named it Checkers. And you know, the kids, like all kids, love the dog, and I just want to say this, right now, that regardless of what they say about it, we're gonna keep it.

Nixon did not have to talk about Checkers, since no one would think he had been wrong to accept the dog. However, the emotional scene that he painted would show he was a good father who loved his daughters, after having earlier praised his wife and assured viewers that he was being kind to his parents. In addition, the many dog lovers who had tuned in could form an instant bond with the Nixons, as many were reduced to tears over the Checkers saga. At the very end of the speech, Nixon asked viewers to "wire and write" the Republican National Committee (RNC) to help them decide if he would remain on the party's ticket. Over 4 million telegrams, letters, and telephone calls poured into the committee, running approximately 200 to one in Nixon's favor. Eisenhower, who was watching the television broadcast, was furious over the call for viewers to write the RNC, since he had thought the decision about Nixon's fate was his to make. He now had no choice but to keep Nixon on the ticket.

Looking back, Nixon believed that Kennedy's wealth and good looks had benefited him, not only in the debates between them but throughout the campaign. Nixon summed up the Kennedy style in a 1983 television interview with Frank Gannon as "suave, smooth, and debonair" that appealed especially to the media "who are frankly more suckers for style than the average people." He went on to complain that, "People aren't going to vote for the man next door."[40] However, it was the "man next door" to whom Nixon wanted to appeal—and whose resentments he wanted to stoke. Thus in *Six Crises*, he stated, seemingly as a matter of fact, that in the 1960 campaign, Kennedy "had unlimited money which already had enabled him to employ a large, skilled staff of organizers, speech writers, pollsters, and others essential for a successful campaign."[41] He did not add that the Kennedy wealth had allowed his opponent to attend expensive Ivy League schools, but in writing about his need to study hard in *Six Crises* to win scholarships he was making such a contrast without actually saying so. At the same time, he depreciated his academic abilities in another pitch to the common man: "I won my share of scholarships . . . in school, not because I was smarter but because I worked longer and harder than some of my more gifted colleagues."[42]

A New Nixon?

Nixon's rejection in November 1960 by approximately 113,000 popular votes—or 0.17 percent of the total cast—was devastating. The Nixons moved back to California, where they built a new house in suburban Los Angeles. Almost immediately, California Republicans began prodding him to run for governor against the very popular Edmund G. "Pat" Brown, arguing that it would be an excellent way for Nixon to keep his hand in politics, and he agreed to do so. Reaching back to his tried-and-true anti-Communist playbook, Nixon tried to hang the charge of being "soft on Communism" around Brown's neck, but it did not work. Most members of the media supported Brown, so it was not surprising that he won by 52 percent to Nixon's 47 percent. What followed was Nixon's sarcastic scolding of the press corps the morning after. He said, "Just think how much you're going to be missing," he announced to them. "You won't have Nixon to kick around anymore, because, gentlemen, this is my last press conference."[43]

Nearly all the media pundits declared Nixon to be dead politically. The next year, he moved to New York City, where he at last became a partner in a Wall Street law firm. Besides his legal practice, Nixon made dozens of speeches around the country in support of Republican candidates and, in the process, collected a mountain of IOUs, which went far in putting him in line for the party's 1968 presidential nomination.

Nixon's media team, led by Roger Ailes, had worked hard to create a "New Nixon." Hopefully, he could come across as a mature senior statesman as opposed to the angry and resentful contender at war with the media. As part of this new persona, Nixon liked to compare himself to President Charles de Gaulle of France, whom he had met several times, and that had led to a sort of mutual admiration. Nixon also owned a copy of de Gaulle's 1932 book of published lectures, *The Edge of the Sword*, which he read and underlined heavily. What especially bonded the two men was the experience of having been defeated politically. De Gaulle had come back to save his country from falling into chaos, a scenario that Nixon, encouraged by de Gaulle, envisioned for himself in 1968. Nixon even tried to imitate de Gaulle's gravitas as the *homme serieux*, the serious man of grandeur, reserve, and poise, who had come back from the wilderness to save his country.[44] To a degree, the new image worked, as the editorial pages of some top metropolitan newspapers began carrying positive stories about Nixon. Only time could tell if he would become America's de Gaulle or if there was really a "New Nixon."

Initially, Nixon and the Republicans assumed they would be going up against incumbent Lyndon Johnson who, having served thirteen months of John Kennedy's unexpired term, was eligible according to the Twenty-Second Amendment to run for two terms in his own right. Johnson won a lopsided victory against Barry Goldwater in 1964, but his popularity had taken a severe beating because of the ongoing and seemingly unwinnable war in Vietnam. Thus, in early April 1968, Johnson announced he would not run again and instead would devote himself to working out a Vietnam peace settlement. Further upsetting expectations was John Kennedy's brother Robert's announcement in mid-March that he would seek the Democratic nomination as an anti-war candidate. It now looked as if Nixon would have to face another matchup against the Kennedy clan's glamour and money. Then, on June 5, Kennedy was assassinated just after winning the California primary, which probably would have secured him the Democratic nomination, even though the primary results did not yet control delegate selections for the nominating conventions of the two parties. With Robert Kennedy now dead, the Democrats nominated Johnson's vice president, Hubert Humphrey, while Chicago police savagely beat peaceful protesters in nearby public parks. Nixon won the Republican nomination handily at their far more placid convention in Miami Beach, Florida.

Humphrey was in the difficult position of having to defend what had become Johnson's war. For the most part, Nixon avoided talking about the war for fear of alienating hawks in both parties, simply saying he had a "secret plan" for ending the conflict. Instead, his main thrust throughout the campaign was to address the fears that many Americans had about civil unrest stemming from the civil rights movement and anti-war protests. Nixon called for law and order and promised, "To bring the country together again." Meanwhile, Governor of Alabama George Wallace, running as an independent, appealed to what he liked to call "ordinary folks" who were sick of being pushed around by "pointy-headed intellectuals, pseudo-intellectual morons telling 'em how to live their lives."[45]

Wallace's appeal to Americans who resented being looked down on and who felt left behind was aimed at the very sorts of people Nixon wished to attract, though he expressed this goal less crudely than Wallace. He reached out to what he would later call the "silent majority," citizens who did not approve of the sexual revolution and the counterculture, who did not participate in antiwar demonstrations, and who did not take part in public discussions.[46] He liked to refer to such people as "middle Americans"—folks, he believed, who were being overshadowed by a caustic media and vocal minorities—the "forgotten men" with whom his father had identified. (Donald Trump would later aim his populist presidential campaigns at similar kinds of people.)

In mid-September, the Gallup Poll showed Nixon ahead by an average of 15 percentage points. Humphrey's main problem was his decision to remain loyal to Johnson's continuing execution of the war, resulting in his being booed and heckled by antiwar protesters most everywhere he went. Then on September 30, in a nationwide televised speech from Salt Lake City, Humphrey called for a complete bombing halt in Vietnam, adding that it could be reversed in case there was no positive response from the other side. Almost immediately, the protests stopped, and support flowed from antiwar groups as well as various factions of the Democratic Party who decided to "come home." Humphrey also appeared more cheerful, more spontaneous, and more genuine than Nixon was. As a result, Humphrey began to rise in the polls, with Gallup reporting him down some eight points by October 21.

Meanwhile, Nixon learned President Johnson had persuaded South Vietnamese President Thieu to join in peace talks. As mentioned in the last chapter, Nixon was terrified that this news would spell his defeat. To prevent this from happening, he had used Claire Chennault of the anti-communist China Lobby to persuade Thieu not to go forward with discussions before the election, with the understanding that a Nixon administration would offer him better terms. Although historians long suspected such interference, there was no proof until the *New York Times* reported in January 2017 that Nixon had personally directed the sabotage.[47] As mentioned in an earlier chapter, Nixon's action to scuttle the peace talks violated the 1795 Logan Act, which makes it a crime for a private US citizen to interfere with negotiations between the United States and a foreign power. For such a violation of federal law, Nixon could have been tried and, if found guilty, sentenced to prison. The popular vote in November was close, with 43.4 percent for Nixon, 42.7 percent for Humphrey—and 13.5 percent for independent candidate George Wallace. Nixon won the Electoral College by 301 to 191.

In attempting to convince voters that there was indeed a "New Nixon," the candidate had steered clear for the most part during the campaign from getting "down and dirty" with his accusations against the Democrats. Instead, Nixon charged his vice president Spiro Agnew, who had been governor of Maryland before his nomination, with leading the verbal assaults against their domestic enemies. Referring to the "Moratorium" against the Vietnam War in October 1969, Agnew declared, "A spirit of national masochism prevails, encouraged by an effete corps of impudent snobs who characterize themselves as intellectuals." Speaking before a Republican dinner at Fort Lauderdale, Florida, in April 1970, he continued his anti-intellectual attacks: "This is the criminal left that belongs not in a dormitory, but in a penitentiary. The criminal left is not a problem to be solved by the Department of Philosophy or the Department of English—it is a problem for the Department of Justice . . ." He added, "Black or white, the criminal left is interested in power. It is not interested in promoting the renewal and reforms that make democracy work; it is interested in promoting those collisions and conflicts that tear democracy apart."[48]

There was, in fact, no New Nixon, and in private, both during and after the presidential election, he was often angry and resentful. He continued to rail against Ivy Leaguers, sneering to assistant Bob Haldeman about what he saw as their effeminacy, as demonstrated by how they "play those frilly games, squash and crew," in contrast to Nixon himself who had played the more manly sport of football at Whittier College.[49] From time to time, Nixon would pound the desk when contemplating appointments and say, "We have too many Ivy Leaguers! No more Ivy Leaguers!"—then turn around and appoint more Ivy League graduates, revealing that he both admired and resented such men.[50] These contradictory feelings may have stemmed from that offer of a Harvard scholarship he had turned down because of family finances. For many years, he had tried to compensate by presenting himself as a person who had risen from humble origins, but the strategy did not work because the resentments continued to gnaw away at him.

Then there was the dichotomy between "common man Nixon" and the pomp he relished as president. He thrilled at the Marine Band's playing "Hail to the Chief," and he ordered White House security officers to wear uniforms with gold braid as if they were royal palace guards, much like what Theodore Roosevelt had done in the early twentieth century, attracting much ridicule in the media against Nixon. On summer evenings, he savored going aboard the presidential yacht for a sail along the Potomac River. He also disdained press conferences, preferring whenever possible to make pronouncements over television from the Oval Office and in that way to avoid answering questions from hated reporters. Also, in imitation of de Gaulle, who used the third person to designate himself, Nixon began using his initials RN in referring to himself with staff, a practice that de Gaulle had adopted in imitation of the Roman Emperor Julius Caesar.[51] Nixon's enthusiasm for the movie *Patton* (1970), which he viewed several times, further reflected his growing authoritarian manner. He also disdained receiving members of Congress at the White House, which greatly undermined his relations with Capitol Hill.

Watergate

In addition, Nixon felt besieged by enemies from all directions and was determined to get even with them. In truth, he reveled in having enemies, which fed his lifelong resentment at supposed unfair treatment and disrespect, and he used his old campaign advisor Murry Chotiner for advice on how to go after them. He would get the IRS to audit the tax returns of foes—real, potential, or imagined. Requests for audits included the returns of Larry O'Brien, who had directed John F. Kennedy's presidential campaign and later became chairperson of the Democratic National Committee. He also wanted the IRS to go after Vice President Hubert Humphrey, Ted Kennedy (who might have presidential aspirations), and Ben Bradlee, executive editor of the *Washington Post.* In addition, he demanded the names of "Jewish contributors to the Democrats" for the IRS to investigate. White House counsel John Dean drew up several "enemies" lists that eventually contained dozens of names. To its credit, the IRS refused to go along with these audit requests.[52] However, FBI director J. Edgar Hoover was more compliant when Nixon asked him to wiretap some thirteen staff members and several newspaper reporters whom he suspected of leaking information.[53]

Nixon's anger over leaks to the media and his determination to stop them set off a cascade of events that led to his downfall.[54] What especially triggered this downward spiral was the publication in 1971 by the *New York Times* and the *Washington Post* of the popularly named Pentagon Papers, officially entitled *United States—Vietnam Relations, 1945–1967: A Study Prepared by the Department of Defense.* Robert McNamara, President Johnson's Secretary of Defense, had ordered the study to give him a better understanding of the origins and evolution of American involvement in Vietnam. Since the study did not go beyond 1967, it in no way implicated the Nixon administration, and, at first, Nixon did not react negatively to it. However, Secretary of State Henry Kissinger was livid when he learned that the study had been leaked to the press, and he insisted that the president had to do something about it.

Once aroused, Nixon reacted by authorizing, on July 24, 1971, a Special Investigations Unit whose purpose was, in his own words, "to stop security leaks and to investigate other sensitive security matters."[55] Nicknamed "the Plumbers" because its job was to plumb leaks from the administration, the unit's first task was to dig up dirt to discredit Daniel Ellsberg, who revealed on CBS News that he had supplied a copy of the Pentagon Papers to the *New York Times.* Not satisfied that the courts would find Ellsberg guilty of espionage, Nixon shouted at White House counsel and assistant John Ehrlichman and Attorney General John Mitchell, "Just . . . convict the son of a bitch in the press."[56]

With Ehrlichman's approval, the Plumbers broke into the office of Ellsberg's psychiatrist and pried open a file cabinet hoping to discover if Ellsberg had confided anything to his therapist that he had not told the press, but they found nothing. In his *Memoirs,* Nixon tried to rationalize the break-in to the psychiatrist's office, writing, "I do not accept that it was as wrong or [as] excessive as what Daniel Ellsberg did . . ."[57] In other words, he was saying that the two wrongs canceled each other out. To punish the *Washington Post* and its publisher Katherine Graham for revealing the *Pentagon Papers,* some pro-Nixon businessmen challenged the FCC licenses of TV stations owned by the *Post* which were important sources of revenue for the company.[58] Nixon was careful not to order any of these activities personally or to know any of the specifics. Rather, Ehrlichman understood what the president wanted and acted accordingly.

As 1972 dawned, Nixon was determined to win reelection and to score an overwhelming, historic victory. The only president to sweep the entire Electoral College had been George Washington, and if Nixon could equal that milestone, it would be sweet revenge against all his enemies. The Committee for the Reelection of the President, headed by Attorney General John Mitchell, would do whatever it could to assure such a sweeping victory. To learn what the opposition was planning, the committee directed the Plumbers to break into the offices of the Democratic National Committee (DNC), located in Washington's Watergate Complex, and to place listening devices on the telephones of the DNC chairman and other party officials. Their break-in on May 26 succeeded, but one of the telephone bugs failed. They went in a second time, on June 17, to make the necessary repair and were seen by a security guard who called the DC police. Two members of the Plumbers group, who were monitoring this second operation from a motel across the street, fled in such a panic that they left behind a stash of consecutively numbered one-hundred-dollar bills, in addition to a notebook with the name of Plumber Howard Hunt and a White House telephone number.

As it turned out, the break-in was unnecessary: Democratic nominee George McGovern, whom some members of his own party considered too liberal, had little chance of winning the election. In addition, Nixon's historic visit to China that February had been a sensation and had sent his approvals soaring. Not surprisingly, he won a smashing victory in November, with 60.7 percent of the popular vote, which was just slightly below Franklin Roosevelt's landslide in 1936 and Lyndon Johnson's blowout win in 1964. Nixon won forty-nine states with 520 electoral votes to McGovern's seventeen—all of them from Massachusetts and Washington, DC. McGovern failed even to carry his home state of South Dakota. Yet Nixon was disconsolate at not equaling Washington's unique victory.

Although Nixon did not specifically order the two break-ins at the Watergate offices of the DNC, it became clear afterward that he directed an extensive cover-up and associated obstructions of justice. Revelations of these actions emerged when a former Haldeman aide named Alexander Butterfield testified before a special Senate "Watergate" committee that Nixon had a secret, voice-activated taping system in the Oval Office. Archibald Cox, who had been appointed a special prosecutor to investigate what had come to be called the Watergate Scandal, promptly subpoenaed the tapes. Nixon refused to turn them over, citing "executive privilege," an ancient doctrine claiming that the presidency cannot operate effectively without a degree of confidentiality.

For Nixon, Cox was the personification of the "East Coast boys" whom he believed had always looked down on him. He had attended a prestigious New England prep school before earning both undergraduate and law degrees from Harvard. If that were not bad enough, Cox was a Kennedy protégé, having served as President Kennedy's solicitor general. On Saturday evening, October 20, 1973, Nixon ordered Attorney General Elliot Richardson to fire Cox. Rather than comply, Richardson resigned. His deputy William Ruckelshaus also resigned when ordered to fire Cox. Finally, Solicitor General Robert Bork carried out the firing. Both print and broadcast media immediately dubbed the event "the Saturday Night Massacre," creating a public relations firestorm against Nixon. However, getting rid of Cox did Nixon no good and he was compelled by the public outcry to appoint a new special counsel. This was Texas lawyer Leon Jaworski, who also demanded the tapes, as did the House Judiciary Committee, which was readying itself for impeachment hearings against Nixon. The Supreme Court, on July 24, 1974, in *United States v. Nixon*, ruled that the president could not use executive privilege to justify refusing to turn over the tapes and directed him to do so, along with various other documents under subpoena.

Revelations in the tapes were devastating. They showed that Nixon had tried to get the CIA to stop the FBI from investigating the break-in, which came to be known as "the smoking gun," and that he had authorized "hush money" to keep the Watergate burglars from implicating the White House in any testimony. In many of the recordings, Nixon used obscene language, made anti-Semitic remarks, and used racial slurs against African Americans and Latinos.

The tapes also showed Nixon continued to believe, as when he was the clever high school debater or the author of the Checkers speech, that he could forge his own truth through words. If he believed something, then it became true for him and for the American people. If so, he might have really believed that he was "not a crook," as he insisted in an infamous televised speech on November 17, 1973. Nor did he consider himself lying when he constantly promised to deliver "peace with honor" in Vietnam, or when he had assured audiences back in the 1950s that domestic Communists were determined to bring him down. In this sense, he was something of what philosophers call a solipsist—that is, people who believe that only their own mind exists, and that any knowledge or beliefs outside it are untrue. Of course, there were other possible reasons for this behavior: He had gotten away with it before; he had learned to spin scenarios to evade his father's wrath; and he was determined to win in the struggle of life even if it meant keeping the truth at bay—from himself as well as from others.

If Nixon needed any reinforcement for not doubting his own words and thoughts, there was his longtime friendship with the Reverend Norman Vincent Peale. While living in New York during the 1960s, he and his family attended services at the Marble Collegiate Church, where Peale was the longtime pastor and who later presided at the White House wedding of the Nixons' daughter Julie.[59] In his sermons, as well as in his best-selling 1952 book, *The Power of Positive Thinking*, Peale stressed the need to believe in oneself and to never give up. "*Always* picture 'success,'" the clergyman wrote, "no matter how badly things seem to be going at the moment." Then there was his advice: "Whenever a negative thought concerning your personal powers come to mind, deliberately voice a positive thought to cancel it out"—and "Do not build up obstacles in your imagination. Depreciate every so-called obstacle."[60] Nixon had come to similar conclusions long before he met Peale, but the clergyman's message surely must have resonated with the president.

However far out of touch with reality Nixon's thoughts and associated actions had taken him, he failed to escape accountability in the end. On July 27, 1974, the House Judiciary Committee voted twenty-seven to eleven, along bipartisan lines, to approve a first article of impeachment accusing the president of obstruction of justice. The committee subsequently voted on two other articles of impeachment—abuse of power and contempt of Congress. A group of Republican lawmakers, headed by Senator Barry Goldwater, went to the White House and pressed Nixon to resign, informing him that the votes were there for the House to impeach and the Senate to convict him, not knowing that the president had already decided to step down. On August 9,

Nixon resigned, and Vice President Gerald R. Ford took the oath of office as president. Nixon's first vice president, Spiro Agnew, had resigned in 1973 after being charged with receiving kickbacks from construction projects while governor of Maryland.

In March 1974, former Attorney General John Mitchell, along with Bob Haldeman and John Ehrlichman, Nixon's most high-ranking staffers, was indicted for conspiracy and obstruction of justice and later, upon conviction, served prison terms. Now the question, following Nixon's resignation, was whether he would face criminal prosecution. President Ford, after being bombarded at every turn during his first month in office about Nixon's legal liability, decided to offer the former president a full pardon. Accepting a pardon, however, is an admission of guilt, since it means that a person has done something illegal for which he or she asks to be pardoned. Nixon did not believe he had done anything wrong other than being stupid for having made the tapes, but facing an ultimatum to sign the pardon, he did so.

Many Americans were outraged at what they saw as a double standard of justice: Nixon had violated both the law and the Constitution and had escaped all punishment while Americans convicted of far lesser offenses went to jail. Many historians have thought that Ford did the right thing to save the nation from being torn apart over seeing a former president prosecuted and possibly sent to prison, but the pardon probably kept Ford from being elected in his own right in 1976. In the aftermath of the Trump presidency, the decision to pardon Nixon may no longer seem to be a wise choice if judicial punishment for Nixon might have served as a warning for Donald Trump.

Some Americans felt comforted that, in the end, the Constitution had prevailed, since Nixon had to resign because of his illegal behavior. However, Nixon never recanted his belief in executive supremacy. During an extensive 1977 interview with talk show host David Frost, aired on both radio and television, Frost asked him about the illegality of his acts. To that, Nixon replied, "Well, when the president does it, that means that it is *not* illegal."[61] Save for the tapes and the revelation of their existence, it is likely that Nixon would have survived as president and gotten away with his serious abuses of power and subversions of the Constitution.

With uncanny insight, James Barber predicted that the country would know other chief executives like Richard Nixon and the grave danger they presented to the nation. "He will be back," Barber wrote. He very nearly got away with establishing a Presidential tyranny in the United States. . . . It is so important to the future of the Presidency to keep it out of the hands of future Nixons . . ."[62] However, even Barber would have had difficulty imagining the threat posed by Donald Trump, whose background and rise to power are examined in the next chapter.

Notes

1 In the words of Laurence Tribe and Joshua Matz in their book *To End a Presidency*, "While Clinton's conduct was faithless to his marriage and to the court in which he testified, it hardly broke faith with the nation as a whole or foreshadowed grave peril

if he remained in office." See Laurence Tribe and Joshua Matz, *To End a Presidency: The Power of Impeachment* (New York: Basis Books, 2018), 21.

2 Barber, *The Presidential Character*, 5–6. Originally published in 1972, *The Presidential Character* is now in its Fifth Edition.

3 Ibid., 7.

4 In his classic work, *Nixon Agonistes* (Boston: Houghton Mifflin Company, 1969 [2002]), author Garry Wills chronicled and examined this phenomenon in a chapter entitled "The Politics of Resentment."

5 Hans L. Trefousse, *Andrew Johnson: A Biography* (New York: W. W. Norton & Company, 1997), 20.

6 Johnson, *Congressional Globe*, 28th Cong., 1st Sess., App. 95–98; *The Papers of Andrew Johnson* (Knoxville: University of Tennessee Press, 1967–1998) 1:133–48.

7 Johnson, Speech at Raleigh, July 24, 1857, *Papers*, 2:476–8.

8 *Congressional Globe*, 29th Cong., 1st Sess., 877–8.

9 Trefousse, *Andrew Johnson*, 148, 155.

10 Johnson, Speech at Nashville, July 4, 1862, *Papers*, 5:231.

11 Johnson, *Papers*, 8:333.

12 Quoted in Trefousse, *Andrew Johnson,* 236.

13 *Myers v. the United States*, U.S. 272 52 (1926).

14 The best, recent biography of Richard Nixon is Thomas, *Being Nixon.*

15 For an insightful analysis of Nixon's family background and it effect on his emotional development, see Fawn M. Brodie, *Richard Nixon: The Shaping of His Character* (New York: W. W. Norton & Company, 1981).

16 Brodie, *Nixon*, 39.

17 Richard Nixon, *RN: The Memoirs of Richard Nixon* (New York: Grosset and Dunlap, 1978), 6.

18 Jessamyn West, quoted in Brodie, *Nixon*, 40.

19 Nixon, *RN*, 6.

20 *Los Angeles Times*, May 10, 1959.

21 Nixon, *RN*, 11.

22 Barber, *The Presidential Character*, 131.

23 Quoted in Jeff Shesol, "The Nixon Memorial," *New Yorker*, August 6, 2014.

24 Quoted in Brodie, *Nixon*, 56.

25 Brodie makes this insightful comparison between these two troubled presidents in her *Nixon*, 84.

26 Quoted in William Saffire, *Before the Fall* (New York: Doubleday, 1975), 8.

27 Barber, *The Presidential Character*, 129.

28 Quoted in Thomas, *Being Nixon,* 22–3.

29 Wills, *Nixon Agonistes* (Boston: Houghton Mifflin, 2002 [1970]), 72–90.

30 Nixon, quoted in Brodie, *Nixon*, 171.

31 Richard Nixon, *Six Crises* (Garden City: Doubleday and Company, 1962).

32 In the book, Nixon covers these crises in six chapters entitled "The Hiss Case," "The Fund," "The Heart Attack," "Caracas," "Khrushchev," and "The Campaign of 1960."

33 Thomas, *Being Nixon*, 53.

34 Nixon, *Six Crises*, 14. See also ibid., 18.

35 Ibid., 11.

36 Nixon, quoted in Jonathan Aitken, *Nixon: A Life* (Washington, DC: Regnery History, 2015), 59–60.

37 Nixon, *Six Crises*, 83.
38 Ibid., 103–4.
39 "Address of Senator Nixon to the American People: The Checkers Speech," The American Presidency Project, September 23, 1952, www.presidency.ucsb.edu/ws/index.php?pid=24485. *The speech can also be seen on YouTube.*
40 Frank Gannon and Richard Nixon, "Real Richard Nixon: Twenty-Eight Days," https://www.c-span.org/video/?321120-1/1983-richard-nixon-frank-gannon-interviews.
41 Nixon, *Six Crises*, 305.
42 Ibid., 295.
43 Nixon, *RN*, 246.
44 *New York Times*, November 12, 1970; Chris Barber, "The New Nixon," The Nixon Library, March 11, 2014; Thomas, *Nixon*, 145, 147, 155, 198, 285.
45 George Wallace, quoted in Rick Pearlstein, *Nixonland: The Rise of a President and the Fracturing of America* (New York: Scribner, 2009), 224.
46 Nixon introduced the term "silent majority" in a speech from the Oval Office on November 3, 1969, in response to demonstrations demanding that he pull the nation out of Vietnam.
47 Peter Baker, *New York Times*, January 2, 2017. The Times reporting was based on the notes of former White House Chief of Staff H. R. Haldeman, which had been deposited in the Nixon Presidential Library and Museum. For a circumstantial discussion of this interference, written before the revelation in the *Times*, see Thomas, *Nixon*, 176–81.
48 Spiro Agnew, *New York Times*, October 20, 1969; *Collected Speeches of Spiro Agnew* (1971), 135.
49 Quoted in Thomas, *Being Nixon*, 418.
50 Ibid.
51 On Nixon's admiration of de Gaulle, see Conrad Black, *Richard Nixon: A Life in Full* (New York: Public Affairs Books, 2007), 579; Schlesinger, *The Imperial Presidency*, 255.
52 Johnnies Mac Walters, who headed the IRS in the early 1970s, was quoted in a *USA Today* article published on May 26, 2013, as saying that he refused to carry out the requested audits from the Nixon administration.
53 Thomas, *Nixon*, 227–8, 292–3, 353.
54 A still valuable contemporary account of Nixon's downfall is the book by Carl Bernstein and Bob Woodward, the Washington Post reporters who were mainly responsible for breaking and investigating the Watergate story: *All the President's Men* (New York: Simon & Schuster, 1974).
55 *New York Times*, July 22, 1973.
56 Quoted in Thomas, *Nixon*, 330.
57 Nixon, *RN*, 514.
58 Woodward and Bernstein, *All the President's Men*, 221.
59 Nixon, *RN*, 360, 362; Thomas, *Being Nixon*, 194.
60 Norman Vincent Peale, *The Power of Positive Thinking* (New York: Simon & Schuster, 2015), 12–13. This book was originally published in 1952 and has sold millions of copies.
61 Quoted in Thomas, *Being Nixon*, 509.
62 Barber, *The Presidential Character*, 144.

10

President or Autocrat

The Survival of American Democracy

If destruction be our lot we must ourselves be its author and finisher. As a nation of free men we will live forever or die by suicide.

Abraham Lincoln, "Address Before the Young Men's Lyceum," 1838

Although Donald Trump begins life in a family with increasing wealth and later boasts of having a personal fortune in the billions of dollars, he is in many ways as resentful when he runs for president as Andrew Johnson or Richard Nixon. Even more than these two predecessors, Trump has an uncanny sense of how to appeal to the insecurities of millions of voters who share his resentments and fears.

The Making of Donald Trump

For Trump, as well as for Richard Nixon and Andrew Johnson, his behavior is closely linked to the formation of his character. Associating Trump's behavior with family dynamics is his niece Mary Trump, who is also a psychologist. Even after accounting for the possibility that her views may have been somewhat colored by her own negative experiences within the family, she provides some of the best available insights into the circumstances of her uncle's childhood, youth, and young adulthood in her book, *Too Much and Never Enough.*[1]On the surface, the circumstances surrounding Donald Trump's birth and upbringing could not have been more promising. When he was born in 1946, his father Fred Trump was already a wealthy real estate developer. That same year Fred was making plans to build a twenty-one-room, red brick, colonial revival house in the then prestigious Jamaica Estates section of New York City's borough of Queens. The house boasted over 4,000 square feet of floor space, with nine-foot columns across the front and a faux coat of arms gracing the pediment above the entrance, the sort of ostentatious display that son Donald would use throughout his adult life in efforts to impress others.

As Donald and his four siblings were growing up, their father devoted himself to amassing greater and greater wealth by putting up apartment buildings mainly in

Brooklyn and Queens for postwar baby boom families. He also joined country clubs where he could entertain clients. Working twelve hours a day, six days a week, he had little time for his family. What mattered to him was making money, and he invariably rated other people by how much money they made. He also had a flair for showmanship, according to his niece, and "often trafficked in hyperbole." To him, "everything was 'great,' 'fantastic,' and 'perfect.'"[2] He never hesitated to brag about himself or admit to a moment's doubt about his latest projects. Norman Vincent Peale's best-selling *Power of Positive Thinking* had much appeal for him, as it had for Richard Nixon. Fred Trump accordingly joined Peale's Marble Collegiate Church in Manhattan. When he and the family attended religious services, it was at Peale's church.

Great family wealth and religious admonitions like Peale's to never doubt oneself are not what children need most to develop into well-adjusted adults. What they require is unstinting parental love and a sense of unconditional support and protection, neither of which young Donald could expect on a regular basis. Fred Trump was far too busy accumulating wealth to show much affection, and in any case, he believed that it was his wife, Mary Anne MacLeod Trump, who should bear all the responsibility for bringing up the children. When Fred did interact with his three sons and two daughters, he expected complete and unquestioning obedience, and when he admonished them, it was usually through sarcasm and ridicule. Their mother did not intervene because she believed her husband should be in charge, as well as because of her chronic ill health that began with serious postpartum complications after the birth of their son Robert. In the words of grandniece Mary Trump, "she was the kind of mother who used her children to comfort herself rather than comforting [the children]." In addition, she was "often unstable and needy, prone to self-pity and flights of martyrdom."[3]

Donald was just two and a half years old when his mother became ill and was not always emotionally available to him, creating feelings of abandonment that his father was temperamentally incapable of understanding or mitigating. Richard Nixon had been older when he experienced abandonment and was at least better able to understand why his mother had to be away from home. Yet both Nixon and Trump, albeit for somewhat different reasons and in somewhat different circumstances, failed to receive the nurturing and love that all children need. Similarly deprived was Andrew Johnson when his widowed mother married again and apprenticed him to a tailor when he was not quite ten years old. In all three cases, the abandonment may well have undermined these future presidents' sense of safety and worthiness of receiving love.

With Donald's mother not "there" for him, Mary Trump reports that he had no choice but to try getting along with his father. Under the circumstances, he and the other four children often resorted to lying to escape their father's scorching verbal censure. Eventually, Donald found favor with Fred by imitating him. This meant being a bully, a braggart, and a person who regarded life as a zero-sum game in which one was either a "winner" or a "loser." As such, Donald was determined to show his father that he had all the makings of a no-holds-barred winner. In contrast, his older brother, Fred, Jr.—known as "Freddy"—was temperamentally a much gentler soul and had neither the interest nor the inclination to follow his father's example. When Freddy failed to be the "killer" Fred Sr. expected him to be and resigned from the family real estate business, Donald gladly took over his brother's role.

Fred Trump accepted Donald's bullying and arrogance toward his younger siblings and classmates, Mary Trump believes, because he could identify with such behavior. Yet, when the private school that Donald attended found his behavior untenable and recommended that he transfer to the New York Military Academy to straighten him out, Fred readily agreed. However, what the rigid discipline at the school seemed to teach Donald was that whoever wielded power, no matter how arbitrary, was the person in control.[4]

After graduating from military school, Donald entered nearby Fordham University in New York's borough of the Bronx. However, he aspired to attend a more prestigious institution and settled on the Wharton School of Business at the University of Pennsylvania in Philadelphia. Worried about a low grade-point average at Fordham, he solved the problem, according to his niece, by paying someone to take the SAT entrance exams for him at a time when photos I.D.s were less common and thus allowed the substitute to pass himself off as Trump. Getting into Wharton under such dubious circumstances may have only reinforced Donald's belief that cheating could pay big dividends.

Fred Trump had long wanted to break into Manhattan real estate, which was more lucrative as well as more prestigious than his projects in the outer boroughs of Brooklyn and Queens. However, he lacked a college degree and the social polish to pull off such a move. He was also a poor public speaker. Now he had a son with an Ivy League degree, who spoke well but shared his chutzpah. Donald now might go where his father could not hope to enter: Fred would be the silent partner who put up the money and would use long-cultivated political connections with the Democrats who ran New York City to ease the way for his son's projects.

Donald's first great real estate coup was buying and remodeling the old Commodore Hotel next to Grand Central Station, which he renamed the Grand Hyatt Hotel and opened in 1980. The money for the project came from his father as well as from bank loans that his father helped to arrange. The Grand Hyatt, shimmering in a sheath of glass and with its gigantic atrium, wowed New Yorkers, including architecture critics, and put Trump on the front page of the *New York Times* as well as numerous other publications.

In 1979, even before the opening of the Grand Hyatt, construction began on Trump Tower in Midtown Manhattan, a fifty-eight-story building completed in 1983 and then the tallest building with all glass sheathing in the city. Trump moved his offices as well as his family into the tower. Two years later, in 1985, he bought the ornate, 126-room Mar-a-Lago estate in Palm Beach, Florida, which had been built by cereal heiress Marjorie Merriweather Post in the 1920s and which Trump turned into a private club and resort. In 1988, back in Manhattan, he bought and renovated the lavish, early twentieth-century Plaza Hotel. By then, Trump had invested heavily in Atlantic City to take advantage of New Jersey's legalization of gambling there in 1976. At one point, he was the owner or part owner of four gambling casinos, but his crown jewel was the Trump Taj Mahal, which opened in 1990. Soaring from the exterior roofs were scores of onion-shaped domes and small minarets, and inside was a 135,000 square-foot casino floor. The total cost was nearly $1 billion, and Trump called it the "Eighth Wonder of the World." As if this were not enough, he had purchased just the year before the Eastern Airlines Shuttle, which operated up and down the Northeast Corridor, and renamed it the Trump Shuttle.

From the very beginning, the "Taj" failed to pull in enough revenue for Trump to make payments on the massive loans he had taken out for it; and in 1991, just a year after it opened, the casino filed for bankruptcy. A year later, Trump was forced to sell Trump Shuttle. In 1995, he had to divest his share in the Plaza Hotel, and a year later, he had to sell his interests in the Grand Hyatt Hotel. Trump saved himself from personal bankruptcy by obtaining loans from family, but six Trump-affiliated companies would eventually go bankrupt. However, these reversals did nothing to tarnish the Trump brand, as he constantly changed the subject by talking about new and exciting plans.

The Taj and the other much vaunted real estate conquests were critical to making Trump into a household name, but far more important in launching him as a celebrity was his publication in 1987 of *The Art of the Deal*, which was part biography and part business and financial advice. The book was a sensation, remaining for fifty-one weeks on the *New York Times* bestseller list. Trump's photo appeared on numerous magazines, and he was a guest on the *Today Show*, the *Phil Donahue Show*, *Late Night with David Letterman*, and *20/20* with Barbara Walters, among others.[5] On the book jacket and title page, the authorship read as "Donald Trump with Toni Swartz." In 2016, Swartz told the *New Yorker* magazine that he and Trump had not actually written the book together but that he, Swartz, was the sole author, a claim backed up by Howard Kaminsky, the former head of Random House, which published the book. Schwartz also told the *New Yorker* that when he found Trump difficult to interview because of his short attention span, he resorted to following him around and listening on an extension line to his phone calls, sometimes asking a few follow-up questions. Still, Trump has always claimed that he alone wrote the book.[6]

In a piece Schwartz later wrote for a collection of essays about Trump's mental health, he reflected further on his experiences in writing the *Art of the Deal*, which largely confirms Mary Trump's analysis of her uncle. He writes that Trump's "worldview was profoundly and self-protectively shaped by his father," who taught him that, "You either dominated or you submitted. You either created and exploited fear, or you succumbed to it." Consequently, Trump had spent his life "seeking to dominate others, whatever that requir[ed] and whatever collateral damage it creat[ed] along the way." Trump also did not appreciate, according to Schwartz, "the qualities that tend to emerge as people grow more secure such as empathy, generosity, [and] reflectiveness, . . . or, above all, a conscience, an inner sense of right and wrong. . . . The life he lived was all transactional."[7]

In addition, Schwartz suspected that Trump suffered from arrested development. He writes, "Beneath his bluff exterior, I always sensed a hurt, incredibly vulnerable little boy who just wanted to be loved." In Schwartz's opinion, this craving to be loved accounted for Trump's endless need for blind loyalty, flattery, and praise, which in turn, "helps to explain his hostility to democracy and a free press—both of which thrive on open dissent."[8]

It is accordingly not surprising that on top of the publicity for *Art of the Deal* and the various grand real estate ventures, a very needy Trump reveled in every scrap of publicity, both good and bad, that he could wring out of local news outlets and especially from the social gossip pages of the tabloid *New York Post*. Glamorous girlfriends, glittering weddings, and delectable details about his two divorces were all grist for the mill. Any day that he was in the news, whether on television or in print, was a good day according to Trump. He even resorted to telephoning media outlets using pseudonyms, including John Miller or John Barron, pretending to give inside information about himself.[9] Trump also licensed his brand on a series of products: There were Trump suits, Trump men's cologne, Trump wines, Trump Vodka, Trump bottled water, Trump steaks, Trump Mortgage, and *Trump Magazine*. The Trump brand was everywhere. The lawsuits and countersuits that Trump constantly filed likewise kept his name circulating around the city. Meanwhile, it was clear that Trump was not following his own advice in *The Art of the Deal*, especially his admonition to "Contain the Costs," as the companies to which he was connected were forced into bankruptcy or were sold to pay massive debts.[10]

Tellingly, according to *New York Times* journalist Timothy O'Brien, who has interviewed and studied the man extensively, Trump had initially thought of attending the University of Southern California to study filmmaking. Later, he came to admire what he called "badass" actors such as Clint Eastwood and Orson Wells. O'Brien quotes Trump as saying, "I loved Orson Wells. He was totally fucked up. He was a total mess. But think of his wives. Think of his hits. . . . He became totally impossible. He thought everybody was a moron. . . ; if he had a budget he'd exceed it by twenty times and destroy everything. He became impossible. I loved that."[11] Given how Trump's life has unfolded, someone reading this quote with Wells' name removed might conclude that Trump was talking about himself.

Then in 2004, an NBC "reality" television series gave Trump the sort of national celebrity status he had always craved. At first, its title was *The Apprentice*, but beginning in 2008 it became *The Celebrity Apprentice*, since the contestants in the second iteration were in fact celebrities from various fields. However, in both cases, the contestants, ranging anywhere from fifteen to eighteen in number, broke into two teams and competed to defeat each other at various set tasks. Each week Trump, sitting in a large red leather boardroom chair, would say, "you're fired" to a contestant he deemed to be a loser. To the last one standing, he would declare, "you're hired." The winning prize during the earlier seasons was a job worth $250,000 to run one of the Trump companies. Later in the *Celebrity Apprentice* version, winners received $250,000 to donate to a charity of their choice. Between 6 and 20 million viewers, depending on the year, watched as "Chairman Trump" doled out rewards and punishments, and in the process gave himself the aura of a reigning business tycoon. In addition, each episode of the *Celebrity Apprentice* series showed the outside of Trump Tower several times, along with well-appointed interior rooms where the two competing teams retreated to plan and conspire. In the process, Donald Trump became one of the best-known individuals in the United States. Of course, like other reality shows, *The Celebrity Apprentice* had nothing to do with reality, since what viewers saw on TV was a massively edited program that was cut and assembled from dozens of hours of filming. In this regard, Trump, like Ronald Reagan, rose to prominence as a television—if not a movie personality as well, as was the case with Reagan.

Yet, even some business schools around the country began to use the *Apprentice* series program as a teaching tool, leading to the idea of Trump University, which opened in 2005 as a for-profit institution offering online courses in real estate, wealth management, and entrepreneurship. The "university" had no accreditation, did not give grades, and did not award diplomas or certificates. Trump appeared in promotional videos promising to share his secrets: "At Trump University we teach success," he insisted, "That's what it's all about. Success. It's going to happen to you." This fake educational venture closed in 2010 amid accusations of fraudulent marketing practices. Facing several class-action lawsuits, Trump settled out of court in 2018 for $25 million.[12]

The 1998 election to the governorship of Minnesota of Jesse Ventura, a former professional wrestler, encouraged Trump to believe that he needed no experience in public office to run for President of the United States as a candidate for the Reform Party, to which Ventura also belonged. He announced his candidacy on *Larry King Live*, a popular evening talk show program at the time, but withdrew from contention, citing divisions within the Reform Party. He had considered running as a Republican in 1988 but decided not to do so because of his increasing debts. He thought about trying again for the presidency in 2004 but did not go through with it since he was launching his reality TV show that year. There was even some talk in Republican circles about his being a viable candidate in 2012.[13] However, most members of the party, along with major media outlets and the public at large, did not take these suggestions seriously, and many even considered them a joke.

The Trump Show

On June 16, 2015, Trump announced he would launch a serious bid for the Republican nomination. A little more than a month later, a Gallup poll indicated that Trump had a name recognition of 92 percent, eleven points higher than Jeb Bush's, despite Bush's famous family name and despite his two recent terms as Governor of Florida. Trump also led all the others who had expressed an interest in running, with Texas Senator Ted Cruz at 66 percent name recognition and Florida Senator Marco Rubio at 64 percent.[14] Trump's celebrity status alone would seem to have given him a distinct advantage over those who could claim a record of public service.

In the end, seventeen other Republicans initially took part in the primary election debates, and from the start, Trump dominated the debate stage and lent an air of *The Celebrity Apprentice* to the events. By winning one state primary after another, he became entitled to stand on stage in the middle of the other candidates. Although he did not say, "you're fired" to the others, he attempted to humiliate his competitors by calling them disparaging names: Jeb Bush was "Low Energy Jeb"; Ted Cruz was

"Lyin' Ted"; and Marco Rubio was "Little Marco." At one debate, Trump declared that Ben Carson was "pathological" and intimated falsely that Ted Cruz's father had been a collaborator in the Kennedy assassination. Television audiences loved the fireworks, and Trump's fans were increasingly impressed by how he took control and dominated the debates.

Trump staged frequent rallies in friendly regions of the country that drew huge crowds. Ever the showman, he realized that if he put on a controversial and exciting performance during these rallies, the cable networks covering them would expand their viewership. Such enlarged TV audiences increased advertising revenue and, in turn, assured that cable outlets would continue to broadcast what had become the "Trump Show." Meanwhile, the other Republican candidates received very little airtime. For example, between August 24 and September 4, 2015, CNN devoted 78 percent of its campaign coverage to Trump, for a total of 234 minutes in contrast to Ted Cruz, who received just seven minutes of coverage.[15] All told, CNN and the other cable stations, which likewise devoted much attention to Trump's campaign, in effect gave him millions of dollars in free advertising.[16]

Despite this coverage, Trump constantly attacked the media, denouncing any critical story as "fake news," shouting insults at reporters covering his appearances, and encouraging the crowd to yell threats and insults at those in the media covering his rallies. He once told a sick joke (that may not have really been a joke) about wanting to kill reporters.[17] At one rally, he called NBC's Katy Tur a liar before millions of viewers, and over Twitter, Trump said she should be fired.[18] His fans loved it. He later admitted to veteran journalist Leslie Stahl that he consistently demeaned and discredited members of the media so "when you write negative stories about me no one will believe you."[19] Nevertheless, Trump had a love/hate relationship with the press: For instance, he often railed against the *New York Times* even though he liked to brag about how often he made front-page news in the *Times*. Like during his days as a real estate developer, he believed that even negative coverage was better than no coverage.

It was also evident to those covering Trump during the campaign that he had no qualms about lying. Indeed, over the years he had freely admitted that telling lies was an important key to his success, in the words of reporter Jonathan Karl, "Like a poker player with a pair of deuces who can convince his opponent he has a full house."[20] Trump also bragged to Barbara Walters during an interview with her on the ABC program *20/20* that he had once deceived a company into believing that a construction project was well underway by telling his contractors to "get every truck you can get. And let us look like we're building the Grand Coulee Dam."[21]

In many respects, opposing Democratic candidate Hillary Clinton personified the social and cultural establishment that Trump's most fervent supporters disliked intensely. Instead of exploring the complexities of their differing views, Trump decided to charge that she was a deeply dishonest and even criminal person. The name he used for her constantly was "Crooked Hillary," mainly because of her use of a private email server to conduct correspondence as Secretary of State. Confusing the matter for the public and helping Trump was the fact that the FBI cleared her of wrongdoing, only to reopen the investigation just eleven days before the election and then to clear her once again two days before voters went to the polls. For months, a favorite chant at every Trump rally—"Lock her up! Lock her up!"—aimed to portray Clinton as a criminal who did not deserve to be in the White House. During one rally, Trump even invited the Russians to find the approximately 30,000 personal emails that Hillary had sent via her server and then had deleted. "Russia, if you're listening," he said, "I hope you're able to find the 30,000 emails that are missing. I think you will be rewarded mightily by our press."[22]

Although the Russians did not locate her missing emails, they did interfere in the election to Trump's benefit. For instance, at 3:00 p.m. on October 7, 2016, the US Director of National Intelligence reported that Russia had hacked the emails of the Democratic National Committee and released them to WikiLeaks, which began posting them. In its statement, the US National Security Agency added that the Russian operation was undertaken to influence the presidential election and that "only Russia's senior-most officials [i.e., Vladimir Putin] could have authorized these activities."[23]

However, the impact of the Russian interference was blunted by the *Washington Post*'s publication of what came to be known as the *Access Hollywood* tape. In it, Trump was heard bragging to program host Billy Bush that his celebrity status allowed him to do anything he wanted to women: "When you're a star, they let you do it. You can do anything. Grab 'em by the pussy. You can do anything."[24] Democrats and Republicans alike believed the tape now doomed Trump's election chances. Trump initially dismissed the tape by saying it was just "locker room banter." A few hours later he released a video statement saying, "I was wrong and I apologize." He then added that what he had said was nothing compared with Bill Clinton's abuse of women and Hillary's supposed shaming of her husband's victims—as if two wrongs made a right. Finally, he signaled that he had no intention of dropping out of the race, declaring, "See you at the debate on Sunday."[25]

The confluence of several events may have saved Trump's chances of winning the election. The *Access Hollywood* tape largely pushed the evidence of Russian interference off the front pages, and Trump cleverly used the tape controversy to attack Hillary Clinton in a way she could not defend herself, lest she pick open all the scabs of the Monica Lewinsky affair and associated scandals involving her husband and other women. If that were not enough, there were the on-again/off-again FBI investigations of Hillary's private email server, which only gave ammunition for Trump to call her a criminal and for crowds to chant "Lock her up." It was in many ways like the "denigrative method" that Richard Nixon had used for years used against his political rivals.

Democratic nominee Hillary Clinton was superbly qualified to be president given her record of public service. She was President Obama's Secretary of State, had served two terms as a US Senator from New York, and was First Lady during her husband Bill Clinton's two terms as president. In addition, she was the first woman nominee for president by a major party. Pollsters, pundits, and most professional politicians (including many Republicans) predicted a Clinton victory. When the results were in, Clinton won the popular vote by nearly 3 million ballots (or 48.2 percent to 46.1 percent). However, she narrowly lost the popular vote to Trump in several key states in the deindustrializing "rust belt" (viz., Pennsylvania, Michigan, and Wisconsin) that had often been in the Democratic column, and thereby lost the electoral vote nationwide. The final electoral tally was 306 for Trump and 232 for Clinton. This election became the fifth time in US history when the winner of the popular vote failed to become president—and the second time in just sixteen years.

Several factors led to Trump's win (at least in the Electoral College, which is what matters). Those who doubted that Trump's outrageous and seemingly immoral behavior would doom his candidacy failed to realize that vast numbers of supporters saw him as their "tough-guy" champion against the urban elites whom they thought looked down on ordinary citizens. In seeming contradiction, the fact that Trump was a wealthy New Yorker only added to his allure as a successful, no-nonsense businessman who knew how to get things done, despite his involvement in bankruptcy several times. Even Trump's lack of a regular and close affiliation with any church, his two divorces, and the accusations of extramarital relationships did not matter to most evangelical Christians because he had announced his opposition to abortion and promised to nominate conservative judges who could overturn the case of *Roe v. Wade*, which in 1973 had legalized abortion.

Some evangelicals, including individuals associated with Jerry Falwell's Liberty University, compared Trump to the sixth-century BCE Persian King Cyrus, an idol-worshipping monarch, whom (as told in the biblical account of Isaiah 45) God had raised up to rescue and rebuild Jerusalem. In other words, the claim was that God could use deeply flawed individuals for his own salvific purposes.[26] For the same reason, it did not matter that Trump hailed from New York City, long considered a veritable Sodom and Gomorrah to many in the heartland of America, or that Trump had behaved in deeply immoral ways according to Evangelical beliefs.

Then there were those who had always voted Republican and who continued to vote for their party's candidate despite misgivings about Trump or simply because they could not imagine casting their ballots for a Democrat, no matter the candidate (a habit that tends to afflict Democrats in reverse). Motivating many Republicans, too, was the belief that Trump would deliver on a big tax cut and repeal various business regulations.

At rally after rally, Trump promised to "Make America Great Again." Its acronym, "MAGA," appeared on hats, shirts, and flags, all of them happily sold to supporters by the Trump campaign. On one level, promising to make America great again did not make much sense at a time when the economy was continuing to expand, with declining unemployment. In addition, the United States remained the most powerful country on the face of the earth, with no other country being close in either soft or hard power.

However, many Trump supporters who were upset about the disappearance of good paying blue-collar jobs in rust belt areas of the country could agree that America was no longer great. They therefore warmed to the candidate's claims that the United States was being "ripped off" by international competitors. The slogan "Make America Great Again" also claimed that the country had been greater in the past before a variety of cultural changes had made many Americans feel angry and threatened. These included issues such as abortion, same-sex marriage, and the increasing number of people in the country who had no religious affiliation. Demographic predictions that whites would become a minority group in just a few decades were additionally unsettling to those who had found identity and pride in being white. Individuals with only a high school education, who increasingly identified with the Republican Party, believed that better educated people in the big cities on the two coasts were mocking them and had far too much influence in American life.

Although few at the time connected the phrase "Make America Great Again" with Ronald Reagan, who had used it frequently during his campaign for president nearly forty years before, both he and Trump were tapping into a strong belief among many that the country had lost its way and needed to restore certain conditions and beliefs. In Reagan's case, there was continuing anger over the civil rights movement, the women's movement, and Vietnam, giving rise to a belief that the period before the 1960s had been more wholesome and promising, despite very real problems in the nation during that earlier time. In Trump's case, he was channeling anger over increasing secularization in the country, an unnecessary war in Iraq, the sub-prime mortgage recession in 2008–09 which punished homeowners, while none of the bankers and Wall Street perpetrators received any punishment, and an increasingly internationalized economy that failed to protect American jobs. In neither case, ironically, had either Reagan or Trump felt the consequences of such changes personally.

Not all Trump supporters were in economic distress; however, and according to author and cultural analyst David Brooks, they included many individuals who were "contractors, plumbers, electricians, middle managers, and small-business owners." In fact, average earnings of Trump supporters were $72,000 a year.[27] What angered many of them, according to Brooks, was their inability to access "the modern meritocracy," which depended on attending a prestigious university and all the connections that came with it, essential to membership in the "creative classes" of media, technology, art, and various avenues of innovation. Brooks concluded that "this situation produces a world in which the populist right can afford to be intellectually bankrupt. . . . They just need to stoke and harvest resentment toward the creative class."[28] The Trump campaign's strategy, according to columnist Ezra Klein, was thus to mobilize this angry base "in order to prevail in a crowded, fractured field [of primary candidates]."[29]

Trump thus successfully tapped into a deep well of anger and discontent among many voters who felt marginalized and locked out of the escalator of social and economic mobility. During the past few decades, in fact, the two major parties had switched places in many respects: Whereas the Republican Party had once attracted a large percentage of voters with a college education—versus Democratic Party voters with less schooling—the balance had flipped. Democrats traditionally had seen themselves as the party of the working class, but the Republicans were now attracting large numbers of blue-collar voters.[30]

In his inaugural address on January 20, 2017, Trump referenced many of these grievances in an unusually dark speech for this occasion: "Politicians prospered, but the jobs left and the factories closed. The establishment protected itself, but not the citizens of our country, . . . and while they celebrated in our nation's capital, there was little to celebrate for struggling families across our land." He then promised, "This American carnage stops right here and right now."[31]

That Trump himself was not a Washington insider had allowed many supporters to conclude that he did not belong to an elite group of politicians who were continuing to ignore their plight. His bashing of immigrants from Latin America throughout the campaign and his espousing the "birtherism" conspiracy, which held that Barack Obama had not been born in the United States and was thus not eligible to be president, had played into those fears of many whites that they were losing their special status in the United States, themes that would continue throughout his presidency.

Throughout the campaign, Trump had nurtured a cult of personality. The rudiments of the cult were already in place when he started the campaigning: He was the all-knowing and all-powerful CEO of the *Celebrity Apprentice* series, as well as the supposed author of the best-selling *Art of the Deal* and a man who had plastered his name all over large buildings and dozens of products. Revealingly, in March 2017, Trump paid a visit to the Hermitage Plantation of former President Andrew Jackson outside Nashville, Tennessee, another chief executive who had forged a cult of personality. The occasion was the 250th anniversary of Jackson's birth; Trump placed a wreath on Old Hickory's grave as taps echoed in the distance. During a short speech, he said he was a "big fan" of Jackson, adding that Jackson had been the "people's president," a role that Trump now sought to play. He had already ordered a portrait of Jackson hung on the wall near his desk in the Oval Office, where it would remain throughout his occupancy of the White House.[32]

Those who were alarmed about the coming Trump presidency, including some Republicans, tried to reassure themselves by hoping that traditional norms and expectations surrounding the office might curb his behavior. In other words, there was the promise of a "New Trump." However, just as there had been no "New Nixon" half a century before, there would be no "New Trump."

Conspiracy, Distortion, and Fear

Significantly, the lies continued immediately after the inauguration. At his very first briefing, Press Secretary Sean Spicer declared that the crowd gathered on the mall below the Capitol for the swearing in was, "The largest audience to ever witness an inauguration—period—both in person and around the globe."[33] Even a cursory glance at aerial photos of the crowd for Trump's inauguration, when compared to those at Obama's inauguration, demonstrated the falsity of Spicer's claims. The following day on the Sunday TV program *Meet the Press*, Trump's senior counselor Kellyanne Conway defended the claims by saying that Spicer had given "alternative facts." Then at an early press conference, Trump claimed that his 306 electoral votes represented the largest victory in the Electoral College since Ronald Reagan when, in fact, Barack Obama and George H. W. Bush both had come into office with higher electoral totals than Trump. In Bush's case, he had won the presidency in 1988 with 426 electoral ballots, 117 more than Trump in 2016. Obama's win in the Electoral College had been 365 to

173, or 192 more than Trump eight years later. Over the next four years of the Trump administration, the *Washington Post* would count over 30,000 false or misleading claims made by the president.[34]

Media assertions that Trump was lying enraged him. He fought back by charging that it was the media who were purveying "fake news," as he had insisted throughout the campaign. He thereby defined himself and his devoted followers as innocent victims of a mendacious body of reporters and editorial writers. On Twitter, which had become the president's favorite tool for direct communications, he denounced the "FAKE NEWS" as "the enemy of the American people." This phrase, "enemy of the people," dated to the French Revolution's "reign of terror" during which political enemies were denounced and then dispatched to the guillotine to have their heads chopped off. Nazi propaganda minister Joseph Goebbels used the epithet against Jews in the lead-up to the Holocaust, and Soviet dictator Joseph Stalin likewise called the millions put to death during his purges "enemies of the people." It is unclear if Trump knew about the ugly history of this phrase. Even if so, he continued to use it against the media, perhaps because he found it effective and perhaps because he had always refused to admit he was wrong as a sign of weakness—or a bit of both.[35]

In dealing with the media as well as other critics, Trump turned to the simplest of defense mechanisms—denial and projection. That is, he denied all charges and projected his own untruths onto others: He was not lying; the pundits and reporters were the liars. At one press conference, he accused the media of creating violence "by not writing the truth," when, in fact, he had been encouraging violence since the beginning of his campaign for president, as when he urged attendees at his rallies to rough up protesters. At the same time, Trump continued to perform what White House correspondent Jonathan Karl has called a "Dr. Jekyll and Mr. Hyde routine" with the media in which he courted their attention while castigating those covering him.[36] In the process, he obtained maximum publicity while satisfying his supporters' craving for "red meat" condemnations of the establishment press. For instance, he lashed out at reporters for asking stupid questions and called them rude, incompetent, disgraceful, and disrespectful. Trump maintained these attacks on the media throughout his presidency, knowing that they would delight his base of support.

As president, Trump continued to play on the anxieties of those who felt threatened by projections that white Americans would become a minority in the United States sometime around the middle of the twenty-first century. During the primary elections, he had attacked Muslim immigration to the United States, and at a rally on December 7, 2015, he called for "a total and complete shutdown of Muslims entering the United States until our country's representatives can figure out what the hell is going on."[37] Trump sensed that fear of Muslims, stoked by the attacks on 9/11, continued to linger. Immigration from Muslim countries also alarmed Christian conservatives who feared for their majority religious status, along with their majority white status. Part of this fear stemmed from the false belief that the United States now had a significantly large Muslim population. Indeed, when asked in a random study to estimate the share of Muslims in the United States population, respondents on average said one out of six, when, in fact, it was one in a hundred.[38] Trump may well not have been familiar with this study, but he had a gut instinct that many Americans feared members of the Muslim faith. He accordingly played on this fear when on January 27, 2017, he issued the first of three executive orders banning the entrance of individuals to the United States from majority Muslim countries, which the Supreme Court upheld in 2018.[39]

During the campaign, he also promised to build an impregnable wall along the whole US-Mexican border, which would keep more people of color from entering the country. At a campaign rally in August 2016, he told the crowd, "We will build a wall on the southern border. And Mexico will pay for the wall—believe me—one hundred percent." "Believe me" had become a signature phrase of Trump's campaign, and his fans *did believe him* "one hundred percent." Of course, there was no way Mexico would pay for the wall, as Trump himself knew very well.[40] Since Mexico was never going to pay for the wall, as president he put his son-in-law Jared Kushner in charge of building some 400 miles of barrier along the southern border in time for the 2020 election when Trump would be running for a second term. Kushner later claimed they had constructed 124.4 miles of wall, but in fact only one mile of it was "new wall." The rest amounted to replacement or repair of an already existing barrier, though Trump continued to insist that great strides had been made on his "big, beautiful wall."[41]

The president was also determined to get tough on undocumented immigrants crossing the southern border. Accordingly, in April 2018, Attorney General Jeff Sessions issued a memo stating that those coming across the border illegally would no longer merely receive a summons to appear in court and then be released until their status hearing. Instead, they would face arrest and incarceration. Since a court ruling in 1997 declared that children could not be in detention for longer than twenty days, they would have to be separated from their incarcerated parents. The results were heart-rending, with scenes on television of small children weeping and wailing for their parents. When Secretary of Homeland Security Kirstjen Nielsen tried to explain immigration law to Trump at a cabinet meeting, he became increasingly angry. Another cabinet member who was there reported to White House correspondent Jonathan Karl that, "the president was so agitated there was legitimate concern about his health—as if he might literally have a stroke right there in the cabinet room."[42]

In fact, Trump was not against all immigrants, especially if they were white people from northern Europe. At an Oval Office meeting with lawmakers in January 2018, he said, "Haiti? Why do we want people from Haiti here? Then they got Africa. Why do we want these people from all these shithole countries here? We should have more people from places like Norway."[43]

Being white—not black or brown (which would include Muslims from the Middle East)—had been a badge of caste superiority from the beginning of American history. It had allowed even the poorest of whites to believe they were superior merely because they were not black or brown. This attitude was especially strong in the South before and after the Civil War, but it was far from absent in the Northern states. Thus, in both sections of the country, there was a strong tendency among whites to identify whiteness as the essence of being American, a belief that continues to lie at the root of "white nationalism." Add to that the assertion that America was a Christian nation in its origins, and one had "white Christian nationalism."

To court white southerners in particular, Trump decried calls for communities throughout the South to take down statues of Confederate generals and various secessionist leaders, which African Americans especially viewed as statements of white supremacy. In a tweet on August 17, 2017, Trump declared, "Sad to see the history and culture of our great country being ripped apart with the removal of our beautiful statues and monuments."[44]

In her book, *Caste*, the journalist and author Isabel Wilkerson describes the crisis that some white, working-class Americans experience when they perceive that people whom they had long considered inferior by mere skin color now have managed to make it into the mainstream; and especially, like President Barack Obama, to become the most powerful person in the world. Wilkerson writes that this perception "left some white working-class Americans in particular, those with the least education and the material security that it can confer, to face the question of whether the commodity that they could take for granted—their skin and ascribed race—might be losing value." She explains further: "Those in the dominant caste who found themselves lagging behind those seen as inherently inferior potentially faced an epic existential crisis. . . . The disaffection is more than economic. The malaise is spiritual, psychological, [and] emotional. Who are you if there is no one to be better than?"[45] Social scientists call this phenomenon "last place aversion."[46] To some, there was even a plot called a white replacement conspiracy. (Fear of losing their racially respected place in America had also been at the root of much of the anger against the Civil Rights movement of the 1960s.)

Meanwhile, continuing reports that Russia had interfered in Trump's favor during the election suggested that he did owe a considerable debt to Russian interests. Such claims especially enraged him, since, if true, they would undermine the legitimacy of his election. Accordingly, he denounced the accusation variously as "the Russian hoax," "fake news," or a "witch hunt." Despite Trump's denunciations, various investigations of Russian interference led to the creation of a special counsel under the Justice Department and headed by former FBI director Robert Mueller, who was a lifelong member of the Republican Party.[47]

The Mueller Investigation, as it was soon called, ran from May 2017 to March 2019. The charge to Mueller was to investigate allegations of "links and/or coordination" between Trump campaign operatives and the Russian government. Mueller also received a mandate to pursue "any matters that arose or may arise directly from the investigations," including possible obstructions of justice by President Trump and members of his administration or election campaign.[48] Mueller's report, dated March 17, 2019, concluded in the first volume of a two-volume report that the social media campaign of the Internet Research Agency, headquartered in Russia, had hacked and then released damaging material from several Democratic Party sources as well as from the Clinton campaign that were intended to benefit Trump in the election. In addition, the agency had made illegal foreign contributions to the US election through buying ads on the social media giant Facebook. However, the report could not establish that the Trump campaign had conspired with the Russian government in its efforts to influence the election.

It was up to newly appointed Attorney General William Barr, who proved to be extremely loyal to President Trump, to decide when and how much of the report to deliver to Congress. Just two days after receiving it and with insufficient time to read and digest the 448-page report, Barr sent a four-page commentary to Congress. In it, he provided greatly distorted interpretations of the document. He reported that there had been no proof of collusion between the campaign and Russian agents, failing to add that the president had withheld evidence that might have demonstrated such connections. Barr also said there had been no obstruction by Trump when the truth was that Mueller had laid out a strong argument for obstruction, adding that he simply could not charge Trump as a sitting president. Barr thus had the "first word," which would be difficult to refute or reverse in the court of public opinion and especially among the president's loyal supporters. Going unmentioned by Barr was that the investigation had resulted in 199 criminal charges against various Trump campaign operatives, leading to thirty-seven indictments or guilty pleas, and to five prison sentences.

In response to Barr's comments, Trump gleefully repeated that there had been "no collusion and no obstruction." The whole thing had been a hoax, Trump trumpeted, "an attempted and failed coup."[49] Barr had delivered handsomely to Trump, who now believed he could wield all levers of presidential power to protect himself. Indeed, Trump's attorneys went so far as to assert in a letter to Mueller in January 2018 that the president could not obstruct justice because the Constitution's provision of a "unitary executive" gave him authority over the entire executive branch, including the Justice Department, and that therefore he had the right to terminate any inquiry.[50] A little over two years later, during a press conference, the president claimed unlimited power, saying, "When somebody's the president of the United States, the authority is total."[51] At least Richard Nixon had waited until he was no longer in office to say on television to David Frost, "Well, when the president does it, that means that it is *not* illegal."[52]

For Trump, his escape from accountability in the Mueller investigation only emboldened him. Just a little over two months after Barr's disingenuous summary of the report, the president made a call on July 25 to Ukrainian President Volodymyr Zelensky asking him to investigate Joe Biden and his son Hunter, who had served on the board of a Ukrainian gas company called Burisma at the same time his father was serving as vice president. The implication was that the senior Biden had used official influence to secure the job for his son, though there has never been any evidence of foul play. Col. Alexander Vindman, a member of the National Security Council who had listened in on the call, was so alarmed about the conversation between Trump and Zelensky that he turned over a complaint to the director of national intelligence. To Vindman, the conversation was "crazy, frightening," and "completely lacking in substance relating to national security."[53]

For Trump's critics, the phone call to Zelensky represented a clear case of bribery, one of the violations listed in the Constitution as grounds for impeachment. In addition, soliciting something of value from a foreign country to assist his bid for reelection would be a violation of federal election law. The House Judiciary Committee, now under the control of the Democrats since their winning control of the lower house in the mid-term elections of 2018, drew up two articles of impeachment in December 2019. These were abuse of power, stemming from the telephone call with Ukrainian President Zelensky, and obstruction of justice because of Trump's refusal to turn over relevant documents or to allow administrative officials to testify in the impeachment probe. On December 18, the full House voted 230 to 197 to impeach Trump and to bind him over to the Senate for trial. Trump repeatedly insisted that he was facing impeachment for simply "making a perfect phone call," but did not offer to explain why he considered it perfect.[54] As expected, the Senate failed on February 5, 2020, to mount the two-thirds vote necessary to convict and remove Trump from office. The tally was fifty-two to forty-eight to acquit on the first article and fifty-three to forty-seven to acquit on the second article. Except for Senator Mitt Romney, who voted guilty on the first article, the voting was strictly along party lines.

After voting for acquittal, Republican Senator Susan Collins announced to the media that Trump had "learned his lesson." Instead, one of the lessons was that impeachment allowed him to raise huge donations from supporters who believed Trump's enemies were simply persecuting him. According to Brad Parscale, Trump's campaign manager, the impeachment and acquittal had given them the means to tap a million more donors.[55] The failed attempt also lifted his approval ratings in predicted "battleground states" in the 2020 presidential election.[56] As time would tell, his acquittal only emboldened Trump to defy any restraints on his authority.

Although not rising to the level of possible impeachment, many critics strongly criticized Trump's handling of the Covid-19 virus as essentially a dereliction of duty, especially given that he knew very early that the epidemic posed a grave threat to the nation's health. For example, in a telephone interview on February 7, 2020, with journalist Bob Woodward, who with Carl Bernstein had been largely responsible for cracking open the Watergate scandal, Trump said of the virus, "It goes through the air. That's always tougher than the touch. . . . But the air, you just breathe the air and that's how it's passed. And so that's a very tricky one. That's a very delicate one. It's also more deadly than even your most strenuous flus."[57] During another interview on March 19 with Woodward, Trump offered an even more detailed understanding of how serious the new virus was: "Part of it's the viciousness. You know when it attacks, it attacks the lungs. . ., and now it's turning out it's not just old people. . . . Just today and yesterday, some startling facts came out. . . . Young people too, plenty of young people." On April 13, he added to Woodward, "It's so easily transmissible, you wouldn't even believe it." Trump also said at a briefing with his health advisors, perhaps with some exaggeration but tellingly, nevertheless, "I've always known this is a—this is a real—this is a pandemic. I've felt it was a pandemic long before it was called a pandemic.[58]

Yet in the weeks and months ahead, Trump would downplay the seriousness of what he knew. In his book *Rage*, Woodward gives many examples of Trump's obfuscation, denial, mistruths, and defensiveness about the Covid threat. Trump claimed, "This is a flu. This is like a flu." And, "When it gets a little warmer, it miraculously goes away." To a group of industry executives, the president insisted, "It's gonna leave. It's gonna be gone. It's gonna be eradicated." He also charged that Democrats were politicizing the issue by criticizing his handling of the pandemic. It was "their new hoax." His excuse for not raising an alarm, he told Woodward during an interview in mid-March, was not to alarm the public: "I wanted to always play it down . . . because I don't want to create a panic." Another reason Trump made light of the pandemic was fear that bad news about it would hurt the good economy, which he was hoping to use as a campaign pitch for a second term. "This is the greatest economy we've ever had," he would say whenever he had the chance, even though the claim was not true in comparison to other periods in US history, an untruth consistent with the sorts of gross mischaracterizations he had made throughout his business career.[59]

From the beginning of the pandemic, Trump was very defensive about the numbers of infected Americans, fearing that any increase would hurt him politically. When he heard plans about evacuating American diplomats and other American citizens from China, Trump exploded: "We're not letting them come back," he said. "You risk increasing my numbers. You won't increase my numbers. . . . Those people shouldn't have been in China in the first place."[60] For similar reasons, he wanted to have cruise ship passengers quarantined on board rather than on shore so that those infected would not have to be counted in the official US numbers—or in what Trump saw as "his numbers."[61] He had never had compassion for others and did not now, even though one of his principal duties as president was to protect the American people and, unofficially, to express his concern for their well-being.

At a reelection rally in Oklahoma in June 2020, Trump even demanded that there be less testing for the virus because he feared the results: "I said to my people, 'Slow the testing down,' because as more tests were conducted, more infections were discovered."[62] Once more, the president thought the disease was all about him, and not about its deadly threat to millions of Americans. And as he had done all his life, he sought to blame others for his own ineptitude, calling the virus the "Kung Flu," a racist slur referring to the origin of the infection in China.[63] He would continue to call it the Kung Flu or the Chinese Flu, as if doing so would absolve him of all responsibility for dealing with it.

Trump's advocacy of unproven or dangerous treatments also placed the public in danger. In early April, for instance, he began to advocate the use of the antimalarial drug hydroxychloroquine to treat the virus. There had been no research trials about its effectiveness against Covid, but the drug was known to cause heart problems in some patients taking it for other applications. At the end of the month, he suggested an even more dangerous cure effected by the injection into the body of powerful and deadly cleaning agents.[64]

By now, Trump was holding nearly daily Covid briefings with his health advisors. Often, he monopolized the podium and had no qualms about contradicting the medical experts. As he boasted to Senator Lindsey Graham, "I'm the one that decides everything."[65] Ever the showman, he liked to brag about the 9 million viewers he claimed were tuning in for each briefing "episode."

When largely peaceful protests broke out in cities around the country in May 2021, in response to a police officer's killing of George Floyd by pressing his knee on Floyd for nearly eight minutes, Trump wanted to send military units into cities where protests had broken out by citing the 1807 Insurrection Act that authorized presidents to deploy active-duty troops and use them domestically by simply declaring that an insurrection had taken place. President Lincoln had used the act to call up 75,000 militia troops in April 1861 after the firing on Fort Sumter at the beginning of the Civil War. Protests over the killing of George Floyd were not remotely similar, and Joint Chief of Staff General Mark Milley told Trump so in no uncertain terms. Secretary of Defense Mark Esper agreed, saying, "Mr. President, there is no need to call up the Insurrection Act." Attorney General Barr was of the same mind, and adamantly so. "If it comes to keeping law and order on the streets," he told Trump, "I would not hesitate to use regular troops . . . if we had to. They're not necessary." He added that the cities could manage the protests on their own: "They have the adequate resources to do it, especially if they used their National Guard or state police."[66]

Still, Esper concluded he had to do something to pacify the president and thereby keep Trump from invoking the Insurrection Act, a tactic that other members of his administration had used on various occasions to keep him from even more reckless actions. To satisfy the president, Esper drew national guardsmen from some ten states to come to Washington because of a Black Lives Matter demonstration on Lafayette Square across from the White House. However, it was US Park Police, leading a group of law enforcement personnel on horseback and in riot gear, who began clearing the square early in the evening of June 1. They used loud explosions accompanied by sparks and smoke. They also shot "pepper balls" that irritated the eyes and noses of protesters. Some of the police pushed people to the ground, while mounted officers herded the crowd through and out of the park. After the park was cleared, Trump made a televised address from the White House Rose Garden in which he threatened to deploy the US military if states and cities refused to restore order, a none-too-veiled allusion to invoking the Insurrection Act.

Those present at the Rose Garden speech were then ordered to line up in a show of force and accompany Trump on a walk across the square to St. John's Church, where a basement fire had been set the night before. Among them were Secretary Esper, Attorney General Barr, Chief of Staff Mark Meadows, Trump's daughter Ivanka and her husband Jared Kushner, and General Mark Milley. Once in front of the church, the president held a Bible (upside down) in the air for two minutes, an awkward and inexplicable gesture. Milley realized almost immediately that he had been used, and the following day he wrote out and signed a public apology, which infuriated Trump.

"Stop the Steal"

Since early in his campaign for president, Trump had been building a cult of personality. At an early rally in January 2016, he boasted, "I could stand in the middle of Fifth Avenue and shoot somebody, and I wouldn't lose any voters, OK?"[67] Although this was an exaggeration, what Trump wanted to convey was that any criticism against him could not undermine support among his passionate followers, given all the love and admiration he enjoyed from them. Unlike his predecessors, Trump also held campaign-type rallies throughout his presidency, and by his fourth year in office, he had taken over the Republican Party to such an extent that it did not have any platform for 2020 besides electing Trump. At rallies, his devoted fans chanted "Trump, Trump, Trump," and believed whatever he said, including what was demonstrably false. Thus, during his campaign for reelection, when he said he could lose only if the election were "stolen," they believed him, and when Trump did lose, they became convinced that he—and they—had been cheated. He especially attacked mail-in ballots, claiming in a tweet during June, and without any evidence, that foreign countries and unspecified "others" would be printing millions of mail-in ballots. His fans readily agreed. "Stop the Steal" became their new mantra.

All the major TV networks pointed out that results might not be known on election day because large numbers of voters would have chosen to vote by mail during the Covid pandemic. In addition, because Republicans were more likely to vote in person, partly because of their party's disparagement of using mail-in ballots, early results might make it look as if Trump were winning reelection.[68] Indeed, when election returns started to come in on the evening of November 3, the picture seemed promising for Trump and the Republicans. A little after midnight, however, the situation looked better for Democratic candidate Joseph R. Biden. Trump was dumbfounded, wondering aloud to staff how he could have been ahead and then appeared to be losing. He either believed or pretended to believe that the later votes coming in were somehow illegitimate.

At 2:30 in the morning of November 4, Trump strode into the glittering East Room of the White House, with "Hail to the Chief" blasting from speakers, where guests had gathered for what they hoped would be a victory party. Angry and indignant and standing at a podium with the seal of the Presidency of the United States affixed to the front of it, he proclaimed, "This is a fraud on the American public. . . . This is an embarrassment to our country. We were getting ready to win this election." He added without any evidence whatsoever, "Frankly, we did win this election. So we'll be going to the US Supreme Court," not realizing that the high court would not take such a case directly but only on appeal from lower courts—if it took the case at all.[69] Still, the president's vociferous claims of fraud from the "bully pulpit" of the White House itself seemed very official and very convincing to millions who had voted for him.

Trump's denials would only intensify in the days and weeks ahead, often buoyed by assurances from political allies such as former New York Mayor and now Trump legal advisor Rudolph Giuliani that he had indeed won and that his victory had been stolen. Vice President Mike Pence, who wanted to keep the support of Trump voters for a possible presidential run in the future, refused to say publicly that his boss had lost. In addition, Trump began to take revenge against members of his administration who had not been supportive enough, firing Secretary of State Mike Esper a week after the election.

It did not matter to Trump or his supporters that he ended up losing to Democrat Joseph Biden by almost 7 million popular votes, or 51.2 percent to 46.9 percent. The electoral totals were 306 for Biden and 232 for Trump. Four years earlier the count was exactly the same, only with Trump winning 306 electoral votes to Hillary Clinton's 232, which Trump had then claimed (falsely) was the biggest victory since Ronald Reagan.

If those diagnosing Trump as an extreme narcissist are correct, his election loss was bound to both infuriate and humiliate him. Accepting that he had been defeated was thus out of the question. Throughout his presidency, he had erupted over the smallest slights, shouting at anyone within earshot.[70]

Trump was now desperate. His entire emotional well-being depended on denying and somehow reversing the election results. Accordingly, he and his supporters challenged election results through the courts in states where he had lost, but their lawsuits failed in more than sixty cases, many presided over by Republican judges. Trump even went so far as to telephone Georgia Secretary of State Brad Raffenperger and ask him "to find" additional votes that would put him over the top in that state. Sidney Powell, another Trump lawyer working in tandem with Rudolph Giuliani, claimed on November 19 that voting machines manufactured by the Dominion Company were part of a worldwide communist conspiracy via "money through Venezuela, Cuba, and likely China" to rig the election against Trump.[71] The fact that Giuliani had been a greatly admired mayor of New York City and earlier a respected US Attorney for the Southern District of New York made him believable to many Trump supporters. One month later, Kash Patel, chief of staff for the acting defense secretary, wanted to use the department's resources to investigate the wacky claim that satellites based in Italy had been employed to tamper with voting machines in the United States.[72] Trump also told several aides that he would simply refuse to leave the White House because of what he insisted was a stolen election.[73]

On December 1, Attorney General Barr, a loyal Republican who had gone out of his way to give legal cover to the administration, told Associated Press Justice Reporter Mike Balsamo that the Department of Justice (DOJ) and the FBI had not detected any fraud in the election that could have altered the outcome. In fact, Barr had violated long-standing Department of Justice rules by approving investigations of alleged voting irregularities before the official certification of electoral votes by Congress. The reason for these rules was so that knowledge of such investigations would not have any influence over public opinion or the carrying out of the regular processes of vote tallying and the appointing of presidential electors. Barr also violated department rules when he acceded to these requests, since purely political communications with the executive branch were also off limits.[74] According to specific DOJ guidelines, "The Department does not have a role in determining which candidate won a particular election, or whether another election should be held because of the impact of the alleged fraud on the election."[75] These limitations had been in place in 1978 following the Watergate scandals.

When the president learned of Barr's comment about there being no significant voting fraud, he was furious and lashed out at the attorney general, telling him he did not need "to say that." Still consumed with anger, he added, "You must have said that because you hate Trump, you must really hate Trump."[76]

After Barr resigned as attorney general on December 23, 2020, White House Chief of Staff Mark Meadows began making requests of Acting Attorney General Jeffrey Rosen to investigate several types of alleged fraud claims.[77] When he did not receive satisfaction from Rosen, he began working through Jeffrey Clark, the Assistant Attorney General for the Civil Division of the DOJ. Disregarding departmental guidelines, Clark met directly with the president in the Oval Office in late December just a few days after Trump and several House Republicans had met with the president to discuss strategies for how to handle the electoral vote counting and certification at the joint session of Congress on January 6. Trump concluded that disrupting this historically pro forma procedure would be his last chance to avoid, in his mind, a colossal humiliation before the entire world. He had always feared being a loser, and now he would be the biggest loser of all.

Clark followed up his meeting with the president by drafting a letter to be sent from Rosen to the legislatures of Georgia, Pennsylvania, Michigan, Wisconsin, Arizona, and Nevada, all of which Trump had lost narrowly, asking them to call special sessions to appoint a different slate of electors than those chosen by popular vote. Hopefully, the result would be conflicting results that Pence could ostensibly use to stall or declare electoral vote submissions to be invalid. Both Rosen and Acting Assistant Attorney General Richard Donoghue refused to sign the letter.[78]

In dozens of tweets to his 90 million Twitter followers, Trump had continued to insist that he had been robbed of victory. Because he spoke with the authority of the presidency, millions of true believers accepted the lie and amplified it as social media exploded with the mantra "Stop the Steal" and accusations that Biden was a usurper. The president also began to rile up his followers to descend on Washington for a protest on January 6. He tweeted on December 19, "Big protest on January 6. Be there, will be wild!" He also primed protesters to see Pence as either a "hero or a villain," saying to the crowd at a rally in Georgia on January 4, "I hope Mike Pence comes through for us. If he doesn't come through, I won't like him very much."[79] On the morning of January 5, Trump tweeted incorrectly, "The Vice President has the power to reject fraudulently chosen electors."[80]

Several of his legal advisors hoped that ever-loyal Vice President Pence, by virtue of his role as presiding officer of the Senate, could be talked into refusing to count and certify the final electoral college results on January 6.[81] Caught in a bind between the electoral law and his desire to placate Trump, Pence phoned former Vice President Dan Quale, explaining that both the president and several legal advisors believed he did have such authority. To such an assertion, Quale correctly answered, "Mike, you have no flexibility on this. None, Zero. Forget it. Put it away."[82] Pence's chief of staff and his legal counsel agreed that the vice president could do nothing to alter the results.

At a White House meeting in Trump's presence where Pence spoke of advice about his inability to do anything other than to certify the electoral votes, legal scholar John Eastman disagreed and offered the vice president an additional option. He could call a pause to the counting so that Republican state legislatures could gather in special sessions to consider sending an alternative slate of electoral votes to Congress. Eastman also falsely asserted that there were dueling slates of electors in various states and that when Pence opened the electoral vote ballots, he could decide on his own which were valid. Trump then said, "You need to listen to John. He's a respected constitutional scholar. Hear him out. Listen, listen to John."[83]

When Pence met with Trump on the evening of January 5, the president urged him to just throw the Biden ballots out and let the House of Representatives decide the winner. In response, Pence again claimed that he was only authorized to count the votes that had come in. Not to be dissuaded, Trump referred to the large crowd that had gathered outside and said to Pence, "What if these people say you do?" The vice president again insisted that he only had the power to count the ballots, to which a furious Trump said, "You don't understand, Mike. You can do this. I don't want you to be my friend anymore if you don't do this. . . . You've betrayed us. I made you. You were nothing. Your career is over if you do this."[84] Pence was learning, as so many others had realized over the years, that loyalty went just one way. He had been painfully subservient to Trump, but the president clearly cared only for himself.

January 6

In the weeks leading to the official certification of electoral votes in Congress on January 6, 2021, Trump had asked supporters who believed his lies about the election to converge on Washington in a "Save America March" to protest the results. "JANUARY SIXTH, SEE YOU IN DC!" he tweeted on December 30. At a rally on the Mall on the morning of the sixth, Trump assured the huge crowd that they had every right to break the law: "When you catch somebody in a fraud," he told them, *"you are allowed to go by very different rules."* Accepting the fraud was out of the question, he added: "*We will never give up.* We will never concede. . . . You don't concede when there's theft involved. . . . Our country has had enough. . . . *[W]e will stop the steal . . ." If not, he declared,* "You will have an illegitimate president . . ., and *we can't let that happen. . . .* [A]nd *if you don't fight like hell, you're not going to have a country anymore."*

The president promised he would lead them personally: "We're going to walk down, and I'll be there with you. . . . We are going to the Capitol . . ." Once there, it would be up to Vice President Pence, who would be presiding over the supposed "fraudulent" certification to stop it. "I hope Mike is going to do the right thing," Trump insisted. "Because if Mike Pence does the right thing, we win the election . . ." Of course, Trump did not go with them, but in urging the crowd onward, he convinced many that they were acting on orders from the president himself, with large numbers shouting at Capitol police who were trying to hold them back, "Our president wants us here." Others were chanting "hang Mike Pence," who was the culprit of the hour for not stopping the certification.[85]

Hundreds of protesters at the Capitol, many of them both angry and armed, forced their way into the building, with the outnumbered and overwhelmed Capitol police unable to stop them. Included were hate groups such as the Proud Boys, QAnon, Oath Keepers, the "boogaloo boys," neo-Nazis, and militiamen. Many carried American flags and Trump banners. One woman waved a flag that read "1776 2.0," as if to say they were there to overthrow a tyrannical government as in the American Revolution. Others carried the Confederate battle flag, which had led armies whose aim was to overthrow the United States government during the Civil War.[86]

The insurrectionists viciously attacked the police, and five people lost their lives on January 6 or in subsequent days as a result of this attack on the citadel of democracy.

Members of both the House and Senate had to be evacuated to safe spaces, and Pence as well as Speaker of the House Nancy Pelosi barely escaped capture and the real possibility of physical harm or even death. National Guard troops and outside police units were curiously slow to respond. Meanwhile, President Trump sat in the White House, fascinated as he watched the riot unfold on television. When House Minority Leader Kevin McCarthy called Trump and said, "You've got to tell them to stop," the president responded, "Well Kevin, I guess these people are more upset about the election than you are."[87] Trump's devoted followers were fighting for him, and the president did not want to do anything to stop them. Later, McCarthy would do a complete about-face and join other Congressional Republicans in agreeing that the election had been stolen.

At 3:13 in the afternoon, Trump finally sent out a tweet in which he asked everyone at the Capitol to remain peaceful. A little over an hour later, he recorded a video outside the White House that was remarkable for his continued denials, lack of any contrition on his own behalf, and ending with praise for the rioters: "This was a fraudulent election," he said, "but we can't play into the hands of these people. We have to have peace. So go home. We love you. You're very special."[88] Three hours later, he sent a message over Twitter, which justified the behavior of the rioters: "These are things and events that happen when a sacred landslide election victory is so unceremoniously & viciously stripped away from great patriots who have been badly and unfairly treated for so long. Go home and remember this day forever!"[89] In Trump's mind, the insurrectionists were patriots fighting for truth and right, actions for which they should be rightfully proud and remember always. Shortly thereafter, Twitter suspended the president's account because of his incitement of violence.

The National Guard finally arrived and secured the Capitol so that the senators and representatives could reassemble to continue the electoral vote count. However, five senators objected to the Arizona vote, which led to an obligatory debate in the House chamber. Later, Senator Josh Hawley objected to the Pennsylvania returns, thereby leading to further debate. Majorities in both the House and Senate voted against the objections, and at 3:40 a.m. on January 7, Biden was certified as the winner.

In the days leading up to the election, US intelligence revealed that the Chinese were afraid Trump might want to start a war with them to rally the voters to his candidacy. Trump had been constantly demonizing China over the Covid virus and there had been tensions over the US Navy's freedom of navigation exercises in the South China Sea. The attack on the Capitol alarmed the Chinese further, for fear that the president might start a war as a way of staying in power. Alarmed by these concerns, General Milley, on January 8, called General Li, his counterpart in China, with whom he had developed a good, long-term relationship. Milley assured General Li, saying, "I want to assure you that the American government is stable and everything is going to be ok. We are not going to attack or conduct any kinetic operations against you. . . . It's going to be ok. We're not going to have a fight."[90] General Li took Milley at his word.

The next day, Milley, who is a keen reader of history, shared some of his thoughts with Bob Woodward about what had happened at the Capitol just days before. He called the rioters domestic terrorists and compared them to the Nazi Brown Shirts, the paramilitary arm of the Nazi Party that had supported Adolf Hitler's rise in Germany. He considered it a "Reichstag moment," as when Hitler had ordered the burning of the German parliament building, which gave him an excuse to assume emergency powers and become the country's dictator. Milley then addressed a public memo to the military. It read, in part, "January 6, 2021 was a direct assault on the US Congress, the Capitol Building, and our Constitutional process." He added, "On January 20, 2021. . . President-elect Biden will be inaugurated and will become our 46th Commander in Chief."[91] Milley took the letter to a meeting of the joint chiefs of the three military services, and each voluntarily signed it.

In the meantime, Milley feared that Trump might go so far as to order a nuclear strike, a worry that Speaker of the House Nancy Pelosi had shared during a telephone call with the general. Believing that the president was "unhinged," she had called Milley to be reassured that Trump acting alone could not order such a strike. He told her there were required procedures and that such a thing could not happen. To make sure, Milley convened a meeting in the Pentagon of senior officers of the National Military Command Center (NMCC) and went over the procedures for launching nuclear weapons. He also insisted that he, as head of the Joint Chiefs of Staff, must be involved directly in the process.[92]

Because of his role in encouraging the assault, the House of Representatives impeached Trump for a second time on January 13, 2021, with ten Republicans joining all 222 House Democrats. The single article of impeachment was "incitement of insurrection." Seven Republican senators voted to convict this second time, but not enough to muster the necessary two-thirds vote to remove the president. The final vote was fifty-seven to forty-three. Failure to convict Trump was no surprise, for no matter what the charges, most Republicans were going to stand by the president, once again suggesting that impeachment was essentially a useless tool among the constitutional checks against presidential abuses of power.

The day before formally charging Trump with insurrection, House leadership under the control of the Democrats formally requested that Vice President Pence invoke the Twenty-Fifth Amendment to the Constitution, ratified in 1967. According to Article 5 of the amendment, the vice president and a majority of the cabinet can hold that the president is unable to discharge the powers and duties of office, in which case the vice president immediately becomes acting president.[93] Pence rejected the request. In any case, it was highly unlikely that a group of Republican cabinet members would vote to remove one of their own because of mental incompetency. In this sense, the Twenty-Fifth Amendment appears to be as moribund as the Constitution's provision for impeachment and removal.[94]

It remained to be seen if some future president, better organized than Trump—or if a reelected Trump—would get away even further with defying all checks on presidential authority and make himself into a genuine autocrat who ends American democracy. However, the possibility of that happening would not merely be the result of Trump's behavior but must be understood within the context of American political history, parallels in other countries, and the changes in recent technology, especially as related to new communication systems, all of which will be considered in the following chapter.

Notes

1 Mary L. Trump, *Too Much and Never Enough: How My Family Created the World's Most Dangerous Man* (New York: Simon & Shuster, 2020).
2 Ibid., 36.
3 Ibid., 23.
4 Ibid., 53.
5 Ibid., 97.
6 Jane Mayer, "Donald Trump's Ghostwriter Tells All," *New Yorker*, July 25, 2016.
7 Tony Schwartz, "I Wrote the Art of the Deal with Donald Trump: His Self-Sabotage is Rooted in the Past," in *The Dangerous Case of Donald Trump*, ed. Bandy Lee (New York: St. Martin's Press, 2017, 2019), 65, 66.
8 Ibid., 67.
9 *Washington Post*, May 13 and June 2, 2016.
10 Donald J. Trump with Tony Schwartz, *Trump: The Art of the Deal* (New York: Random House, 1987 [2015]), 61–3.
11 Timothy L. O'Brien, *Trump Nation: The Art of Being the Donald* (New York: Grand Central Publishing, 2005), xii–xiii.
12 See John Cassidy, "Trump University: It's Worse Than You Think," *The New Yorker*, June 2, 2016; Ian Tuttle, "Yes, Trump University Was a Massive Scam," *National Review*, February 26, 2016; and O'Brien, *Trump Nation*, 34.
13 *New York Times*, February 14, 2000, *USA Today*, June 15, 2015.
14 *Politico*, July 24, 2015.
15 Ezra Klein, *Why We're Polarized* (New York: Avid Reader Press, 2020), 165.
16 For a colorful yet piercing analysis of the Trump campaign see Katy Tur, *Unbelievable: My Front Row Seat to the Craziest Campaign in American History* (New York: Dey Street Books, 2017).
17 See Jonathan Karl, *Front Row at the Trump Show* (New York: Dutton, 2020), 39–40.
18 Tur, *Unbelievable*, 91.
19 Trump told Lesley Stahl that he bashes the press to discredit negative stories (cnbc.com)
20 Karl, *The Trump Show*, 4.
21 Quoted in ibid.
22 *New York Times*, July 28, 2016.
23 Karl, *The Trump Show*, 60.
24 Ibid., 59.
25 Ibid., 64.
26 *New York Times*, December 31, 2018.
27 Evan Osnos, *Wildland: The Making of America's Fury* (New York: Farrer, Straus and Giroux, 2021), 278.
28 David Brooks, "Blame the Bobos," *The Atlantic*, September 2021, 65, 66.
29 Klein, *Why We're Polarized*, 191.
30 For an insightful analysis of these shifts, see Gerald F. Seib, *We Should have Seen it Coming: From Reagan to Trump—A Front Row Seat to a Political Revolution* (New York: Random House, 2020), 228–33.
31 *Politico*, January 20, 2017.
32 *The Tennessean*, March 15, 2017.

33 Karl, *The Trump Show*, 119.
34 *The Washington Post*, January 24, 2021.
35 Karl, *The Trump Show*, 142–6.
36 Ibid., 244, 247.
37 *New York Times*, December 7, 2015.
38 Osnos, *Wildland*, 8.
39 The case is *Trump v. Hawaii* (2018).
40 Osnos, *Wildlands,* 55.
41 See Bob Woodward, *Rage* (New York: Simon & Schuster, 2020), 264–6; *New York Times*, December 22, 2016.
42 Karl, *The Trump Show*, 287. See also ibid., 284–9.
43 *Vox*, November 20, 2018.
44 *New York Times*, August 20, 2017.
45 Isabel Wilkerson, *Caste: The Origins of Our Discontents* (New York: Random House, 2020), 183.
46 Osnos, *Wildland*, 231.
47 For the most complete account, see Andrew Weissmann, *Where the Law Ends: Inside the Mueller Investigation* (New York: Random House, 2020).
48 *New York Times*, May 17, 2017; Rod J. Rosenstein, May 17, 2017, "Order No. 39-2017: Appointment of Special Counsel to Investigate Russian Interference with the 2016 Presidential Election and Related Matters."
49 Woodward, *Rage*, 314.
50 Quoted in *New York Times*, June 2, 2018.
51 Quoted in ibid., April 14, 2020.
52 Quoted in Thomas, *Being Nixon*, 509.
53 *New York Times*, October 8, 2019.
54 Quoted in Carol Leonning and Philip Rucker, *I Alone Can Fix It* (New York: Penguin Press, 2021), 24.
55 Woodward, *Rage*, 269.
56 Leonning and Rucker, *I Alone Can Fix It*, 51–2.
57 Woodward, *Rage*, xix. This interview, like all the others quoted in the book, were audio recorded.
58 Ibid., 285, 315.
59 Woodward, *Rage*, xviii, 235, 244, 252, 254, 285–6, 287–8, 321.
60 Leonning and Rucker, *I Alone Can Fix It*, 42.
61 Ibid., 76.
62 Quoted in Ibid., 201.
63 Ibid.
64 *The Guardian*, April 7, 2020; *Los Angeles Times*, April 14, 2020; *New York Times*, April 7 and April 26, 2020.
65 Woodward, *Rage*, 317.
66 Ibid., 99.
67 *Washington Post*, January 23, 2016.
68 See Jonathan Karl, *Betrayal: The Final Act of the Trump Show* (New York: Dutton, 2021) 119–21.
69 Bob Woodward and Robert Costa, *Peril* (New York: Simon & Schuster), 133.
70 Ibid., 6–7.
71 Sidney Powell, quoted in Karl, *Betrayal*, 147.

72 Karl, *Betrayal*, 173.
73 *New York Times*, November 4, 2024.
74 These rules had been spelled out during the Trump administration in a Memorandum from White House Counsel Donald F. McGahn II to All White House Staff, January 27, 2017.
75 Dep't of Justice, Federal Prosecution of Election Offenses at 84 (8th ed., December 2017), https://www.justice.gov/criminal/file/1029066/download.
76 Woodward and Costa, *Peril*, 170.
77 These activities are laid out in Majority Staff Report, Senate Committee on the Judiciary, "Subverting Justice: How thee Former President and His Allies Pressured DOJ to Overturn the 2020 Election," October 7, 2021, https://democracy4all.org/2021/10/07/full-text-subverting-justice.
78 "Subverting Justice," 19, 24, 28, 34, 37, 38; *Washington Post*, August 4, 2021: *New York Times*, October 3, 2021 and July 3, 2021. See also Karl, *Betrayal*, 250–4.
79 "Red Flag," *Washington Post*, October 31, 2021.
80 Quoted in Karl, *Betrayal*, 271.
81 This certification on January 6 was in accordance with Congress's Vote Count Act of 1887.
82 Quoted in Woodward and Costa, *Peril*, 199.
83 Quoted in ibid., 226.
84 Quoted in ibid., 229, 231.
85 These quotations from Trump are from the *New York Times*, January 10, 2021.
86 For a timeline on how the January 6 attack on the Capitol unfolded, see *New York Times*, August 15, 2021 and October 17, 2021.
87 Quoted in Woodward and Costa, *Peril*, 248.
88 Quoted in ibid., 254.
89 Quoted in Karl, *Betrayal*, 301.
90 Quoted in Woodward and Costa, *Peril*, 129.
91 Quoted in Ibid., xix, 274.
92 Ibid., xxvi–xxvii.
93 Amendment XXV, Section 3, Ratified February 10, 1967.
94 Karl, *Betrayal*, 308–12.

11

American Monarchy

Premonitions and Reforms

An ancient maxim from the English Common Law meaning that the monarch cannot be held legally accountable for any action or decision.

"The King Can Do No Wrong"

Warnings

Many writers have warned about the possible demise of democracy both at home and abroad, so that in some respects, a president like Donald Trump should not be a complete surprise. Among them is Sinclair Lewis in his 1935 novel, *It Can't Happen Here*, a chilling if imagined account of a fascist takeover in the United States by the fictional US Senator Windrip, who promises to bring back prosperity and restore American greatness, and who becomes president after defeating Franklin Roosevelt in his bid for reelection in 1936.[1] Winthrop's installation of a fascist government in the United States does not result initially from any sort of coup because a coup is unnecessary, given that the groundwork has already been laid by the beliefs of a majority of the American people, which Windrip has understood for many years. He has spelled it all out in his book, *Zero Hour*, which has become a "Bible" to his followers and a not too subtle comparison to Adolf Hitler's *Mein Kampf*.

In the fictional *Zero Hour*, Windrip makes populist appeals to people who have not done well in life by castigating the wealthy and well-educated. "I'd rather bring more johnnycake and beans and spuds into the humble cabin of the Common Man," he writes, "than a twenty-four-carat, college graduate, ex-cabinet member statesman . . ."[2] He goes on to extoll the virtues of small, rural communities in contrast to the wickedness of large East Coast cities: "In the little towns, ah, there is the abiding peace that I love, and that can never be disturbed by even the noisiest Smart Alecks from these haughty megalopolises like Washington, New York, & etc."[3] Windrip is confident these same common people are devoted to the old-time religion with its emphasis on a literal and inerrant reading of Scripture, salt-of-the-earth Americans who will join him in fighting "the pusillanimous, mendacious, destructive, tom-fool Higher Critics [of the Bible], so-called . . ."[4]

White nationalist pronouncements also figure in his message: "My one ambition is to get all Americans to realize that they are, and must continue to be, the greatest race on the face of this old Earth . . . -though, of course, all this does not apply to people who are racially different from us . . ." However, being the right type of American, he adds, erases all meaningful differences that "there may be among us, in wealth, knowledge, skill, ancestry, or strength."[5] Given this genuine kind of American superiority, Windrip is an isolationist in foreign policy and Windrip dismisses, "All this nonsense of wasting our time at Geneva [with the League of Nations] . . ."[6]

Six years after the appearance of Sinclair Lewis's *It Can't Happen Here*, psychologist Eric Fromm, a Jewish refugee from Nazi Germany to the United States, used the insights of social psychology to analyze the appeal of autocracy. In his 1941 book, *Escape from Freedom*, Fromm attributed the appeal of autocracy to the realities of modernism, which, beginning with the Renaissance, offered individuals the possibility to shape their own lives in contrast to the ascribed roles of earlier times, especially during the Middle Ages.[7] Now individuals could plausibly use talent and individual initiative to mold themselves and go as far as ability and hard work might take them. However, Fromm also believed such individualism could result in "growing isolation, insecurity and thereby growing doubt concerning one's own role in the universe, the meaning of one's life, and with all that a growing feeling of one's own powerlessness and insignificance as an individual."[8] Although liberated to forge one's own way in the world, the individual was also "freed from those ties which used to give him security and a feeling of belonging. . . . The world ha[d] become limitless and at the same time threatening."[9]

It was apparent by the early 1940s, when Fromm was writing, that the great majority of individuals in industrialized countries were in no position to make themselves successful economically but were most probably cogs in some massive capitalistic enterprise that could collapse in the face of an economic depression or structural unemployment. The consequences for individuals caught up in this downward slide were, in Fromm's words, "aloneness, fear, and bewilderment," and "people cannot stand it forever." They therefore "must try to escape from freedom altogether," and "the principal social avenues of escape in our times are the submission to a leader."[10] This submission requires giving up "the independence of one's own individual self" and fusing "one's self with somebody or something outside oneself in order to acquire the strength which the individual self is lacking."[11] In the process, the follower feels connected to a glorious future: "By becoming part of a power which is felt as unshakably strong, eternal, and glamourous, one participates in its strength and glory."[12] The leader of such a movement becomes for the frightened and disaffected "a magical helper."[13]

In *The Origins of Totalitarianism* (1951), author Hannah Arendt also took up the bewildering aspects of the modern world and its threats to democracy. Especially alarming to her was how this condition allowed leaders to get away with massive lies. As she explained, "The [modern] masses are obsessed by a desire to escape from reality because in their essential homelessness they can no longer bear its accidental, incomprehensible aspects . . ." Thus, "the masses' escape from reality is a verdict against the world in which they are forced to live and in which they cannot exist . . ." If they are faced with a choice between bewildering and threatening reality "or bowing down before the most rigid, fantastically fictitious consistency of an ideology, the masses probably will always choose the latter . . ."[14] Arendt adds that "a lying world of consistency . . . is more adequate to the human mind than reality itself [by which] through sheer imagination, uprooted masses can feel at home and are spared the never-ending shocks which real life and real experiences deal to human beings and their expectations."[15] Buttressing this propaganda of lies in both Hitler's Germany and in Stalin's Soviet Union was the assertion that the leader "is always right." The leader has all the answers; he alone can protect his people and lead them into a glorious future.[16]

In the early to mid-1960s, historian Richard Hofstadter used social psychology to plumb some disturbing aspects of American culture that reveal how citizens of this country have long been susceptible to believing in conspiracies and lies, along with how the perils of modernity have exacerbated tribalism. He offered these views in his book, *Anti-Intellectualism in American Life*, and in his essay, "The Paranoid Style in American Politics." In *Anti-Intellectualism*, Hofstadter looked at a long history in the United States of group hatreds combined with beliefs in nefarious conspiracies. "There has always been in our national experience," he wrote, "a type of mind which elevates hatred to a kind of creed." As a result, "group hatreds take a place in politics similar to the class struggle in some other modern societies." What is more, these hatreds are "filled with obscure and ill-directed grievances and frustrations, with elaborate hallucinations about secrets and conspiracies . . ."[17]

A decade later, historian Arthur M. Schlesinger, Jr., in the last chapter of his 1973 book, *The Imperial Presidency*, focused on two dangers to American democracy, as then presented by the Nixon White House. These were the creation of what Schlesinger called a "plebiscitary presidency" combined with an unhealthy public reverence for presidents and the presidency, which Nixon had taken to new heights.

Schlesinger described this first danger, that of the Plebiscitary Presidency, by saying, "The President, instead of being accountable every day to Congress and public opinion, would be accountable [only] every four years to the electorate . . . and would govern, as much as he could through decree"—that is, through executive orders.[18] This lack of accountability was particularly evident during the ongoing Cold War when presidents presided more or less single-handedly over issues of war and peace in what amounted to an American empire, both formal and informal, and hence gave rise to an imperial presidency.

The second danger stemmed from what Schlesinger described as an undue reverence for the presidency and presidents. "The age of the imperial Presidency," he observed, "had in time produced the idea that the run-of-the-mill politicians, brought by fortuity to the White House, must be treated thereafter as if they had become superior and perhaps godlike beings."[19] As prime exhibits, there were Nixon's love affair with the presidential yacht, his directive that the White House police should dress like palace guards, and his insistence that the Marine Band announce him on every possible occasion by playing *Hail to the Chief*. More alarming were Nixon's assertions of a blanket executive privilege whereby he refused to turn over virtually all documents to Congressional committees whether they genuinely involved either national security or sensitive domestic issues.

At the end of the book, Schlesinger delivered a prescient warning: "We have noted that corruption appears to visit the White House in fifty-year cycles," referring to the Harding scandals in the early 1920s and the Watergate scandal in the early 1970s. He concluded "that exposure and retribution inoculate the Presidency against its latent criminal impulses for about half a century." Thus, "around the year 2023 the American people would be well advised to go on the alert and start nailing down everything in sight."[20] This was a haunting prediction, given Donald Trump's claim in 2019 at a rally during his first term as president, "I have the right to do whatever I want as president."[21] Richard Nixon had made the same claim in 1977, three years after being forced out of office, in a televised interview with David Frost: "Well, when the president does it, that means that it is *not* illegal."[22]

Failure of Accountability

Events following Trump's defeat for reelection and failures to hold him accountable appear to show that both Trump and Nixon had been correct. In the days immediately after the attack on the Capitol on January 6, 2021, both popular and political opinion hold that Donald Trump is finished as a public figure in the United States. Yet the US Senate fails to convict Trump following his impeachment by the House for his leading role in the attack on the Capitol, and the Justice Department fails to act against the former president for over two years. Equally belated is Georgia's judicial system in charging Trump and several associates for their illegal efforts to change the presidential election vote in that state. Also tardy is a federal indictment against the former president for taking hundreds of classified documents with him to his private home in Florida and refusing to turn them over to the National Archives, as required by federal law via the Presidential Records Acts passed by Congress in 1978 and 2018. In New York, a little over two years after Trump has left office, a state court indicts him for financial fraud related to paying hush money to a porn star to conceal a sexual relationship. Only this New York case will result in a conviction but without any penalty involving jail time or fines at sentencing just ten days before Trump is inaugurated for a second term as the nation's forty-seventh president, itself an unimaginable event given the January 6 assault on the Capitol four years earlier and its attempts to overthrow the results of the 2020 presidential election. And seeming to give him protection from any prosecution for what he might do in a second term is the Supreme Court case of Donald *Trump v. United States*, handed down on July 1, 2024, which rules that presidents enjoy legal immunity for all official acts while in office. Without doubt, Trump will insist that anything he does as president qualifies as an official act. As with the kings of old, the court has ruled, in effect, that, "The President Can Do No Wrong."

The delays in the two federal court cases against Trump seem especially perplexing. For instance, anyone other than Trump who had taken classified documents and refused to turn them over would probably have been arrested immediately, very likely charged with a serious crime, and very likely sentenced to prison. However, the US Department of Justice believed that a former president should be treated with the sort of deference unavailable to most anyone else, a jarring example of a double standard of justice. Then, even after a federal grand jury indicted Trump in West Palm Beach, Florida, in June 2023 on what came to be known as the "documents case," Federal District Judge Eileen Cannon, a Trump appointee, slow-walked the case by hearing endless appeals. In August 2024, just three months before the presidential election, she dismissed the entire case, with the groundless claim that Special Counsel Smith had been appointed illegally. And with Trump's election to a second term, the case was dropped by the Justice Department, which was preparing to appeal Cannon's ruling.[23]

The failure of the Justice Department to wait until November 2023 to charge Trump with orchestrating the attack on the Capitol seems even more perplexing. One explanation holds that Attorney General Merrick Garland wanted to pursue the case "up the chain" by first arresting and trying the individuals who had attacked the building on January 6 before going after Trump himself. Or it may have been that conventional wisdom held Trump was finished as a politician and that the country did not need to fear the possibility of his running for and winning another term in the White House. It also appeared that top Justice Department officials and the FBI did not want to look "too political" by quickly charging Trump.[24]

However, pressuring the attorney general to act were ten televised hearings in 2022 by a bipartisan committee of the House of Representatives about the January 6 attack, which interviewed hundreds of witnesses, some of whose sensational testimony appeared in these televised hearings. Based on what it concluded to be overwhelming evidence, the committee made a series of criminal referrals in December to the Justice Department that included Trump himself. A month earlier, in November, the attorney general appointed Jack Smith as special counsel to investigate Trump's role on January 6. Smith was a seasoned prosecutor who had most recently served as chief prosecutor at the International Court of Justice at The Hague in the Netherlands. On November 15, 2022, just three days before Smith's appointment, Trump announced that he would run again for president in 2024, an unusually early announcement for presidential candidates.

Trump immediately denounced the actions of the justice department as a "witch hunt," insisting that the Biden administration was engaged in political persecution and claimed personal martyrdom, charges that he repeated throughout his second campaign for the White House and that his devout followers believed without question. He similarly denounced the other cases against him, with similar positive effect on supporters. Trump also saw winning a second term as a "get out of jail" card, given the Supreme Court's granting of presidential immunity from prosecution. And when Trump won the election in November, Smith dropped the prosecution for January 6 but succeeded in releasing a comprehensive and damning report about the case on January 14, 2025, just days before the inauguration. Smith concluded that he had built a strong case against Trump, writing in the report, "Indeed, but for Mr. Trump's election and imminent return to the presidency, this office assessed that the admissible evidence was sufficient to obtain and sustain a conviction at trial."[25]

Trump Redux

Trump had won the popular vote by 77,266,801 ballots to Democratic candidate Kamala Harris's 74,931,313—or 49.9 percent to 48.4 percent. Trump's popular vote victory was thus small at just 1.5 percent, equivalent to Richard Nixon's similarly unimpressive margin in 1968. And because of votes for third-party candidates, Trump did not receive a majority of the popular tally, though he has repeatedly claimed to have been handed a strong mandate. With an electoral vote of 312 to 226—for a margin of eighty-six votes—his victory in the Electoral College was also smaller than several recent presidents, including Barack Obama, Bill Clinton, and George H. W. Bush.[26]

During several discussions with my colleague Jeffrey Carroll of the Political Science Department, the two of us agreed that it would take many months to sort out all the reasons for Trump's victory. However, some explanations are becoming apparent. One is that Democrats across the country, in urban areas as well as in suburbs, failed to turn out in as many numbers as in 2020. For example, counties yielding the largest victories for Democrat Joseph Biden in 2020 produced 1.9 million fewer votes for Harris, including the Philadelphia and Detroit metropolitan areas, which have long been Democratic Party strongholds, though the reasons for these discrepancies remain unclear.[27] Then there are those who apparently voted for Trump because they did not believe that he would do many of the alarming things he had threatened during the campaign, such as placing significant tariffs on various countries, seeking retribution against critics and political enemies, and pardoning everyone convicted in the federal courts for storming the Capitol.[28]

The hoped-for women's vote against Trump because of Harris's gender, as well as due to Trump's appointment of Supreme Court Justices who overtured *Row v. Wade* in 2023, which had legalized most abortions nearly half a century earlier, also failed to galvanize women sufficiently against Trump.[29] Women did vote for Harris by six points over Trump in 2024, but less than their ten-point margin for Biden over Trump in 2020.[30] Men voted for Trump by eleven points in 2024 in comparison to just two points in 2020. Trump did especially well with men under forty-five, who went from voting for Biden by eight points to voting for Trump by eight points in 2024, a swing of some sixteen points overall. Increased support among men for Trump also extended to Black and Latino men. The precise reasons for these shifts remain unclear at the time of this writing.

Probably of great significance was President Biden's announcement on April 25, 2023, that he would run for a second term, despite earlier statements defining himself as a one-term, transitional occupant of the White House. This announcement came despite worries about both his cognitive and physical health, which would later be revealed as having been covered up by family and staff.[31] Biden went on to run virtually unopposed in the Democratic presidential primaries and received the party's nomination. However, a disastrous performance in his televised debate against Trump on June 27, 2024, which only emphasized his various infirmities, led to calls from leading Democrats for him to withdraw from the race, which he did three weeks later, on July 21, 2024. In leaving the race, Biden recommended Vice President Harris as his heir apparent. Harris was left with only a little over three months to mount a campaign. Another handicap that she had to face was her close association with an incumbent president who had declining approval ratings at a time when many Americans wanted change. Whether a longer campaign would have led her to victory is uncertain. Also impossible to know is whether another and more successful Democratic candidate might have emerged from the primary process if Biden had decided not to run again.

The economy seems to have been a factor in Trump's win even though the United States could boast the strongest economy in the world, with rising GDP, a soaring stock market, low unemployment, and declining inflation. But these facts meant little to those who were angry about higher grocery prices that had persisted from higher inflation in the aftermath of Covid. That presidents can do little or nothing about food prices—or prices in general—meant nothing to many voters.[32]

Making no difference in the outcome, at least among the MAGA faithful, as well as for most Republicans, were the criminal indictments and convictions against Trump. In addition to seeing him as a victim and martyr, according to Jack Goldsmith, a Harvard Law professor and assistant attorney general under George W. Bush, "The electorate does not care, as it once did, that a president [should] pay fealty to law and other traditional expectations of the office." Such an attitude would have horrified the delegates to the Constitutional Convention.[33]

A very telling *New York Times* article by Dan Barry and Alan Feurer explained in detail how Trump, "Flipped the Script and Made Jan. 6 an asset." According to them, "What began as a sustained attempt to absolve Mr. Trump of responsibility for Jan. 6 gradually took hold, as his allies in Congress and the media played down the attack and redirected blame to [non-existent] left-wing plants, Democrats, and even the government." In the process, "Violent rioters—prosecuted, convicted and imprisoned—somehow became patriotic martyrs. . . . It neatly fit the persecution narrative that binds Mr. Trump to many of his faithful."[34] And if those who had been prosecuted were innocent victims, then it could be argued that Trump was an innocent victim as well.

Trump also claimed that a near assassination of him at an outdoor presidential campaign rally in Butler, Pennsylvania on July 13, 2024, was further evidence of martyrdom and victimhood. He vowed during a speech at the Republican National Convention five days later that he would not speak about the incident again, "Because it is actually too painful to tell." Yet over the next twelve weeks, he spoke about it constantly, blaming the attempt to kill him, without a shred of evidence, on the Democrats, the "Deep State," the Marxists, and the news media. "Their rhetoric," he insisted during an interview on pro-Trump Fox News, "is causing me to be shot at, when I am the one who is going to save the country."[35] He also vowed to return to the scene in Butler as an example of his promise to 'Fight! Fight! Fight! and did so on October 6 despite the danger. Since Trump probably escaped death by having turned his head slightly as the bullet approached, he and many of his supporters insisted that God had intervened to save him.[36]

In addition, Trump painted a dark picture of the United States, especially if Harris were elected. The country would face economic ruin, there would be a Third World War including a nuclear holocaust, murderous immigrant gangs would rampage all over the land, factories would close, and farmers would lose their land, all part of an "economic bloodbath"—echoes of Trump's 2016 campaign and of his "American carnage" remarks in his first inaugural address.[37]

Throughout the campaign, he told attendees at rallies, "I am your retribution," and promised to intimidate and punish anyone he believed had been opposing or working against him. He called for former President Barack Obama to be tried before "military tribunals" and threatened to go after Facebook founder Mark Zuckerberg for supposedly assisting state and local governments during the 2020 election.[38] He also called for the arrest of his former chief of staff, Marine General John F. Kelly, who told a *New York Times* reporter on the record that Trump would rule like a dictator. According to Kelly, "The former president is in the far right area; he is certainly an authoritarian, admires people who are dictators [and] he has said that. So certainly he falls into the general definition of fascist, for sure."[39]

During his inauguration address on January 20, 2025, Trump painted a dark picture of his country, as he had eight years earlier in his first inaugural address. He claimed that his election was "a mandate to completely and totally reverse a horrible betrayal and all of these many betrayals that have taken place. . . . From this moment on, America's decline is over." Turning to what he believed was his own persecution, he vowed that "the vicious and unfair weaponization of the Justice Department and of our government will end." And referencing the assassination attempt on him during the campaign, he insisted, "I felt then, and I believe even more so now, that my life was saved for a reason. I was saved by God to make America great again.[40]

In his invocation at the inauguration, the Reverend Franklin Graham, son of the famous evangelist Billy Graham, compared Trump to Moses, who had delivered the Jewish people out of Egypt back to their Promised Land of Israel. Accordingly, God had saved Trump's life, "and raised him up with strength and power by his mighty hand."[41] This conclusion by Graham, combined with Trump's own insistence that God had saved his life to "Make America Great Again," may well have been interpreted by some to mean that Trump was president "by divine right," much like Europe's monarchs of old. It was a claim that some Americans had made about both Washington and Lincoln, and an assertion that Woodrow Wilson had reportedly made about himself.

Within days—and in some cases hours—of his inauguration, Trump issued executive orders that appeared on the face of them to be either illegal or unconstitutional. For instance, on the afternoon of his inauguration, on January 20, he signed an executive order ending birthright citizenship for children born in the United States to undocumented immigrants, despite its obvious violation of the Fourteenth Amendment, which guarantees citizenship to "all persons born or naturalized in the United States and subject to the jurisdiction thereof." Three days later, a federal judge blocked enforcement of the order, but the case was likely to end up in the Supreme Court, which has often been sympathetic to Trump.[42] On January 24, Trump dismissed as many as seventeen inspectors general, who exercise oversight of federal government departments, despite an act of Congress just two years before that requires presidents to give Congress a thirty-day advance notice before any such dismissals. The act also requires "detailed and case-specific reasons" for any dismissals.[43]

Then on January 27, Trump issued an order to "freeze" trillions of dollars in federal grants and loans that Congress had already authorized, an action that amounted to an illegal impoundment of funds and that clearly violated the 1974 Impoundment Control Act, passed in reaction to President Richard Nixon's impoundment of some billions of dollars then appropriated by the legislative branch. The Trump administration rescinded the order in the wake of chaos and widespread protests over the withdrawal of funding for numerous social programs, along with a blocking order from a federal district judge.[44] The much-vaunted separation of powers—and with them, the hoped-for checks and balances put forth at the Constitutional Convention 238 years earlier to restrain presidential abuses of power—were being challenged as never before. It remained to be seen if Trump would defy court orders in the future, including those from the Supreme Court, as Andrew Jackson had done, thereby touch off a serious Constitutional crisis.

Especially alarming was Trump's firing of Justice Department prosecutors and CIA agents because they had worked on criminal investigations of the president, a naked act of retribution. He also directed his new Justice Department to investigate and prosecute those who had worked on the various federal court cases against him.[45] These acts of retribution, following up on vows to do so during the campaign, do much to explain why President Biden issued preemptive pardons to members of his family. He also gave such pardons to Dr. Anthony Fauci, Retired General Mark Milley, and former Congresswoman Liz Cheney, whom Trump had threatened many times to prosecute.

Perhaps most troubling of all, on the afternoon of his inauguration, Trump issued pardons to nearly 1,600 persons who had been arrested or convicted of attacking the Capitol on January 6, 2021, including those who had violently assaulted police officers, resulting in four deaths. In many ways, this action was a continuation of Trump's denial that anything illegal had occurred on that day and, once more, his personal claims of innocence. In any case, wielding the pardon power in this way clearly violated the intent of the authors of the Constitution, who had granted the pardon power to presidents as a way of correcting unduly harsh sentences or as a means of recognizing errors in judicial proceedings that courts would not or could not correct.

Remaining, however, is the haunting question as to how millions of voters could have ignored or denied the facts of the violent attempts on January 6 to overturn the results of an honest and legitimate election, given the overwhelming evidence of eyewitnesses, hundreds of hours of video, and the admissions of the perpetrators in court, or in some cases, to friends and family members. A reference earlier in this book to the power of "cognitive dissonance," a universal human tendency to reject information that challenges strongly held beliefs, offers some valuable insights. Elaborating on this tendency is a book by Mark Lilla entitled *Ignorance is Bliss: On Wanting Not to Know*. By questioning long-held beliefs, Lilla writes, "people risk upsetting ideas they've built their lives around, with no guarantee of finding satisfying new ones."[46] They also risk humiliation, if only to themselves, of admitting that their strongly held beliefs are in fact false.

These strong tendencies to reject information that challenges firmly held beliefs are an important reason why any negative news about Trump was and continues to be rejected by his fervent followers. At the same time, there are those who admire Trump's "bad behavior," as referenced by an earlier reference to Ruth Marcus's *The Drama of Celebrity*. To quote Marcus again, "Defiant Celebrities appeal not only to the marginal and the outcast, but to anyone who has ever wanted to bypass conventions, gatekeepers, and experts . . ."[47]

Also discussed earlier is the reality that millions of voters are devoted to various "information silos," whether from cable news or social media. Indeed, making social media even more troubling was the announcement in January 2025 by Mark Zuckerberg, CEO of Meta, which owns Facebook, Instagram, WhatsApp, and Threads, that they would now loosen restrictions on their apps on how people can talk about contentious issues. Meta also deleted its fact-checking programs, which had targeted misinformation, replacing them with a dubious reliance on users to correct falsehoods.[48]

Half a century ago, Nixon nearly got away with his depredations. If not for an observant security guard at the Watergate complex who called the police, or if not for the revelation of the president's secret tapes, Nixon would have remained in the White House to finish his second term. Despite this sense of relief at the time of Watergate that "the Constitution had worked," James David Barber's haunting prediction in his book *Presidential Character* should not have been ignored. Nixon "will be back," he wrote. "He very nearly got away with establishing a Presidential tyranny in the United States. . . . It is so important to the future of the Presidency to keep it out of the hands of future Nixons . . ."[49] Were Barber writing today, he would no doubt add, "and out of the hands" of people like Donald Trump.

The factors that had led to Nixon and then to a more dangerous Trump will not easily disappear: Photography, film, television, and more recently social media are not about to vanish as tools for gaining and maintaining varying degrees of celebrity and personality cults. Political polarization, which does not lend itself to effective checks on presidential abuse of power, will likely remain so long as Americans are closely divided along cultural lines. Attempts to win elections through voter suppression will also continue as strategies for winning the presidency while subverting democracy, unless there is, at the very least, new voting rights legislation at the national level. In addition, the Electoral College will continue to tempt parties to challenge the legitimacy of presidential elections in cases where the difference of a few thousand (or even a few hundred votes or less) in several states can mean winning the White House despite losing the popular vote by much larger margins nationwide, an outcome that the delegates to the Constitutional Convention could not have fathomed.

A Call for Reform

Of greatest importance, there needs to be a Constitutional amendment to abolish the Electoral College, or short of that, the implementation of a sufficient number of state legislatures to agree that their electoral votes would go to whichever presidential candidate wins the popular vote nationwide. Congress must also renew the Voting Rights Act to combat voter suppression by the states so that citizens can freely exercise their right to check presidential misbehavior at the ballot box, which, among other matters, would require legislation to address the Supreme Court case of *Shelby County v. Holder* (2013).[50] The Supreme Court also needs to overturn the 2010 case of *Citizens United v. Federal Election Commission*, which allows unlimited amounts of money to be donated to campaigns through Political Action Committees, including anonymity for contributions if so desired. The court also must overturn the 2024 case of *Donald Trump v. the United States*, in which the justices granted presidents legal immunity for any acts committed while in office.

Congress also needs to pull back or greatly restrict the many emergency powers it has granted to presidents, including the power to levy tariffs. It should also codify the emolument clause in Article I, Section 9 of the Constitution, which forbids any person holding office from accepting gifts from foreign powers (which would include the president) to include non-monetary assistance to interfere with American elections. Legislators also need to amend and strengthen the War Powers Act of 1973 to curb presidential commitment of armed forces, as well as the Impoundment Act of 1974, which restricts presidents from spending funds already appropriated by Congress. They also need to restrict the pardon power to cases that truly merit it because of clear injustice or extreme sentences and the like. Presidents should also be forbidden by legislation to maintain direction of any business, to use the office to gain monetary rewards, and be required to submit copies of their income tax returns.

Undoubtedly, the low level of public knowledge about the Constitution and the American system of government is a continuing problem when it comes to checking presidential overreach. Before 1960 or so, most states required their public schools to teach at least three separate courses in civics or government, depending on the names assigned to them. Today, however, only nine states plus Washington D.C. require one year of civics or government classes, thirty states require only half a year for these subjects, and eleven states have no requirements at all for such offerings. Not surprisingly, a 2024 survey by the US Chamber of Commerce revealed that 70 percent of adults could not even name the three branches of government.[51] It is thus no wonder that at least half the electorate is not alarmed at Trump's abuses of executive power or aware of the role that checks and balances are supposed to play in preventing them.

At the same time, presidents need to retain sufficient power to cope with the manifold issues at home and abroad that only a president can lead in solving or at least managing. The task will be to allow presidential authority to meet present and future needs without threatening or destroying American democracy, a delicate balance that the delegates to the Constitutional Convention sought to create. Ultimately, the system must depend on the goodwill and restraint of presidents to honor a system of checks and balances, since, short of the highly unlikely prospect of impeachment and removal—or the serious threat thereof—neither the legislative nor judicial branches of government can realistically compel them to honor checks and balances. In this sense, and especially with the modern presidency which is armed with the "bully pulpit" of powerful communications platforms, there is no longer the oft-touted, co-equal system of checks and balances, if there ever was one concerning the presidency.

Sincere study and debate will be required in the months and years ahead to propose and implement reforms to guard the American presidential system from a future of autocratic or dictatorial rule. In the meantime, one can only hope that the federal courts, and especially the United States Supreme Court, will attempt to rein in abuses of executive power before too much damage is done, or before too many precedents are established that cannot be easily reversed. Failure to do so threatens to obliterate Lincoln's "government of the people and by the people [the American democracy] and for the people [the American republic]."

Notes

1 Sinclair Lewis, *It Can't Happen Here* (New York: Signet Classics, 2014 [1935]).
2 Ibid., 44.
3 Ibid., 163.
4 Ibid., 118.
5 Ibid., 69.
6 Ibid., 91.
7 Eric Fromm, *Escape from Freedom* (New York: Henry Holt and Company, 1994 [1941]).
8 Ibid., 35.
9 Ibid., 62.
10 Ibid., 133.
11 Ibid., 140.
12 Ibid., 154.
13 Ibid., 175.
14 Hannah Arendt, *The Origins of Totalitarianism* (New York: Houghton Mifflin Harcourt Publishing Company, 1994 [1951]), 532.
15 Ibid., 353.
16 Ibid., 383.
17 Richard Hofstadter, *Anti-Intellectualism in American Life*, in *The Library of America* edition of his collected works, ed. Sean Wilentz (New York: Library Classics of the United States, Inc., 2020), 42.
18 Schlesinger, *The Imperial Presidency*, 377.
19 Ibid., 410.
20 Ibid.
21 *Business Insider*, July 23, 2019.
22 Quoted in Thomas, *Being Nixon*, 509.
23 *New York Times*, August 29, 2024. For a thorough account and analysis of these indictments, see Melissa Murray and Andrew Wiseman (New York: W. W. Norton & Company, 2024).
24 *Politics*, August 2, 2023; *Crime and Justice News*, August 17, 2023; Carol Lenning and Aaron C. Davis, "FBI Resisted Opening Probe into Trump's Role in January 6 for More than a Year," *Washinton Post*, June 20, 2023.

25 Quoted in *New York Times*, January 15, 2025.
26 *Washington Post*, January 20, 2025.
27 Michael C. Bender, *New York Times*, November 12, 2024.
28 Ibid., October 15, 2024.
29 The name of the case that overturned Row v. Wade is *Dobbs v. Jackson*.
30 *New York Times,* November 13, 2024.
31 Ibid., January 18, 2025.
32 See charts on the economy in Ibid., December 29.
33 Quoted in Ibid. by Peter Baker, January 13, 2025.
34 Ibid., January 5, 2025; Maryann Cousins, "2024-Election Survey: Gender and Age Analysis of 2024 Election Results," December 12, 2024; 2024 Post-Election Survey: Gender and Age Analysis of 2024 Election Results.
35 *New York Times*, September 19, 2024.
36 Ibid., October 5, 2024.
37 Ibid., October 2, 2024.
38 Ibid., September 11, 2024.
39 Ibid., October 24, 2024.
40 The complete text of Trump's 2025 inaugural address appeared in the *New York Times* on January 21 of that year.
41 "Rev. *Franklin Graham's Prayer at Trump's Inauguration*," *Prayer Prompt*, January 20, 2025; *New York Times*, January 20, 2025.
42 *New York Times*, January 24, 2025.
43 Ibid., January 26, 2025.
44 Ibid., January 29 and 30, 2025.
45 *New York Times*, Editorial Board, February 2, 2025.
46 Mark Lilla, *Ignorance and Bliss: On Wanting Not to Know* (New York: Farrar, Straus and Giroux, 2024), 47.
47 Marcus, *The Drama of Celebrity*, 26.
48 *New York Times, January 12, 2025.*
49 Barber, *The Presidential Character*, 144.
50 *New York Times*, September 10, 2021. See also Bob Bauer and Jack Goldsmith, *After Trump: Reconstructing the Presidency* (Washington, DC: Lawfare Press, 2020).
51 Sarah Shapiro and Catherine Brown, "A Look at Civics Education in the United States," *American Educator*, Summer 2018.

Bibliography

Aitken, Jonathan. *Nixon: A Life*. Washington, DC: Regnery History, 2015.

Ambrose, Stephen E. *Nixon: The Education of a Politician, 1913–1962*. New York: Simon and Schuster, 1987.

Applebaum, Anne. *Twilight of Democracy: The Seductive Lure of Autocracy*. New York: Doubleday, 2020.

Arendt, Hannah. *The Origins of Totalitarianism*. New York: Houghton Mifflin Harcourt Publishing, 1984.

Bagehot, Walter. *The English Constitution*. London: Chapman Hall, 1867.

Baker, Jean Harvey. *The Stevensons*. Woodstock: Foul Play Press, 1997.

Baker, Peter. *Days of Fire: Bush and Cheney in the White House*. New York: Doubleday, 2013.

Baker, Peter, and Susan Glasser. *The Divider: Trump in the White House, 2017–2021*. New York: Doubleday, 2022.

Barber, James David. *The Presidential Character*. New York: Routledge, 2020 [1971].

Barnouw, Erik. *Documentary: A History of the Non-Fiction Film*. Oxford: Oxford University Press, 1993.

Ben-Ghiat, Ruth. *Strongmen: Mussolini to the Present*. New York: W. W. Norton & Company, 2021.

Berg, A. Scott. *Wilson*. New York: G. P. Putnam's Sons, 2013.

Bernstein, Carl, and Bob Woodward. *All President's Men*. New York: Simon & Schuster, 1974.

Black, Conrad. *Franklin Delano Roosevelt: Champion of Freedom*. New York: Public Affairs, 2003.

Boorstin, Daniel J. *The Image: A Guide to Pseudo Events in America*. New York: Vintage Books, 1961.

Borneman, Walter R. *Polk: The Man Who Transformed the Presidency and America*. New York: Random House, 2008.

Bowen, Catherine Drinker. *Miracle at Philadelphia: The Story of the Constitutional Convention*. Boston: Little, Brown and Company, 1965.

Bowen, Mark, and Matthew Teague. *The Steal: The Attempt to Overturn the 2020 Election and the People Who Stopped it*. New York: Atlantic Monthly Press, 2022.

Bowles, John B. Jefferson: *The Architect of American Liberty*. New York: Basic Books, 2017.

Brodie, Fawn. *Thomas Jefferson: An Intimate Portrait*. New York: W. W. Norton & Company, 1974.

Brodie, Fawn. Richard Nixon: *The Shaping of His Character*. New York: W. W. Norton & Company, 1981.

Brooks, David. "Blame the Bobos." *The Atlantic*, September 2021.

Chernow, Ron. *Alexander Hamilton*. New York: Penguin Books, 2005.

Coblenz. Michael. "The Fight Goes on Forever: Limited Government and the First Bank of the United States." *Southern Illinois University Law Review*, 2015.

Collier, Peter, and David Horwitz. *The Kennedys: An American Drama*. New York: Summit Books, 1984.
Contosta, David R. *America's Needless Wars: Cautionary Tales of US Involvement in the Philippines, Vietnam and Iraq*. Amherst: Prometheus Books, 2017.
Contosta, David R. *Henry Adams and the American Experiment*. Boston: Little, Brown and Company, 1980.
Contosta, David R. Rebel Giants: *The Revolutionary Lives of Abraham Lincoln and Charles Darwin*. Amherst: Prometheus Books, 2008.
Cooper, Phillip J. *By Order of the President: The Use and Abuse of Executive Direct Action*. Lawrence: University Press of Kansas, 2004.
Corwin, E. S. *The President's Control of Foreign Relations*. Princeton: Princeton University Press, 1917.
Cosgrove, Kenneth M. *Donald Trump and the Branding of the Presidency*. London: Palgrave Macmillan, 2022.
Curtis, James C. *Andrew Jackson and the Search for Vindication*. Boston: Little, Brown and Company, 1976.
Dallek, Robert. *An Unfinished Life: John F. Kennedy, 1917–1963*. Boston: Little, Brown and Company, 2003.
Dalton, Kathleen. *Theodore Roosevelt: A Strenuous Life*. New York: Vintage Books, 2004.
Dean, John. *Blind Ambition*. New York: Simon and Schuster, 1976.
De Backer, Charlotte S. J. "Blinded by Starlight: An Evolutionary Framework for Studying Celebrity, Culture, and Fandom." *Review of General Psychology*, 2012.
Donald, David Herbert. *Lincoln*. New York: Quadrangle Books, 1995.
Donovan, Robert J. *PT 109: John F. Kennedy in World War II*. New York: McGraw-Hill, 1961.
Dueholm, James A. "Lincoln's Suspension of Habeas Corpus." *Journal of the Abraham Lincoln Association*, Summer 2008.
Ellis, Joseph E. *American Sphinx: The Character of Thomas Jefferson*. New York: Basic Books, 1998.
Ellsberg, Daniel. *Secrets: A Memoir of Vietnam and the Pentagon Papers*. New York: Viking, 2002.
Elson, Ruth Miller. *American Schoolbooks in the Nineteenth Century*. Lincoln: University of Nebraska Press, 1964.
Feldman, Noah. *The Broken Constitution*. New York: Farrer, Straus, and Giroux, 2021.
Ferling, John. *The Ascent of George Washington*. New York: Bloomsbury Press, 2009.
Fielding, Raymond. *The American Newsreel: A Complete History, 1911–1967*. Jefferson: McFarland, 2011.
Frank, Justin A. *Trump on the Couch: Inside the Mind of the President*. New York: Penguin Random House, 2018.
Frick, Daniel. *Reinventing Richard Nixon*. Lawrence Kansas: University Press of Kansas, 2008.
Friedel, Frank. Franklin D. Roosevelt: *A Rendezvous with Destiny*. Boston: Little, Brown and Company, 1990.
Fromm, Eric. *Escape from Freedom*. New York: Henry Holt and Company, 1994 [1941].
Fukuyama, Francis. *The End of History and the Last Man*. New York: Free Press, 2006 [1992].
Gartner, John D. *In Search of Bill Clinton*. New York: St. Martin's Press, 2008.

Goldman, Eric F. *The Tragedy of Lyndon Johnson*. New York: Alfred A. Knopf, 1969.
Goldzwig, Steven R. *Truman's Whistle-Stop Campaign*. College Station: Texas A&M University Press, 2008.
Gore, Albert A. "The Impact of Television on the Conduct of the Presidency, 1947–1969." Harvard University Senior Thesis.
Hagedorn, Hermann. *Leonard Wood: A Biography*. New York: Harper and Brothers, 1931.
Hamilton, Alexander. *Papers of Alexander Hamilton*. New York: Columbia University Press, 1961–1987.
Hargreaves, Mary H. M. *The Presidency of John Quincy Adams*. Lawrence: University Press of Kansas, 1985.
Heckscher, August. *Woodrow Wilson: A Biography*. New York: Charles Scribner's Sons, 1991.
Herndon, William. *Herndon's Informants: Letters, Interviews, and Statements about Abraham Lincoln*. Urbana: University of Illinois Press, 1998.
Herndon, William. *Herndon's Life of Lincoln*. New York: Da Capp Press, 1983 [1888].
Hofstadter, Richard. *Anti-Intellectualism in American Life*. New York: Library Classics of the United States, 2020 [1963].
Howe, Daniel Walker. *The Political Culture of American Whigs*. Chicago: University of Chicago Press, 1979.
Isikoff, Michael, and David Corn. *Hubris*. New York: Crown Publishers, 2007.
January 6 Report by the House January 6th Committee, forward by Ari Melber. New York Harper, 2022.
Jefferson, Thomas. *Writings of Thomas Jefferson*. Jefferson Memorial Association, 1903.
Jewitt, Caitlin. *The Primary Rules: Parties, Nominations, and Presidential Nominations*. Ann Arbor: University of Michigan Press, 2019.
Johnson, Andrew. *The Papers of Andrew Johnson*. Knoxville: University of Tennessee Press, 1967–1998.
Kalb, Marvin. *The Road to War: Presidential Commitments Honored and Betrayed*. Washington, DC: Brookings Institute Press, 2013.
Kaplan, Fred. *John Quincy Adams: American Visionary*. New York: Harper Perennials, 2015.
Karl, Jonathan. *Betrayal: The Final Act of the Trump Show*. New York: Dutton, 2021.
Karl, Jonathan. *Front Row at the Trump Show*. New York: Dutton, 2020.
Katyal, Neal. *Impeach: The Case Against Donald Trump*. Boston: Houghton Mifflin Harcourt, 2019.
Kendrick, Alexander. *The Would Within: America in the Vietnam Years, 1945–1974*. Boston: Little, Brown and Company, 1974.
Klein, Ezra. *Why We're Polarized*. New York: Avid Reader Press, 2020.
Kohlsaat, H. H. *From McKinley to Harding: Personal Recollections of Our Presidents*. New York: Charles Scribner's Sons, 1923.
Kornacki, Steve. *The Red and the Blue: The 1990s and the Birth of Political Tribalism*. New York: HarperCollins, 2018.
Lee, Bandy, ed. *The Dangerous Case of Donal Trump*. New York: St. Martin's Press, 2017.
Leonning, Carol, and Philip Rucker. *I Alone Can Fix It*. New York: Penguin Press, 2021.
Levitsky, Steven, and Daniel Ziblatt. *Tyranny of the Minority*. New York: Crown Publishing Company, 2023.
Lewis, Sinclair. *It Can't Happen Here*. New York: Signet Classics, 2014 [1935].

Lichuaco, Marcel P., and Moorefield Story. *The Conquest of the Philippines by the United States, 1898–1925*. New York: G. P. Putnam's Sons, 1926.

Lijphart, Arend, ed. *Parliamentary Versus Presidential Government*. Oxford: Oxford University Press, 1992.

Lilla, Mark. *Ignorance and Biss: On Not Wanting Not to Know*. New York: Farrar, Straus and Giroux, 2024.

Lincoln, Abraham. *Collected Works of Abraham Lincoln*. New Brunswick: Rutgers University Press, 1953.

Linz, Juan Jose. "The Perils of Presidentialism." *Journal of Democracy*, Winter 1990.

Linz, Juan Jose, and Arturo Valenzuela. *The Failure of Presidential Democracy*. Baltimore: Johns Hopkins University Press, 1994.

Lippmann, Walter. *Public Opinion*. Middletown: Renaissance Classics, 2002 [1922].

Logevall, Frederick. *JFK: Coming of Age in the American Century*. New York: Random House, 2020.

Lubell, Samuel. *The Future of American Politics*. New York: Doubleday and Company, 1951.

Maclay, William. *Journal of William Maclay*. New York: D. Appleton and Company, 1890.

Madison, James, Alexander Hamilton, and John Jay. *The Federalist Papers*. Middletown: Black & White Publications, 2015.

Madison, James, Alexander Hamilton, and John Jay. *Notes of the Debates in in the Federal Convention of 1787*. Athens: Ohio University Press, 1985.

Madison, James, Alexander Hamilton, and John Jay. *The Papers of James Madison*. Charlottesville: University of Virginia Press, 1979.

Madison, James, Alexander Hamilton, and John Jay. *The Writings of James Madison*. New York: G.P. Putnam's Sons, 1909–1910.

Maraniss, David. *First in His Class: The Biography of Bill Clinton*. New York: Simon & Shuster, 1995.

Marcus, Sharon. *The Drama of Celebrity*. Princeton: Princeton University Press, 2019.

McDougal, Walter. *Throes of Democracy: The American Civil War Era, 1829–1877*. New York: Harper Perennials, 2009.

McGinnes, Joe. *The Selling of the President 1968*. New York: The Trident Press, 1969.

McKeever, Porter. *Adlai Stevenson: His Life and Legacy*. New York: William Morrow and Company, 1989.

McKinley, William. *Speeches and Addresses of William McKinley*. New York: Doubleday & McClure, 1900.

McNeal, R. A. "Nicholas Biddle, Anacharis, and the Grand Tour." *Pennsylvania Magazine of History and Biography*, July 1996.

Meacham, Jon. American Lion: *Andrew Jackson in the White House*. New York: Random House, 1976.

Meacham, Jon. *Destiny and Power: The American Odyssey of George Herbert Walker Bush*. New York: Random House, 2015.

Meacham, Jon. *Thomas Jefferson: The Art of Power*. New York: Random House, 2012.

Miller, Nathan. *Theodore Roosevelt: A Life*. New York: William Morrow and Company, 1992.

Mitchell, Greg. *Tricky Dick and the Pink Lady*. New York: Random House, 1998.

Morris, Edmund. *Dutch: A Memoir of Ronald Reagan*. New York: Random House, 1999.

Morris, Edmund. *Theodore Rex*. New York: Random House, 2001.

Moss, George Donelson. *Vietnam: An American Ordeal.* Upper Saddle River: Prentice Hall, 2002.

Murray, Melissa, and Adrew Weissman. *The Trump Indictments.* New York: W. W. Norton & Company, 2024.

Nixon, Richard. *RN: The Memoirs of Richard Nixon.* New York: Grosset and Dunlap, 1978.

Nixon, Richard. *Six Crises.* Garden City: Doubleday, 1962.

Obama, Barack. *The Audacity of Hope: Thoughts on Restoring the America Dream.* New York: Three Rivers Press, 2006.

Obama, Barack. *Dreams of My Father: A Story of Race and Inheritance.* Preface to the Fourth Edition. New York: Three Rivers Press, 2004.

O'Brien, Timothy L. *Trump Nation: The Art of Being the Donald.* New York: Grand Central Publishing, 2005.

Osnos, Evan. Wildland: *The Making of America's Fury.* New York: Farrer, Straus and Giroux, 2021.

Parton, James. *Life of Andrew Jackson.* New York: Mason Brothers, 1863.

Peale, Norman Vincent. *The Power of Positive Thinking.* New York: Simon & Schuster, 2015 [1952].

Perlstein, Rick. *Nixonland: The Rise and the of a President Fracturing of America.* New York: Scribner, 2009.

Pessen, Edward. *The Log Cabin Myth: The Social Backgrounds of Presidents.* New Haven: Yale University Press, 1984.

Peterson, Merrill D. *Lincoln in American Memory.* New York: Oxford University Press, 1994.

Postman, Neil. *Amusing Ourselves to Death: Public Discourse in the Age of Show Business.* New York: Penguin Books, 2005 [1985].

Rakove, Jack N. *Original Meanings.* New York: Vintage Books, 1996.

Randall, Willard Sterne. *Thomas Jefferson: A Life.* New York: Henry Holt, 1993.

Ricks, Thomas E. *First* Principles: *What the American Founders Learned* from *the Greeks* and *Romans.* New York: HarperCollins, 2020.

Rimini, Robert V. *Andrew Jackson.* New York: Harper and Row, 1999.

Rimini, Robert V. *John Quincy Adams.* New York: Times Books, 2002.

Roosevelt, Theodore. *An Autobiography.* New York: Charles Scribner's Sons, 1913.

Roosevelt, Theodore. *A Compilation of Messages and Speeches of Theodore Roosevelt, 1901–1905.* New York: Bureau of National Literature and Art, 1906.

Roosevelt, Theodore. *Letters of Theodore Roosevelt.* Cambridge, MA: Harvard University Press, 1951–1954.

Roseboom, Eugene H. *A History of Presidential Elections.* New York: The Macmillan Company, 1970.

Rossiter, Clinton. *Constitutional Dictatorship.* Princeton: Princeton University Press, 1948.

Saffire, William. *Before the Fall.* New York: Doubleday, 1975.

Schieffer, Bob, and Paul Gates. *The Acting President: Ronald Reagan and the Supporting Actors Who Helped Him Create the Illusion That Held American Spellbound.* New York: E. P. Dutton, 1989.

Schlessinger, Arthur M. *The Age of Jackson.* Boston: Little, Brown and Company, 1945.

Schlessinger, Arthur M. *The Imperial Presidency.* Boston: Houghton Mifflin Company, 1973.

Schlessinger, Arthur M. *A Thousand Days: John F. Kennedy in the White House.* Boston: Houghton Mifflin Company, 1965.

Schwartz, Barry. *George Washington: The Making of an American Symbol*. New York: Free Press, 1987.
Schwartz, Frederick A. O., Jr., and Aziz Z. Hug. *Unbalanced: Presidential Power in Time of Terror*. New York: The New Press, 2008.
Shales, Amity. *Great Society: A New History*. New York: HarperCollins, 2019.
Shapiro, Sarah, and Catherine Brown. "A Look at Civics Education in the United States." *American Educator*, Summer 2018.
Skowronek, Stephen. *The Politics Presidents Make: Leadership from John Adams to Bill Clinton*. Cambridge, MA: Harvard University Press, 1997.
Slonim, Shlomo. "The Electoral College at Philadelphia." *Journal of American History*, June 1986.
Smith, Jean Howard. *Eisenhower in War and Peace*. New York: Random House, 2012.
Snyder, Timothy. *On Freedom*. New York: Crown, 2024.
Snyder, Timothy. *On Tyranny: Twenty Lessons from the Twentieth Century*. New York: Crown, 2017.
Steel, Ronald. *Walter Lippmann and the American Century*. Boston: Little, Brown and Company, 1980.
Teachout, Zephyr. *Corruption in America*. Cambridge, MA: Harvard University Press, 2014.
Thach, Charles C. *The Creation of the Presidency*. Indianapolis: Liberty Fund, 2007.
Thomas, Evan. *Being Nixon: A Man Divided*. New York: Random House, 2016.
Toobin, Jeffrey. *True Crimes and Misdemeanors: The Investigation of Donald Trump*. New York: Doubleday, 2020.
The Tower Commission Report: The Full Text of the President's Special Review Board. New York: Bantam Books/New York Times Books, 1987.
Trefousse, Hans L. *Andrew Johnson: A Biography*. New York: W. W. Norton & Company, 1997.
Tribe, Laurence, and Joshua Matz. *To End a Presidency: The Power of Impeachment*. New York: Basic Books, 2018.
Truman, Harry S. *Memoirs: Years of Trial and Hope*. Garden City: Doubleday, 1956.
Trump, Donald with Tony Schwartz. *The Art of the Deal*. New York: Random House, 1987.
Trump, Mary L. *Too Much and Never Enough: How the Family Created* the *World's Most Dangerous Man*. New York: Simon & Schuster, 2020.
Waltzer, Michael. *Just and Unjust Wars*. New York: Basic Books, 2007.
Warner, Margaret Garrard. "Bush Battles the Wimp Factor." *Newsweek*, October 19, 1987.
Washington, George. *The Papers of George Washington: Confederation Series*. Charlottesville: University of Virginia Press, 1992–1997.
Weissman, Andrew. *Where the Law Ends: Inside the Mueller Investigation*. New York: Random House, 2020.
White, Theodore S. *Making of the President 1960*. New York: Harper Perennials, 2009 [1961].
White, Theodore S. *Making of the President 1964*. New York: Harper Perennials, 2009 [1965].
Wilkerson, Isabel. *Caste: The Origin of Our Discontents*. New York: Random House, 2020.
Williams, T. Harry. *The History of American Wars from 1745 to 1918*. Baton Rouge: Louisiana State University Press, 1981.
Wills, Gary. *Nixon Agonistes*. Boston: Houghton Mifflin, 2002 [1969].

Wilmerding, Lucius. *The Electoral College*. New Brunswick: Rutgers University Press, 1958.
Wilmot, Rufus. *The Republican Court, Or, American Society in the Days of Washington*. New York: D. Appleton and Company, 1856.
Wilson, Woodrow. *Congressional Government: A Study in American Politics*. Boston: Houghton Mifflin Company, 1885.
Wilson, Woodrow. *Constitutional Government in the United States*. New York: Columbia University Press, 1908.
Woodward, Bob. *Rage*. New York: Simon & Schuster, 2020.
Woodward, Bob, and Robert Costa. *Peril*. New York: Simon & Schuster, 2021.

Index

About the Author

David Contosta, Ph.D. is Professor of History and Chair of the History Department at Chestnut Hill College in Philadelphia. He is the author of twenty-five books that include publications of national and international interest. Among these are *Henry Adams and the American Experiment*, *America in the Twentieth Century*, *The Private Life of James Bond*, *Rebel Giants: The Revolutionary Lives of Abraham Lincoln and Charles Darwin*, and *America's Needless Wars.*

In addition, Contosta has published several books about people and places in the Philadelphia area. Among these are *Suburb in the City: Chestnut Hill Philadelphia* and *Metropolitan Paradise: Philadelphia's Wissahickon Valley* (co-authored with Carol Franklin). Most recently, he published a personal memoir entitled *An American Childhood* (co-authored with Philip Hazelton) and a first novel, *Happenstance*, set largely in the Philadelphia region.

Contosta has co-produced, written, and/or appeared in several documentary films and has been interviewed many times on both radio and television. He has also lectured at Nanjing University in China and at Pyeongtaek University in South Korea and has been a Visiting Research Professor at Cambridge University in England, as well as a Fulbright Scholar to France.

www.ingramcontent.com/pod-product-compliance
Ingram Content Group UK Ltd.
Pitfield, Milton Keynes, MK11 3LW, UK
UKHW020216290926
15470UKWH00001B/218

9 781666 944426